CLARENDON l
Edited
TONY HONORÉ AN ⊔ ᴋAZ

CLARENDON LAW SERIES

The Concept of Law
by H. L. A. HART

Introduction to the Law of Contract (4th Edition)
by P. S. ATIYAH

Introduction to Roman Law
by BARRY NICHOLAS

An Introduction to the Law of Torts (2nd Edition)
by JOHN G. FLEMING

Constitutional Theory
by GEOFFREY MARSHALL

Legal Reasoning and Legal Theory
by NEIL MacCORMICK

Natural Law and Natural Rights
by JOHN FINNIS

The Law of Property (2nd Edition)
by F. H. LAWSON and BERNARD RUDDEN

An Introduction to Administrative Law
by PETER CANE

Bentham and the Common Law Tradition
by GERALD J. POSTEMA

Conflicts of Law and Morality
by KENT GREENAWALT

The Foundations of European Community Law (2nd Edition)
by T. C. HARTLEY

The Principles of Criminal Evidence

A. A. S. ZUCKERMAN

CLARENDON PRESS • OXFORD

1989

Oxford University Press, Walton Street, Oxford OX2 6DP

Oxford   New York   Toronto
Delhi   Bombay   Calcutta   Madras   Karachi
Petaling Jaya   Singapore   Hong Kong   Tokyo
Nairobi   Dar es Salaam   Cape Town
Melbourne Auckland

and associated companies in
Berlin   Ibadan

Oxford is a trade mark of Oxford University Press

Published in the United States
by Oxford University Press, New York

British Library Cataloguing in Publication Data
Zuckerman, A. A. S.
The principles of criminal evidence.—
(Clarendon law series)
1. England. Criminal courts. Evidence. Law
I. Title
344.205'6
ISBN 0-19-876103-1
ISBN 0-19-876234-8 Pbk

Library of Congress Cataloging-in-Publication Data
Zuckerman, A. A. S.
The principles of criminal evidence/A. A. S. Zuckerman.
—(Clarendon law series)   Includes index.
1. Evidence, Criminal—Great Britain.   I. Title. II. Series.
KD8371.Z77   1989   345.41'06—dc19   [344.1056]   88-26999
ISBN 0-19-876103-1
ISBN 0-19-876234-8 (pbk.)

Set by Graphicraft Typesetters, Hong Kong
Printed in Great Britain by Biddles Ltd
Guildford and King's Lynn

Acknowledgements

I WAS invited to undertake this book by Professor H. L. A. Hart, who was at the time the editor of the Clarendon Series and who gave me help and encouragement in commenting on early drafts. In the early stages I also benefited from the views of Professor E. Harnon of the Hebrew University of Jerusalem, Mr L. Jonathan Cohen of The Queen's College, Oxford, and Mr A. Ligertwood of Adelaide University. I was able to complete a full draft of the work through the assistance of the British Academy which granted me a Research Readership during the academic years 1985 to 1987.

I owe a debt of gratitude to a number of people. Mr P. Healy, of Wolfson College, Oxford, made helpful comments on the first three chapters, and the whole draft was subjected to extensive critical scrutiny by Ms D. J. Birch of Nottingham University, Mr Justice Hoffmann, Mr A. Stein of University College, London, and Professor W. Twining of University College, London. Their wise counsel and their innumerable suggestions spared me many mistakes and inconsistencies.

Professor T. Honore, of All Souls College, Oxford, who read the final draft on behalf of the Clarendon Series, exposed many weaknesses in its structure and shortcomings of style and gave me invaluable help in improving the book. Professor J. Raz, of Balliol College, Oxford, made many important points which helped me clarify my own attitude in several respects.

Mr K. Gledhill assisted me throughout by substantive and stylistic comments and by checking references. Ms S. Taverne helped improve the structure and style of the book.

My acknowledgements would be seriously wanting if I did not record my deep debt to Professor Sir Rupert Cross who guided my first and insecure steps in the law of evidence, who encouraged me to undertake the present work, and whose own contribution to the law of evidence has influenced every serious work written on this topic since the publication of the first edition of *Cross on Evidence* in 1958.[1]

A.A.S.Z.

University College, Oxford,
1989

---

[1] The last edition of this work to be prepared by Professor Cross himself was the fifth edition of 1979, to which reference will be made whenever attention is drawn to Professor Cross's own views; otherwise references will be to the recent edition, which was prepared by Mr C. Tapper.

Contents

Table of Cases

Table of Statutes and Statutory Instruments

I

A Law of Criminal Evidence

THE LAW OF EVIDENCE AND THE CRIMINAL PROCESS

The law of evidence regulates the process of adducing evidence for the purpose of proving disputed facts. When a court of law sets out to decide whether a disputed event took place as party *A* contends or, on the contrary, as party *B* argues, the court is concerned to find the truth about that event. But there are many ways of determining the truth.

The doctor, the scientist, the journalist, and the historian are also interested in finding the truth about facts, yet each of these adopts different procedures to that end. The procedure that each follows is influenced by the purpose for which the investigation is carried out and by the conditions under which it is done. If the purpose is to produce an account for the next day's newspaper, a journalist will obviously carry out more limited investigations than would, for example, a historian whose time-scale and purpose are different. If the journalist's facts prove to be wrong, it would not necessarily be a valid criticism to say that he had not conducted as full an investigation as a historian would have done, but it would be perfectly in order to criticize him for not following the procedures dictated by the professional standards of his calling. We may wish to take the matter further and enquire whether the standards of the journalistic profession are adequate. But in this regard too the fact that they are different from those of the historian's does not, by itself, provide a reason for disapproval.

Like any procedure for determining the truth about events, the legal process also has to be evaluated against the background of its additional aims, its circumstances, and the resources devoted to it. Apart from the ascertainment of truth, the aims of the legal process are clearly different from those of journalistic investigation or historical research. For example, the law may desire to provide special facilities for litigants, such as the means of obtaining evidence in support of their case, or it may attempt to devise a mechanism for a fair distribution between the litigants of the risk of mistakes in adjudication. Clearly the first stage in the evaluation of the legal process must consist in discovering the general principles which underpin the rules governing litigation in the courts. These principles are not ready-made; we have to derive them by examining the practices of the courts. Once we have identified the general principles reflected in judicial practice, we are in a position to consider how effectively the courts promote their own principles and, indeed, whether these principles are defensible.

As soon as we enquire about the aims and principles of the legal process of fact-finding, we discover that there is not just one legal procedure for determining facts but many. There are criminal proceedings and civil proceedings. Within the criminal process there are jury trials and magistrate trials. Outside the criminal process there are trials in the High Court of Justice and many other proceedings, such as arbitration proceedings, administrative proceedings, industrial-relations tribunals, and different disciplinary tribunals. Each procedure will have its distinctive features and will reflect the underlying concerns of the substantive law which the particular procedure is concerned to apply.[1] The law of evidence, as it is traditionally conceived, does not deal with every single legal procedure; it is confined to criminal and civil proceedings in the superior courts of the land and in magistrates' courts. However, even those procedures that the traditional law of evidence encompasses are so diverse as to make it impossible to observe any general underlying principles that might give coherence to this body of law. There are at least

---

[1] For challenges to the independence of the law of evidence from the substantive law see: Llewellyn, *Jurisprudence* (1962), 439; Packer, 'Two models of the criminal process', 113 University of Pennsylvania L Rev 1 (1964); id., *The Limits of the Criminal Sanction* (1968); Griffith, 'Ideology in criminal procedure of a "Third Model" of the criminal process', 79 Yale L J 359 (1970); G. Fletcher, *Rethinking Criminal Law* (1978), ch. 8; L. Fuller, 'The forms and limits of adjudication', 92 Harv L Rev 353 (1978); P. Arenella, 'Rethinking the functions of criminal procedure: the Warren and Burger courts' competing ideologies', 72 Georgetown L J 185 (1983). For a criticism of the current methodology see: Twining, 'Identification and misidentification in legal processes: redefining the problem', in Lloyd-Bostock and Clifford (eds.), *Evaluating Witness Evidence* (1983), 255.

two distinct procedures, the criminal and the civil, which are not only governed by different rules but also reflect entirely different concerns.

This is not to say that the criminal and civil modes of trial have nothing in common. Both types of proceedings share some features which are fundamental to the English system of adjudication. Both procedures are adversarial in the sense that the judge leaves it to the parties to determine the confines of the dispute and pursue its resolution as they choose, subject only to rules of fair play.[2] Both trial processes are oral and public in nature, in the sense that evidence and argument are presented orally to the court which is open to the public. However, although these characteristics are common it is impossible to overlook the deep differences between the law of evidence in criminal jury trials and civil cases.

Serious criminal prosecutions are tried by a judge sitting with a jury while the vast majority of civil cases, however serious, are tried by judge alone.[3] In criminal cases the facts need to be proved beyond all reasonable doubt. In civil actions they may be proved on the balance of probabilities. The hearsay rule applies in criminal cases but not, to all intents and purposes, in civil ones.[4] The requirements for the corroboration of witnesses are entirely different in criminal cases from those in civil cases. Unlike the position in civil cases, in criminal trials the rules concerning past crimes of the accused and his confession occupy a central position. The privilege against self-incrimination is predominantly found in the criminal process.

In civil litigation most disputes regarding evidence are occupied with the parties' right of access to evidence, mainly in the hands of the opponent, and with the means of securing it. There

---

[2] For an interesting comparison of the adversarial and inquisitorial philosophies see Damaska, 'Evidentiary barriers to conviction and two models of criminal procedure . . .', 121 University of Pennsylvania L Rev 506 (1973).

[3] Magistrates' courts have jurisdiction both over less-serious offences and over some civil matters. Here although the mode of trial is similar in civil and criminal trials the rules of evidence are different; criminal proceedings are by and large governed by the rules applicable to jury criminal trials.

[4] This rule excludes out-of-court statements when adduced as proof of the truth of facts stated therein; see Ch. 11.

is a general trend towards a merging of the rules of evidence and the rules of discovery, which were traditionally considered to be rules of procedure and not of evidence.[5] By contrast, in the criminal trial the right of access to information in the possession of the accused is severely curtailed by the privilege against self-incrimination. Moreover, even those rules that are said to apply in both forms of trial often undergo special modification when employed in criminal cases. For instance, legal professional privilege and public-interest immunity are capable of being overridden in a criminal trial by the need of the accused to establish his innocence. Similarly, a particular presumption, such as the presumption of legitimacy, may have a different effect in a criminal case from its effect in a civil case.

Such extensive differences between the law governing criminal and civil cases could hardly be accidental. A number of important factors set apart our criminal and civil procedures. Unlike the civil trial, the criminal trial is not concerned with resolving a dispute between symmetrically competing claims,[6] but is devoted to an examination of the conduct of the accused. Its object is to determine whether the accused has transgressed a criminal prohibition and whether he should be punished.[7] The proceedings take the form of a charge brought by the state against an individual. The law-enforcement agencies are involved not only as litigants before the court but also as investigators and, as such, have very considerable power over the individual before the trial. A pronounced imbalance exists therefore between the law-enforcement agencies and the individual. On the one hand are ranged the investigative and prosecuting authorities of the state and, on the other, there is the individual accused. This imbalance calls for special measures to ensure that the individual suspect or accused is protected from abuse by the organs of the state. The most prominent of these measures is the privilege against self-incrimination. An accused need not, either before or during the trial, account for his

---

[5] This is particularly notable in the development of Anton Piller orders, which are designed to secure evidence from destruction or suppression by the opponent.

[6] Most, though not all, civil trials are concerned with competing claims regarding the same object. When this is not the case, as in administrative proceedings, the procedure will reflect this aspect.

[7] The same is true of certain disciplinary procedures.

actions; the prosecution has to prove his guilt without any right to call upon him to provide evidence. Nor may the prosecution usually call the accused's spouse as a witness without the latter's consent. Confessions are subject to judicial control and illegally obtained evidence is liable to exclusion in certain circumstances.

The object of the criminal trial is to punish offenders. Punishment can deprive the accused of his most cherished right: his personal freedom. But the consequence of punishment can exceed the material disadvantage represented by the sanction of incarceration or fine. It can mark the convict with a moral condemnation that may hurt more than imprisonment and could inflict permanent injury upon the convict's self-respect and standing in the community.[8] A legal system which respects the rights of the individual has to devise a criminal procedure that affords due protection from punishment to the innocent citizen and the law of criminal evidence includes several measures for achieving this end.

It is an important function of the criminal process to promote observance of the law. To this end its verdicts have to command public approval. Hence not only must the criminal process protect the innocent but it must also be seen to be doing so. There is, however, no external test for judging whether a criminal verdict reflects the truth. The past cannot, as it were, be revived for the purpose of checking conformity between the facts as they really happened and as they have been reflected in the verdict of the court. In this regard a judicial determination of the facts is like any other judgment about the past; it can be assessed only by the strength of its own persuasive power. It follows that public confidence in the criminal verdict has to be vested in the process as such. This is achieved by the use of the jury system, which ensures that factual judgment, and some non-factual judgment too, is formed according to the ordinary citizen's view of the world.

Public confidence in the administration of criminal justice depends also on its ability to provide the community with satisfactory protection from crime. The public need for protec-

---

[8] For a discussion of the difference between punishment and other unpleasant treatment see Ten, *Crime, Guilt, and Punishment* (1987).

tion from crime receives little direct acknowledgment in discussions of individual rules but it is central to the operation of the criminal law of evidence and its manifestations can be observed in the qualifying effect that it has upon many rules, such as the privilege against self-incrimination.

In civil procedure, where the aim is essentially to settle disputes between citizens, hardly any of these concerns figure to any important extent.[9] Since the civil process is not principally concerned with affording the individual protection from the state's organs, it does not have to adopt special measures to protect the innocent from punishment or reflect the community's need for protection from crime.

There has not always been such a clear distinction between criminal and other kinds of proceedings. Until relatively recently the facts were determined by a jury in both criminal and civil cases. In both most exclusionary rules applied equally. However, as a result of numerous reforms, starting in the middle of the nineteenth century, criminal proceedings have been set on a separate course. This divergence reflects the special functions of our system of criminal justice.

Consequently, whatever might have been the case half a century ago, it would be idle to pretend that today there is only one law of evidence subject merely to variations in criminal and civil proceedings. The law of criminal evidence has an independence of purpose and a cohesion of principle such that it requires a discrete treatment. This book is confined to a discussion of the law of criminal evidence.

THE RELATION BETWEEN GENERAL PRINCIPLES AND JUDICIAL PRACTICES

A critical exposition of the law of criminal evidence has to be conducted by reference to its general principles. Foremost amongst them is, naturally, the desire to discover the truth.

[9] For a general outline of the civil procedure see Sir Jack Jacob, *The Fabric of English Civil Justice* (1987), ch. 1. See also K. E. Scott, 'Two models of the civil process', 27 Stan L Rev 937 (1974–5), and the distinction drawn there between a 'conflict-solving' function and a 'behavior-modification' function.

This desire assumes a special significance in the criminal trial because it represents more than a disinterested wish that verdicts concerning criminal charges should correspond with the truth. Rather, it reflects the powerful public interest in bringing offenders to justice in order to protect the community from crime. We may therefore refer to this principle in terms of the public interest. In addition to this principle there are two other principles which stand out when we examine the criminal procedure, as will have become clear: the principle of protecting the innocent from conviction and the principle of maintaining high standards of propriety in the criminal process.

The principle of protecting the innocent from conviction finds expression in several rules that exclude relevant evidence, such as evidence which may create prejudice against the accused, as well as in the requirement of proof beyond reasonable doubt. It is important to appreciate that what is meant by 'innocent' is innocent of the offence for which the accused is being tried. In the course of his trial, an accused may be revealed to have committed other offences. The law's commitment to the protection of the innocent also extends to such an accused and safeguards have been erected against the risk that he may be convicted not because he has committed the crime charged but because he has done some other discreditable act. Amongst these safeguards is to be found the rule that excludes evidence when its prejudicial effect outweighs its probative force, i.e. evidence that may lead the trier of fact to judge the person rather than his act.

The principle of maintaining standards of propriety in the criminal process finds expression in that great English institution: the privilege against self-incrimination. It also has important manifestations in the procedure for obtaining confessions from suspects in custody and in relation to the attitude of the courts to evidence obtained in breach of the rules of search and seizure which are designed to protect the citizen from undue interference or abuse by the state.

Although the existence of these general principles is widely acknowledged, their operation in the day-to-day practice of the courts is often overlooked because of excessive emphasis on legal definition in the exposition of the law of evidence. A textbook on evidence will normally allude to the rationale behind a particular rule of evidence, but will then tend to present the rule as self-sufficient and as capable of application in its own terms, regardless of its rationale. Very often, however, an examination of the case law will show that the practice of the courts does not conform to these definitions. The principal reason for this is that when a court decides, for example, whether to admit a particular piece of evidence, it will consider not only the received definition of its admissibility but also the need to secure evidence of crime.

A central feature of the law of criminal evidence is therefore to be found in the interplay between these three major principles and in the continual need that the courts experience of striking a balance between their competing demands. In particular situations the need to protect the innocent from conviction might require steps which are inconsistent with the public interest in punishing offenders. For example, the more stringent the requirement of proof of guilt, the more likely it is that some guilty persons will escape punishment. Similarly, a conflict may arise between the rules governing search and seizure and the need to secure evidence of crime.

A methodology that tends to distil fixed definitions of admissible and inadmissible evidence from the practices of the court does not allow sufficiently for the courts' desire to reflect the public interest in convicting offenders. For example, it is said that the rule against hearsay excludes statements made out of court which are adduced as evidence of the truth of that which they state, regardless of their probative weight and reliability. For this view to constitute a correct representation of the law the exceptions to the rule would have to be equally well defined and similarly independent of probative force, because if high reliability constituted an exception, the rule could not be said to be insensitive to reliability. We shall see, however, that this is far from being the case since the most important exception to the rule, the *res gestae* exception, is largely a matter of probative force. Furthermore, hearsay is often admitted by the use of a number of other relatively open-ended exceptions and also by judicial interpretation of the rule itself in terms of probative reliability rather than by reference to its formal definition. Commentators, and sometimes the judiciary, tend to assume that decisions to admit evidence that falls within the formal definition of prohibited hearsay are unjustified. But it is more realistic to conclude that when all the different devices for admitting hearsay are taken into account the description of the rule in terms of its current definition is misleading: it wrongly insulates the exposition of the rule against hearsay from the discretion which the courts exercise in order to admit evidence which is highly reliable and which is necessary for the proof of guilt. An accurate account of the hearsay practice must reflect this factor not as an inexplicable aberration but as an integral and comprehensible function of judicial discretion. It is only when we have a comprehensive view of the practice of the courts in relation to hearsay that we are able to make a correct assessment of the extent to which the innocent are protected from unreliable but incriminating evidence of this sort.

In order to understand properly the practice of the courts both in relation to the privilege against self-incrimination and in relation to illegally obtained evidence we have to take into account the force of the public interest in punishing the guilty. An examination of the operation of the privilege against self-incrimination will reveal that the real protection from self-incrimination that it affords to suspects is minimal. This is due to the countervailing pressure exerted against it by the need to obtain evidence of crime. The same pressure affects the admissibility of illegally obtained evidence. By outlawing, for example, illegal searches in certain situations the legislature has indicated that it is prepared to forgo the evidence of crime that such searches may reveal. It might be said that it therefore follows that when evidence has been obtained by an illegal search, it must be excluded. However, such a view would ignore the fact that once evidence of guilt has come to light, the resistance to a return to the *status quo ante* and to the release of the offender is very great and cannot be brushed aside by an appeal to the original illegality of the search.

The traditional exposition of the law of evidence creates an unnecessary dichotomy between rules and discretion. Most of the rules of evidence do not in fact provide fixed definitions of acceptable or unacceptable practices but rather lay down guidelines for decisions, which have to be made after consideration of various factors.[10] In some areas this is already accepted as being the case.[11] For example, evidence of the accused's past convictions is admissible only if its prejudicial effect is outweighed by its probative weight. Clearly, the discretion that the judge has in this matter is not open-ended. He cannot decide to admit the evidence once he has reached the conclusion that the prejudicial effect exceeds the probative contribution of the evidence in question. The law has settled the principle that if there is an unwarranted risk of prejudice the evidence must be excluded and the judge is merely given the task of deciding whether this is the case.[12]

When we come across discretion to exclude evidence, it is necessary to identify the factors that need to be considered in the exercise of the discretion. So far as prejudicial evidence is concerned, we need to pinpoint what is meant by prejudice and to assess the effectiveness of the measures that have been taken to avoid prejudice. The risk of prejudice can, as we will see, consist not only in overestimating the probative significance of past convictions but also, and perhaps more seriously, in the risk that a jury will convict because its members disapprove of the accused or because they decide that he does not deserve to be given the benefit of doubt. Once we have identified these risks we will be in a better position to determine how effective have been the measures to safeguard the accused from them and, indeed, the extent to which the courts have striven to counteract them not only in relation to the admissibility of past misdeeds but also in other contexts which give rise to the similar risks. A clear appreciation of the nature of the risk to the accused should also enable us to develop countermeasures for limiting it.

[10] By a fixed definition is meant a legal definition the application of which is a matter of 'either or'; that is, either the situation falls within the definition of the rule, in which case a certain result will follow, or it does not, in which case such a result will not follow. An example of such rule is provided by the traditional explanation of the traditional hearsay rule. Either a piece of evidence falls within the definition of hearsay, in which case it is inadmissible, or it does not, in which case it is admissible.

[11] For a survey of the instances where discretion has received recognition see Pattenden, *The Judge, Discretion, and the Criminal Trial* (1982).

[12] An illuminating analysis of the constraints under which judges exercise their discretionary powers will be found in: Galligan, *Discretionary Powers: A Legal Study of Official Discretion* (1986).

The common depiction of the law of evidence as a collection of inflexible legal definitions of acceptable and unacceptable practices has given rise to many situations where the application of these definitions creates injustice. Judicial discretion is sometimes used as a moderator of the rigour of the fixed definitions in order to prevent the more extreme forms of injustice. This ever-increasing appeal to discretion in the traditional exposition raises an obvious question: What is the difference between a fixed rule that may be a side-stepped by the exercise of discretion when justice so requires and a declaration that the matter is governed by discretion to see that justice is done? Put differently, if the aim is to reach a sensible and just solution to a practical problem, would it not be simpler merely to outline the aims that the judge must achieve and leave it to his good judgment how best to do so in any concrete situation? We shall find that in many contexts an explanation of the existing law in terms of such discretion is much more accurate than an exposition based on strict definitions of permissible and impermissible practices.

It might be suggested that judicial discretion, however circumscribed, is inadequate for promoting protection of the innocent from conviction or for the preservation of standards of propriety in the investigation of crime. Strict and binding legal definitions, it might be said, offer more reliable instruments to that end. However, if we assess the contribution that binding definitions have made towards promoting the general principles of the criminal process of fact-finding we find them wanting. The reason is simple: the courts refuse to observe strict definitions when they consider the result of observance unsatisfactory. As we have just seen, much hearsay evidence is admitted despite the strictures of the formal definition and the limitation on the formal exceptions to this definition. Similarly, the privilege against self-incrimination affords the suspect in custody a freedom to decline answering police questions, but no rule has yet been devised, in this or any other country, for ensuring that the suspect has a genuine choice in the matter. There are, as we shall see, many other examples of deviation from the formal definitions in the actual practice of the court.

Indeed, the existence of strict definitions can be said to have undermined the protection of the innocent from conviction and the maintenance of standards of propriety in the criminal process. Definitions often provide the courts with an excuse for concealing the real reasons for their decisions by enabling them to take refuge in refined technical distinctions. This used to be the position, as we shall see in Chapter 12, with prejudicial evidence before the House of Lords' decision in *Boardman* v. *DPP*.[13] Evidence of the accused's past crimes was admissible if it fell into certain pre-defined categories. In reality these categories gave the trial judge extensive discretion and relieved him of the need to justify his decision to admit prejudicial evidence by reference to its real contribution to the proof of the accused's guilt. This is still the position in regard to hearsay evidence.

Rather than describe the law of criminal evidence in terms of rules, while at the same time allowing the judge considerable freedom in sidestepping them, we should account for the law in terms of the principles that guide the courts in the exercise of discretion. For instance, in relation to hearsay we will still maintain a principle of excluding hearsay but we will also give the judge discretion to admit it if it is of sufficient reliability and if it does not expose the innocent accused to an unwarranted risk of being convicted. Decisions concerning hearsay will therefore have to be justified on a case-by-case basis. Thus we will ensure that, instead of finding a convenient and often spurious exception for the purpose of admitting evidence, the trial judge has to consider the interest of the individual accused in a more open and reviewable manner.

It might be argued that discretion would undermine certainty and predictability in the conduct of criminal proceedings. The reverse is the case. At present definitions of admissible and inadmissible evidence give the impression of predictability but, as we have seen, the courts do not always follow these definitions with the result that they do not provide a reliable guide to the likely outcome. An acknowledgment of discretion will bring into the open the full range of the considerations that affect judicial decisions and their articulation will provide us with better means of predicting their future course.

Today many judges are unaware of the extent of the dis-

---

[13] [1974] 3 All ER 887.

cretion they possess and they are consequently discouraged from paying close attention to the general principles according to which it should be exercised. Thus the admissibility of hearsay, for instance, depends on how familiar the trial judge is with the manipulative techniques of this rule. An open acknowledgment of discretion will contribute to the development of the judicial instinct. Once the exercise of discretion comes to be accepted as one of the indispensable tasks of the trial judge, greater attention will have to be given to the principles guiding it. The development of guidelines for the exercise of discretion, far from weakening the protection of the innocent or undermining standards of propriety, for example, will promote better awareness of these important principles.

THE EFFECTS OF THE INSTITUTIONAL STRUCTURE OF TRIAL BY JURY

Serious criminal trials in England take place before a judge sitting with a jury. This mode of trial by jury exerts an important influence on the structure of the law of criminal evidence. Another feature of our mode of trial consists in its adversarial character, which also makes itself felt in the various practices developed within the framework of the law of evidence.

So far as trial by jury is concerned, the involvement of lay persons in adjudication fulfils an important social and political function by introducing into the process of fact-finding and law-application popular experience of the world and prevailing standards of morality. The task of the jury is not only to determine what happened but also to apply the law. We shall consider later the reasons for entrusting these tasks to ordinary citizens. It is sufficient to observe here that the jury fulfils a supervisory role in the criminal process in that it is given an opportunity, if not always a right, to express disapproval of the conduct of the case against the accused or of the criminal law itself. However, this also creates special problems with regard to the maintenance of proper standards in adjudication.

Broadly speaking, the judge controls the evidence presented before the jury and the jury returns a verdict of 'guilty' or 'not guilty' on the basis of the evidence so presented. The division of functions between judge and jury sometimes necessitates two-level rules; that is, rules that are partly directed to the judge and partly to the jury.[14]

For instance, in relation to certain inherently unreliable witnesses the judge must instruct the jury that, in the absence of corroboration, it is dangerous to convict on the basis of these witnesses' testimony. However, while the judge clearly has to administer this warning, there are no means of ascertaining whether the jury has understood its significance nor any procedure for ensuring that the jury has taken heed. It follows that emphasis must be placed on the clarity, the reasonableness, and the comprehensibility of the warning. This factor has, however, been overlooked because of a tendency to detach the discussion of the practice of the courts from its procedural context. Emphasis tends to be placed instead upon the form of the direction that the judge has to administer, so much so that judges have come to feel bound by precedent to pronounce incantations that are more likely to confuse than to guide. It is clearly fruitless to treat the judicial duty to warn the jury against a certain form of unwarranted reasoning in terms of an obligation to utter some settled form of words irrespective of whether it makes sense in the circumstances. A warning to the jury concerning the danger of relying on certain suspect witnesses, for example, must be capable of persuading the jury to adopt a certain mode of reasoning and to this end it has to be capable of making sense to ordinary persons.[15]

The fact that the jury has the power to apply the law according to prevailing standards necessitates the development of measures for controlling this power. We would not wish, for example, the jury to find an accused guilty on less than proof beyond reasonable doubt because the accused has a criminal record and does not, by popular standards, deserve the benefit of doubt. To forestall this possibility a judicial instruction has to appeal to the jury's moral sense in a persuasive manner. We shall see that here too the discussion in decided cases and

---

[14] For a description of the various technical devices employed by legal provisions regarding evidence see McNamara, 'The canons of evidence: rules of exclusion or rules of use?', (1985–6) 10 Adelaide L Rev 341.

[15] See Ch. 10 on corroboration.

commentaries is often dominated by the form that a warning has to take rather than by its goal, with the result that the courts have thereby undermined their own ability to promote the legal standards that the law proclaims.

Although much of the criminal law of evidence is intimately connected with the dual character of the adjudicator in trial by jury, it would, however, be a mistake to suppose that if criminal trials were conducted by judge alone the law of evidence would become redundant. The general concerns that have been outlined would still require procedural solutions. Nor is it obvious that in a trial by professional judges it would be easier to safeguard the innocent from conviction or the accused with a criminal record from prejudice. Indeed, the reverse might well be true. In a trial by judge alone it would not be easy to keep the judge ignorant of evidence that was found unworthy of admission. Nor would there be as wide an opportunity as there is at present to articulate the reasons for admitting or excluding a piece of evidence.

The adversarial nature of the trial gives the prosecution and the accused freedom in the choice of the issues to be tried and in the means by which to prove their respective cases. But this freedom cannot be unlimited, otherwise it will give undue scope for abuse. Accordingly the courts have evolved a number of practices for preventing misuse of the adversarial freedom by, for example, extending the dispute beyond what is strictly necessary in order to create confusion or prejudice. These practices are frequently conceived as fixed rules that govern the course of the presentation of evidence by the parties at the trial. We shall see, however, that the trial judge is not provided with a legal definition of what counts as abuse and is not relieved from the need to assess the utility of a given course of action proposed by one party against its disutility in terms of waste of time and the creation of confusion. In this regard too we will find that the judicial task is a demanding one and that the trial judge is often called upon to make difficult assessments of competing considerations.

By removing much of the dichotomy between rules and discretion we should be able to achieve a simplified account of the law of evidence. Many decisions will come to be viewed not as elaborations or refinement of rules, and thus as a binding precedent, but as instances of the exercise of judgment in the application of some general principles, such as the balancing of prejudicial effect and probative weight or the assessment of the likely probative contribution of a piece of evidence relative to the risk of confusion and waste of time attendant on its admission. The criminal law of evidence is sufficiently developed for it to be adequately explained without constant reference to the detail of decided cases. Hoffmann ascribed to the law of evidence the evolutionary tendency which Sir Peter Medewar had described in natural sciences:

The factual burden of a science varies inversely with its degree of maturity. As a science advances, particular facts are comprehended within, and therefore in a sense annihilated by, general statements of steadily increasing explanatory power and compass—whereupon the facts need no longer be known explicitly, i.e. spelled out and kept in mind. In all sciences we are being progressively relieved of the burden of singular instances, the tyranny of the particular. We need no longer record the fall of every apple.[16]

The law of evidence is now ready to relegate a number of 'apples' from the repository of valid rules to the annals of historical curiosity.

THE ORGANIZATION AND SCOPE OF EXPOSITION

Although this book does not deal with every single rule of criminal evidence, it does aim to examine the main features of the proof of guilt in jury trials. English law is the principal object of this examination but the problems that our courts have encountered are not unique and attention is often drawn to developments in other jurisdictions, particularly in the United States where many topics have benefited from extensive commentary.

The work is organized in three parts. The first part deals with the nature of trial by jury and the mechanisms of judicial control over the jury. Chapter 2 makes the point that the jury is not exclusively concerned with determining what happened, but

---

[16] (1978) 94 LQR 457, 459.

also has a role of interpretation which involves the exercise of non-factual judgment. Chapter 3 discusses the reasons for placing persons accused of serious crime in the charge of the jury and draws attention to some ramifications of these reasons for the law of evidence. Thereafter the discussion turns to a description of the more practical aspects of judicial control over the jury. Chapter 4 deals with the notions of relevance and admissibility and explains the judge's task in considering whether the evidence adduced by the parties is sufficiently relevant to be placed before the jury and in determining how and when to withhold from the jury issues for which insufficient evidence has been presented. Chapter 5 discusses the opinion rule and describes the measures adopted to prevent usurpation of the jury's function and the preservation of lay standards in the determination of facts and in the application of law. Chapter 6 outlines the concept of judicial notice and its use to ensure that the process of proof is confined only to those facts about which there is a genuine dispute. The concluding chapter of this part, Chapter 7, returns to judicial supervision and deals with some special policies that judges have evolved for preventing abuse of the adversarial process by waste of time, the creation of confusion, or the distortion of testimony.

The second part is devoted to the various devices employed to protect the innocent from conviction. The outstanding principle of protection is the requirement of proof beyond reasonable doubt as a condition of a verdict of guilty. Since the technique of imposing the burden of proof and the device of presumptions are used for allocating the risk of losing the case, it is necessary to explain these concepts before turning to their concrete application in criminal cases; accordingly, Chapter 8 provides a general explanation of these notions. Chapter 9 then examines the meaning of the requirement of proof beyond reasonable doubt. Proof beyond reasonable doubt is, as we have seen, only one of several measures taken to protect the innocent—the others include: the requirements of corroboration, discussed in Chapter 10, the rule against hearsay, examined in Chapter 11, and the principles governing the admission of prejudicial evidence, treated in Chapters 12 and 13.

The concluding part deals with various aspects of the moral acceptability and legitimacy of the criminal process. Chapter 14 outlines the limitations on the compellability of certain groups of witnesses and Chapter 15 is devoted to the privilege against self-incrimination. Finally, Chapter 16 discusses the problem of illegally or improperly obtained evidence.

What has been omitted is not necessarily unimportant. To provide an idea of the criteria for omission a number of instances may be mentioned.

The rules of evidence in magistrates courts are held, on the whole, to be the same as in trial by jury. Seeing the close connection between the institution of the jury and many of these rules the justification for equal application is by no means self-evident. However, the law concerning magistrates' courts is left outside the scope of this book because trial by jury brings out most prominently the problems of the protection of the innocent, the need for moral acceptability of the process, and the countervailing public interest in convicting offenders.

There is another important matter which is omitted in the present book: convictions resulting from pleas of guilty, which constitute the vast majority of convictions. Clearly here too there is a need to protect the innocent from conviction (not every plea of guilty is a genuine admission), and to maintain a high standard of moral acceptability (which may at times be undermined by plea-bargaining). These aspects have been left out because they require extensive consideration of out-of-court processes which would be better undertaken in a separate work. The doctrines of double jeopardy and of issue estoppel are similarly omitted because they do not deal with the actual process of fact-finding.

Lastly, there are a number of rules the main application of which is in civil proceedings but which have limited scope in criminal trials, such as legal-professional privilege and public-interest immunity. These too have been omitted, save for some general remarks.

2

Fact and Interpretation

THE LOGIC OF FACT-FINDING

Inferences from evidence are drawn according to ordinary common sense. This is the type of logical process that we employ in any form of practical inquiry into facts and it normally takes an inductive, rather than a deductive, form.[1] Deductive inferences are drawn from their premises as of necessity. To take the classical example: all men are mortal, Socrates is a man, therefore Socrates is mortal. This form of syllogistic inference, as may be seen from the example, does not reveal anything new; it merely spells out what is already contained in the premises. To affirm the premises and deny the conclusion would amount to a contradiction.

Inductive reasoning takes a different form. The inferred conclusion does not follow from the premises as a matter of necessity. Suppose the question is whether a certain person is a law student, and the evidence is that that person was seen in a library. If that were all we knew about the person, no inference could be drawn either way. But suppose we also know that 90 per cent of the persons using that particular library are law students. We can now say that there is a 90 per cent probability that the person in question is a law student.[2] Unlike the inferences of deductive logic, inductive reasoning produces only probability of a higher or lower value. Although we are justified in arriving at the conclusion that the person in question is very

---

[1] For a discussion of the significance of this distinction in the context of fact-finding in the law see *Wigmore on Evidence*, Tillers Rev, vol. 1A, s. 30.

[2] In mathematical calculus probabilities are expressed on a scale ranging from nought to one, the two extremes denoting, respectively, the certainty of the negative and affirmative assertions. In our example we can say that there is 0.9 probability that the person was a law student. For a simple explanation of the mathematical calculation of probabilities see Sir Richard Eggleston, *Evidence, Proof and Probability*, 2nd edn. (1983), ch. 2.

probably a law student, he may turn out not to be one. This possibility in no way affects the correctness of our inference of probability from the given premises.

The reliability of our inference in this example is influenced by the extent to which the statistical generalization is well supported and the degree to which it is sensitive to variations in the circumstances. If the generalization that 90 per cent of the library-users are law students was based on a count taken over a short period, it might reflect an unusual concentration of law students in the library at the time of the count. To the extent that the generalization is based on a wider sample and is less sensitive to variation in the relevant circumstances, we would be able to place greater confidence in it. But this confidence is not easily expressible in numerical terms.[3]

Although numerical values have been used in the above example little use is made of them in litigation because we rarely have statistical data about common occurrences. We do not know, for example, how frequently instances of flowerpots falling into the street are caused by negligence, nor do we have statistics to indicate what proportion of persons with a shifty look are liars. Ordinarily we are only able to call on rough assumptions about the likely course of events. In most cases that come before the courts the trier of fact is left to gather these generalizations from his own knowledge. The adjudicator would take, for instance, the fact that the accused ran away from the scene of the crime as an indication, albeit inconclusive, of the accused's possible guilt, using the assumption that people who behave in this way are generally guilty. Similarly, when confronted with oral testimony, the trier of fact has to employ prevailing assumptions concerning the indicators of truth-telling.[4] He brings to the judicial exercise the store of assumptions which he has absorbed from his intellectual, social, and cultural background. Some of these may be universal, such as our notions of gravitation; others may be more confined to time and place, such as the supposition that London underground trains are full of passengers during the rush-hour period.[5]

---

[3] L. Jonathan Cohen, *The Probable and the Provable* (1977), ch. 3.

[4] For an analysis of reasoning by reference to common-sense generalizations, see: J. L. Mackie, *The Cement of the Universe* (1974), ch. 3; also Ekelof, 'Free evaluation of evidence', 8 Scandinavian Studies in Law 47 (1964).

[5] See the discussion of these matters in Ch. 6.

While the great majority of generalizations are brought into the arena by the trier of fact, some will be introduced by the parties by means of expert evidence, such as medical information concerning the likely cause of death given certain circumstances. But whether a generalization is part of the adjudicator's background knowledge or whether it is brought to his attention along with the rest of the evidence, its function is exactly the same: to facilitate the drawing of inferences and assess their probability.

At a theoretical level there is a dispute whether the reasoning employed in the adjudication of facts conforms to the canons of the mathematical calculus of probabilities, or whether it conforms to some other kind of logic.[6] The ramifications of this dispute need not concern us here but it is important to consider the extent to which the trier of fact is called upon to do more than assess the probative support generated by the evidence placed before the court.

TRUTH AND CLASSIFICATION IN JUDICIAL FACT-FINDING

The distinction between law and fact lies at the basis of adjudication and has important implications.[7] The law has to be applied to the facts of the case which are either admitted by the parties[8] or have to be ascertained by the court. The law determines which types of facts give rise to rights and duties or have some other legal significance. The facts of the individual case are not themselves created by the law but exist independently of the law. When the facts are disputed, the function of the legal process is merely to find out what these facts are—namely,

---

[6] The principal exponent of the non-mathematical thesis is Jonathan Cohen, *The Probable and the Provable* (1977). See also Tribe, 'Trial by mathematics: precision and ritual in the legal process', 84 Harv L Rev 1329 (1971). For exposition of the mathematical thesis see Finkelstein, *Quantitative Methods in the Law (1978)* and Eggleston, *Evidence, Proof and Probability*, 2nd edn. (1983). For a recent rehearsal of the debate see 66 Boston University L Rev 377 ff. (1986). For a comprehensive review of the modern theories of proof see *Wigmore on Evidence*, Tillers Rev, vol. 1A, ss. 30–37.7.

[7] Much of the ground covered here is discussed in my paper: 'Law, fact or justice', 66 Boston University L Rev 487 (1986). See also J. Jackson, 'Questions of fact and questions of law', in Twining (ed.), *Facts in the Law* (1983), 85.

[8] Formal admissions may be made under s. 10 of the Criminal Justice Act 1967.

what happened—so that the appropriate legal results may then follow.[9]

To distinguish between law and fact is to draw a distinction between the question of what happened and the legal consequence of that which happened. The latter question is governed by normative rules laid down by the lawmaker or by morality. When we consider the legal consequences of what happened we aim to determine what the law requires the citizen or the court to do. To ascertain the facts, it is said, we only have to follow the forms of reasoning which are employed in any form of factual inquiry.[10] But, as we shall shortly see, this is a misleading oversimplification of what is involved in the ascertainment of facts in the courts.

Constitutive Facts and Evidential Facts

We may distinguish two types of facts which differ according to their function in a legal case.[11] The first type consists of constitutive facts.[12] These are facts to which the law attaches some consequence; for example, a person who intentionally kills another is guilty of murder. The courts exist to adjudicate only upon factual disputes which are of concern to the legal system: disputes that involve legal rights, duties, or have other legal consequences. Hence they are concerned with the ascertainment of constitutive facts.[13] The second type consists of evidential facts. These are facts which are presented to the tribunal for the

---

[9] Other principles that rest on the distinction include the following: the litigants must plead facts and not law; the jury decides questions of fact while questions of law are left to the judge; decisions on the law give rise to binding precedent, decisions on the facts do not; the former may be challenged on appeal but not, generally, the latter.

[10] Thayer, *A Preliminary Treatise on Evidence at Common Law* (1898), 265.

[11] The term 'fact' extends to include events, beliefs, and other states of affairs.

[12] Other terms are also employed for this purpose, such as ultimate, material, operative, or dispositive facts.

[13] As Thayer put it: 'When it is said that a fact is for the jury, the fact intended . . . is that which is in issue, the ultimate fact, that to which the law directly annexes consequences'. Thayer, *A Preliminary Treatise on Evidence at Common Law* (1898), 197. Constitutive facts are often couched in terms of the relevant rules, such as, for instance, 'offer', 'acceptance', 'trespass', and so on. This explains why in describing the facts for the purpose of litigation we often have recourse to legal notions.

purpose of establishing constitutive facts (or facts from which constitutive facts may be inferred); for example, the fact that the accused's fingerprints were found on a gun might enable us to infer that he killed the victim. This example, like most cases in court, involves a number of steps. A police officer produces a gun in court and testifies that he found it at the scene of the crime. An expert testifies that he found a fingerprint on the gun and that he identified it as belonging to the accused. The gun and the testimony concerning it are evidential facts. From this the jury infers other evidential facts: that the accused's fingerprint was indeed on the gun and that the accused fired the gun. Finally, the jury comes to a conclusion about the constitutive fact: that the accused killed the victim. Although it is imperative to distinguish between evidence before the court (testimony, documents, objects, etc.) and inferences drawn from it on the way to a finding about the constitutive facts, no special terminology has been employed for this purpose, trusting that the distinction can be made clear without it. Explaining the notion of an evidential fact Hohfeld wrote: 'An evidential fact is one which, on being ascertained, affords some logical basis—not conclusive—for inferring some other facts. The latter may be either a constitutive fact or an intermediate evidential fact.'[14]

Hohfeld was careful to specify the kind of inference he had in mind. He emphasized that it was a mistake to suppose that the constitutive facts stated in a criminal charge were proved by the facts that happened in reality; rather, he pointed out, the latter were the constitutive facts themselves. Thus, in a trial in which the accused is charged with burglary by entering a building and stealing therein, the fact that he put his arm through the window is not proof of entry, it is itself the entry, the constitutive fact. Yet the move from the statement 'X put his arm through the window' to the conclusion 'X entered the building' is also governed by some rules. Hohfeld implied that the rules pertinent to this move were different from the rules involved in inferring a constitutive fact from an evidential fact.

The first move, from the witness's statement to the conclusion that something was the case, is governed by what Thayer called

---

[14] *Fundamental Legal Conceptions* (1923), 34.

'logic and common-sense'.[15] The relation of an evidential fact (the witness's statement) to the fact it tends to prove (that X put his arm through the window) is referred to as relevance. One fact is relevant to another if the existence of the former increases the probability of the latter's existence or non-existence.

The second move, from 'X put his arm through the window' to 'X entered the building', is a different question.

In our example, the accused can be convicted only if putting his arm through the window amounts to the constitutive fact of 'entry'. But how do we find out whether it does?

The Problem of Classification and of Application of Law

In litigation the tribunal has to identify the constitutive facts before it can attach legal consequences to them. The definition of a crime may contain terms such as 'setting fire' to something, 'threatening', 'injuring', 'killing', and the like. Determining the scope of such terms is not necessarily straightforward nor is it a peculiarly legal problem. Supplying one with potatoes usually involves bringing the potatoes to one's house and leaving them there. But, as Elizabeth Anscombe explained, this is only generally the case for there are exceptional circumstances where these actions will not amount to supplying the potatoes, as where the purported supplier sends somebody to remove them shortly after they have been left at the house in question.[16] She goes on to say that

There can be no such thing as an exhaustive description of *all* the circumstances which theoretically could impair the description of an action of leaving a quarter of potatoes in my house as 'supplying me with a quarter of potatoes'. If there were such an exhaustive description, one would say that 'supplying me with a quarter of potatoes' *means* leaving them at my house, together with the absence of any of those circumstances. As things are, we could only say 'It means leaving them . . . together with the absence of any of the circumstances

---

[15] Thayer, *A Preliminary Treatise on Evidence at Common Law* (1898), ch. 6, p. 263.
[16] 'On brute facts', (1958) 18/3 Analysis.

which would impair the description of that action as an action of supplying me with potatoes'; which is hardly an explanation.

The question of whether our accused 'entered' the building when he put his arm through the window is therefore a question of classification. There are a number of ways of dealing with such a problem. It may be left to be determined by the common usage of the word 'entering'. If, however, putting one's arm through a window does not count as entering in common parlance, the trier of fact may nevertheless be asked to decide whether it should count as entering for the purpose of burglary; in which case the question will fall to be decided as a matter of policy. Alternatively, the law itself may take up this problem and lay down that for the purpose of the offence of burglary putting one's arm through a window is 'entering'. Whichever method is employed, the determination of whether putting one's arm through the window amounts to entry is decidedly not a question that can be answered by finding out what happened.

A question of classification will typically arise at the end of an evidential process of inference and will be concerned with a constitutive fact. In the example just mentioned the question of whether the accused's act amounted to entry has to be answered only once we have inferred from the evidence that the accused did indeed put his arm through the window. But a question of classification can arise in the course of the inferential process. For example, part of the evidence against the accused is that a person, since deceased, said that he saw a tall man outside the relevant window. A question arises whether this statement can apply to the accused who is only five foot ten. The question of whether putting one's arm through the window amounts to burglary and the question of whether a five foot ten person may be described as tall are clearly governed by different considerations. The former is a question about what the law forbids while the latter is a question about what the deceased meant to convey by his statement.

When, as is frequently the case, the trier of fact has to decide whether the accused has inflicted 'grievous bodily harm' or has committed an act which is proximate enough to the commission of an offence to count as a criminal attempt, the issue before the

court will typically involve both factual inference and classification.[17] Questions of this type are described in legal practice as
questions of fact. These include, for example, whether a certain
activity amounts to 'trade',[18] whether a certain conduct is 'dishonest',[19] or amounts to 'insulting behaviour',[20] or whether an
activity was carried out for 'immoral purposes'.[21]

This characterization conflates the two kinds of reasoning we
have been discussing: for whether a certain activity is to be
considered as 'trade', as 'dishonest', etc. cannot always be free
of policy considerations and cannot necessarily be determinable
only by the facts that happened. Such questions may require
the tribunal to decide the scope of the legal prohibition.[22] If this
kind of question is left to the trier of fact, as is usually the case,
it follows that the function of this trier of fact is not confined to
deciding what happened but extends to decisions regarding the
appropriate consequences of the facts it finds.

Questions of classification of the kind we have been discussing may have to be resolved by reference to a diversity of
standards. Dishonesty, for example, will be resolved according

---

[17] It may be doubted, in the particular circumstances of an individual case,
whether the leaving of the potatoes at the defendant's house should count as
supplying them to him, but before we can resolve this doubt we must decide
whether the potatoes were indeed left at the defendant's house. In other words, the
question about 'supplying' arises only once we have decided that the potatoes were
left at the house.

[18] *Edwards* v. *Bairstow* [1955] 3 All ER 48, 56. Lord Radcliffe said: 'All these cases
in which the facts warrant a determination either way can be described as questions
of degree and, therefore, as questions of fact.' The same view is expressed by Lord
Hailsham LC in *Cole Bros Ltd* v. *Phillips* [1982] 2 All ER 247, 253. Accordingly
questions admitting of only one answer are characterized as questions of law. This
puts theory on it head. Facts either existed or they did not. By contrast, the law can
take different forms. On characterizing questions of degree as questions of fact see
W. A. Wilson, 'Questions of degree', (1969) 32 MLR 361.

[19] In *Feely* [1973] 1 All ER 341 it was decided that dishonesty, for the purpose of
the Theft Act 1968, was a question of fact to be determined by the jury.

[20] *Brutus* v. *Cozens* [1972] 2 All ER 1297, decides that this is also a question of fact
for the jury.

[21] *Gray* (1982) 74 Cr App R 324.

[22] See discussion by Mureinik, 'The application of rules: law or fact?', (1982) 98
LQR 587; Griew, 'Directions to convict', [1972] Crim L Rev 204; McConville,
'Directions to convict: a reply', [1973] Crim L Rev 164; Glanville Williams, 'Law
and fact', [1976] Crim L Rev 472. For a discussion of whether the law itself may be
regarded as a fact see A. R. White, 'Fact in the law', in Twining (ed.), *Facts in the
Law* (1983), 108; Tillers, 'The value of evidence in law', (1988) 89 NILQ 167.

to the current precepts of morality. By contrast, whether the victim suffered grievous bodily harm will have to be determined by reference to popular standards of gravity which will reflect the current state of medicine. We shall see in the next chapter that questions of classification are sometimes reserved for the judge as problems of interpretation of law and at other times they are left to the jury as problems of application of law. What is important to note here is that however these questions are described, they involve more than merely finding out what happened.

'Particular fact situations', Professor Hart wrote, 'do not await us already marked off from each other, and labelled as instances of the general rule, the application of which is in question; nor can the rule itself step forward to claim its own instances.'[23] The definitions of criminal offences, in common with most other rules of law, are open-textured, allowing 'at the point of actual application, a fresh choice between open alternatives'.[24] In principle, however, the open texture of rules does not necessarily have to result in the trier of fact bringing to bear his own interpretation on the legal terminology. It is possible to draw a line between fact-finding (in the sense of what happened) and interpretation and to confine the role of the jury to the former. We could devise a procedure whereby the disputed facts were isolated prior to being brought before the trier of fact. On a murder charge, for example, the prosecution's case may hinge on the presence of the accused in a certain place at a crucial time. The trier of fact could be kept ignorant of the nature of the charge and be asked to pronounce only on the issue of the accused's presence. In this way we would not only release the trier of fact from applying the law to the facts (here, deciding whether the conduct of the accused amounted to the offence of murder) but also insulate the process from many external influences. The knowledge, for example, that the accused is a bad person may naturally prejudice the adjudicator.

But even if such a system of isolation of fact from value were practically feasible, it would hardly be attractive. This is because we require more of the trier of fact than this kind of

---

[23] *The Concept of Law* (1961), 123.   [24] Ibid. 125.

fact-finding out of context.[25] We expect a criminal verdict to carry moral weight as well as factual accuracy. In England this moral dimension is created by a procedure which makes the trier of fact understand the gravity of the accusation brought against the accused and the seriousness of the consequences for the accused, should the accusation be proved.[26]

[25] It is doubtful whether a system of strict isolation would appeal to the public even if it were statistically provable that in a long run of cases we would obtain more factually correct decisions by such a method of trial. Verdicts produced by a system that can measure nothing except the probabilities of purely factual evidence might not be capable of fulfilling the social functions required from judicial decisions. See Nesson, 'The evidence or the event? Or judicial proof and the acceptability of verdicts', 98 Harv L Rev 1357 (1985).

[26] It is interesting to note that in civil cases there is a reluctance to determine important points of legal principle as preliminary issues on assumed facts. Even in civil litigation there is a tendency to fashion the legal principle as close as possible to its factual context.

3

The Jurisdiction over Fact and Interpretation in Trial by Judge and Jury

FACTUAL AND NON-FACTUAL DIMENSIONS OF JURY ADJUDICATION

There is a general common-law principle that questions of fact are tried by the jury and questions of law by the judge. This principle is said to be subject to occasional exceptions. However, many questions of classification and interpretation which go beyond just learning what happened are designated as questions of fact and are as a result placed within the jury's province.[1] There is some recognition that the law–fact distinction is unsatisfactory as a definition of the jurisdictional divide because the jury's power extends beyond the facts and into the law.[2] Early generations of judges recognized that the jury had some power over the law. Lord Mansfield wrote that 'by means of a general verdict they [the jury] are entrusted with a power of blending law and fact, and following the prejudices of their affections or passions.'[3]

A number of factors combine to make up the jury's power to exercise non-factual judgment. The first concerns the jury's interpretive role. Problems of interpretation left to the jury include the determination of the scope of 'threatening, abusive or insulting' behaviour;[4] of 'grievous bodily harm';[5] of whether

---

[1] See Cornish, *The Jury* (1968), 102.

[2] Lord Diplock thought that there was 'a risk of confusion even in the minds of lawyers themselves as to the respective functions of judge and jury in a criminal trial, if we classify as questions of law all those matters which it is for the judge to decide, and as questions of fact all those matters which he must leave to be decided by the jury.' *DPP* v. *Stonehouse* [1977] 2 All ER 909, 918; also discussion in Thayer, *A Preliminary Treatise on Evidence at Common Law*, (1898), ch. 5.

[3] *Shipley* (1784) 4 Douglas 73, 163. See discussion in Devlin, *The Judge*, 1981, 117 ff.; Green, verdicts *According to Conscience* (1985).

[4] Public Order Act 1936, s. 5; *Brutus* v. *Cozens* [1972] 2 All ER 1297.

[5] For the purpose of aggravated assaults under ss. 18 and 20 of the Offences against the Person Act 1861.

'an act is more than merely preparatory to the commission of the offence' with the attempt of which the accused is charged.[6] To illustrate the jury's ability to shape the law we need only mention two examples. The first concerns the element of 'dishonesty' in theft and other related offences.[7] It is for the jury to decide whether the accused was dishonest and the jury's decision must be made according to 'the ordinary standards of reasonable and honest people'.[8] The dishonesty requirement is additional to the *mens rea* requirement of intention.[9] Thus rather than draw clear lines of criminality in the area of theft and deception, the legislature leaves it to the jury to decide whether conduct conforming with the basic elements of the offence deserves punishment because it is dishonest.[10]

Another instance of the infusion of the jury's moral sense into the definition of a criminal offence is also provided by statute. Section 14 of the Sexual Offences Act 1956 makes it an offence 'for a person to make an indecent assault on a woman'. According to the recent House of Lords decision in *Court*, indecency means 'conduct that right-thinking people will consider an affront to the sexual modesty of a woman'.[11] Lord Griffiths emphasized the jury's role in thus defining this offence:

It seems natural to me that this extra element [i.e. *additional to the mental element required for the commission of an assault*] should be that which constitutes the essence of the offence, namely an intent to do some-

---

[6] Criminal Attempts Act, 1981, s. 1; for comments on the jury's role see *DPP* v. *Stonehouse* [1977] 2 All ER 909.

[7] See in particular ss. 1 and 15 of the Theft Act 1968 and the Theft Act 1978.

[8] *Ghosh* [1982] 2 All ER 689, 696.

[9] In theft, for example, the basic mental element is an intention permanently to deprive the owner of the property in respect of which the accused is charged; Theft Act 1968, s. 1. In the offence of evasion of liability by deception under s. 2(1)(*b*) of the Theft Act 1978 the basic *mens rea* is an intention to make permanent default. In these offences a conviction will not take place unless the jury were also satisfied that the accused's conduct was dishonest.

[10] These offences are concerned with the protection of property, which includes real and personal property and other intangible property; Theft Act 1968, s. 4(1). Since the offences of theft and deception cover a large range of violations of proprietary rights there was probably no practical way of devising a definition capable of capturing all conduct popularly regarded as criminally reprehensible and, at the same time, excluding conduct that is not so regarded. Hence it was right that the legislature should qualify criminality by reference to the moral standards of the community.

[11] [1988] 2 All ER 221, 223.

thing indecent to a woman in the sense of an affront to her sexual modesty or, in other words, an intent to do that which the jury find indecent.[12]

The jury's interpretive function is not always that wide and the construction of many other terms, such as 'malice aforethought', is reserved for the judge.[13] There is therefore no *a priori* definition of the border between the two jurisdictions. To find out whether a certain issue is for the jury or the judge we have to fall back on tradition and decided cases.

A second factor that enhances the jury's scope for non-factual judgment is the finality of acquittals. In England, the United States, and most commonwealth jurisdictions, there can be no appeal against a jury verdict of acquittal. In 1724 Pratt CJ declared: 'It was never yet known that a verdict was set aside by which the defendant was acquitted in any case whatsoever, upon a criminal prosecution.'[14]

Lastly, the criminal procedure makes it difficult to disentangle factual from non-factual judgment by requiring the jury to pass a verdict of guilty or not guilty upon the charge as a whole rather than find the existence of individual factual elements of the offence charged.[15] As long ago as 1670 Vaughan CJ held in *Bushell's case*:

That decantatum in our books, *ad quaestionem facti non respondent judices, ad quaestionem legis non respondent juratores*, literally taken is true: for if it be demanded, what is the fact? the judge cannot answer it: if it be asked, what is the law in the case, the jury cannot answer it. . . . In

---

[12] [1988] 2 All ER 223.

[13] Even where a question of interpretation is reserved for the judge, there will always be room for jury interpretation too because, as we have seen, problems of interpretation can arise at lower levels of the description.

[14] *King* v. *Jones* (1725) 8 Mod 201, 208. For the historical background see: Thayer, 'Law and fact', 4 Harv L Rev 147 (1890); Cornish, *The Jury* (1968), 116 ff.; Devlin, *The Judge* (1981), ch. 5. See also Kadish and Kadish, *Discretion to Disobey* (1973), 162. Not all lawyers approve of this power: Griew, 'Directions to convict', [1972] Crim L Rev 204; for a reply see McConville, 'Directions to convict: a reply', [1973] Crim L Rev 164. It is notable that no such principle existed in favour of the verdict of a civil jury which could be overturned if contrary to the law. For discussion see: Devlin, *Trial by Jury* (1956), 89–91; Scheflin and Van Dyke, 'Jury nullification: the contours of a controversy', 43 Law and Contemp Prob 51 (1980).

[15] Weinstein, 'Some difficulties in devising rules for determining truth in judicial trials', 66 Col L Rev 223, 238 (1966); Cornish, *The Jury* (1968), 122.

special verdicts the jury inform the naked fact, and the Court deliver the law. . . . But upon all general issues . . . the jury . . . resolve both law and fact complicately . . . so though they answer not singly to the question what is the law, yet they determine the law in all matters where issue is joyn'd, and tryed in the principal case, but where the verdict is special.[16]

The rule is no different today. In Lord Devlin's words, the 'principle [is] that no man is guilty unless he is so found, not upon this or that issue but upon the *whole crime*'.[17]

We may conclude that under our system of criminal justice fact-finding and interpretation of law are so interwoven in the criminal procedure that it is sometimes difficult to discern where fact ends and law or morality begin. Intention, for instance, is a central requirement in the more serious offences. Yet that 'X intended to wound' is not a straightforward fact. It requires interpretation against the background of both the agent's own mental and moral make-up and the community's moral conventions.[18]

THE SIGNIFICANCE OF THE RIGHT TO TRIAL BY JURY

Having outlined the extent of the power possessed by the jury we have to draw a distinction between what it is within the jury's power to do and what it is right that it should do. The fact that the jury's acquittal cannot be overturned does not necessarily imply that a jury which acquits is always right. We may still say: the jury has acquitted, its verdict is final, but it was wrong for it so to do.[19]

No one would suggest that a jury may acquit for any reason it

---

[16] (1670) Vaughan 135, 143. See discussion in Devlin, *The Judge* (1981), ch. 5.

[17] Devlin, *The Judge* (1981), 143. General verdicts are not obligatory but special verdicts upon individual issues are discouraged. *Archbold's Pleading, Evidence and Practice in Criminal Cases*, 42nd edn. (1985), 516–17. For historical discussion see Milsom, 'Law and fact in legal development', (1967) University of Toronto L J 1.

[18] See discussion in P. Arenella, 'Rethinking the functions of criminal procedure: the Warren and Burger courts' competing ideologies', 72 Georgetown L J 185 (1983).

[19] It is consistent to hold that the jury is duty-bound to exercise its judgment within certain constraints and, at the same time, that for reasons of policy we will not interfere with a verdict of acquittal even where the jury has breached its duty.

chooses but in practice it is not easy to disentangle the exercise of the power to acquit from what it is right for the jury to do. Juries are asked to return a general verdict of guilty or not guilty and are neither required nor allowed to give reasons for their verdicts. Thus it is difficult, if not impossible, to ascertain whether a verdict rests on a finding of fact or on non-factual judgment and, if the latter, whether the non-factual judgment is permissible. There are, however, situations where it is clear that a jury has acquitted in the face of adequate proof of the commission of the offence charged because the jury has considered the prosecution of the accused unjust, as in some recent prosecutions under the Official Secrets Acts. How should we characterize such verdicts? The juror's oath is: 'I will faithfully try the defendant and give a true verdict according to the evidence'.[20] Should we say that members of the jury acted wrongly because they did not abide by their oath? Sometimes we would certainly say so. But on other occasions an acquittal contrary to the evidence might meet with public approval because the jury expressed a widely held moral disapproval of an unjust law or an unjust prosecution. While it might be said that the verdict was legally wrong, because the jury did not abide by the oath, we might also allow that the jury was morally conscientious.

This leads us to the reasons for vesting such powers in the jury. Modern justifications for the jury system do not single out the jury as peculiarly able to interpret the law correctly.[21] Nor, we should note, is it claimed that juries possess special qualities that make them a particularly accurate instrument for discovering the truth. Lord Devlin stresses the ability of juries to do justice according to the 'merits' and not just according to the law.[22] By this he means that the jury has the power to determine the case according to extra-legal considerations. For example, Lord Devlin explains that '[i]t is generally accepted that a jury will tend to favour a poor man against a rich man:

---

[20] Practice Note [1984] 3 All ER 528.

[21] For a survey of the literature see: Baldwin and McConville, *Jury Trials* (1979), 135; Kalven and Zeisel, *The American Jury* (1971).

[22] *Trial by Jury* (1956), 151–8; id., *The Judge* (1981), 84 ff.; Damaska, *The Faces of Justice and State Authority* (1986), ch. 1.

... because ... there is a feeling that a rich man can afford to be less indifferent to the misfortune of others than a poor man can be.'[23] The acceptance of this consideration is all the more telling since it runs counter to the legal principle which holds that the relative wealth of the parties is irrelevant. Making a similar point in relation to the American jury, Winter wrote that 'the jury may be viewed as one of those institutions in the criminal process with discretion to exercise leniency'.[24] It is thought an advantage that the jury should have considerable power to regard certain facts as material to its decision even when those facts do not formally affect the legal consequences, and sometimes even to exercise its power to disregard the law altogether.[25]

The principal reason for assigning this role to a group of twelve ordinary citizens is the need to secure public confidence in criminal verdicts.[26] Given that no external mechanism exists for checking the accuracy of judicial fact-finding, confidence has to be vested in the body making the decision.[27] There is a mutual dependence between belief in the correctness of factual decisions and trust in the body making them and its wisdom.

Trial by jury secures public trust in the criminal process in a number of related ways. First, as Lord Devlin wrote, the

jury is the means by which the people play a direct part in the application of the law. . . . Constitutionally it is an invaluable achievement that popular consent should be at the root not only of the making but also of the application of the law. It is one of the significant causes of our political stability.[28]

---

[23] Devlin, *Trial by Jury* (1956), 155.

[24] Winter, 'The jury and the risk of nonpersuasion', 5 Law and Society 335, 340 (1971).

[25] For empirical investigation of this aspect see: Kalven and Zeisel, *The American Jury* (1966), ch. 15; also Lempert, 'Uncovering "non-discernible" differences: empirical research and the jury-size cases', 73 Mich L Rev 643 (1975).

[26] Hart and McNaughton, 'Evidence and inference in the law', in D. Lerner (ed.), *Evidence and Inference* (1958), 48, 52. For a general discussion of the importance of procedure in obtaining public confidence see W. H. Simon, 'The ideology of advocacy', [1978] Wis L Rev 29.

[27] 'even in connection with the visible and tangible facts of a particular case, it is constructive truth—the verdict of the jury . . . that must pass as the unchallengeable truth.' N. Isaacs, 'The law and the facts', 22 Col L Rev 1, 6 (1922).

[28] *The Judge* (1981), 127.

Secondly, by involving ordinary citizens in the criminal trial we make the community's own standards of justice and morality an arbiter of guilt or innocence. To quote Lord Devlin again:

> It is not a perverse acquittal that an innocent man is looking for when he asks for trial by jury, but a trial by men and women of his own sort. A professional man accused of a professional offence is not said to be seeking a perverse acquittal when he demands to be tried by men of his own profession. He is invoking the obverse of the right which enables the ordinary man charged with an ordinary offence to demand trial by ordinary men and not by a professional. Each is seeking the application to his case of a set of standards which he believes will be better understood and applied by one tribunal as by the other.[29]

By means of the jury system we ensure that our criminal-trial system does not become detached from popular perceptions of right and wrong and does not thereby lose the public support which is so important to its effective operation. We have already seen how this is achieved in relation to the offence of theft, where popular notions of honesty have to determine the criminality of an otherwise prohibited act. Of equal, if not greater, significance, is the recent development in relation to the mental element of murder. The moral difficulties in deciding whether foresight of death should suffice as *mens rea* for this offence have led the courts to place the question of intention in the lap of the jury rather than attempt to settle it themselves. Buxton has observed that 'intention in the criminal law is now in effect not an issue of law at all, but rather an issue of fact, to be determined by the jury without theoretical speculations and thus without theoretical guidance from the judge.' Far from regarding it as an abandonment of responsibility, Buxton welcomes this development because 'shared values and assumptions about the implications of actions and the circumstances in which those actions occur may be a safer guide to culpability than analytical

---

[29] Ibid. 141–2; also E. P. Thompson, 'Subduing the jury', *London Review of Books* (4 and 18 Dec. 1986). This outlook receives acknowledgment in the Attorney General's 'Guidelines on Jury Checks', (1981) 72 Cr App R 14, para. 5(b), where it is assumed that the jury has the function of 'reflecting the broad spectrum of the views and interests in the community'; Cornish, *The Jury* (1968), 126, and interesting discussion in *Adams* v. *Texas* 448 US 38 (1980).

deductions from generalised verbal definition.'[30] Trust in the criminal system is secured by the fact that the jury applies standards of adjudication which are both generally familiar and widely accepted.[31]

An example of the jury's ability to promote a public sense of security may be seen in the reaction to disturbing instances of unreliability of police testimony. Recently English juries have shown a marked reluctance to convict on the uncorroborated evidence of policemen.[32] Juries have also tended to show their mistrust for the enforcement of the Official Secrets Acts through a widespread reluctance to convict in prosecutions under these acts.[33] Professor Cornish concluded from his investigations into the English jury that 'a provision of which juries will not approve is unlikely to be regularly enforced'.[34]

Jury-trial can provide opportunity for a moral test of innocence. This point is illustrated by Lord Devlin's account of the trial of Dr John Bodkin Adams in 1957. Bodkin Adams, a medical practitioner, stood accused of the murder of a Mrs Morrell, who had been his patient. During the preliminary

---

[30] 'Some simple thoughts on intention', [1988] Crim L Rev 485, 495. See also Duff, 'The obscure intentions of the House of Lords', [1986] Crim L Rev 771. Where trial of fact does not take place, as where the accused pleads guilty, the system allows greater scope for divergence from popular perceptions of justice, e.g., in plea-bargaining situations.

[31] See Cornish, *The Jury* (1968), 126. There are other methods of enhancing public trust. Offences of lesser seriousness are tried in magistrates' courts where lay justices try both the law and the facts. Other legal systems too have found it necessary to devise ways of achieving this end, as Prof. Stein has shown in *Legal Institutions, The Development of Dispute Settlement* (1984), 39, 44.

[32] Especially when such evidence consisted of an alleged confession. Interestingly neither judges nor lay magistrates seem similarly troubled. See also Glanville Williams, 'Letting off the guilty and prosecuting the innocent', [1985] Crim L Rev 115, and comment by Worboys, 764.

[33] A less laudable instance of jury reluctance to convict concerns drunken driving; *Cracknell* v. *Willis* [1987] 3 All ER 801, 804. There also appears to be a reluctance to convict policemen accused of committing offences in the course of their duties; see Glanville Williams, 'Letting off the guilty and prosecuting the innocent', [1985] Crim L Rev 115, 116.

[34] Cornish, *The Jury* (1968), 116. Lord Goff testifies, and seemingly approves, of jury refusal to convict of murder, in the face of indisputable intention on the part of the accused to cause grievous bodily harm, because of common-sense reluctance to regard such state of mind as justifying a verdict of murder; 'The mental element in the crime of murder', (1988) 104 LQR 30, 49. However, the supreme court of Canada has strongly disapproved of an express invitation to a jury to ignore the law: *Morgentaler* (1988) 62 CR (3d) 1.

proceeding two other murder charges were levelled against the accused but were later dropped. Before and during the trial widespread rumours prevailed that the accused had murdered many other patients for personal gain. In his memoirs of the trial Lord Devlin, who tried the case, draws an analogy between the conduct of this case and the old forms of trial.[35] For the trial by battle, he explains, the Crown selected one champion in the form of a charge related to the death of Mrs Morrell. Since the accused was acquitted this champion was defeated. But Lord Devlin stresses that the accused was not altogether cleared because he declined to enter the witness-box, which Lord Devlin compares to the trial by ordeal. He sets out the effect of the accused's failure to testify as follows:

As for the ordeal, the accused declined it. The only way in which he could have challenged his invisible foes [*the public rumours*] was by going into the witness-box and submitting to cross-examination. He could not, of course, have been cross-examined on anything except the Morrell case. The result of the test would have depended not so much upon the content of his answers as upon his demeanour and what he showed of himself to the public. Certainly he had something to explain in the Morrell case and his explanations would have had to have been plausible. If they were and if he had been acquitted, the British public would have acquitted him of all else because he had faced the music. Refusal of the ordeal left him with a verdict of Non-Proven on all that was rumoured or alleged and untried as well as in the trial itself.[36]

To be believed by a jury seems tantamount to receiving a special moral dispensation.[37] Such dispensation, however, can only be given to an accused who enters the witness-box and exposes his entire character to examination before a jury so as to enable the latter to evaluate his conduct.

In the United States the awareness of the contribution of juries has found expression in decisions concerned with jury-composition and in the debate about the role of juries in

---

[35] *Easing the Passing* (1985) 197.   [36] Ibid.

[37] It is not suggested that jury verdicts always have this effect. It is doubtful that the force of verdict rests, as Professor Nesson suggests, in the fact that the jury saw the accused but not the public and that therefore the latter is bound to accept the judgment of the former; 'The evidence or the event? On judicial proof and the acceptability of verdicts', 98 Harv L Rev 1357, 1370 (1985).

capital-punishment trials. The Supreme Court has held that an accused has a right that his jury be selected from a representative cross-section of the community. Failure to do so amounts to a denial of the right to jury-trial and of due process.[38] Justice Marshall wrote:

When any large and identifiable segment of the community is excluded from the jury service, the effect is to remove from the jury room qualities of human nature and varieties of human experience, the range of which is unknown and perhaps unknowable. . . . exclusion deprives the jury of a perspective on human events that may have unsuspected importance in any case that may be presented.[39]

'Human qualities' play a crucial rule in relation to capital punishment. In certain American jurisdictions the jury is charged with the task of sentencing in capital trials, as well as with the determination of guilt. On these occasions the jury has to make certain assessments of the facts and choose between capital punishment and life sentence. A protracted debate has taken place about whether exclusion from the jury of persons who object to capital punishment is constitutional. *Witherspoon* v. *Illinois*[40] decided that such exclusion was unconstitutional.[41] The debate reached a climax in 1980 in *Adams* v. *Texas*.[42] Under the Texas procedure once the jury convict of murder they are asked three questions: first, whether the killing was deliberate, secondly, whether the accused would continue to be a threat to the community, and, thirdly, whether the accused's conduct was unreasonable in response to any provocation. If they answered all in the affirmative the death penalty followed. In *Adams* jurors who could not undertake that the mandatory death penalty or life imprisonment would not affect their deliberations on any issue of *fact* were excluded. The Supreme Court held that the exclusion was unconstitutional. Speaking for the majority, Justice White addressed himself to the jury's function in answering the above questions and said:

[38] *Taylor* v. *Louisiana* 419 US 522 (1975).
[39] *Peters* v. *Kiff* 407 US 493, 503–4 (1972).
[40] 391 US 510 (1968).
[41] For a somewhat different view see *Bumper* v. *North Carolina* 391 US 543 (1968).
[42] 448 US 38 (1980).

In essence, Texas juries must be allowed to consider 'on the basis of all the relevant evidence not only why the death sentence should be imposed, but also why it should not be imposed', *Jurek* v *Texas* . . . This process is not an exact science and the jurors unavoidably . . . exercise a range of judgment and discretion while remaining true to their instructions and their oaths.[43]

Justice Renquist, in a minority, was quick to point out that

the court's observations in this regard are as true when applied to the initial determination of guilt as they are when applied to the sentencing proceedings. In either determination, a juror is required to make 'unscientific' determinations and to exercise a good deal of discretion within the boundaries of his or her oath.[44]

It is doubtless true that the choice between life imprisonment and the death sentence requires a good deal more value-judgment than the primary determination of guilt. Nevertheless, the American debate is instructive in that it illustrates the point that the combination of fact-finding and of non-factual judgment is a central feature of our criminal procedure.

In the criminal field there are two central social concerns in relation to which the jury can reflect public sentiment: the need to protect innocent people from conviction and punishment and the need to protect the community from crime. However, these two social concerns are not necessarily complementary.[45] They may argue for different standards of fact-finding because the more we protect innocence by increasing the standard of proof of guilt the fewer guilty people we are likely to convict, and the weaker will the protection from crime be.[46]

A thorough assessment of the advantages and disadvantages of the jury system requires an analysis of the objects of adjudication which is beyond the scope of this work. Nor is it possible to discuss here the empirical evidence about the extent to which juries are swayed by non-factual considerations or, indeed, the

[43] *Adams* v. *Texas* 448 US 38, 46.

[44] Ibid. 54. More recently the Supreme Court seems to have somewhat retreated from the liberal standard set up by the majority in *Adams*: *Wainright* v. *Witt* 469 US 412 (1985); *People* v. *Brown*, argued in the Supreme Court in Dec. 1986.

[45] This point will be discussed in Ch. 9.

[46] Posner, 'An economic approach to legal procedure and judicial administration', 2 Journal of Legal Studies 399 (1973).

reasons for which the legislature or the judiciary defer to jury judgment on particular non-factual issues. The aim is limited to drawing attention to the general significance and value that attach to trial by jury and to the procedural devices that call for lay judgment in the ascertainment of facts and in the interpretation of law, and even allow moral judgment to override the law in favour of acquittal.[47] This procedure gives the jury an opportunity to strike a balance between the community's need for protection from crime and the need to protect the innocent. But the extent of the jury's power also makes it necessary to place a rein on a jury's freedom to be swayed by moral considerations. We must therefore turn to the mechanism by which this is achieved.

THE JUDGE'S SUPERVISORY ROLE

The task of controlling the jury's freedom falls primarily upon the trial judge. He fulfils this role by determining the range of the evidence upon which the jury is called to return a verdict. Much of the criminal law of evidence is occupied with principles by which judges limit the breadth of the events to be placed before the jury and the evidence to be assessed by them. These principles form the subject of several later chapters. Here it is only necessary to outline the areas with which these principles are concerned so as to provide an idea of the extent of the judicial contribution to the fact-finding process.

The judge carries out the primary filtering of evidence to be admitted in the case. This filtering is governed to a large extent by principles of utility. Evidence which is irrelevant, in the sense that it does not tend to prove or disprove any fact in issue, will of course be excluded. But even relevant evidence may be excluded if its probative contribution is likely to be negligible in relation to the waste of time and the trouble that may be caused by its admission.[48] At times the trial judge's task is to assess the

---

[47] The existence of at least some moral licence to disregard the law increases the jury's power because deviation from the law can be justified.

[48] Some of the practices concerning admissibility have developed into definite rules, such as the rule against hearsay, discussed in Ch. 11. Not all the exclusionary rules that once existed continue to subsist. Some, such as the best-evidence rule, have died a quiet death and have been replaced by tests of sufficiency of probative weight. See *Garton* v. *Hunter* [1969] 1 All ER 451; *Kajala* v. *Noble* (1982) 75 Cr App R 149; *Wayte* (1983) 76 Cr App R 110.

prejudicial potential of evidence adduced by the prosecution and admit it only if its probative weight exceeds its prejudicial effect. Thus judges may forbid disclosure of the accused's previous crimes or of other discreditable conduct on his part.[49]

When determining admissibility, the judge may need to conduct a factual investigation himself. For instance, it is for the judge to determine whether a witness possesses sufficient mental capacity to justify reception of his testimony.[50] Similarly, before admitting in evidence a confession attributed to the accused the judge has to determine whether the circumstances of his interrogation rendered his confession unreliable.[51]

By requiring the judge to decide what should and what should not go before the jury two objectives are achieved. First, the jury is spared distraction by trivial and unhelpful evidence and is enabled to concentrate attention on the most significant evidential aspects. Secondly, the judge is in a position to limit the scope of jury discretion by excluding unduly prejudicial evidence such as information about the accused's previous crimes. In this way he can forestall the possibility that the jury would base their verdict on the accused's record.[52]

The judge does not confine himself to examining individual pieces of evidence, he also has to decide whether the cumulative probative potential of the evidence is sufficient to allow the case to be submitted to the jury's decision. There are two stages at which such a decision might have to be taken. At the end of the

[49] See Chs. 12 and 13.

[50] Children and Young Persons Act 1933, s. 38. For the procedure of ascertaining the competence of witnesses see *Archbold's Pleading, Evidence and Practice in Criminal Cases*, 42nd edn. (1985), 377–80.

[51] The Police and Criminal Evidence Act 1984, s. 76 (see Ch. 14). To this end the judge will hold a fact-finding hearing in the absence of the jury. On such occasions the question may arise whether the judge is bound by the exclusionary rules: whether he is precluded from receiving evidence that may not be presented to the jury. Prof. Cross thought that the judge was not bound by these rules; *Cross on Evidence*, 5th edn. (1979), 68. It is more probable that the answer depends on the nature of the rule. It is unlikely, for example, that in determining the reliability of a confession the judge is free to have regard to prejudicial evidence.

[52] See discussion in Ch. 12. When the judge hears argument or evidence on admissibility, the hearing takes place in the absence of the jury if prejudicial matters are likely to come up, as when the accused's criminal record or the admissibility of his confession are in question. But when no prejudicial evidence is involved the hearing is held in the presence of the jury; see, for instance, *Reynolds* [1950] 1 All ER 335. But see *Goldstein* [1983] 1 All ER 434.

prosecution's case the accused may submit that there is no case to answer. This submission asserts that the prosecution has not adduced sufficient evidence to justify a conviction even if its evidence is believed. If the submission is accepted the judge will direct the jury to acquit. A similar test may have to be applied to the entire body of the evidence when both parties have presented their cases in order to determine whether there is sufficient evidence to allow the case to go to the jury or whether the judge should order an acquittal.[53]

It is relatively easy for the judge to control what goes before the jury by means of excluding evidence or by altogether withdrawing the case from the jury. What is far more demanding an exercise is to exert some influence on what the jury do with the evidence that has been admitted in the case. The judge has considerable opportunity to influence the jury by his comments upon the evidence during the case and in the course of the summing up to which members of the jury have to be treated before retiring for their deliberation. In this summing up the judge will set out the elements of the offence charged and the facts which the jury must find in order to convict. He will explain the nature of the burden of proof which the prosecution has to discharge. Above all, the summing up

should ... include a succinct but accurate summary of the issues of fact as to which a decision is required, a correct but concise summary of the evidence and the arguments on both sides and a correct statement of the inferences which the jury are entitled to draw from their particular conclusions about the primary facts.[54]

The instrument employed for placing a rein on the jury's freedom to be swayed by inappropriate considerations in reaching their verdict consists therefore in verbal directions addressed by the judge to the jury. Unfortunately, the effectiveness of judicial directions has been somewhat undermined by insufficient appreciation of the overall function of the jury.

---

[53] These matters are discussed in Ch. 4 where we shall also see that there is room for further judicial intervention on appeal on the grounds that the verdict is unsafe or unsatisfactory.

[54] *Lawrence* (1981) 73 Cr App R 1, 5. 'Primary facts' refer in all probability to evidential facts. When expressing their view about the evidence judges tread carefully because juries are known to resent being told what to do and could well return a verdict which is the opposite of the one pressed by the judge.

DIRECTIONS ADDRESSED TO THE WILL AND
EXPLANATIONS ADDRESSED TO THE UNDERSTANDING

The development of the means of controlling the jury's power has been retarded by the prevalence of two assumptions: that the jury is exclusively or predominantly a trier of fact and that the jury can be made to obey unquestioningly the trial judge's instructions. To some extent the first assumption has encouraged the second. The assumption that the jury has no business in adjudication except to determine the facts has too readily led judges to believe that a jury can be instructed to obey directions on how to proceed in relation to matters that are not strictly confined to factual inferences. Attempts to rule juries by such directions must clearly be less effective than explanations that appeal to the jury's understanding and engage their approval. To do the latter, one has to be aware of the subtle ways in which non-factual judgment influences the ascertainment of facts.

The fact that the jury's function is not strictly confined to ascertaining what happened is well acknowledged in practice. Prosecution and defence counsel alike are aware of the relationship between the moral and political outlook of individual jurors and the trial's outcome.[55] In the public debate about the right to trial by jury those arguing against its erosion do not rely on the jury's ability to determine objective truth accurately. Rather, their argument is founded upon the desire to be judged by reference to the current social standards.[56]

By contrast, within the law of evidence there is a dogged reluctance to accept the role of the jury as more than factfinder. The persistence of the twin assumptions about the jury's

---

[55] The significance of moral outlook in jury verdicts received open recognition in the debate about the propriety of jury vetting. Cf. *Crown Court at Sheffield, ex parte Brownlow* [1980] 2 All ER 444, 452–4, 455–6, where the Court of Appeal described as unconstitutional the practice of investigating the criminal records of prospective jurors with a view to excluding them from the jury panel, except in limited situations. See also: *Mason* (1980) 71 Cr App R 157; 'Attorney General's Guidelines on Jury Checks', [1980] 2 All ER 457; and earlier discussion regarding the jury selection in the United States, Ch. 3, text corresponding to n. 38.

[56] Thompson, 'Subduing the jury', *London Review of Books* (4 and 18 Dec. 1986); Nicol, Official secrets and jury vetting, [1979] Crim L Rev 284; D. Wolchover, 'The right to jury trial', 136 NLJ 530 (1986).

function and its pliability are largely responsible for the sense of mystification that is sometimes expressed about jury reasoning. Professor Cross wrote:

It must be admitted . . . that no discussion of the law of evidence in criminal cases will ever be completely satisfactory until we have some idea of the extent to which the average jury understands the directions which the law requires the judge to give, and whether jurors are as comprehending, uncomprehending or prejudiced as some of the rules of evidence suppose.[57]

This sense of ignorance is largely unrealistic. After all, we have trial by jury so that verdicts will be returned according to the prevailing standards of reasoning. Doubts concerning jury understanding of directions are wrongly addressed when they are directed at the ability of juries to comprehend. The proper object of these doubts should be those judicial directions, of which there is a substantial number, which common sense finds difficult to digest. A few examples will suffice to illustrate this point.

Until 1972 judges had to instruct juries that testimony which required corroboration could not in law corroborate another witness whose testimony also required corroboration. Such direction was clearly contrary to common sense. Suppose that witness *A* gives an account of the events in issue. *A* is a child whose evidence might be unreliable and therefore requires corroboration. Witness *B* is then called and he gives an account that confirms *A*'s account in every detail. *B* is an accomplice of the accused and therefore also requires corroboration. In common sense, if *A* and *B* are independent witnesses (in the sense that they could not have influenced each other), the conformity of their respective accounts corroborates or confirms each of their accounts. To instruct the jury otherwise would be something that they would find difficult, perhaps even impossible, to comprehend. But we do not need much research to know this. The fault in this case lies not with the jury but with the law that makes such a demand. Although that particular rule no longer subsists, there are other aspects of the law of corroboration

---

[57] *Cross on Evidence*, 5th edn. (1979), 64. For an examination of jury thinking see Cornish and Sealy, LSE Jury Project, 'Juries and the rules of evidence', [1973] Crim L Rev 208.

which still make impractical demands from people who are guided by common sense.[58]

Another example concerns the practice of 'refreshing' memory. When a witness no longer remembers a car registration number he fleetingly observed many months before, he is allowed to refresh his memory from a note he made of the number. Yet the law decrees that the jury must be instructed that the evidence of the number is not the note but the witness's testimony which repeats the content of the note, regardless of the fact that the witness remembers nothing of the note's contents.[59]

Sometimes juries are instructed that they may take into account the accused's previous crimes when assessing the credibility of his denial of guilt but must not use his criminal record in determining his guilt.[60] It is very much to be doubted that the judges giving such an instruction would be any better able to obey it. A similar doubt may be entertained in relation to directions under section 27(3) of the Theft Act 1968. On a charge of handling stolen goods previous convictions for similar offences are admissible to prove the accused's knowledge that the goods were stolen. But the jury must be instructed not to take such convictions into account on the issue of the accused's possession.[61]

Merely to entertain doubt as to whether juries can follow instructions which defy reason seems unduly cautious. It is almost certain that they cannot.[62] But this does not provide a reason for questioning the suitability of jurors as triers of fact but rather furnishes reasons for questioning the suitability of those instructions: a point Bentham made close to two centuries ago.

The central theme of Bentham's work on evidence is, in

---

[58] See *DPP* v. *Hester* [1972] 3 All ER 1056 and further discussion in ch. 10.

[59] Of course the witness would usually remember that he made the note and could authenticate it, but to tell a jury that an authenticated note is proof of the facts stated therein would infringe the rule against hearsay; see discussion in Ch. 6.

[60] See further discussion in Ch. 12 and 13.

[61] Due to the impractical nature of this direction trial judges sometimes exclude such evidence altogether: *List* [1965] 3 All ER 710, dealing with the statutory predecessor of the Theft Act. This subject is discussed in Ch. 12.

[62] See Jerome Frank, *Law and the Modern Mind*, Anchor books edn. (1963), 195; Criminal Law Revision Committee, 11th Report, cmnd. 4991, para. 25..

Twining's terminology, the 'anti-nomian thesis'.[63] It holds that rules of law that attempt to direct how evidence should be used in reaching a conclusion are more liable to lead the trier of fact astray than to a correct determination of the issue.[64] Legal rules that require the judge to tell the jury that this or that evidential use of a piece of evidence is forbidden are ineffectual because they often conflict with the jury's function of deciding according to their common sense. At present a jury may be told to convict if they believe the accused's guilt beyond reasonable doubt; the same jury may be told also not to give credence to such and such evidence. One can order a person to act but one cannot order (or even force) a person to believe and hence an instruction not to believe the believable is as ineffective as an instruction to believe the unbelievable.[65] Bentham understood well that mandatory instructions can be effectively addressed to the will ('Do this or that') but not to the understanding ('Believe this or that').[66]

In dealing with the law of criminal evidence we shall have numerous opportunities to notice how the two misconceptions just discussed have affected judicial control over the jury. Many attempts to confine the non-factual judgment of the jury have foundered as a result of a persistent reluctance to acknowledge the intricate ways in which our system of criminal justice allows non-factual and extra-legal judgment to permeate into the ascertainment of the facts. Juries should certainly be helped to reason correctly, but various judicial dictates have proved inadequate help because of their failure to engage the jury's understanding.

---

[63] Twining, *Theories of Evidence: Bentham and Wigmore* (1985), 66.

[64] *Rationale of Judicial Evidence*, (1827), vol. 3, pp. 219 ff.

[65] One can instruct the jury to proceed as if they held a certain belief, but the effectiveness of such instruction is very doubtful.

[66] See Bowring edn, vol. 6, pp. 151–2, and Twining, *Theories of Evidence: Bentham and Wigmore* (1985), 67.

4

Relevance, Admissibility, and Judicial Control

As we have seen, judicial control over the fact-finding process in jury-trials is exercised to a large extent through the filtering of the evidence to be presented before the jury and by withholding cases from jury adjudication. This chapter outlines the concepts involved in this exercise, of which the most important are relevance and admissibility.

RELEVANCE AND ADMISSIBILITY

Inferences from evidence are drawn according to ordinary logic so that only data which in ordinary reasoning count as evidence for a disputed proposition should be allowed to be presented at the trial. This is the rule of relevance. In Stephen's phraseology, relevance denotes that

any two facts ... are so related to each other that according to the common course of events one either taken by itself or in connection with other facts proves or renders probable the past, present or future existence or non-existence of the other.[1]

Neither the need for relevance nor its definition is a peculiarly legal matter, as Thayer pointed out:

There is a principle—not so much a rule of evidence as a proposition involved in the very conception of a rational system of evidence, as contrasted with the old formal mechanical systems—which forbids receiving anything irrelevant, not logically probative.[2]

---

[1] Digest, 12th edn. art. 1.
[2] *Preliminary Treatise on Evidence* (1898), 264. See also Montrose, 'Basic concepts of the law of evidence', (1954) 70 LQR 527. For a comprehensive survey see *Wigmore on Evidence*, Tillers Rev., vol. 1A, 37.

However, it does not follow from the fact that relevance is determined by the logic of inductive reasoning that considerations peculiar to the legal process do not impinge on the acceptability of evidence in the courts. On the contrary, most of the law of evidence consists of principles which alter the course of free proof. The most basic of these devices is the test of admissibility, by which evidence is tested for its qualification to be admitted in a court of law.

A distinction is commonly drawn between relevance and admissibility. Relevance is said to be entirely governed by logic whereas admissibility is thought to be a matter of law.[3] Both of these assumptions are liable to mislead if left unqualified.

The test of relevance operated by the courts is more complex than is usually assumed due to institutional constraints. The ascertainment of facts under any system of inquiry, be it legal or otherwise, is bound to be affected by the conditions under which the inquiry is conducted, by the character of its functionaries, by the methods employed, and, not least, by the purpose for which it is carried out. One of the most obvious constraints is that of resources. Criminal cases of a serious nature are tried before a judge and a jury consisting of twelve lay members of the community. This composition of the court may not be the most conducive to the ascertainment of truth. Truth may be more readily discovered by twenty-four jurors instead of twelve or two or three professional judges instead of one. But accuracy is not the only concern of the legal system.[4] In deploying the inevitably limited resources allocated to the Lord Chancellor's office accuracy is only one amongst several considerations; others include the speed of adjudication and the availability of persons for jury service.

Institutional constraints do not end with the organization of the courts but continue to exert their influence throughout the process of trying an issue of fact. The constraints of cost and time have several consequences in the context of judicial pro-

---

[3] *Phipson on Evidence*, 12th edn. para. 153. 'Admissibility' is sometimes used as denoting that a piece of evidence is both relevant and that it does not infringe any legal rule of exclusion. Thus while no irrelevant evidence can never be admissible, relevant evidence may still be inadmissible.

[4] Dworkin, *A Matter of Principle* (1985), 72.

ceedings. Litigants cannot be allowed to take disproportionate amounts of the court's time, because this will deny the same facility to others. The rich litigant must not be allowed to waste time and augment cost so as to exhaust the poorer litigant or the coffers of the state. Lastly, the purpose of adjudication is not only to ascertain the facts but also to resolve the charge as promptly as possible so as to put to rest public concern about criminal activity. Promptness is necessary if wrongs are to be effectively remedied, if social tensions are to be relieved, and if crime is to be effectively combated.[5]

A constraint of a different kind is imposed by the limitation of the human mind. There is an inevitable limit to the amount of evidence that a person, however experienced and talented, can digest. In piling up evidence, albeit relevant, a point will come where any further piece of evidence may detract from, rather than increase, the correctness of the final assessment.

The risk of overburdening the trier of fact is not only a function of the number of witnesses called but also of the extent to which their reliability may be tested. Suppose that the witness for the prosecution testifies that the accused struck the first blow. The credibility of the witness is clearly important and the accused proposes to challenge the witness's record for accuracy by showing that a month earlier the witness made a mistake in observing some other event from a similar distance. However, this course gives rise to a new dispute over what happened on the previous occasion, which is otherwise unrelated to the present issue. Clearly, the more such side-issues are allowed, the more likely it becomes that the trier of fact will be distracted and reach a mistaken conclusion on the main issue.[6]

It follows that in determining whether a certain piece of evidence should be admitted into the trial the judge has, first, to consider whether the evidence bears a logical relationship to the issue and, if it does, whether it makes a sufficient contribution to what is already known to justify the loss of time and the

---

[5] For discussion see Fuller, 'The forms and limits of adjudication', 92 Harv L Rev 353 (1978); Eisenberg, 'Participation, Responsiveness, and the Consultative Process, etc'. 92 Harv L Rev 410 (1978); Scott, 'Two models of the civil process', 27 Stan L Rev 937 (1974–5).

[6] *Agassiz* v. *London Tramway Co* (1872) 21 WR 199.

trouble that its reception might cause.[7] Thus the question of
relevance in legal proceedings does not only involve a determination of whether the evidence affects the probability that the
event at issue occurred but also whether it affects it sufficiently
to be worthy of admission. 'The degree of relevance needed to
qualify for admissibility is not', as Hoffmann put it:

a fixed standard, like a point on some mathematical scale of
persuasiveness. It is a *variable* standard, the probative value of the
evidence being balanced against the disadvantages of receiving it such
as taking up a lot of time or causing confusion.[8]

If the judge is to decide whether a piece of evidence is likely
to make a sufficient probative contribution, he has to assess its
potential probative weight.[9] The difference between assessment

---

[7] Bentham was the first to explore the relationship between the admissibility of
evidence and its utility; Bentham, *Rationale of Judicial Evidence* (1827), vol. 4, bk. IX,
p. 477. In *A–G* v. *Hitchcock* (1847) 1 Exch 91, 105, Rolfe B remarked that '[i]f we
lived for a thousand years instead of about sixty or seventy, and every case was of
sufficient importance, it might be possible and perhaps proper . . . to raise every
possible inquiry as to the truth of statements made . . . In fact mankind finds it to be
impossible.' See also *Hollington* v. *Head* (1858) 4 CB (NS) 388, 391 per Willes J. For
discussion of relevance see Michael and Adler, 'The trial of an issue of fact', 34 Col
L Rev 1224, 1462 (1934), and Hoffmann, 'Similar facts after *Boardman*', (1975) 91
LQR 193, 204–5. The conjunction of a test of utility with a test of relevance is of
course not a peculiarly legal necessity. It arises in all practical inquiries.
[8] Op. cit. 205. See also, USA, Uniform Rules, Rule 45, which lays down: 'the
judge may in his discretion exclude evidence if he finds that its probative value is
substantially outweighed by the risk that its admission will (a) necessitate undue
consumption of time, or (b) create substantial danger of undue prejudice or of
confusing the issues or of misleading the jury; or (c) unfairly and harmfully surprise
a party who has not had reasonable opportunity to anticipate that such evidence
would be offered.' See also Federal Rules of Evidence (R. D. 1971) 403, which
makes exclusion mandatory when probative value is substantially outweighed by
the danger of unfair prejudice, confusion of issues, or misleading the jury, but
discretionary in the case of other dangers. Cf *Wigmore on Evidence*, Tillers Rev, vol.
1A, ss. 28, 37.4. This is essentially a Benthamic view. It is Bentham's philosophy
that the ascertainment of truth must take into account not only rectitude of decision
but also its timely utility; *Rationale of Judicial Evidence* (1827), vol. 1, pp. 31 ff.;
Twining, *Theories of Evidence: Bentham and Wigmore* (1985), 91.
[9] Weight consideration is inevitable in determining relevance. Suppose that the
issue is whether the accused was in a certain town at a certain time. The prosecution offers to show that a spent train ticket to that town was later found in the
accused's coat. This evidence is relevant because we are able to appeal to the
generalization that people in possession of spent train tickets have usually used
them for the nominal destination. The evidence is relevant because it is capable of
producing a probability regarding the issue. Its probability is its weight. We may
say, therefore, that it is relevant because it has a weight.

by the judge and assessment by the jury lies in the purpose and method of the assessment. The judge is not concerned to estimate the final weight of any piece of evidence, let alone the probative outcome of the whole of the evidence. At the admissibility stage he is only concerned to make a rough and ready estimate of the potential contribution that the evidence in question might make and whether it is substantial enough to justify admission. The admissibility test is therefore a composite test made of a mesh of considerations of logical probabilities and of practical utility. By contrast the jury's primary duty is to examine the entire body of evidence in order to decide whether or not the charge against the accused has been proved.

On some occasions the potential contribution of the evidence adduced will be immediately apparent to the judge; for example, the testimony of an eyewitness to the disputed event. At other times its potential will only emerge from a juxtaposition of the evidence in question and other pieces of evidence or known facts. If, upon the presentation of an individual piece of evidence, the judge is in doubt about its relevance, he will ask the party offering it how it relates to the rest of the evidence he plans to adduce. If a publican claims that the brewer supplied him with bad beer, then the fact that the same brewer supplied another pub with bad beer might not be of sufficient weight to be admissible. But it would become sufficiently weighty if it is also shown that it was one of five incidents of supply of bad beer by the same brewer in the same neighbourhood within the space of a day.[10]

The law does not provide rules by which to determine whether a piece of evidence has sufficient probative potential to justify its reception.[11] The self-same piece of evidence in support of the self-same proposition may be sufficient in one set of circumstances but not in another. To quote Thayer:

---

[10] Cf. *Holcombe* v. *Hewson* (1810) 2 Camp. 391.

[11] It is possible to translate the constraints of time and confusion into fixed rules of law. We may, for example, make a rule that no trial should last more than two days or that no party should call more than four witnesses. Although such rules will save time they will be insensitive to the additional function of the court, that of reaching a correct conclusion. For the view that the law does lay down rules in this regard see *Wigmore on Evidence*, 3rd edn. (1940), vol. 1, s. 12, p. 298. For commentary see: Twining, *Theories of Evidence: Bentham and Wigmore* (1985), 154; *Wigmore on Evidence*, Tillers Rev, vol. 1, sec. 12 nn.

[The evidence] must not barely afford a basis for conjecture, but for real belief; it must not merely be remotely relevant, but proximately so. Again, it must not unnecessarily complicate the case, or too much tend to confuse, mislead or tire . . . the jury, or to withdraw their attention too much from the real issues of the case. Now in the application of such standards as these, the chief appeal is made to sound judgment; to what our lawyers have called, for six or seven centuries at least, the discretion of the judge. Decisions on such subjects are not readily open to revision; and, when revised, they have to be judged of in a large way; this is expressed by saying that the question is whether the discretion has been unreasonably exercised, has been abused.[12]

Although precedent cannot obviate a case-by-case assessment of sufficiency of relevance, past decisions can help to identify goals or policies which need be pursued in the reception of evidence. They inform us of the importance of factors such as the avoidance of confusion, of proliferation of issues, and of the saving of cost.

There is, however, one aspect of admissibility that is a matter of law in the sense of being governed by rules. To be admitted evidence must not only be of sufficient probative potential, it must also not be specifically excluded by a rule of law.[13] As we shall see, some rules exclude certain types of evidence irrespective of weight while others require the judge to strike a balance between weight and prejudicial effect.

Some writers have suggested that the concepts of relevance and of admissibility do not comprehend all the basic concepts in this field. It is said that there is a further concept to be reckoned: materiality.[14] 'Materiality' is supposed to denote that the fact in support of which evidence has been adduced is of legal consequence in the proceeding. A question of materiality in this sense is not really a question about evidence. As we have seen, the trial of fact is concerned solely with ascertaining those facts

---

[12] *Treatise*, 516.

[13] These are commonly referred to as 'exclusionary rules'. Strictly speaking, these are not rules of admissibility because they only ordain exclusion not inclusion; if a piece of evidence is not so excluded its admissibility would depend on it being sufficiently relevant.

[14] See James, 'Relevance, probability and the Law', 29 Calif L Rev 689 (1941); Montrose, (1954) 70 LQR 527. Cf. *Wigmore on Evidence*, 3rd edn. (1940), vol. 1, s. 12, p. 296.

which the substantive law fixes as giving rise to legal results, and about the existence of which there is a dispute between the parties. No other facts may be the subject of a trial of fact.[15] Since 'relevance' is a relative term, it can only be relative to facts in issue. If evidence is not relevant to one of these facts, it will be excluded and we do not need a concept of materiality to tell us this.[16]

'NO CASE TO ANSWER'

Between the admissibility stage and the verdict there is an intermediary stage at which a decision about the evidence has to be taken.[17] At the end of the case for the prosecution, before the accused is required to present his defence, the judge may be required to consider whether the prosecution has submitted sufficient evidence to justify putting the issue to the jury.[18] If the judge concludes that the prosecution has not done so, he will stop the trial and direct the jury to acquit.[19] The test formulated by Professor Cross is that the judge must

inquire whether there is evidence which, if uncontradicted, would justify men of ordinary reason and fairness in affirming the proposition which the proponent is bound to maintain, having regard to the degree of proof demanded by the law with regard to the particular issue.[20]

[15] As a matter of general principle the courts will not entertain hypothetical questions: *Re Barnato* [1949] ch. 258.
[16] If the concept of materiality is put forward as a test for ascertaining which factual elements are required by the substantive law for any legal result, then the question is one of interpretation of the substantive law and not about the evidence in the case.
[17] For a discussion of a further stage see next section.
[18] The prosecution's duty to produce sufficient evidence is sometimes referred to as a duty to make out a 'prima-facie case'.
[19] The need for a decision on this matter usually arises on a plea of 'no case to answer' put forward by the accused at the close of the prosecution's case. But even in the absence of such submission the judge must consider whether the prosecution has made out a prima-facie case, for otherwise the accused has a right not to be put to his defence: *Abbott* [1955] 2 All ER 899, 903. See Glanville Williams]1965] Crim L R 343 and 410. On the duty of the judge to ensure that justice is done according to the law, irrespective of submissions from accused see: *Stirland* v. *DPP* [1944] AC 315, 327–8 per Viscount Simon LC; P. M. North, '*Rondel* v. *Worsley* and criminal proceedings', [1968] Crim L R 183.
[20] *Cross on Evidence*, 5th edn. (1979), 77. See also Edwards, (1970) 9 Western Australia L Rev 169.

Accordingly, the prosecution must adduce evidence capable of producing in the mind of an ordinary person conviction beyond reasonable doubt. Where the prosecution fails to adduce evidence in support of one of the elements of the offence or where the prosecution adduces evidence which is incapable of leading to the conclusion of guilt there will clearly be no case to answer.

It has been said that in determining whether there is a case to answer the judge does not weigh the evidence and does not assess the credibility of witnesses but only determines whether the required minimum of evidence has been adduced.[21] This statement is misleading. A certain amount of weighing is unavoidable at this stage because the trial judge has to form a view whether the evidence could potentially produce conviction beyond reasonable doubt.[22] Suppose that the case for the prosecution rests on one witness who alternately affirms and denies that he saw the witness commit the offence. The judge is likely to hold that no reasonable jury could possibly convict on such evidence precisely because its probative weight is negligible.

The courts are uncertain how to treat mistaken rejection of a plea of 'no case to answer'. The difficulty concerns the situation where the judge wrongly rejects the accused's submission at the end of the prosecution's case, and in the course of his defence (or as part of a co-accused's case) other incriminating evidence is revealed which fills the gap in the prosecution's case. The question inevitably arises: Should the Court of Appeal quash the conviction?[23]

There are two schools of thought. The first is that on appeal the court must consider the evidence as a whole and that a

---

[21] *Barker*, unreported, per Lord Widgery CJ quoted in *Mansfield* [1978] 1 All ER 134, 140.

[22] See J. C. Wood, 'The submission of non case to answer in criminal trials: the quantum of proof', (1961) 77 LQR 491.

[23] Section 2(1) of the Criminal Appeal Act 1968, which deals with curable mistakes by the trial judge, has no application in this situation. It lays down 'that the Court may, notwithstanding that they are of opinion that the point raised in the appeal might be decided in favour of the appellant, dismiss the appeal if they consider that no miscarriage of justice has actually occurred.' Had the accused's submission of 'no case' been accepted, there would have been a directed acquittal. See *Abbott* [1955] 2 All ER 899, 902, construing the predecessor of the present provision.

conviction will be quashed only if it is unsafe or unsatisfactory on the totality of the evidence, including that which was adduced by the defence.[24] A second school of thought is supported by cases holding that as the accused had a right to be acquitted at the end of the prosecution's case, his conviction must therefore be quashed.[25]

Two competing factors are involved here. On the one hand, there is the principle that the accused has a right to say: 'If the prosecution can prove my guilt let it do so. I need do nothing to help it'. Consequently, once the prosecution's case has collapsed, the accused has a right to be acquitted without being put to his defence.[26] On the other hand the accused was, in fact, convicted on perfectly admissible evidence, and to acquit him now is to set free a person about whose guilt there is no doubt. Our courts seem to have given prominence to the latter factor and have upheld convictions where guilt appeared evident but not otherwise.[27] This approach is to be preferred because it gives due weight to the public interest in the conviction and

[24] *George* (1908) 1 Cr App R 168; *Pearson (No. 1)* 1 Cr App R 77, quoted in *Payne* v. *Harrison* [1961] 2 All ER 873; *Jackson* (1910) 5 Cr App R 22; *Fraser* (1911) 7 Cr App R 99; *Power* [1919] 1 KB 572.

[25] *Joiner* (1910) 4 Cr App R 64; *Abbott* [1955] 2 All ER 899. The former case was explained away in *Power* [1919] 1 KB 572. It has been suggested that the distinction between the two groups of decisions is that in the former the accused himself supplied incriminating evidence after the prosecution's case while in the latter the additional evidence was given by a co-accused who threw the blame on the accused; the authority is *Payne* v. *Harrison* [1961] 2 All ER 873 which was, however, a civil case and involved different considerations from those applicable in a criminal case; see *ibid.* 877. The neatness of the distinction is somewhat spoiled by *Power*, a case belonging to the first group, where the incriminating evidence was also supplied by a co-accused, albeit called as witness for the accused. It is difficult to see how this distinction can justify a different reaction to a mistaken rejections of 'no case' submissions.

[26] In *Abbott* [1955] 2 All ER 899, 903; Similarly, if the accused has pointed to sufficient evidence in the prosecution's case indicating the possibility of self-defence and the prosecution has failed to adduce evidence to rebut it, the judge must withdraw the case from the jury and not deny the accused the choice of whether or not to defend himself: *Hamand* (1986) 82 Cr App R 65 (see also Ch. 9). Unlike the position in criminal cases, in civil cases the judge need not rule on a defendant's submission of 'no case to answer' unless the latter elects not to give evidence. See also Wood, 'The submission of no case to answer in criminal trials . . .' (1961) 77 LQR 491.

[27] *Joiner* (1910) 4 Cr App R 64, does not fit into this explanation. Perhaps it was for this reason that it was not followed in *Power* [1919] 1 KB 572.

punishment of offenders, and avoids the unedifying spectacle of acquitting an accused whose guilt has been in fact proved.[28]

It is to be noted that the trial judge may withdraw not only the entire charge from the jury but he may also withdraw a specific issue. The accused, for example, bears the burden of establishing the defence of insanity. If he fails to adduce *prima facie* evidence to sustain his plea, the judge will instruct the jury to dismiss the plea without considering it.

THE TEST OF 'UNSAFE OR UNSATISFACTORY'

There is a further stage at which the trial judge may be asked to decide whether the case should be withdrawn from the jury: after both the prosecution and the defence have presented their respective cases. Section 2(1)(a) of the Criminal Appeal Act 1968 provides that the Court of Appeal 'shall allow an appeal against conviction if they think . . . that the conviction should be set aside on the ground that under all the circumstances of the case it is unsafe or unsatisfactory'.[29] At one stage it was thought that an analogous test had to be applied by the trial judge in deciding whether to let the case go to the jury because a conviction based on evidence that cannot safely support a guilty verdict is bound to be quashed on appeal. A trial judge, it may be said, should not allow the jury to return a verdict of guilty which is bound to be quashed later.[30]

In *Galbraith*[31] the Court of Appeal has rejected this view, explaining that if the trial judge were allowed to consider whether a conviction would be unsafe or unsatisfactory he would inevitably be applying his views to the weight of the

---

[28] Different considerations may obtain where the trial judge rejected the accused's submission of 'no case' not in the mistaken belief that the prosecution has made out a *prima facie* case but because he felt that the accused should be made to answer the accusation all the same.

[29] This provision was first enacted by s. 4(1) of the Criminal Appeal Act 1966. This provision replaced s. 4(1) of the Criminal Appeal Act 1907 which empowered the court to quash a conviction if it thought it to be unreasonable or incapable of being supported by the evidence.

[30] *Mansfield* [1978] 1 All ER 134. For commentary see Devlin Committee on Evidence of Identification, para. 4.67.

[31] [1981] 2 All ER 1060.

evidence, which he must not do.[32] This explanation is unsatisfactory for, as we have just seen, a certain amount of weighing is inevitable. Indeed, some weighing of evidence is sanctioned by the very tests formulated in *Galbraith* itself:

(a) Where the judge comes to the conclusion that the Crown's evidence, taken at its highest, is such that a jury properly directed could not properly convict upon it, it is his duty, upon a submission being made, to stop the case. (b) Where however the Crown's evidence is such that its strength or weakness depends on the view to be taken of a witness's reliability, or other matters which are generally speaking within the province of the jury and where on one possible view of the facts there *is* evidence upon which a jury could properly come to the conclusion that the defendant is guilty, then the judge should allow the matter to be tried by the jury.[33]

The Court of Appeal's approach in *Galbraith* may be supported on the grounds that since an acquittal is not subject to appeal, a mistake by the trial judge in withdrawing the case from the jury is irredeemable. Thus, it could be said, except in extreme cases of insufficient evidence (falling under head (a) above) it is prudent to leave the final assessment of whether the evidence is safe and satisfactory to the Court of Appeal.[34]

The *Galbraith* policy of reserving the 'safe and satisfactory' test to the appellate instance suffers, however, from an almost fatal flaw: appellate judges are very reluctant to review factual decisions. Their reluctance is understandable in view of the fact that our procedure is essentially oral, making it difficult for a judge who sits on appeal to pass judgment on the basis of the written record. Even when the evidence is wanting on paper, appellate judges tend, understandably, to assume that if the jury was prepared to rely on it, there must have been something in the appearance of the witness or the way in which the

---

[32] [1981] 2 All ER 1061.

[33] [1981] 2 All ER 1062. For review of the authorities see Pattenden, 'The submission of no case to answer . . . , [1982] Crim L Rev 558.

[34] It should be noted that the Court of Appeal has further powers of review, such as the power to hear fresh evidence in exceptional circumstances; Criminal Appeal Act 1968, s. 23; *Parks* (1960) 45 Cr App R 1. Having heard fresh evidence it may quash the conviction or order a new trial; s. 7 of the 1968 Act.

evidence was given to provide added weight.[35] Given that the trial judge has heard the evidence and is better placed to assess its strength, it would be better to allow him to apply the test under consideration leaving the appellate court with an opportunity for a second opinion.

[35] This point is illustrated by the reluctance of appellate courts to quash convictions based on visual identification notwithstanding the notorious unreliability of such evidence. See Twining, 'Identification and misidentification . . .', in Lloyd-Bostock (ed.), *Evaluating Witness Evidence* (1983), 255; Gross, 'Loss of innocence: eyewitness identification and proof of guilt', 16 Journal of Legal Studies 395 (1987).

5

Opinion: Probative Utility and
Lay Standards

Witnesses, according to legal tradition, are allowed to testify to facts but not to their opinions. The jury must draw its own inferences from the facts stated by the witness; the witness has to confine himself to recounting what happened.

However, 'opinion' is an ambiguous term. Most factual reports of witnesses involve opinion. I observe the back of a person with a stoop walking across the road and decide that it is my friend X. When I testify that I saw X across the road, I do not just report what I saw but also the opinion I formed about what I saw. As Thayer observed, '[i]n a sense all testimony to matter of fact is opinion evidence; i.e. it is a conclusion formed from phenomena and mental impressions'.[1] Yet clearly the law does not mean to exclude my testimony. Although most lawyers would accept that in the absence of a legal definition of 'opinion' the distinction between statements of fact and of opinion cannot govern admissibility, the rule excluding opinion evidence continues to be described in terms of this distinction. The highest claim that seems to be made for it is that it appears to work because it is 'laxly applied'.[2] But what is important is to know what lies behind this uneven application of the rule or, in other words, what are the considerations that govern admissibility or inadmissibility.

On examination, hardly any decision will be found to turn

---

[1] Thayer, *A Preliminary Treatise on Evidence at Common Law* (1898), 524. See also *Wigmore on Evidence*, Chad Rev, vol. 7, s. 1978. '[T]he testimony of any witness', Weinstein observed, 'describes the combination of himself and the event'. Weinstein, 'Some difficulties in devising rules for determining truth in judicial proceedings', 66 Col L Rev 223, 231.
[2] Cowen and Carter, *Essays on the Law of Evidence* (1956) 164. See also Heydon, *Evidence, Cases and Materials*, 2nd edn. (1984) 367.

exclusively on the fact-opinion distinction. When early judges rejected opinion they did so, as Wigmore pointed out, because they regarded the statement of opinion as a mere guess or a belief not dictated by observation; but they did not disparage statements of opinion resting on 'an inference or conclusion from personally observed data'.[3] This is just as true today. Broadly speaking, opinion evidence is excluded either because it makes an insufficient probative contribution or because it is felt that the formation of opinion should, in the circumstances, be left to the court. Hence the opinion rule may be seen as expressing a preference for 'the more concrete description to the less concrete, the direct form of statement to the inferential',[4] and for reserving to the court the process of inference wherever feasible.

An example will illustrate the idea of probative usefulness as a function of specificity. In a case involving a charge of causing the death of a pedestrian by reckless driving a witness testifies that he was present at the scene and that he believes that the accused was responsible for the accident. No sensible adjudicator would return a verdict on the basis of this testimony because it is expressed in such general terms that we cannot be sure of its meaning. If the witness says that the accused drove recklessly, the statement is a little less vague in that it suggests a criterion of blame; but it does not take matters far because we do not know the witness's standards for appropriate driving; nor does the witness explain his grounds for believing that the accused was reckless. If the witness goes on to say that the accused drove too fast, we would learn the factual grounds for his assessment. But this still does not enable the court to judge what happened; we do not know how fast the accused drove. It is only when the witness states his assessment of the accused's speed that the adjudicator begins to be able to form a view about the event in question.

This is so not because the statement is one of pure fact and expresses no opinion. Clearly, the witness's view of the speed at which the accused drove relies on conscious or unconscious inference and extends beyond the report of crude physical sen-

---

[3] *Wigmore on Evidence*, Chad Rev, vol. 7, s. 1917, p. 5.
[4] *McCormick on Evidence*, 3rd edn. (1984), 30.

sations. Specificity enables the trier of fact to test the witness's view about the speed. It draws attention to the faculties involved in the witness's assessment and enables the adjudicator to gauge its reliability.[5] Specificity also ensures that the witness stops short of expressing his view about the appropriateness of the accused's conduct and leaves it to the court so to do. After all it is the function of the court to pass judgment on the appropriateness of the accused's conduct.

The perception of a state of affairs can be reported at different levels of generality and from the point of view of different interests. Up to a point, the more specific an account of observation is the more we can concentrate on its components in order to estimate its reliability.[6] But there comes a point beyond which it is both impractical and undesirable to insist on further specificity in the description of perceptions. Visual identification consists of an inference from minute perceptions which it is neither easy nor instructive to break down into their constituent components. Even if a witness were able to describe the minutiae of his impressions, his description would not be nearly as informative as a statement such as 'The man I saw was X', or pointing at a man and saying 'The man I saw is over there.'[7] However, no rule of law can provide a precise definition of the optimal point of specificity or usefulness for all instances of evidence. Wigmore wrote that

We are dealing merely with a broad principle that, whenever the point is reached at which the tribunal is being told that which it is itself

---

[5] The witness may, for instance, be asked to estimate the speed of other moving cars or he may be asked about his qualifications to form this kind of judgment. An eyewitness assessment of speed is normally rough and unreliable. The courts are therefore not permitted to rely on the uncorroborated accounts of eyewitnesses: Road Traffic Regulation Act 1967, s. 78A, inserted by s. 203 of Road Traffic Act 1972.

[6] In *Davies* [1962] 3 All ER 97, 98, a case involving a charge of driving while unfit due to drink, Lord Parker CJ disapproved of asking the witness to state whether the accused was unfit to drive a car due to drink. But he held that 'a witness can quite properly give his general impression whether the accused had taken drink', adding that the witness 'must describe . . . the facts on which he relies'.

[7] This is not to say that the witness should not be questioned as to his reasons for believing that he saw X. Such questioning might reveal the causes of potential mistakes, such as the false belief that X always wore a certain distinctive garment.

entirely equipped to determine without the witness' aid on this point, his testimony is superfluous and is to be dispensed with.[8]

An informative explanation of the opinion rule is one that brings out the two aspects that lie at its foundation: the principle of probative usefulness and the principle that the accused's conduct should, as far as practicable, be assessed by the court and not by the witness. The main manifestations of the latter principle are to be observed in relation to expert evidence.

EXPERT EVIDENCE: THE GUIDING PRINCIPLE

The greater part of the case-law is concerned not with the fact–opinion distinction but with a different question altogether: the scope for expert evidence.[9] English law, it seems, has always been prepared to accept the opinions and conclusions of experts in matters which require specialized knowledge or training and which the judge and the jury cannot be expected to possess.[10] An expert may be asked to draw conclusions from facts that he himself has observed. A pathologist who has examined a corpse may testify as to the likely cause of death. Alternatively, an expert may be required to form a view on the basis of facts supplied by others. A pathologist may be asked for his opinion about the cause of death given that a body was found to bear certain marks.

While the employment of experts is both necessary and desirable, it is nevertheless fraught with risks, which the courts strive to minimize. In our adversarial system the parties themselves

---

[8] *Wigmore on Evidence*, Chad Rev, vol. 7, s. 1918, 11–12. See Rule 701 of the United States Federal Rules of Evidence: 'If the witness is not testifying as an expert, his testimony in the form of opinions or inferences is limited to those opinions or inferences which are (a) rationally based on the perception of the witness and (b) helpful to clear understanding of his testimony or the determination of a fact in issue.' A similar attitude is displayed by Canadian case of *Graat* v. *R.* (1982) 144 DLR (3d) 267.

[9] See, for example, Keane, *The Modern Law of Evidence* (1985).

[10] *Buckley* v. *Rice-Thomas* (1554) 1 Plowd 118, 124; *Folkes* v. *Chadd* (1782) 3 Doug KB 157; Best, *The Principles of the Law of Evidence*, 12th edn. (1922), 436; Learned Hand, 'Historical and practical considerations regarding expert testimony', 15 Harv L Rev 40 (1901) Hammelmann, 'Expert evidence', (1947) 10 MLR 32.

employ the experts and, naturally, pay their fees. Consequently the scope for bias, conscious and unconscious, is considerable. Taylor wrote:

it is often quite surprising to see with what facility, and to what an extent their views [*of experts*] can be made to correspond with the wishes or the interests of the parties who call them. They do not, indeed, wilfully misrepresent what they think, but their judgments become so warped by regarding the subject in one point of view, that, even when conscientiously disposed they are incapable of forming an independent opinion.[11]

The difficulty is augmented by a further factor. When the determination of an issue requires specialized knowledge, neither the jury nor the judge are likely to be able to subject expert testimony to searching scrutiny. In theory Lord President Cooper may have been right to say of experts that

[t]heir duty is to furnish the judge or jury with the necessary scientific criteria for testing the accuracy of their conclusions, so as to enable the judge or jury to form their own independent judgment by the application of these criteria to the facts proved in evidence.[12]

But in practice this is rather unrealistic. As Learned Hand observed, we call experts because the trier of fact is not competent to judge on the matter. How can we, then, expect the trier of fact to adjudicate between conflicting expert opinions?[13] There is therefore a risk that a jury's decision may be influenced less by the merits of the opinions advanced than by the self-confidence and apparent respectability of those who advance them.

For these reasons the courts try to limit the scope for expert

---

[11] *Treatise on the Law of Evidence*, 12th edn. (1931) 59. See also *McCormick on Evidence*, 3rd edn. (1984), 42. Even lawyers, who are after all officers of the court, cannot help judging matters from their clients' point of view: *Columbia Picture Industries* v. *Robinson* [1986] 3 All ER 338, 370, 375.

[12] *Davie* v. *Edinburgh Magistrates* [1953] SC 34, 40.

[13] Historical and practical considerations regarding expert testimony, 15 Harv L Rev 40, 54–5 (1901). See also Hammelmann, 'Expert evidence', (1947) 10 MLR 32. In certain tribunals, such as employment and discrimination, experts are involved in a judicial role. Whether experts should be also used to advise juries on contentious matters should, perhaps, be also considered; see Basten, 'The court expert in civil trials', (1977) 40 MLR 174.

evidence to issues which the court feels incompetent to judge. Lawton LJ explained the limitation and its reasons in *Turner*:

> If on the proven facts a judge or jury can form their own conclusions without [expert] help, then the opinion of an expert is unnecessary. In such a case if it is given dressed up in scientific jargon it may make judgment more difficult. The fact that an expert witness has impressive scientific qualifications does not by that fact alone make his opinion on matters of human nature and behaviour within the limits of normality any more helpful than that of the jurors themselves; but there is a danger that they may think it does.[14]

EXPERT STANDARDS AND LAY STANDARDS IN ADJUDICATION

The accused in *Turner* pleaded provocation to a charge of murder but his plea was rejected and he was convicted for murder. He appealed on the grounds that the trial judge wrongly rejected the evidence of a psychiatrist who proposed to testify that the accused was very likely to be provoked by his girl-friend's admission of infidelity. Dismissing the appeal Lawton LJ said that 'jurors do not need psychiatrists to tell them how ordinary folk who are not suffering from any mental illness are likely to react to the stresses and strains of life.'[15] The Court of Appeal declined to follow the Privy Council's decision in *Lowery* v. *R*.[16] In *Lowery* L and K were charged with a murder which could have been committed by both of them together or by one of them alone. It was held that the trial judge had rightly allowed K to call psychiatric evidence in order to show that he had a weak and easily dominated personality, that L was aggressive, and that, therefore, the crime was more likely to have been committed by L.[17]

---

[14] *Turner* [1975] 1 All ER 70, 74.   [15] Ibid.

[16] [1973] 3 All ER 662.

[17] Prof. Cross thought that *Lowery* was distinguishable on the ground that L had already put his character in issue and the evidence merely went to rebut L's version; *Cross on Evidence*, 5th edn. (1979), 444–5. Carter explains the apparent inconsistency by suggesting that Turner was normal whereas in *Lowery* the evidence was directed to show abnormality; Carter, *Cases and Statutes on Evidence* (1981), 522.

The different outcome in these two cases is not necessarily objectionable. Admissibility depends, as we have seen, on probative usefulness. If a decision on the admissibility of particular expert evidence were binding, future courts would be obliged to admit expert evidence even where expertise has turned out to be unreliable. Psychiatry, with which the last two cases were concerned, is far from being a precise and reliable science and its contribution to our understanding of the mind may vary greatly. The fact that in *Lowery* v. *R.* a judge in Victoria thought that it would be helpful for a jury to know how a psychiatrist viewed the personalities of two accused who conducted a cutthroat-defence can hardly provide compelling reason for a judge in England to admit psychiatric testimony on the issue of provocation.

There is, however, another dimension to the problem of expert evidence and on this one might expect some judicial consistency. The decision to admit or reject expert evidence on a certain issue is not only a function of whether it can contribute to the determination of truth by supplying knowledge which the judge and the jury do not possess. A much more important and troublesome question is whether it is proper to bring to bear on an issue which is not strictly an issue of fact an expert body of opinion rather than to leave the matter to be determined by lay standards. The fact that psychiatry is a study of mental processes does not of itself dictate that psychiatric evidence must be admissible on an issue of provocation. This issue requires a decision whether the accused had lost control over himself as a result of provocation. But there are degrees of loss of control and it is possible that the ordinary man's standards of what amounts to loss of control are different from those of psychiatrists. Hence the question whether to accept psychiatric evidence on provocation may involve a choice between different standards of judgment.[18]

In *Stamford*[19] the issue was whether an article was 'indecent or obscene'. The court rejected an application by the defence to

---

[18] Lawton LJ made it clear in *Turner* that he was rejecting psychiatric standards as a matter of principle and preferring the application of popular standards to the issue; [1975] 1 All ER 70 at 74, 75.

[19] [1972] 2 All ER 427.

call an expert witness to explain the meaning of these words. The expression 'indecent or obscene' denotes moral judgment. The function of forming a judgment of this type is clearly entrusted to the jury rather than to experts. Lord Morris of Borth-y-Gest stressed this point in another case where he said that

> Even if accepted public standards may to some extent vary from generation to generation, current standards are in the keeping of juries, who can be trusted to maintain the corporate good sense of the community and to discern attacks upon values that must be preserved.[20]

This outlook stands in marked contrast with the earlier case of *DPP* v. *A and BC Chewing Gum Ltd*[21] where the accused was charged under section 4(2) of the Obscene Publications Act 1959, with publishing obscene battle cards which were sold to children together with bubble gum. The trial judge allowed the prosecution to tender the evidence of child psychiatrists as to the likely effect of such cards on children. The Divisional Court confirmed this ruling on the grounds that juries did not have as much knowledge of the minds of children as of those of grown ups and that 'when you are dealing...with children...any jury and any justices need all the help they can get'.[22] It is doubtful whether psychology is sufficiently advanced to provide a more accurate estimate of social effect than ordinary common sense. Furthermore, the central question here, as in the previous cases, was one of moral judgment. For these reasons, presumably, the case has been distinguished in most decisions that have dealt with this type of issue.[23] Indeed, in *DPP* v. *Jordan* Lord Dilhorne expressed direct disapproval of *A and BC Chewing Gum Ltd* when he said:

> If an article is not manifestly obscene as tending to deprave or corrupt, it seems to me somewhat odd that a person should be liable to

---

[20] *Shaw* v. *DPP* [1962] AC 220, 292. See also *DPP* v. *Jordan* [1977] AC 699. A similar line was taken in relation to the statutory phrase 'calculated to deprave or corrupt': *Anderson* [1971] 3 All ER 1152. See also *Calder and Boyars Ltd* [1968] 3 All ER 644.

[21] [1967] 2 All ER 504.   [22] Ibid. 506 per Lord Parker CJ.

[23] See *Stamford* [1972] 2 All ER 427. See also: *Anderson* [1971] 3 All ER 1152.

conviction for publishing obscene matter if the evidence of experts in psychiatry is required to establish its obscenity.[24]

A judge deciding whether expert opinion should be accepted as an arbiter of a certain matter has to consider the state of public opinion on the point. If the community has come to defer to professional standards on the matters in question, the courts will normally follow suit. Medical evidence is admissible on matters of health because we accept the authority of the medical profession in this regard. Psychiatry has not yet attained a like acceptance. Psychiatric evidence is admissible on the issue of insanity[25] but not, as we have seen, on the mental state of a normal person. It is arguable that the distinction is irrational; for to understand abnormality psychiatry has first to master the normal mental processes. However, as long as the community does not defer to psychiatry on matters such as intention and credibility, the scope for expert evidence on such matters must remain limited[26] and judicial differences of opinion, of the kind we came across in *Turner* and *Lowery*, are to be expected. Only when public opinion is clear one way or another can we demand consistency from the courts.

The divergence between expert and jury standards helps to explain one particular difficulty, commonly referred to as the problem of expert evidence on the ultimate issue. It has been supposed on occasion that expert opinion on the existence or non-existence of a constitutive fact, such as intention to kill in murder or entry in burglary, is inadmissible.[27] It is doubtful whether such a rule has ever been in operation,[28] but there are good reasons why courts should wish to be cautious in admitting expert opinion on the elements of the offence charged. Suppose that the required element of *mens rea* is an intention to kill and the issue in the case is whether the accused fired his gun intentionally. If the court were to proceed on the strength

[24] *DPP* v. *Jordan* [1976] 3 All ER 775, 782.
[25] *Holmes* [1953] 2 All ER 324; even where insanity is the ultimate issue.
[26] In at least one jurisdiction in the United States expert evidence has been admitted on credibility: *State* v. *Chaplle* 660 P 2d 1208, 1217 (1983).
[27] The constitutive facts in criminal prosecutions are the elements of the offence and the facts giving rise to excuse from liability.
[28] Cases purportedly supporting it are often explicable on different grounds. See *Wigmore on Evidence*, Chad Rev, vol. 7, s. 1921.

of an expert who states that the accused fired intentionally, an impression might be created that the decision against the accused was taken not so much by the jury as by the psychiatrist.

Expert opinion concerning the elements of the offence may sometimes be rightly said to amount to usurpation of the court's own jurisdiction in those circumstances. But this is not because we have an absolute objection that the testimony of a witness should virtually settle the issue in the case.[29] What we object to in certain cases is rather that the final judgment will be reached not according to the standards of the jury but according to some other standards.[30] The danger of usurpation is particularly poignant where common-sense standards differ from specialist standards and where the latter do not command general public acceptance. That this is the core of the concern was made clear by an American court when it declared that:

> When a standard, or a measure, or a capacity has been fixed by law, no witness whether expert or non-expert . . . is permitted to express an opinion as to whether the person or the conduct, in question, measures up to that standard; on that question the court must instruct the jury as to the law, and the jury draw its own conclusion from the evidence.[31]

The policy of maintaining jury standards in criminal adjudication does not require a rule forbidding expert evidence on the elements of the offence. Indeed, the trend is to repudiate any such rule.[32] The policy of maintaining jury standards only

---

[29] Where the only issue is the identity of the accused, it is perfectly in order for an expert to testify that the person who committed the crime must have been the accused because of certain traces left by the offender.

[30] It is no historical accident that in the very case which the sovereignty of the jury to acquit according to their lights was established Vaughan CJ declared that it is for the witness to testify to fact and for the jury to draw inferences from them: *Bushell's case* (1671) Vaugh 135.

[31] *Grismore* v. *Consolidated Products Co* 5 NW 2d 646, 663 (1942). It is doubtful whether the same rule can obtain in relation to expert evidence on an issue of professional negligence.

[32] Rule 704 of the American Federal Rules of Evidence that lays down that 'testimony in the form of an opinion or inference otherwise admissible is not objectionable because it embraces an ultimate issue'. See also the Canadian case of *Graat* v. *R.* (1982) 144 DLR (3d) 267, and discussion in *Cross on Evidence*, 6th edn. (1985), 445–8. Section 3 of the Civil Evidence Act 1972, which governs the position in civil cases in England, imposes no limitation in respect of the ultimate issue; see also s. 5 of the Act and Law Reform Committee, 17th Report, Evidence of Opinion and Expert Evidence (1970), cmnd. 4489.

dictates vigilance against extending the scope of expert evidence, whether on the fulfilment of the elements of the offence or any other issues, beyond matters on which the community as a whole regards experts as suitable arbiters.

THE FACTS OF THE CASE AND THE FACTS OF EXPERTISE

Once it has been decided to admit expert evidence, a number of precautions are taken to ensure that the evidence makes a worthwhile contribution to the fact-finding process. For instance, a person called as an expert must be shown to have some special skills, if not a professional qualification, on the matter on which he is to testify. However, the requirement of a special qualificaton is laxly observed and the testing of the expert's professional ability is mainly carried out in the cross-examination of the expert.[33] Of more important consequence is the courts' insistence on maintaining a distinction between the expert's theory and the disputed facts.

Suppose that the issue in a case concerns the cause of a person's death. A pathologist who has performed an autopsy may testify both to the condition in which he found the corpse and about the probable cause of death to be inferred from that condition. A pathologist who has not himself seen the corpse may only express a view about the probable cause on the hypothesis that the body was in a certain state. The distinction is important because of the danger that the jury may infer that the body was in fact found in a certain state merely because an expert witness based his theory on such a hypothetical state of affairs.

It is important to realize that the facts of the case, such as the condition of the corpse in the above example, and the expert's theory concerning these facts are not the only factors involved in expert testimony. There is a third factor: the facts of the expertise. Suppose that our expert testifies that on examining the corpse he observed spots of a particular character. The presence of the spots is clearly a fact of the case and they are

---

[33] *Phipson on Evidence*, 13th edn. (1982), 572.

indicative of the cause of death which is in issue. Suppose now that the expert goes on to say that he has learnt from observing other corpses that this type of spot is almost always associated with, say, poisoning. He further adds that the professional literature on the subject confirms his theory of causal connection. The expert's former observations and the state of the professional literature also concern facts.

The distinction between the facts of the case and the facts of the expertise is not a distinction between statements of fact and of opinion. The facts of the expertise will usually be embedded in the expert's theory but they are facts as any other fact. Moreover, just as the facts of the case may be in dispute so may the facts of the expertise; experts may, for example, be divided on the results of experiments conducted in their field.[34] The distinction has a procedural function. It differentiates the procedure applicable to the proof of the facts of the case from the procedure involved in establishing the facts of expertise.

The facts of the case must be proved according to the normal rules of evidence. In our example, if the parties are divided on whether the deceased's body bore certain marks or not, the existence of the marks must be proved by legally admissible evidence and according to the usual standards. Proof of the facts of the expertise is not subject to all the rules of evidence. For example, the results of experimental evidence may be proved by hearsay evidence. Such proof would usually consist of references to professional literature even where this involves hearsay upon hearsay.[35]

The reason for the procedural differentiation lies in the way in which expert opinion is formed. Scientific or other expert generalizations are arrived at by open debate in the field in question. Before a generalization is adopted it is usually tested

---

[34] In *H* v. *Schering Chemicals Ltd* [1983] 1 All ER 849, the issue concerned the effect on the plaintiff of a drug manufactured by the defendants. The plaintiffs were allowed to adduce the results of investigations into other instances of the use of the drug although the correctness of the results of these other investigations was in dispute.

[35] See *Abadom* [1983] 1 All ER 364; *H* v. *Schering Chemicals Ltd* [1983] 1 All ER 849; Pattenden, 'Expert opinion evidence based on hearsay', [1982] Crim L Rev 85; *McCormick on Evidence*, 3rd edn. (1984), 38; Note, 'Inadmissible evidence as a basis for expert opinion', 40 Van L Rev 583 (1987). For a discussion of the rule against hearsay see Ch. 11.

and subjected to scrutiny so that flaws are likely to be exposed. It is therefore improbable that a further investigation in a court of law will add much to the professional knowledge concerning the factual bases of scientific generalization. Disputes about the factual justification of generalizations may arise between opposing experts in court but little would be gained if the courts attempted to settle them by the machinery of judicial fact-finding and according to the strict rules of evidence.[36]

[36] At times there will be a further reason why a judicial investigation of the facts from which the expert draws his conclusions would be unnecessary. In *Abadom* [1983] 1 All ER 364, an expert was allowed to testify what quantity of a particular type of glass was in use. The expert based his opinion on data accumulated by the Home Office. Even if a few individual entries in the Home Office records had been inaccurate, the general picture was likely to remain unaffected.

6

Judicial Notice

THE PROBLEMS ADDRESSED BY THE DOCTRINE OF
JUDICIAL NOTICE AND THEIR SOLUTION

When drawing inferences from evidence the trier of fact inevitably uses generalizations concerning the normal course of
events. He will assume, for instance, that non-perishable goods
do not disappear of their own accord or that a double-decker
bus cannot be driven over waterlogged fields. In gauging the
reliability of testimony he will make assumptions about the
usual signs of truth-telling. However, the use by the trier of fact
of his knowledge of the world raises a number of problems.

The right to be heard is clearly one of the more basic rights of
a person accused of crime.[1] Hence to deny an accused person
the opportunity to challenge the factual assumptions on which
his conviction may rest would constitute a serious injustice. To
afford a party an opportunity of challenging his opponent's case
the law ordains that issues of fact must be decided only upon
evidence that the litigants have placed before the court.[2]

Three problems may arise in this regard. First, if the trier of
fact must decide according to the evidence in the case, is he still
allowed to have recourse to his general knowledge? The second
problem concerns admissibility. We have seen that evidence

---

[1] This is true whether we consider this right to be grounded on a utilitarian
calculation and hence justified by its tendency to produce a factually correct result
or whether we regard the right to be heard as an end in itself. For a survey of the
debate see Bayles, 'Principles for legal procedure', 5 Law and Philosophy 33 (1986).
Of particular interest are: Summers, 'Evaluating and improving legal process: a
plea for "process values"', 60 Cornell L Rev 1 (1974); Tribe, *American Constitutional
Law* (1978), 503; Dworkin, *Matter of Principle* (1985), 98.

[2] This was not always the case in English law. At one time jurors were expected
to resolve the dispute on the basis of their own knowledge of the disputed facts:
Holdsworth, *A History of English Law*, vol. 1, 7th edn. (1956), 317; Manchester,
'Judicial notice and personal knowledge', (1979) 42 MLR 22. See also Jenks,
'According to the evidence', in *Cambridge Legal Essays*, (1926), 191.

presented in court is subjected to tests of admissibility but the general knowledge used by the trier of fact is obviously not subject to these tests. The last problem follows from the jurisdictional division between judge and jury: Is the judge entitled to instruct the jury to take certain facts as given, when it is for the jury to decide the facts?

Where there can be no reasonable dispute between the parties, it is wasteful to insist on a full trial of fact.[3] To require a party to prove a matter which is patently a foregone conclusion is to impose on him an unnecessary burden. The doctrine of judicial notice relieves the parties from the necessity of proving facts that are not reasonably disputable and thereby also solves the three problems just mentioned. When an indisputable fact is taken for granted, it clearly cannot be said that one or the other of the parties has been deprived of an opportunity to advance his case. The requirements of admissibility do not obtain in relation to facts that need not be proved because they are not capable of reasonable dispute.[4] Lastly, indisputability removes the difficulty about jurisdiction: where there is no genuine dispute, there is nothing to refer to a jury for decision and the trial judge may instruct the jury to accept the facts as proven.[5]

The test of indisputability, therefore, authorizes the judge to dispense with proof of facts which are indisputable either because they are generally considered as true in the community or because they may be reliably ascertained from sources that are widely accepted as correct.[6] For example, judicial notice has

---

[3] Though of course evidence will have to be called if the judge does not possess knowledge of an indisputable fact. In *Ingram* v. *Percival* [1968] 3 All ER 657, Lord Parker CJ approved of a decision by magistrates to take judicial notice of local tides, although saying that where the justices do not have the requisite knowledge, the matter must be proved by evidence.

[4] In relation to indisputable facts there is no need to safeguard against waste, confusion, mistake, or prejudice.

[5] This principle insures that juries do not reach conflicting decisions in relation to facts that are commonly regarded as beyond dispute; such conflicts could undermine public confidence in the judicial process.

[6] See discussion by Morgan, 'Judicial notice', 57 Harv L Rev 269 (1944) and comment by K. C. Davis, *Administrative Law Text*, 3rd edn. (1972), 314. Generality of knowledge may be confined to a locality. Thus a court may take judicial notice of local conditions; *Dennis* v. *A J White & Co* [1917] AC 479, 492; *Ingram* v. *Percival* [1969] 1 QB 548; [1968] 3 All ER 657; *Keane* v. *Mount Vernon Colliery Co* [1933] AC 309.

been taken of the fact that two weeks is too short a period for human gestation,[7] that the University of Oxford exists for the advancement of learning,[8] and that a postcard is likely to be read by people other than the addressee.[9] Verification by reference to indisputable sources takes place where, for example, the court has to ascertain on which day 1 January 1973 fell, or historical facts such as the date on which the USA declared war on Japan, or the geographical location of places. For the purpose of informing itself of such matters the court may have access not only to reliable documentary sources but also to experts.[10]

Unfortunately the courts have not always confined themselves to a test of disputability. In *Wetherall* v. *Harrison*,[11] the issue was whether the accused had a good medical reason for refusing to give a blood sample. A medical witness for the prosecution testified that he had not. The justices found that, in the light of their own experience in the matter, the defendant may well have had a good medical reason for refusing. Lord Widgery CJ explained that while a magistrate is forbidden to use his knowledge in order to contradict evidence given in court he may use his knowledge to assess the evidence adduced before him.[12]

This distinction is untenable. Where, for instance, an accused testifies that he was not in Piccadilly at a certain time, a juror is clearly forbidden to determine the issue on the basis that he himself saw the accused in Piccadilly at the relevant time, even though he is merely using his knowledge to decide that the accused is lying. The juror may not use his knowledge because the accused has not been given an opportunity to contest the juror's information. In *Wetherall* v. *Harrison* if the justices were in possession of some information bearing on the issue, fairness

---

[7] *Luffe* (1807) 8 East 193.

[8] *Re Oxford Poor Rate Case* (1857) 8 E & B 184.

[9] *Huth* v. *Huth* (1915) 3 KB 32.

[10] As it would do, for instance, in order to inform itself of a professional practice; *Davey* v. *Harrow Corp* [1958] 1 QB 60; *Re Rosher* (1884) 26 Ch D 801. See also *McQuaker* v. *Goddard* [1940] 1 KB 687; [1940] 1 All ER 477.

[11] [1976] 1 All ER 241.

[12] On this basis the Court of Appeal concluded that the magistrates had used their knowledge legitimately; [1976] 1 All ER 244.

demanded that the prosecution be notified of the information so that it might challenge it. Had the Court of Appeal not been distracted by a distinction between information used as evidence and information used for assessing evidence it would not have been led into error.

The law requires an adjudicator who proposes to reject a factual proposition for which evidence is adduced to notify the affected party so that the party may have an opportunity to support his case.[13] In *Blick*[14] the accused explained his presence at the scene of the robbery by saying that he was visiting a public lavatory. A juror informed the judge that the lavatory was closed at the time whereupon the judge invited the prosecution to call evidence on the point so that the juror's information might be investigated by both parties in open court. In another case it was emphasized that the trier of fact must not produce from his personal knowledge evidence 'with which the parties have not had an opportunity of dealing'.[15]

Consequently adjudicators need to notify the parties of an intention to rely on information possessed by them where the information is neither incontestable nor widely known.[16]

Whether a fact is reasonably disputable depends on the state of knowledge at the time and place of the trial. What may

[13] *Fox* v. *Wellfair* [1981] Com L R 140. The trier of fact in this case was an arbitrator. Specialist tribunals, such as industrial tribunals, are expected to rely on their expertise in the field of their jurisdiction, but they continue to be bound by the general principle of fairness.

[14] (1966) 50 Cr App R 280.

[15] *Hammington* v. *Berker Ltd* [1980] 1 ICR 248, 252. See also Jackson, 'Expertise or evidence?', (1982) 98 LQR 192; *Reynolds* v. *Llanelly Associated Tinplate* [1948] 1 All ER 140.

[16] Rule 10(1) of the American Uniform Rules of Evidence takes matters further by requiring judges to give notice in all circumstances. This seems excessive because fairness does not always necessitate notification. The existence of a formal requirement might well become the source of unnecessary technical disputes. The Federal Rules of Evidence adopt a more flexible approach. Rule 201(b) defines a fact of which judicial notice may be taken as 'one not subject to reasonable dispute in that it is either (1) generally known within the territorial jurisdiction of the trial court or (2) capable of accurate and ready determination by resort to sources whose accuracy cannot reasonably be questioned'. Rule 201(e) complements this by providing that 'a party is entitled upon timely request to an opportunity to be heard as to the propriety of taking judicial notice and the tenor of the matter noticed. In the absence of prior notification, the request may be made after judicial notice has been taken.' See *Wigmore on Evidence*, Chad Rev, vol. 9, s. 2565.

reasonably be in dispute today may cease to be so at some future time. It follows that a decision to take judicial notice of a certain fact cannot conclude the matter once and for all.[17] If it did, we would have had to say that a decision to take judicial notice of fact X creates an irrebuttable presumption of law that X is the case.[18]

However, this does not preclude conformity between different decisions on the same subject-matter. As long as a fact is indisputable it will be recognized as such by different courts. Indeed, an attempt by a party to dispute what is not reasonably disputable may verge on abuse of process; as where a litigant insists that his adversary prove that human gestation cannot take place in two weeks when the former only means to make litigation more cumbersome for his adversary. But the position would be quite different if a future litigant were in a position to challenge the common assumption about human gestation by reference to some new scientific development. Where a party has reason to dispute what has been regarded as indisputable, he will have in effect to this prove the hitherto held assumption.

MATTERS IMPROPERLY DESCRIBED AS PERTAINING TO JUDICIAL NOTICE

There are a number of matters which are inappropriately discussed in connection with judicial notice. It is said that judges take judicial notice of the law of the land or that courts are presumed to know the law so that it need not be proved according to the ordinary rules of evidence.[19] However, as McCormick has observed, '[t]he recognition appears to be growing . . . that

---

[17] The notion that rulings on judicial notice give rise to binding precedent is connected with the theory, discussed in Ch. 3, that the judge decides questions of law, leaving questions of fact to the jury. It may therefore be thought that a decision to take judicial notice of a certain fact creates a binding precedent as being a decision on the law. However, this reasoning is wrong given that not all decisions reserved to the judge result in binding precedent. Whether, for instance, a given piece of evidence is sufficiently relevant falls to be decided by the judge without his decision becoming a binding precedent.

[18] For an instance of law-making under the guise of judicial notice see n. 21 below.

[19] *Cross on Evidence*, 5th edn. (1979), 155.

the manner in which the law is insinuated into the judicial process is not so much a problem of evidence as it is a concern better handled within the context of the rules pertaining to procedure'.[20]

When a court decides that a flick-knife—any flick-knife and not just the one seized from the accused in question—is an offensive weapon for the purpose of section 1(1) of the Prevention of Crime Act 1953, and that future courts may take judicial notice of this fact, as did the Court of Appeal in *Simpson*,[21] the court simply lays down the law and does not find facts.[22] It is, therefore, a pity that the term 'judicial notice' appears in a number of English statutes in the sense in which it was used in *Simpson*.[23]

Nor is there any advantage in treating notice taken of certain political matters, such as the relationship between the United Kingdom and other states, in conjunction with judicial notice. In *Duff Development Co.* v. *Government of Kelantan*[24] the independence of Kelantan was in issue. The House of Lords decided that the proper way of proceeding was 'to take judicial notice of the sovereignty of a State, and for that purpose ... to seek information from a Secretary of State; and when information is obtained the court does not permit it to be questioned by the parties.'[25] The courts have proceeded in this way on matters such as the continuance of the Second World War,[26] diplomatic

---

[20] *McCormick on Evidence*, 3rd edn. (1984), 921–2.

[21] [1983] 3 All ER 789.

[22] In the United States a distinction is drawn between 'adjudicative facts' and 'legislative facts'. The former are facts concerning a particular event in litigation, for example, the date on which an offence took place. The latter concern states of affairs which are relevant to the interpretation and development of the law, for example, in deciding whether flick-knives are offensive weapons it is relevant to know how often flick-knives have been used offensively. See K. C. Davis, 'An approach to problems of evidence in the administrative process', 55 Harv L Rev 364 (1942); 'Judicial notice', 55 Col L Rev 945 (1955); and see 'Comment, The presently expanding concept of judicial notice', 13 Vill L Rev 528 (1968). For more recent discussion see K. C. Davis, 'Facts in lawmaking', 80 Col L Rev 931 (1980); Federal Rules of Evidence, The Advisory Committee's Note on Rule 201, 56 FRD 183, 201.

[23] See, for example, the Interpretation Act 1978, s. 3; the European Communities Act 1972, s. 4(2); and discussion in *Cross on Evidence*, 5th edn. (1979), 157. Sometimes, statute provides that the court is to take judicial notice of certain official acts. The effect of such provisions is to lay down substantive rules of law.

[24] [1924] AC 797.   [25] [1924] AC 797, 805–6.

[26] *R* v. *Botrill, ex parte Kuechenmeister* [1946] 1 All ER 635.

status,[27] and the recognition of a foreign state.[28] The principle involved in seeking ministerial guidance in these cases is not concerned with ascertaining facts at all. Rather, it is concerned with jurisdiction: the principle holds that it is the government and not the court that determines the state of foreign relations, even for the purpose of litigation.

Lastly we must deal with the question of whether evidence is admissible to rebut matters judicially noticed. Thayer and Wigmore thought that such evidence was admissible. Morgan and Maguire considered that it was not.[29] The question appears difficult because it addresses itself to different matters at one and the same time. The first is: May a judicially noticed fact be rebutted by evidence? The second question is: May evidence be adduced to settle the factual content of judicial notice?

If we approach the first question with the test of reasonable disputability the answer is straightforward. A fact is either disputable or it is not. If it is not, then no dispute arises once judicial notice has been taken of it and no evidence is adduced in rebuttal. If it is reasonably disputable, judicial notice cannot settle the dispute and the matter is open to be contested in the ordinary way.

The second question presents a wholly different problem: granted that judicial notice may be taken of a fact, may evidence be adduced to prove that fact? Suppose that the state of the tide at a certain coastal point on a certain day is relevant in a trial. Since the times of the high and low tide are not really disputable judicial notice may be taken on the matter. For that purpose the trial judge may consult a tide-table or an expert. The parties may, at this point, challenge the table used or the expert called. If the parties do so, they clearly raise an issue of fact. But the issue here will not be the correctness of a proposition of fact of which judicial notice has already been taken, but rather what should be the proposition to be adopted.[30] Once

---

[27] *Engelke* v. *Musman* [1928] AC 433.

[28] *Carl Zeiss Stiftung* v. *Rayner and Keller (No. 2)* [1967] 1 AC 853.

[29] The relevant refs. are collected in *McCormick on Evidence*, 3rd edn. (1984), 930–4.

[30] It may happen that in an attempt to determine the authoritative source for some particular information it is discovered that the matter is not really indisputable, in which case the matter will have to be tried in the ordinary way. Thus if it is learnt that different tide-tables give different information the time of the relevant tide will have to be proved in the ordinary way.

this dispute is settled, for example by accepting a certain tidetable as authoritative, the statement of fact to be judicially noticed becomes identified and this is the end of the matter.

It is possible that the puzzle we have been discussing is the product of the convention that the topic of judicial notice deals with 'matters which need not be proved by evidence'.[31] This convention is somewhat misleading because, as we have seen, evidence may be required to establish a judicially noticeable fact, for example, an authoritative work of reference. The important feature of the doctrine is not that it dispenses with evidence but that it dispenses with the ordinary procedure of proof in relation to indisputable facts. This explains why in trial by jury the determination of judicial notice is left to the judge, whose task it is to determine the choice of procedure.

THE STORE OF KNOWLEDGE BELOW THE SURFACE

In practice the procedure of taking judicial notice does not succeed in drawing attention to all or even most of the generalizations employed by the trier of fact. All inferences from evidence entail reliance on generalizations but only very few of these are expressly authorized as matters of judicial notice. The vast majority of generalizations remain unstated in court even when they are far from self-evident.

An example will illustrate this point. A is charged with the murder of V. The prosecution proves that V had insulted A. The relevance of insult is that it proves a motive. Motive is relevant because, at the very least, it is assumed that on the whole a crime is not committed without a motive. The attribution of probative weight to insult involves a number of steps. First, it is assumed that V's insult offended A. Secondly, that the offence may have created in A a lasting ill-feeling towards V. Lastly, given this ill-feeling, that A is more likely to have committed the murder than if he had no such feeling. Yet none of these assumptions is beyond dispute. The tendency of individuals to take offence varies greatly, as does the lasting power of offence

---

[31] *Cross on Evidence*, 5th edn. (1979), 153.

taken. More importantly, the vast majority of people who take offence and harbour ill-feeling do not avenge themselves by taking life. It is clear therefore that the probative force commonly attributed to the sort of generalizations used in this simple example is debatable.

Quite often assumptions made in the course of the trial are subconscious. This is especially true of assumptions about truth-telling. The trier of fact judges veracity from, amongst other factors, the witness's demeanour. But generalizations about the significance of this or that trait of conduct will often remain hidden not only from the parties but also from the trier of fact himself. Furthermore, a decision to believe a witness may be made for reasons which are not susceptible to this kind of analysis at all.[32] Thayer showed awareness of the pervasive and, at the same time, elusive nature of the general assumptions from which we reach conclusions when he wrote:

In conducting a process of judicial reasoning, as of other reasoning, not a step can be taken without assuming something which has not been proved; and the capacity to do this, with competent judgment and efficiency, is imputed to judges and juries as part of their necessary mental outfit.[33]

While the extent to which unstated assumptions affect our inferences from evidence is well recognized, the role of stereotyping and the connection between this and our sense of morality is far less appreciated. For instance, in 1935 Alma Rattenbury and George Stoner were accused of murdering Alma Rattenbury's husband.[34] At the time the two accused were having a sexual affair. Mrs Rattenbury was thirty-eight and Stoner eighteen. It was assumed that Mrs Rattenbury bore a

---

[32] Jerome Frank wrote that the adjudicator's 'decisional process, like the artistic process, involves feelings that words cannot ensnare'; *Courts on Trial* (1949), 173. See also Hutcheson, 'The judgment intuitive: the function of the "hunch" in judicial decisions', 14 Cornell L Q 274 (1929).

[33] Thayer, *A Preliminary Treatise on Evidence at Common Law* (1898), 279–80. See also Davis, 'A system of judicial notice based on fairness and convenience', in his *Perspectives of Law* (1964), 69, 73; Levin and Levy, 'Persuading the jury with facts not evidence: the fiction-science spectrum', 105 University of Pennsylvania L Rev 139 (1956).

[34] An account of the trial by F. Tennyson Jesse may be found in J. Mortimer (ed.), *Famous Trials* (1984), 15.

heavier guilt due to the belief that the sin of a wife was greater than that of her lover and that a person of thirty-eight ought to know better than take a boy lover. In addition, the age difference led to the assumption that she was the dominant partner. Yet the assumption that older women dominate younger men is far from obvious.[35] The commentator Tennyson Jesse went so far as to suggest that 'there is no woman so under the dominion of her lover as the elderly mistress of a very much younger man.'[36] Another assumption which played a role in this trial was that, whatever the circumstances, women want to marry their lovers. It was accordingly assumed that Mrs Rattenbury plotted with her lover to kill her husband in order to clear the way for their marriage. However, Tennyson Jesse is quite right to point out that, in the circumstances, this assumption was ill-founded because her husband allowed Mrs Rattenbury considerable freedom and there was little to be gained by her from marrying a poor person twenty years her junior, and much to be lost.[37] Nevertheless, the role that stereotyping and moral judgment played in those proceedings was not exceptional. Tennyson Jesse drew attention to the custom of English courts, which has changed little since that trial, 'to animadvert upon the moral qualities, or lack of them in a person accused of crime'.[38]

Sounding a sceptical note about generalizations Twining writes:

In respect of any . . . generalization one should not assume too readily that there is in fact a 'cognitive consensus' on the matter. The stock of knowledge in any society varies from group to group, from individual to individual and from time to time. Even when there is a widespread consensus, what passes as 'conventional knowledge' may be untrue, speculative or otherwise defective; moreover, 'common-sense generalizations' tend not to be 'purely factual'—they often contain a strong mixture of evaluation and prejudice, as is illustrated by various kinds of social, national and racial stereotypes.[39]

---

[35] The same assumption was prominent in the trial of Bywaters and Thompson; see Twining, *Theories of Evidence: Bentham and Wigmore*, 143.

[36] Rattenbury and Stoner, in Mortimer (ed.), *Famous Trials* (1984) 25.

[37] Ibid. 47 ff.   [38] Ibid. 49.

[39] *Theories of Evidence: Bentham and Wigmore* (1985), 146.

It can hardly be doubted that the regularities that we attribute to the world around us, especially those concerned with
human conduct and intentions, are not always founded in scientific observation and at times reflect emotional expectations.[40]
Wigmore sought to minimize the risk of ill-founded generalizations affecting the outcome of the trial. In his book *The Science
of Judicial Proof* (1937), he wrote:

What is wanted is simple enough in purpose—namely, some method
which will enable us to lift into consciousness and to state in words the
reasons why a total mass of evidence does or should persuade us to a
given conclusion, and why our conclusion would or should have been
different or identical if some part of that total mass of evidence had
been different. The mind is moved; then can we not explain why it is
moved? If we can set down and work out a mathematical equation,
why can we not set down and work out a mental probative equation?[41]

Wigmore sought to devise a system by which every single
move from evidence to conclusion would be laid out, recorded,
and analysed. The rough method to this end is the 'narrative
method' which arranges 'all evidential data under some scheme
of logical sequence, narrating at each point the related evidential facts, and at each fact noting the subordinate evidence on
which it depends; concluding with a narrative summary.'[42]
However, Wigmore felt that this method could not completely
overcome the shortcomings of our present practice. For effective
and rigorous analysis he developed his 'chart system'. This
system makes use of special symbols, invented by Wigmore for
the purpose of plotting the relation of every bit of evidence to
every other piece of evidence and between these and the issues.
By outlining the connections between each piece of evidence
and the issue one necessarily brings out the assumptions employed to sustain these connections.[43]

---

[40] See also Weinstein, 'Some difficulties in devising rules for determining truth in
judicial trials', 66 Col L Rev 223, 232 (1966).

[41] *Science of Judicial Proof* (1937), 8. Wigmore's theory has been recently rescued
from obscurity by Prof. Twining in *Theories of Evidence: Bentham and Wigmore* (1985),
ch. 3.

[42] *Science of Judicial Proof* (1937), 7. For an interesting contribution on coherence
see D. N. MacCormick, 'Coherence in legal justificaton', in Krawietz *et al.*, *Theorie
der Normen* (Berlin, 1984), 37.

[43] Different kinds of evidential support have their distinct notation. Thus we find
notations for conjunction, corroboration, convergence, and catenate inferences. For
an outline see Twining, *Theories of Evidence: Bentham and Wigmore*, 125 and app.

The treatment of even a simple case with the chart method involves long and complex chains of notations and is probably beyond the capacity of most people who have not been educated to lay out their thoughts in this way. It is clearly unsuitable for a jury system of trial because jurors lack both the training and, as the law stands, the opportunity to engage in such a task.[44] We are faced in this respect with a choice between trial by professional judges who will give comprehensive reasons for their verdicts and lay juries who will not. The reasons for preferring trial by jury were discussed in chapter 3. Here it is only necessary to emphasize a few points.

Given that the assessment of evidence by the trier of fact is bound to be influenced by his mental make-up as well as by his general knowledge and experience there is a lot to be said for deferring to the ordinary citizen in the determination of facts because his knowledge is likely to represent the experience and outlook of wide sections of society. By contrast, a professional judiciary will tend to reflect a much narrower view of the world. In his recent book *The Faces of Justice and State Authority*,[45] Damaska observes:

Long terms of office create the space for routinization and specialization of tasks. Routinization of activity implies that issues that come before the official are no longer apprehended as representing a unique constellation of circumstances calling for 'individualized justice'. Choices are narrowed: while there may be many ways to go about solving a problem, only one emerges as habitual. A considerable degree of emotional disengagement also becomes possible. Specialization implies, of course, that only certain factors—those within a narrow realm—play part in decision making. As a consequence of habitualization and specialization, a professional's official and personal reactions part company: he acquires the capacity of anesthetizing his heart, if necessary, and of making decisions in his official capacity that he might never make as an individual.

Hence even if it is possible for judges to achieve a greater degree of articulation of the assumptions that lie behind their inferences than the untrained juror, the gains would be out-

---

[44] Jurors do not take notes during the trial, they are not provided with a transcript, and they are forbidden to seek outside advice in their deliberations.

[45] (Yale University Press, 1986), 19.

weighed by the loss of the plurality of social outlook and experience which the latter brings with him.

It appears, however, that even professional judges are very reluctant to provide a detailed account of their factual reasoning.[46] This resistance may well be due to a belief in the futility of such exercises. The construction of a full and detailed inferential map that marks the evidence and all possible routes to the issues is a very time-consuming task and it is far from clear that its results justify the delay and the expense that would inevitably be involved.

What is then the relationship between the doctrine of judicial notice and the vast number of assumptions that we all make in the analysis of facts? One thing is clear, it is not the function of the doctrine of judicial notice to draw attention to every factual assumption that is involved in the inferential process. We have to accept that this process is carried out against the background of a large number of unstated assumptions about the course of nature. The function of the doctrine is therefore much more limited. It is to bring into the foreground assumptions about the world when there are some special reasons for doing so. These reasons may lie in the limited accessibility of some facts, such as an indisputable but obscure piece of scientific information. At other times judicial notice merely identifies the sources of indisputable information, such as calendars and tide-tables. But it cannot guarantee that the adjudicator is aware of every assumption he makes, let alone that every assumption is well grounded.

---

[46] In *Varndell* v. *Kearney & Trecker Marwin Ltd* [1983] ICR 683, 693 Eveleigh LJ thought that since there was no appeal on findings of fact there is no need for 'a detailed recitation of the evidence'. Similarly, in *Union of Construction Allied Trades and Technicians* v. *Brain* [1981] ICR 542, 551, Donaldson LJ said that 'it would be a thousand pities if . . . reasons [for decisions of fact] began to be subjected to detailed analysis and appeals were to be brought based upon such analysis'. See also *Morris* v. *London Iron and Steel Co* [1987] 2 All ER 496.

7

Presentation of Evidence: Litigants' Freedom and Judicial Control

INTRODUCTION

At the basis of our trial procedure lies the idea that the court's function is confined to adjudication on the disputed issues while the litigants are left free to conduct their case. It is they who join issues and choose on what to litigate. It is they who call evidence in support of their assertions, present it, and subject each other's evidence to tests of reliability. The judge is supposed to remain aloof from the cut and thrust of the contest.[1]

However, a litigant is not completely free to pursue his ends to the disadvantage of his opponent. For instance, the prosecution is required to inform the defence of the witnesses it proposes to call, of the existence of witnesses who possess material information but whom the prosecution does not intend to call, of the fact that its witnesses have made previous inconsistent statements, and of witnesses' previous convictions.[2] Although the accused has no general duty to disclose his intentions in advance of the trial, his freedom is not always unlimited; he must, for instance, give notice of his intention to call alibi evidence.[3]

---

[1] As Prof. Cross put it, the 'elucidation of facts by means of questions put by the parties or their representatives to witnesses summoned, for the most part, by them, called mainly in the order of their choice, before a judge, acting as an umpire rather than an inquisitor, is the essential feature of the English "adversary" or accusatorial system of justice.' *Cross on Evidence*, 5th edn. (1979), 219.

[2] See Criminal Justice Act 1977, s. 48; 'Guidelines on the disclosure of "unused material" to the defence . . .', [1982] 1 All ER 734; *Archbold's Pleading, Evidence and Practice in Criminal Cases*, 42nd edn. (1985), 328–38. See also interesting discussion in Note, 'The prosecution's duty to disclose to defendants pleading guilty', 99 Harv L Rev 1004 (1986).

[3] Criminal Justice Act 1967, s. 11. It would, however, be a rare case for the court to prohibit an accused from adducing alibi evidence on the grounds of non-compliance with the notice requirement; *Archbold's Pleading, Evidence and Practice in Criminal Cases*, 42nd edn. (1985), 473.

Nor is the theory of judicial passivity entirely correct.[4] Generally speaking, the trial judge has the responsibility of ensuring that adversarial freedom is not abused and that the parties and their advocates present their cases with propriety, fairness, and economy. The principal instrument at the judge's disposal, in addition to his considerable moral authority over the conduct of the proceedings, is his jurisdiction over admissibility.[5] We have already seen that the trial judge sifts the evidence adduced by the parties and admits only evidence of acceptable probative weight. This chapter discusses the presentation of evidence and some aspects of judicial control over this process.

THE ORDER OF PRESENTATION

A central feature of the criminal trial is its reliance on oral evidence. Most of the evidence is adduced through the testimony of witnesses who appear before the court and either testify from their own recollection of events or produce documents (or other objects) to the authenticity of which they depose.[6] Some rules are necessary to regulate the order and manner of presentation so that the process may be conducted efficiently and economically.

A criminal trial begins with an opening speech by the prosecutor who then proceeds to present his evidence. When the prosecutor has closed his case, it is the accused's turn to present his own case. If the accused intends to testify, he is normally required to do so before any other witnesses for the defence.[7]

---

[4] For a description of aims of judicial intervention in the presentation of the case see *Matthews* [1984] 7 All ER 823. The judge has, for instance, the power to call witnesses without the parties' consent. In civil cases the judge may call witnesses of his own initiative only with the consent of the parties: *Re Enoch and Zartesky* [1910] 1 KB 327. Although in criminal proceedings he does not require the parties' consent, his freedom is confined and is in practice rarely used. See *Archbold's Pleading, Evidence and Practice in Criminal Cases*, 42nd edn. (1985), 481, and *Kooken* (1982) 74 Cr App R 30.

[5] For a discussion of the controls over the judicial conduct of the trial see A. Samuels, 'Judicial misconduct in the criminal trial', [1982] Crim L Rev 221.

[6] In certain exceptional circumstances witness statements may be taken before the trial and adduced at the trial in the form of depositions. See *Archbold's Pleading, Evidence and Practice in Criminal Cases*, 42nd edn. (1985), 348, 355 ff.

[7] Police and Criminal Evidence Act 1984, s. 79.

After the case for the defence, the prosecutor has a right to make a closing speech in which he may comment on the evidence as a whole. The defence may then make its closing speech. Whether or not the defence has called evidence, it always has the right to the last word.[8]

The party calling a witness, or his advocate, will examine the witness-in-chief with a view to eliciting information favourable to the party's case. The witness will then be cross-examined by the opponent with a view, usually, to discrediting him or to extracting information that is unfavourable to the proponent's case. Since the examination of witnesses is done by interested litigants, the courts have had to evolve practices to prevent abuse. These practices are usually described in terms of rules but, as we shall see presently, this is often misleading.

EXAMINATION-IN-CHIEF

Examination-in-chief is said to be governed by four rules: first, the rule forbidding leading questions; secondly, the rule prescribing what kind of documents may be used in order to help the witness refresh his memory; thirdly, the rule forbidding questions calculated to show that the witness had made previous statements to the same effect as his testimony; and, fourthly, the rule forbidding a party to cross-examine his own witness in order to discredit him. However, a review of practice suggests that the permissibility of these devices is discretionary.

Leading Questions

A witness is summoned either by the prosecution or the defence[9] and furnishes information in reply to questions from the party who summoned him. Naturally, a party calls a witness only if the party believes that the witness can advance his cause. This party has a strong interest in securing the hoped-for

---

[8] Criminal Procedure Act 1865, s. 2. The right of an accused to call witnesses or to address the jury may be curbed if used for improper purposes: *Morley* [1988] 2 All ER 396.

[9] Subject to the judicial power to call witnesses; see *Archbold's Pleading, Evidence and Practice in Criminal Cases*, 42nd edn. (1985), 481.

testimony and there is a danger that the party would try to induce the witness to say not so much what the latter believes as what the former wishes to hear. As Best wrote:

the party calling a witness has an advantage over his adversary, in knowing beforehand what the witness will prove, or at least is expected to prove; and ... if he were allowed to lead, he might interrogate in such a manner as to extract only so much of the knowledge of the witness as would be favourable to his side, or even put a false gloss on the whole.[10]

The so-called rule forbidding leading questions draws attention to the need to prevent such a practice. A leading question is one which suggests to the witness that a specific answer is desired of him.[11] At times, however, leading questions are allowed. Sometimes it is permissible to draw the witness's attention to the required answer, as when a witness is asked to provide specific information about which there is no real dispute. Clearly, a forbidden question is not one which takes a particular form (i.e., it suggests the answer) but one which is directed to an improper end. Hence the test is whether the question put to the witness is likely to distort the witness's testimony on a disputed fact in which case it will be forbidden.[12]

Refreshing Memory

While a party may not, generally speaking, suggest to his witness what to say, the witness may require help in remembering the events in question. One way of providing such help is by showing the witness a document recording the events. This method presents an obvious risk: the more a witness relies on a document, the more he is likely to be influenced by what he reads; beyond a certain point the document itself rather than the witness's account becomes the source of the information.

Wigmore thought that a distinction should be drawn between situations where a document does in fact evoke a present recollection of an event, and situations where it does not have

---

[10] *Principles of the Law of Evidence*, 5th edn. (1870), 802.
[11] *Cross on Evidence*, 5th edn. (1979), 226; *McCormick on Evidence*, 3rd edn. (1984), 11.
[12] For discussion see Glanville Williams, *The Proof of Guilt*, 3rd edn. (1963), 93.

this effect. Documents in the first category, he thought, should not be subject to any restriction, while documents in the latter should be regarded as hearsay and admitted in evidence only under a well-defined exception to the hearsay rule.[13] English law, however, recognizes that in most situations this distinction is hard to draw. It therefore pursues a practical approach designed to close the main avenues for insinuating information for which the witness cannot vouch.

First, to counteract improper preparation of witnesses before the trial it is laid down that if, prior to being called, a witness has been allowed to consult statements he made to the police, the prosecution must notify the defence that this has been done.[14] Such notice should enable the defence to discover the extent to which a witness speaks from his own recollection. Secondly, in order to ensure that a witness is not influenced by extraneous information, the law insists that only documents that have been made at, or close to, the time of the events in question, and have been written by the witness himself or under his supervision may be shown to the witness.[15] Thirdly, documents used for refreshing memory must be given to the opponent, who may then cross-examine the witness on them, and to the trier of fact.

The first and third safeguards are straightforward because they require the giving of notice and the handing over of documents respectively. The second safeguard is not so simple. The requirement of contemporaneity is strictly observed only when there is doubt whether the document really revives a present memory in the witness.[16] Where, at the sight of a document, a witness is clearly made to recollect the event in all its relevant details, the use of documents which were not prepared by the witness or under his supervision is sometimes allowed.[17] By

---

[13] *Wigmore on Evidence*, Chad Rev, vol. 3, s. 754, 754A. For the present purposes we may take this rule to mean that a statement, other than one made by a witness giving evidence at the trial, which is tendered as evidence of the facts stated therein is inadmissible. For discussion of the effect of the hearsay rule on the practice of using documents for the purpose of refreshing memory see Ch. 11.

[14] *Richardson* [1971] 2 All ER 773; *Westwell* [1976] 2 All ER 812.

[15] *A-G's Reference No 3 of 1979* (1979) 69 Cr App R 411.

[16] The less the witness could be expected to remember the greater the insistence on contemporaneity: Newark and Samuels, [1978] Crim L R 408–9.

[17] *Doe d. Church and Phillips v. Perkins* (1790) 3 T R 749.

contrast, where, as is commonly the case, it is not clear whether the witness speaks from his own memory or merely repeats the information from the document, the courts show greater insistence that the document should have been made, or verified, by the witness close to the time at which he observed the facts.[18]

We may conclude that the underlying purpose of judicial supervision of the practice of refreshing memory is to ensure that parties do not introduce evidence which does not originate from the witness and for which he is not answerable.

Previous Consistent Statements

A party calling a witness has, naturally, an interest in supporting the witness's credibility. To further this end a party may be tempted to show that the witness had related the same story out of court. There are a number of good reasons for discouraging such a practice. First, in most instances proof of a consistent statement will add little weight to the witness's testimony and will therefore be superfluous. Secondly, the introduction of such statements will often raise unnecessary side-issues and cause confusion and delay. Lastly, there is a danger that such statements would be used to bolster artificially the credibility of the witness.[19]

As a general measure of prudence, judges have for a long time tended to disallow a party from eliciting from his own witness the fact that the latter had previously made statements consistent with his present testimony. This judicial practice has given rise to the belief that there is a cut-and-dried rule of law to this effect. Since it cannot be ignored that on occasion judges have allowed the introduction of consistent statements, it is said that admissibility in these instances is due to three special rules

---

[18] *A-G's Reference (No. 3 of 1979)* (1979) 69 Cr App R 411. It has been decided that a witness may also refresh his memory from a document which was made by another at his dictation, though without his supervision, provided the maker read it out to the witness: *Kelsey* (1982) 74 Cr App R 213.

[19] Especially through previous statements specially designed for this purpose. See *Fox* v. *General Medical Council* [1960] 3 All ER 225; *Corke* v. *Corke and Cook* [1958] 1 All ER 224. For this reason the rule is sometimes described as the rule against self-corroboration, or the rule against self-serving statements.

of exception.[20] First, a prior statement is admissible for the purpose of rebutting a suggestion that the witness has recently invented his story.[21] Secondly, a prior statement is admissible to prove a complaint made by the victim of a sexual assault soon after the incident in support of the victim's testimony.[22] Lastly, it is thought permissible to elicit previous consistent statements when they formed an integral part of a relevant transaction.

In a thorough trawl of the case-law Gooderson has shown that previous consistent statements have been allowed in many more situations than just these.[23] Statements made by the accused on his arrest or on the recovering of property from him, to mention two instances, have been admitted.[24] It is easy to see that the instances of admissibility, whether within or without the 'exceptions', have a common denominator: sufficient probative significance of the statement admitted. We may therefore say that admissibility is a function of probative contribution. If this is the case, it is better to abandon the idea of a rule of inadmissibility which is subject to special exceptions.

Instead we should accept that judges are not handed ready-made solutions for deciding admissibility in these circumstances. Essentially the judicial task here is no different from the task of determining whether any other piece of evidence makes a sufficient contribution to the elucidation of the issues to justify its admission. The recognition that the guiding principle is sufficiency of probative value does not entail that trial judges will now have to devote more time to the admissibility of consistent statements. Judges may continue to proceed on the general assumption that such statements are on the whole useless. But trial judges have no permanent dispensation from

---

[20] *Phipson on Evidence*, 13th edn. (1982), 788–90; *Archbold's Pleading, Evidence and Practice in Criminal Cases*, 42nd edn. (1985), 402–5.

[21] *Coll* (1889) 25 LRIr 522; *Ahmed* v. *Brumfitt* (1967) 112 Sol J 32.

[22] *Lillyman* [1896] 2 QB 167; *Osborne* [1905] 1 KB 551.

[23] 'Previous consistent statements', [1968] CLJ 64. For a review see also: *Phipson on Evidence*, 13th edn. (1982), 788.

[24] It has recently been held that when an incriminating statement is adduced by the prosecution which also contains exculpatory explanations by the accused, the jury are entitled to treat the latter as evidence of their truth: *Sharp* [1988] 1 All ER 65; *Hamand* (1986) 82 Cr App R 65. See Elliott and Wakefield, 'Exculpatory statements by accused persons', [1979] Crim L Rev 428.

fresh assessment of the probative value of previous consistent statements[25]

Hostile Witnesses

Although a party summons a witness only if he believes that witness to possess information favourable to his case, there is no guarantee that the witness will impart the hoped-for information. If the witness does not meet the party's expectations, that party will wish to press the witness by cross-examining him. Cross-examination is the method, as we shall presently see, by which one party may challenge his opponent's witnesses. This is commonly done by asking a witness searching questions with a view to casting doubt on his powers of perception and memory, imputing mendacity, undermining his moral credentials, and extracting from him information unfavourable to the party that called him.

A party is generally forbidden to cross-examine his own witness for two principal reasons. First, if a party suspects that a person is not credible, he should not call that person to testify and should avoid wasting the court's time.[26] Secondly, it is unfair that a person should be summoned to testify only to have aspersions cast upon his credibility by the party calling him. In some situations, however, adherence to this prohibition may itself become a source of unfairness.

Where a witness is reluctant or evasive to the point of refusing to obey his duty to divulge information in his possession, the

---

[25] For a useful summary of the considerations involved in admitting previous statements to rebut suggestion of recent invention see *National Defendant* v. *Clements* (1961) 104 CLR 476. It is said that, due to the rule against hearsay, when previous consistent statements are admitted they are not to be taken as evidence of facts stated; *Wallwork* (1958) 42 Cr App R 153. This view is now open to doubt. In *Sharp* [1988] 1 All ER 65, the prosecution adduced a statement made by the accused to the police which was partly inculpatory and partly exculpatory. The House of Lords held that the exculpatory part was to be given its full evidentiary value even to the extent of being regarded as evidence of the truth of that which the exculpatory part asserted; see n. 35 below. This matter is further considered in Ch. 11, which deals with the hearsay rule.

[26] This is not to say that a party is bound by unfavourable evidence given by his own witnesses. He is allowed to call other witnesses to give a different account; though not for the purpose of showing that his earlier witnesses are the kind of people who should not be believed on their oath.

party who called him clearly needs some means of pressing his questions. The practice in such situations is for the judge to declare the witness to be hostile and allow cross-examination by the party who summoned the witness. Whether or not the witness's responses justify cross-examination is something that the judge has to decide in the light of the circumstances before him.[27]

Cross-examination of one's own witness, unlike ordinary cross-examination, must be confined to attempts to elicit information from the witness, and must not be directed to showing that the witness is the kind of person who cannot be believed on his oath.[28]

CROSS-EXAMINATION

Introduction

The most effective method for testing a witness's evidence is cross-examination. The cross-examiner may use tactics designed to extract disclosures which the witness is reluctant to make, to prompt contradiction, to undermine confidence, to cast doubt on honesty and reliability, and generally to try and detract from the value of the testimony which the witness has

---

[27] The results of rigid adherence to the rule forbidding a party to impeach his own witness has led to its abrogation in the United States; *McCormick on Evidence*, 3rd edn. (1984), 84–5. Rule 607 of the Federal Rules of Evidence provides that '[t]he credibility of a witness may be attacked by any party, including the party calling him'. As long as the English approach remains flexible enough, it is preferable to either a complete prohibition or to unlimited licence to impeach one's own witness. English law should, however, follow the American example in one respect. In the United States an accused is allowed to cross-examine his witness if the latter unexpectedly gives evidence capable of incriminating the accused; *Chambers* v. *Mississippi* 410 US 284 (1973). In England it is not enough that the witness has given unfavourable evidence in order to justify cross-examination by the accused, the witness has to be evasive. The American approach is more consonant with the principle that the accused must have an opportunity to challenge the evidence against him.

[28] Criminal Procedure Act 1865. For difficulties of interpretation see *Cross on Evidence*, 5th edn. (1979), 252–5. Like the cross-examination itself, the use of previous statements is subject to judicial permission. Criminal Procedure Act 1865, s. 3; *Booth* (1982) 74 Cr App R 123. See text corresponding to n. 57 below.

given in-chief.[29] While such impeachment methods are useful for ascertaining the truth, they may become oppressive and limits have to be placed on the cross-examiner's freedom.[30]

Relevance to Issue and Relevance to Credibility[31]

A distinction has developed between adducing evidence to undermine a witness's credibility and adducing evidence to the issue. This distinction is taken to justify a restriction upon the cross-examiner's freedom.[32] It is said that as a general rule a party who cross-examines a witness is not entitled to call independent evidence to show that the witness is unreliable because such evidence is not relevant to an issue in the case but only to the witness's credibility.

We have seen that, other things being equal, all relevant evidence is admissible unless its contribution to the ascertainment of truth is outweighed by considerations of confusion, cost, and delay. Since there are no special considerations of policy that require the exclusion of evidence adduced to contradict a witness, we are entitled to assume that the justification of the present rule rests on the supposition that evidence which merely tends to discredit a witness makes, on the whole, insufficient probative contribution to warrant its reception.

This assumption is unfounded. Let us take the case in which the only issue is the offender's identity and the only evidence for the prosecution is *W*'s testimony who claims to have observed the accused from thirty yards. The accused adduces evidence to show that *W* cannot see beyond ten yards. According to the rule we are discussing this evidence is inadmissible because it is only relevant to credit of the witness and not to the issue of the commission of the offence. By contrast, if the accused calls

---

[29] In the absence of special circumstances, failure to cross-examine the opponent's witness will be taken as an indication of acceptance of the witness's testimony. See *Browne* v. *Dunn* (1894) 6 R 67, 75.

[30] The legal profession has laid down guidelines to moderate attacks upon witnesses. The Bar Council's rules warn, for example, against 'questions which are only intended to insult or annoy; and against unnecessary or unreasonable suggestions of misconduct or bad character; *Phipson on Evidence*, 13th edn. (1982), 807.

[31] See my paper 'Relevance in legal proceedings', in Twining (ed.), *Facts in Law*. (1983).

[32] This distinction also provides the rationale of a number of other practices; see Ch. 21 and 13 dealing with similar-fact evidence and ss. 1(*e*) and (*f*), respectively, of the Criminal Evidence Act 1898.

evidence to show that he was a close friend of the victim, this evidence will be admissible because it is relevant to the issue; it makes it less probable that the accused would harm his friend. Yet the evidence of motive is far less significant in this case than *W*'s ten-yard eyesight. It would not be irrational for the trier of fact both to believe that the accused was the victim's friend and to conclude that the accused committed an offence against the friend. But if the trier of fact believes that *W* could not have observed the offence, a conviction could not properly take place. It can hardly be maintained that evidence affecting credibility is as a general rule less important than evidence which impinges directly on an issue.

If our object is to arrive economically at factually correct conclusions, admissibility should depend on the degree to which evidence contributes towards this end. Since the distinction between relevance to credibility and relevance to issue does not reflect a divergence in probative force we should not allow it to govern admissibility.[33]

The validity of the distinction between relevance to credibility and relevance to issue may also be questioned at a more fundamental level. One fact is relevant to another when it renders the existence of the other more probable. The fact that the witness says: 'The man who committed the offence was the accused' is relevant because it renders it more probable that the accused was the offender. However, *W*'s testimony could have this effect only if it has some credibility. If the testimony has no credibility at all, for example, because it is the blabber of a madman, it is irrelevant. It follows that the connecting link between *W*'s testimony and the conclusion based on it is credibility. In other words, the relevance of a witness's testimony is embedded in his credibility, actual or potential.[34] Credibility is

---

[33] It is true, as we shall shortly see, that the extremity of the *Hitchcock* rule (see n. 40 below), and therefore of the implications of the distinction between relevance to issue and relevance to credit, is subject to a number of exceptions. However, unless we choose to regard the exceptions as open-ended, the rule produces injustice whenever its application results in the exclusion of evidence that is not allowed in by an exception but which is of considerable probative significance.

[34] Credibility refers here to the probative weight that may be given to the testimony of a witness. In this sense a witness's testimony may lack credibility even if we do not think that he is lying; as where we have come to the conclusion that the witness did not see what he believes he saw. For a distinction between concluding that a witness is in fact wrong on a particular point and concluding that due to his unreliable character we cannot rely on him see Ch. 13.

not something separate (a separate issue) which is somehow suspended between the witness's statement and the fact asserted therein. *W*'s ten-yard eyesight does not pertain to something which is different from the relevance of *W*'s testimony to the issue. When it is shown that our witness cannot see beyond ten yards, this factor becomes subsumed in the evidence we have for identification. Once the ten-yard limit has been proved we say that the evidence of identification consists in the testimony of a witness who claims to have identified the offender from thirty yards when in fact he can see nothing beyond ten yards.

In what sense can it be said that *W*'s eyesight is not directly relevant to the issue? It is not directly relevant in the sense that the range of *W*'s eyesight neither increases nor decreases the probability that the accused committed the offence charged. But in this sense it is not merely not directly relevant, it is wholly irrelevant. To deny direct relevance (which is implied in the assertion of indirect relevance used in this context) is to address a question which is of no consequence or interest: What is the probability that the accused committed the offence given that *W* cannot see beyond ten yards? The question of consequence is a different question: What is the probability that the accused committed the offence given that *W* says he saw him doing so from a distance of thirty yards when *W* cannot see beyond ten yards? Suppose that our witness testifies: 'I saw the accused, but I am not sure'. The qualifying words are as much a part of the evidence which goes to the issue as the opening words. Similarly, if *W* were to testify: 'I cannot usually see beyond ten yards but on this occasion I identified the accused from thirty yards', we cannot say that only the second part of this sentence is relevant to the issue but not the first.[35]

---

[35] In *Sharp* [1988] 1 All ER 65, 71, Lord Havers said 'that a jury will make little of a direction that attempts to draw a distinction between evidence which is evidence of facts and evidence in the same statement which whilst not being evidence of facts is nevertheless evidentiary material of which they may make use in evaluating the evidence which is evidence of the facts.' However, in *Lui Mui Lin* v. *R The Times* (26 Oct 1988) it has been held that an inadmissible confession of an accused may be used by a co-accused for the purpose of cross-examining the accused and that the jury must be told not only that the confession is not evidence of the facts admitted in it, but also that it may only be taken into account for judging the credibility of the accused's evidence against the co-accused and not his credibility in denying his own guilt. This direction can only confuse.

True, the information concerning the witness's eyesight is significant only because the witness has testified and we want to know what credence we can give to his testimony. Put differently, the relevance of the information concerning eyesight is contingent on the witness having given evidence. But such contingency will be found in all instances of circumstantial evidence. Suppose the issue is whether the accused was in a certain place at a certain time. The fact that a car bearing a certain registration number was seen at the scene of the crime is relevant to his presence only if the accused uses a car bearing that number. But it would be absurd to insist that because the accused's use of the car is not directly relevant to the issue but only to the credibility (or probative weight) of the sighting of the registration number at the scene it has a different kind of relevance. By the same token, *W*'s eyesight is not of a different kind of relevance merely because it is contingent on *W* having testified.

Proof of Previous Inconsistent Statements and Other Discrediting Facts

A common method of challenging a witness during cross-examination is to suggest to him that he has made out of court a statement inconsistent with his account at the trial.[36] If the witness denies having made an inconsistent statement the question arises whether the cross-examiner may prove the statement.[37]

An unrestricted licence to prove previous inconsistent statements could lead to confusion and waste of time. Suppose that a prosecution witness identifies the accused. In the course of cross-examination the witness is asked by the defence whether he has admitted having made a mistaken identification on a previous and unrelated occasion and he denies such an admis-

---

[36] See, for instance, *Hart* (1932) 23 Cr App R 202. Sometimes the law imposes restrictions on the scope of such examination as does, for example, s. 2 of the Sexual Offences (Amendment) Act 1976, discussed below.

[37] It should be noted that, due to the rule against hearsay discussed in Ch. 11, previous statements of the witness are not allowed to be taken as proof of any matters stated in them; *Prefas and Bryce* (1988) 87 Cr App R 111. However, this may no longer be the case in view of *Sharp* [1988] 1 All ER 65; see n. 35 above. See also Criminal Law Revision Committee, 11th Report, para. 257.

sion. May the defence prove the admission of mistake? To enable the trier of fact to draw any useful conclusion from this inconsistent statement the defence will have to prove not only the making of the statement but also that it was true (in the sense that the witness's previous identification was wrong) and that the circumstances of the previous identification were similar to the circumstances under consideration. Otherwise proof of a previous mistake will merely show that which is already known: that the witness is not infallible.

Although the admissibility of inconsistent statements usually receives separate treatment in books on evidence, it is merely one aspect of the more general problem: the extent to which a party may adduce evidence to discredit the opponent's witnesses. The defence, in our example, may wish to give evidence of a previous mistaken identification by the witness although the latter has never said that he had been mistaken. Since both the admissibility of an inconsistent statement and of other matters relating to credibility pose a similar problem it is useful to deal with them together.

At present admissibility is largely governed by the distinction between relevance to issue and to credibility. According to *A-G* v. *Hitchcock* a party is free to call independent evidence to contradict his opponent's witness if such proof concerns the main issue but not if it concerns only a collateral matter. Pollock CB explained:

The test of whether an inquiry is collateral or not is this: if the answer of a witness is a matter which you would be allowed on your own part to prove in evidence—if it have such a connection with the issues, that you would be allowed to give it in evidence—then it is a matter on which you may contradict him.[38]

This rule produces the absurd result, discussed earlier, that the accused is not allowed to adduce evidence to show that the witness cannot see from the distance from which he claims to have observed the event in issue. Not surprisingly, the *Hitchcock* rule has often been disregarded when justice so demanded.[39]

---

[38] (1847) 1 Exch 91, 99. The *Hitchcock* rule is also known as the rule concerning the finality of a witness's testimony on collateral questions.

[39] For an illustration of unwavering faith regardless of consequence see the Australian case of *Piddington* v. *Bennett Wood Properties Ltd* (1940) 63 CLR 533.

The received wisdom is that deviation from this principle is only authorized under four exceptions beyond which proof of matters going to credit is inadmissible.[40]

The first of these exceptions concerns previous convictions of the witness. If during cross-examination a witness denies that he has been convicted of a criminal offence, his conviction may be proved.[41] The second exception allows the cross-examiner to prove that the witness is biased against his party.[42] A third exception sanctions proof that the witness has a reputation for untruthfulness, and a fourth allows medical evidence showing him to be unreliable.[43]

If proof of collateral matters were confined to these four categories, much important evidence would be excluded. For this reason, presumably, Professor Cross thought that while the *Hitchcock* rule was broadly satisfactory it had to be regarded as subject to an open list of exceptions.[44] This view is calculated to maintain the rule while, at the same time, allowing deviation from it whenever justice so requires. But it leaves one pondering the difference between saying that a new exception to the rule may be made where justice so requires and saying that collateral evidence is always admissible where justice requires.

Rather than rely on a rule subject to an open-ended list of exceptions it would be more satisfactory to state the position in a way that offers guidance for the unusual (or 'exceptional') situation as well as for the run-of-the-mill case. This can be achieved by an explanation that amplifies the purpose of the

---

[40] *Archbold's Pleading, Evidence and Practice in Criminal Cases*, 42nd edn. (1985), 413–4; *Phipson on Evidence*, 13th edn. (1982), 816; Murphy, *A Practical Approach to Evidence* (1980), 392.

[41] Criminal Procedure Act 1865, s. 6. Sections 4 and 5 of the Act govern the admissibility of previous inconsistent statements generally, but are not thought to differ from the common law. Questions about spent convictions are prohibited in civil proceedings: s. 4(1) of Rehabilitation of Offenders Act 1974. In criminal proceedings they are allowed but discouraged: s. 7(2) of the Act and Practice Direction by the Lord Chief Justice of 30 June 1975; see *Phipson on Evidence*, 13th edn. (1982), 819.

[42] *Thomas* v. *David* (1836) 7 C & P 350; and discussion in *Phipson on Evidence*, 13th edn. (1982), 818.

[43] See *Phipson on Evidence*, 13th edn. (1982), 819–20.

[44] *Cross on Evidence*, 5th edn. (1979), 265. Wigmore preferred to leave the matter to the good judgment of the trial judge: *Wigmore on Evidence*, 3rd edn. (1940), vol. 3, s. 1003. Cf. Stephen, *Digest of the Law of Evidence*, 12th edn. (1946), arts. 143–4.

judicial power to allow or disallow evidence on collateral issues. Such explanation may be found in the speech of Lord Pearce in *Toohey* v. *Metropolitan Police Commissioner*:

The only general principles which can be derived from the older cases are these. On the one hand, the courts have sought to prevent juries from being beguiled by evidence of witnesses who could be shown to be, through defect of character, wholly unworthy of belief. On the other hand, however, they have sought to prevent the trial of a case becoming clogged with a number of side issues, such as might arise if there could be an investigation of matters which had no relevance to the issue save in so far as they tended to show the veracity or falsity of the witness who was giving evidence which *was* relevant to the issue. Many controversies which might thus obliquely throw some light on the issues must in practice be discarded, because there is not an infinity of time, money and mental comprehension available to make use of them.[45]

In that case the two accused, who were charged with assault with intent to rob one *M*, alleged that they had found *M* drunk and hysterical and were only helping him home. *M*, on his part, claimed that he had been attacked by the accused. The issue was whether *M*'s admitted state of hysteria was caused by an assault or whether, on the contrary, the hysteria made him imagine an assault. The accused wished to ask a police surgeon, who examined *M* shortly after the incident, whether in his view the hysteria was caused by drink and whether *M* had a tendency towards hysteria. The trial judge disallowed the question as being contrary to authority. Overruling this decision the House of Lords held that it was 'allowable to call medical evidence of mental illness which makes a witness incapable of giving reliable evidence'.[46]

Some writers confine the decision to medical evidence affecting the reliability of a witness.[47] But on this view the wife of the witness who testifies to having identified the accused from thirty yards cannot testify that her husband cannot see from that distance because she lacks medical qualifications. This can hardly be the law.

---

[45] [1965] 1 All ER 506, 511.   [46] Ibid. 512.

[47] *Phipson on Evidence*, 13th edn. (1982), 820; *Archbold's Pleading, Evidence and Practice in Criminal Cases*, 42nd edn. (1985), 420.

It has to be accepted that there is no rule, of the *Hitchcock* type, that defines in advance when evidence may be admitted to contradict a witness and when it may not. Admissibility depends on whether the evidence in question can make sufficient contribution to the determination of the issue. If, after giving due consideration to the danger of confusion and to the time and cost involved in its reception, the judge concludes that the proffered evidence can make a significant contribution, he must admit it. Again the judge's task is no different from his general duty to put evidence through a test of sufficiency of relevance.

The price exacted by the notion that admissibility is governed by a rule emerges from decisions such as *Busby*.[48] The accused was charged with offences of burglary and handling. The evidence against him consisted mainly of statements he had made to the police and of statements attributed to him by fellow prisoners. His defence was that the police had fabricated the statements and had offered inducements to his fellow-prisoners. Cross-examining the police officers, counsel for the accused suggested to them that they had threatened one of the defence witnesses in order to deter him from testifying in the accused's favour. When the witness in question was called by the defence, counsel proposed to ask him in-chief whether the officers had approached him with a request to change his account. The trial judge felt bound by authority to rule out this question on the grounds that it went to credit of the officers and did not go to the issue. The Court of Appeal held that the question should have been allowed because:

If true, it would have shown that the police were prepared to go to improper lengths in order to secure the accused's conviction. It was the accused's case that the statement attributed to him had been fabricated, a suggestion which could not be accepted by the jury unless they thought that the officers concerned were prepared to go to improper lengths to secure a conviction.[49]

As a result of the trial judge's improper exclusion of the defence evidence, convictions on six offences of burglary and

---

[48] (1982) 75 Cr App R 79. See also *Marsh* (1986) 83 Cr App R 165.
[49] *Busby* (1982) 75 Cr App R 79.

four of handling were quashed. However, it would be unfair to blame the trial judge entirely for this outcome. If trial judges are told that the matter is governed by a rule of law, they will necessarily regard themselves bound by decisions that interpret or apply the rule.[50] As long as the courts continue to pay homage to the *Hitchcock* rule and to the distinction between relevance to credibility and relevance to issue trial judges are liable to be led astray.

There are some indications that this misleading distinction is losing its attraction for the courts. In *Viola*[51] the accused pleaded consent to a charge of rape and wished to cross-examine the complainant on: (1) whether a few hours before the alleged offence she had made sexual advances to two casual visitors; and (2) whether a few hours after the incident she entertained a naked man in her house. The trial judge, relying on section 2 of the Sexual Offences (Amendment) Act 1976, disallowed the questions. Section 2(1) forbids evidence concerning 'any sexual experience of a complainant with a person other than' the accused without leave of the judge. Section 2(2) goes on to add that '... the judge shall give leave if and only if he is satisfied that it would be unfair to that defendant to refuse to allow the evidence to be adduced or the question to be asked ...'

Lord Lane CJ said that while the judge must, under section 2, disallow questions which merely go to credit, he should allow questions which

are relevant to an issue in the trial in the light of the way the case is being run, ... as opposed merely to credit, ... because to exclude a relevant question on an issue in the trial ... will usually mean that the jury are being prevented from hearing something which, if they hear it, might cause them to change their minds about the evidence given by the complainant.

---

[50] In the instant case the trial judge's mistake lay, according to the Court of Appeal, in his failure to appreciate the effect of a decision of forty-six years of age upon an earlier decision one-hundred-and-thirty-five years old. The current editor of *Cross on Evidence* considers *Busby* to have been wrongly decided because of inconsistency with a case decided in 1811: 6th edn. (1985), 290. As it happens *Busby* is in line with *Hitchcock* where both Pollock CB and Alderson B said that where a witness denies having offered a bribe to another witness contradictory evidence may be adduced.

[51] [1982] 3 All ER 73.

If the subsection must not cause injustice then, clearly, it must not sanction exclusion of any evidence which might materially affect the outcome, whether it be considered relevant to issue or to credit.[52]

In the event the Court of Appeal decided that the above questions were admissible because they

> went to the question of consent and were matters which could not be regarded as so trivial or of so little relevance as for the judge to be able to say that he was satisfied that no injustice would be done to the appellant by their exclusion . . .[53]

If, one may ask, the test boils down to the justice or injustice of exclusion, would it not be preferable to discard the unfruitful distinction between relevance to issue and to credibility altogether?[54]

Placing the test on a footing of probative usefulness will clarify the position regarding a number of statutory provisions in this field. First, the criterion would be the same whether the matter falls to be decided under section 2 of the 1976 Act or outside it. Secondly, the operation of the Criminal Procedure Act 1865, will become straightforward. Section 4 of the 1865 Act allows the cross-examiner to prove that the witness made a previous inconsistent statement. According to section 3 of the same Act, previous inconsistent statements may be put to hostile witnesses only by leave of the judge.[55] If admissibility is a function of probative significance, the outcome will be the same under both sections.[56]

In conclusion, the position regarding evidence on collateral matters can be much simplified by two simple devices. First, we

---

[52] The Lord Chief Justice seemed to concede as much, ibid. 77.

[53] Ibid. 79.

[54] Lord Lane CJ observed in *Viola* that it was wrong to talk of discretion in relation to s. 2 of the Sexual Offences (Amendment) Act 1976 because if the judge 'comes to the conclusion that he is satisfied that it would be unfair to exclude the evidence, then, the evidence has to be admitted . . .', ibid. 73, 77. See also *Cox* (1987) 84 Cr App R 132.

[55] *Booth* (1982) 74 Cr App R 123.

[56] If on an application under s. 3 the judge decides that the prior statement can make a material contribution he will have to admit it. And, vice versa, although no leave is required under s. 4, the judge should still refuse to allow proof of a previous statement when it can make no real contribution to the elucidation of the issues.

must avoid unnecessary distinctions such as that which leads to separate treatment being accorded to the admissibility of previous inconsistent statements and of other evidence designed to discredit a witness. Whenever a party proposes to call evidence to discredit a witness, whether by proving his previous inconsistent statements or by proving other facts pertaining to his reliability, the problem is identical.

Secondly, we must discard the notion that such admissibility is governed by a special rule. Judges may sensibly continue to assume that evidence called for the sole purpose of contradicting or discrediting a witness is on the whole useless, but it is incumbent on them to exercise their own judgment when this assumption is reasonably questioned. Decided cases constitute a repository of experience and can provide useful examples of how judges have dealt with similar problems in the past, but in the final resort admissibility must depend on the trial judge's assessment of the probative value of the evidence in question.[57]

---

[57] It would also be useful to discard misleading terminology. It is said that 'answers given by a witness to questions put to him in cross-examination concerning collateral facts must be treated as final'; *Cross on Evidence*, 6th edn. (1985), 282–3. The cross-examiner who disputes the witness's answers may state his disagreement and may seek to have them contradicted by other witnesses who can testify to the same event; it is better to avoid the term 'finality' in this regard.

8

Burden of Proof and Presumptions as Risk-Allocation Techniques

The aim of this chapter is to introduce the notions of burden of proof and presumptions. These notions are not, of course, confined to criminal evidence but are employed extensively throughout the litigation process and the exposition includes some illustrations from the civil law where risk-allocation techniques are more extensively used.

In the adversarial trial the judicial role is essentially passive. The trier of fact approaches the factual dispute with an open mind, leaving it to the parties to present their evidence and persuade the court of the existence of the facts necessary to their case. This system requires rules that determine what should happen if a party fails to persuade the court of a fact that is necessary to that party's case. Rules allocating the burden of proof provide the answer in such situations. They determine which litigant has to prove the constitutive facts and the degree of probability which such proof has to reach. In effect, these rules allocate the risk of losing the case should a party fail to prove a constitutive fact.[1]

For instance, the law of contract lays down that a person who lends money to another (i.e. hands over money under a legally binding agreement that it should be repaid) is entitled to repayment of the loan. Suppose that at the end of the trial the court is

---

[1] The following sources have proved invaluable in the writing of this section: *Wigmore on Evidence*, 3rd edn. (1940), vol. 9, ss. 2485 ff.; Stone, 'A comment on *Joseph Constantine Steamship Line Ltd* v. *Imperial Corporation Ltd*', (1944) 60 LQR 262; Denning, 'Presumptions and burdens', (1945) 61 LQR 379; Bridge, 'Presumptions and burdens', (1949) 12 MLR 273; Glanville Williams, *Criminal Law, The General Part*, 2nd edn. ch. 23.

left in doubt as to whether *B* has failed to repay the £100 which *A* lent him. A choice will then have to be made whether to give judgment for the plaintiff, or for the defendant, or to follow Solomon's principle and divide the object of contention.

Clearly, any course taken involves a risk of handing down a wrong judgment in the sense of doing one of the parties out of what is in fact his right. If we say, as we generally do, that the plaintiff wins if he proves his case on the balance of probabilities, which for the sake of argument we may regard as 55 per cent probability, it follows that we are prepared to accept a 45 per cent risk that the decision against the defendant in that case is a wrong one.[2] Burdens of proof and presumptions provide the means by which the substantive law allocates the risk of losing the case.

The simplest technique for allocating this risk consists of laying down that unless the party claiming the enforcement of a right proves, to a certain degree of probability, the facts giving rise to his right, the court will refuse to help him. This device is referred to as the 'legal burden' or the 'burden of persuasion' or the 'probative burden'. The first term emphasizes the dependence of the burden on the substantive law, while the last two stress the need to produce sufficient proof to produce a certain degree of assurance in the adjudicator's mind.[3] Henceforth the burden requiring the proponent to prove his case to a certain degree of strength will be referred to as the probative burden.[4]

Since a belief in the truth of a proposition can be held with various degrees of confidence, this burden needs to specify the level of confidence which the proof has to produce in the trier of

---

[2] It must not, however, be assumed that 45 per cent or so of all civil cases are wrongly decided. It is very probable that in many civil cases the plaintiff achieves more than a preponderance of probabilities, quite likely even proof beyond reasonable doubt, in others plaintiffs may achieve some 80 per cent or 70 per cent probabilities so that the overall rate of untrue conclusions in civil cases will be much lower than 45 per cent.

[3] It should be borne in mind that hardly any terms in this field have generally accepted meanings and it therefore is always advisable to examine the precise meaning implied in the particular usage.

[4] As the probative burden that lies on the prosecution in a criminal case requires proof beyond reasonable doubt, we may refer to this burden as a burden of persuasion.

fact.[5] Common-sense assessments of probabilities are not expressible in precise numerical terms, as we have seen in Chapter 2, and the law can therefore set only rough probabilistic requirements. Basically there are two such standards: proof on the balance of probabilities and proof beyond reasonable doubt. The first standard requires that the proponent show that it is more likely than not that his version of the facts is right, while the latter requires, as we shall see in Chapter 9, that the trier of fact is left with no reasonable doubt in his mind as to the correctness of the facts in respect of which this burden lies.

The probative burden obtains in respect of particular issues or facts. Failure to discharge the burden results in the proponent losing on that particular issue. This may mean losing the case as a whole, but not necessarily so. If our plaintiff fails to prove on the balance of probabilities that he handed over the money to the defendant his claim will, obviously, be dismissed. But suppose the defendant, in addition to denying receipt of the money, also claims that he was coerced into signing an agreement to repay the sum. In this last respect the probative burden rests on the defendant. Failure by him to convince the court on the balance of probabilities need not necessarily result in judgment against him, since the plaintiff could still fail to discharge his burden to show that the defendant received the money. We should, therefore, only speak of a probative burden in relation to a particular issue or fact.[6]

There is a further technique for allocating the risk of losing the case, commonly referred to as the 'burden of adducing evidence' or the 'evidential burden'. This burden imposes an obligation to adduce some evidence in support of the existence of some facts in issue, without imposing any duty to generate any particular degree of confidence in the adjudicator's mind.

---

[5] The evaluation of evidence in the courts is fundamentally subjective: McBaine, 'Burden of proof: degrees of belief', 32 Calif L Rev 242 (1944); Kaye, 'The paradox of the gate-crasher and other stories', [1979] Ariz St U L J 101. For a discussion of subjective and objective probability theories in the judicial context see: Twining, 'Debating Probabilities', (1980) 2 Liverpool L Rev 51.

[6] In criminal cases, as we shall see later, the prosecution generally bears the burden of proving all the elements of the offence with which the accused is charged. Consequently, it is sometimes said that the prosecution bears the burden of persuasion on the case as a whole but there are exceptions to the general rule.

The probative value of evidence required to discharge this burden will vary according to whether the party bearing the burden of adducing evidence also carries the probative burden or not.

A few examples will clarify this. It is normal, though by no means universal, for the party bearing the probative burden in respect of a given issue to bear the burden of adducing evidence as well. The prosecution normally carries the burden of proving all the ingredients of the offence charged. If the charge is murder, the prosecution has to prove, *inter alia*, that the accused caused the victim's death. The burden of adducing evidence means that the prosecution must present evidence which, if believed, is sufficient to entitle a reasonable person to infer that the accused caused the death. If it fails to do so, it will fail on that issue at that early stage and the accused will not be called upon to answer the charge.[7]

Suppose now that in response to a murder charge the accused claims that the killing was done in self-defence and that it was, therefore, justifiable. On this issue too the prosecution bears the burden of persuasion in that it has to prove beyond reasonable doubt, if self-defence is in issue, that the accused did not act in self-defence. But it is the accused who bears the burden of adducing evidence of self-defence in the first place. That is, the accused must show some evidence of self-defence or else the judge will instruct the jury not to consider the defence. Since the accused does not bear a probative burden on the issue of self-defence he need only produce evidence which could, if believed, create a reasonable doubt that he might have acted in self-defence. Consequently the nature of the burden of adducing evidence[8] varies according to whether the party bearing it also bears the probative burden and, quite possibly, also according to the standard of proof required by the given probative burden.

The purpose of imposing the burden of adducing evidence on a party who does not bear a probative burden on the issue in question, is to prevent that party from troubling the trier of fact with claims that are unsupported by evidence. In our last

---

[7] See also discussion of the plea of 'no case to answer' in Ch. 4.
[8] Which is sometimes referred to as the burden of raising the issue.

example, the trier of fact will not have to deal with the defence of self-defence unless there is some evidence to support it and the prosecution will be relieved from the need to disprove every conceivable defence that the accused might possibly raise. The imposition of a burden of adducing evidence on the defence in respect of self-defence inevitably imposes on the accused some risk of losing the case.[9]

When the burden of adducing evidence is imposed on the proponent bearing the probative burden, its purpose is to relieve the opponent from the need of defending himself unless the proponent has adduced evidence capable of discharging his probative burden.[10]

Before leaving simple burdens, two further terms need be mentioned. One sometimes comes across the expression 'provisional burden' or 'tactical burden'. These terms are sometimes used to denote the burden of adducing evidence, but they are also used in another sense which is best conveyed by an example. Suppose that on a charge of murder the prosecution has called a witness who testifies that he saw the accused deliver the fatal blow. In doing so the prosecution has discharged its burden of adducing evidence in respect of the killing. Since the burden of persuasion also rests on the prosecution in this respect, the accused may refrain from adducing any evidence to the contrary in the hope that the jury will disbelieve the prosecution's witness. An accused who adopts this course runs, of course, the risk that the jury will be persuaded by the witness. It is said that such an accused bears a 'provisional' or a 'tactical' burden by taking the risk of not adducing contradicting evidence. These terms merely describe the exigencies of litigation and do not denote any formal technique of risk allocation.

---

[9] The fact that the accused is unable to discharge the burden of adducing evidence of self-defence does not necessarily entail that he did not act in self-defence. Situations where the accused might have a genuine defence but no evidence to support it are rare; he could assert his defence by testifying. Such circumstances may exist, however, as where the accused suffers from amnesia; *Critchley* [1982] Crim L Rev 524.

[10] The burden of adducing evidence imposes no further risk on the party bearing the probative burden as he has, in any event, to produce evidence that would generate sufficient confidence in the adjudicator.

PRESUMPTION: THE BASIC TECHNIQUE[11]

Three basic techniques for distributing the risk of losing the case have been described so far: allocation of the probative burden, the determination of the degree of proof required to discharge this burden, and the allocation of the burden of adducing evidence. These techniques may be used in a more complex manner by employing the device of presumption. 'Presumption', like so many other terms in this field, is used in several senses. For the time being we are interested in the central sense which denotes a rule of law whereby on proof of one fact (the 'basic fact') by the proponent the court is duty-bound to find the existence of another fact (the 'presumed fact'), unless the contrary is proved by the opponent or, as is sometimes the case, unless the opponent adduces evidence to the contrary.

Suppose, for example, that the plaintiff's claim depends upon him being the legitimate son of the deceased. Legitimacy depends on two factors: first, being the natural child of the deceased, and, secondly, having been born to the lawfully wedded wife of the deceased during her marriage to him. The presumption of legitimacy relieves the plaintiff from the need of proving the first element, if he has first proved the second element. If the plaintiff proves that he was born during his mother's marriage to the deceased, the court will find that he was the deceased's legitimate son, unless the defendant proves that the plaintiff was in fact begotten by another man. In respect of birth during wedlock, the plaintiff bears both the probative burden and the burden of adducing evidence. Only once he has discharged these burdens will he benefit from the presumption.

In this instance the probative burden resting on each party requires proof on the balance of probabilities.[12] However, the technique of presumption may also be used to distribute the burden of adducing evidence. Suppose that the proponent's case requires him to prove that a certain person who purported to

---

[11] For interesting discussion see: Ulman-Margalit, 'On presumptions', (1983) 80 Journal of Philosophy 143.

[12] Until the Family Law Reform Act 1969, s. 26, proof beyond reasonable doubt was required from the party challenging the presumption.

act as a public officer was duly appointed. An appointment is valid if, first, it was made by an authorized body, and, secondly, this was done in the legally prescribed form; the burden of persuasion rests on the proponent in this respect. The presumption of *omnia praesumuntur rite esse acta*[13] relieves the proponent from adducing evidence to prove these two factors in the first instance. If he shows that the person in question purported to act in the requisite capacity, the court will find that the person in question was duly appointed, unless the opponent produces some evidence that he was not. When the opponent has produced sufficient evidence of lack of authority, the court will decide in favour of the proponent if, and only if, he discharges his probative burden and proves a valid appointment. Sufficient evidence means, in this instance, evidence from which the absence of a due appointment may be inferred.

Two practical aspects need mentioning. First, the assessment of the evidence at the trial is not done piecemeal and the trial does not stop in order to determine whether the proponent has discharged his burden in respect of the basic fact or whether the opponent has succeeded in producing sufficient evidence to rebut the presumed fact. Nor does it stop to see whether a party has discharged his burden of adducing evidence on an isolated issue. The proponent will usually know from the pleadings, in civil cases, or from the conduct of the case, in criminal cases, which course the opponent proposes to take. He will, if he can, not merely rely on the force of presumption but also try to strengthen his case regarding the presumed fact by adducing positive evidence on the point.

Secondly, it is open to the opponent to challenge not only the presumed fact but also the basic fact. To revert to an earlier example, a defendant may try to avoid the effect of the presumption of legitimacy by showing that the plaintiff was not born during lawful wedlock, as well as, or instead of, proving that the plaintiff was not the deceased's son. If the defendant prevents the plaintiff from proving birth during lawful wedlock (the basic fact), he will have won on the issue of legitimacy even although he may have failed to discharge the burden resting on him in respect of fatherhood (the presumed fact).

---

[13] All acts are presumed to have been done rightly.

TERMINOLOGY AND CATEGORIES OF PRESUMPTIONS

As set out above, the technique of presumptions provides an uncomplicated method of distributing the risk of losing the case in respect of different facts which need to be proved in a criminal or civil trial. The nature of individual presumptions is easily described by outlining the basic and the presumed facts, by stating the type of burden in relation to each of them, and by indicating which parties bear the burden. Unfortunately this straightforward method is not always followed and a myriad of terms is employed. Most of these terms are neither generally accepted nor consistently used. A terminological explanation is therefore necessary.

The word 'presumption' is used to describe a number of different things. At times we come across expressions such as the 'presumption of innocence' or the 'presumption of sanity'. The first usually conveys the idea that in criminal cases the probative burden in respect of the accused's guilt rests on the prosecution. The second indicates that the burden of proof in respect of the defence of insanity is on the accused. In neither case is the burden of proof contingent on proof of a basic fact and there is no need to use the word 'presumption' in this context at all.

One sometimes comes across what is known as the classical classification of presumptions, by which presumptions are divided into three groups. First, presumptions of fact. These refer to situations in which, as a matter of common sense and not by force of law, the court may draw a certain factual inference from the existence of a certain set of facts. For example, on a charge of handling stolen goods, if the accused fails to provide a credible explanation for his possession of recently stolen goods there is said to arise a presumption of guilty knowledge.[14] This merely means that the jury may, as a matter of ordinary logic, infer the accused's knowledge that the goods were stolen. 'Presumption of fact' thus refers to circumstances which commonly occur in conjunction.[15] In this sense we may come across the 'presump-

---

[14] *Cross on Evidence*, 5th edn. (1979), 49.
[15] For instance where fact B may be inferred from fact A because A and B commonly occur together and B seldom occurs without A.

tion of continuance' whereby the trier of fact may infer the existence of a state of affairs from its existence at an earlier point in time. For instance, it may be inferred that a person was alive at a certain time from the fact that he was alive a short time before. In none of these cases is there any formal risk distribution because inferences are left to be drawn in the normal way.[16]

The second classical category consists of 'irrebuttable presumptions of law'. Upon the proof of certain facts the court is duty-bound to find the existence of another set of facts, irrespective of the true state of affairs. For example, it is an irrebuttable common-law presumption that all persons know the law. It is obvious that this is not a rule about the distribution of the risk of judicial mistake in the ascertainment of the true state of affairs. It is simply an awkward way of expressing the substantive rule that ignorance of the law is no defence.[17]

While the two foregoing categories are not presumptions in the central sense mentioned at the outset, the third category in this classification does cover presumptions in this central sense. This category, 'rebuttable presumptions of law', comprises all that is included in our central sense: rules whereby on proof of a basic fact a conclusion as to the presumed fact must be drawn, in the absence of evidence or proof, as the case may be, to the contrary. In order to draw attention to the difference between presumptions which distribute the probative burden and presumptions which distribute the burden of adducing evidence, proposals for more accurate terminology were at one time put forward by Lord Denning and by Professor Glanville Williams.[18]

Professor Williams speaks of presumptions which, upon proof of the basic facts, cast a burden of adducing evidence on the opponent as 'evidential presumption', while to a presumption

---

[16] The same goes for the usage, more prevalent in older cases, of describing the tendency of certain proven facts to support a certain conclusion as giving rise to a presumption in favour of the conclusion.

[17] For further instances see *Phipson on Evidence*, 13th edn. (1982), 1047.

[18] Denning, Presumptions and burdens, (1945) 61 LQR 379; Glanville Williams, *Criminal Law, The General Part*, 2nd edn. ch. 23; also Bridge, 'Presumptions and burdens', (1949) 12 MLR 273; Rankin, 'Presumptions and burdens', (1946) 62 LQR 135.

casting the probative burden he refers as 'persuasive presumption'. Lord Denning, for his part, describes the latter as 'compelling presumption'. However, none of these terms is well established in legal usage and for the sake of clarity it is always advisable to spell out the consequences of any particular presumption.

GENERAL THEORIES CONCERNING PRESUMPTION: A SENSELESS QUEST

The Relativity of Presumption

Traditionally the subject of presumptions has been considered to present enormous difficulties of exposition and analysis.[19] These difficulties are largely due to an unrealistic or misguided belief that the whole subject of presumptions could and should, in principle, be reduced to a comprehensive and coherent system of rules of general application. At the root of this belief lies a resistance to accepting presumptions for what they are: techniques, and no more, for allocating the risk of losing the case.

How the risk of losing on a given issue should be distributed is a question that can only be answered by the substantive law. For instance, the presumption of legitimacy, discussed earlier, arises in that form from the law of persons and has to do with the welfare of children, the obligations of marriage and the like, as well as with the general probabilities concerning legitimacy.[20] It is the policies of the family law that dictate the risk allocation and the technique to be employed for that purpose. The technique itself, the permutations upon the burden of proof, cannot determine when this or that risk allocation is appropriate.

While no one disputes that individual presumptions are the creatures of substantive law it is felt at times that the law of evidence should bring some order into the entire subject of

---

[19] Morgan warned that 'Every writer of sufficient intelligence to appreciate the difficulties of the subject matter has approached the topic of presumptions with a sense of hopelessness, and has left it with a feeling of despair.' 'Presumptions', 12 Washington L Rev 255 (1937).

[20] *Piers* v. *Piers* (1849) 2 HLC 331, 380–1.

presumptions by devising a system for the grouping of all presumptions.[21] Others believed that much confusion will be
avoided by a generally accepted terminology.[22] It is doubtless
true that ambiguity of terms can result in ambiguity about the
exact effect of individual presumptions but all that is required
to secure clarity and certainty is for the lawmaker to state
whether it is the probative or the evidential burden that is
involved in any individual presumption and the degree of probative force required to discharge the relevant burden. Beyond
that it is difficult to see what further contribution the law of
evidence can make in this respect.

This point can be illustrated by looking at the presumption of
res ipsa loquitur.[23] The basic facts of the presumption are, first,
that the plaintiff suffered damage, secondly, that the damage
was caused by an object or an activity which was under the
exclusive control of the defendant, and, thirdly, that the incident was such as usually happens through lack of care by those
in control. Proof of these basic facts is said to give rise to a
presumption that the accident was caused by the defendant's
negligence.[24] While the basic and presumed facts are fairly
clear, the exact probative effect of this presumption is doubtful.
There seems to be judicial support for three different views.[25]
Some cases suggest that this is merely a presumption of fact, a
common-sense guide to reasoning without any legally binding
effect.[26] The second view is that the presumption merely casts
the evidential burden on the defendant and that all he has to do
in order to discharge it is to adduce evidence capable of supporting an inference that he was not negligent. The third view is
that, on proof of the basic facts, the probative burden is imposed on the defendant to disprove negligence on the balance of
probabilities.

To settle which of these interpretations should be adopted the
court or the lawmaker will have to consider which technique

---

[21] Denning, 'Presumptions and burdens', (1945) 61 LQR 382.
[22] *Cross on Evidence*, 5th edn. (1979), 121.
[23] The thing speaks of itself.
[24] Street, *The Law of Torts*, 7th edn. (1983), 124.
[25] The authorities are reviewed in *Cross on Evidence*, 6th edn. (1985), 136.
[26] Thus the basic facts will usually support a conclusion of negligence but need
not if, in the circumstances, the basic facts do not warrant such conclusion.

will best serve the relevant policies of risk allocation in the law of negligence. The imposition of the legal burden on the defendant, once the basic facts have been proved, may be considered to be more conducive to the observance of high standards of care and, therefore, to afford greater protection to the public. Against this it might be argued that a burden of persuasion imposes far too heavy a liability on, say, industry and that such onerous liability might hinder economic progress. On considering these policies we may well conclude that it is undesirable that the presumption should have the same effect in all situations. We may, for example, decide that in relation to road accidents and industrial accidents the probative burden should be imposed on the defendant but that in the case of, say, professional conduct (such as the medical and legal professions) a probative burden would be excessive and that no more than an evidential burden should rest on the defendant. Clearly, the matter can only be settled in the light of the policies of the law of negligence, and the study of presumptions in other fields, such as criminal presumptions, cannot advance the process of determining the content of this presumption.

Considerations of policy may affect the operation of the same presumption in different fields. The presumption of legitimacy will again serve as illustration. If, in a civil case, the proponent proves that a child was born in lawful wedlock, the court must find that the child is legitimate unless the opponent proves, on the balance of probabilities, that it was not the husband's child. But the self-same presumption will be found to have a very different effect if legitimacy happens to be an issue in a criminal case. As Professor Cross pointed out, if on a charge of incest with his daughter the accused contends that although born in wedlock the child was not his, he will have to do no more than adduce evidence that suggests a reasonable possibility of illegitimacy.[27] This is so because the presumption is overtaken by the cardinal principle of criminal justice that no person may be convicted unless his guilt has been proved beyond reasonable doubt. By the same token, when the presumption operates against the prosecution (as where the prosecution's case is that although the child was born to the wife of another, she is in

---

[27] *Cross on Evidence*, 5th edn. (1979), 127.

reality the accused's daughter), it is not enough for it to prove the accused's parenthood on the balance of probabilities, which would be enough to rebut the presumption in a civil case. The prosecution will have to prove the accused's parenthood beyond reasonable doubt.[28]

The relativity of presumptions may also be illustrated by reference to the presumption of marriage. This lays down that on proof of a marriage ceremony the court must find that the marriage conformed with the requisite formalities and that it was, therefore, valid in form. The probative burden is on the opponent to prove the opposite.[29] When, however, the prosecution in a criminal case relies on that presumption, a lighter burden is imposed on the accused. To rebut the presumption he need only adduce evidence capable of raising doubt concerning the formal validity of the marriage. Thereafter the prosecution retains the burden of proving formal validity beyond reasonable doubt. It is clear therefore that the rules governing presumptions are not universal rules. As rules of substantive law they are encased in their respective fields, and their operation will sometimes alter when transposed to a different field of law where different principles may be at work.

No Law of Conflicting Presumptions

The belief that there is scope for a general law of presumptions has led to some odd legal theories. One such theory concerns 'conflicting presumptions'. This topic deals with situations where two or more presumptions arise in connection with the same set of facts, each of which dictates a different allocation of the burden of proof. For example, in *Monckton* v. *Tarr*[30] the plaintiff claimed workmen's compensation in 1930 on the ground that she was the widow of the deceased workman. She had gone through a marriage ceremony with the deceased in 1913. The defendants contended that this marriage was void since the deceased was already married at the time, having married A.J. in 1895. A.J. was alive at the time of the proceedings. The plaintiff met this contention by arguing that A.J. was

---

[28] Ibid. See also *Hemmings* [1939] 1 All 417.
[29] *Cross on Evidence*, 5th edn. (1979), 134–6.   [30] (1930) 23 BWCC 504.

herself already married when she purported to marry the deceased in 1895, having married D.C. in 1882. D.C. deserted A.J. in 1887 and there was no evidence whether he was alive at the time of the 1895 ceremony. There is a presumption of marriage which holds that once a ceremony of marriage is proved it must be assumed that the marriage was essentially valid (as distinguished from formally valid) in the sense that the parties had the capacity to marry. The presumption in favour of the 1913 ceremony conflicted with that of the 1895 ceremony, for if the latter was a valid marriage the former could not have been.[31]

Writers on evidence have attempted to devise rules for solving such conflicts. Yet to assume the possibility of a universal theory governing conflicts of presumptions is as illusory as to assume one governing the presumptions themselves. The presumption of marriage, for instance, is a rule of family law. It is designed to increase the protection of matrimonial rights. In a case such as *Monckton* v. *Tarr* there is a conflict between the need to protect the rights arising from an apparent former marriage and the need to protect the rights arising from an apparent later marriage. The substantive law may well resolve this conflict by providing, as was decided in that case, that none of the ceremonies should get preferential treatment and that the plaintiff must prove her case without the help of any presumptions. But there may well be other solutions.[32] Each solution will necessarily be governed by the relevant substantive law and not by some general theory of evidence.

The Distinction between Probative Weight of Basic Facts and the Effect of Presumptions Arising From Them

It is important to distinguish between the probative force of the basic facts of a presumption and the legal effect that attaches to it. A confusion between the two could lead to the conclusion that some presumptions are artificial or arbitrary. There is, for

---

[31] In this case different instances of the same presumption came into conflict, but there could be cases where conflict arises between wholly different presumptions.

[32] See, for example, *Taylor* v. *Taylor* [1965] 1 All ER 872 and see Heydon, *Evidence, Cases and Materials*, 2nd edn. (1984), 61–3.

instance, a common-law presumption of death which arises on proof of the basic facts: (*a*) that there is no evidence that *A* was alive for seven years; (*b*) that there were persons who were likely to hear from him and that they did not do so within those seven years; and (*c*) that due inquiries were made.[33] Upon proof of these basic facts death will be presumed unless the opponent adduces evidence from which the contrary might reasonably be inferred. It might be said that this presumption is artificial because absence in similar circumstances for six years and eleven months is no less probative than absence for seven years and one day.

Such a claim proceeds from the view that the presumption attempts to reflect the probative force of the basic facts. If that were the case the presumption would indeed be artificial. However, a presumption hardly ever comes into existence merely in order to reflect the probative weight of the basic facts: common sense could be relied upon to achieve this result. A presumption is a technique whereby the substantive law can distribute the risk of losing on a given issue. Thus in the case of prolonged absence there is a need to resolve rights which have remained suspended due to the protracted disappearance of a person. It is clearly undesirable to allow the rights of an absent person to remain indefinitely suspended. There is, therefore, nothing arbitrary or artificial about the need to limit the duration of time for which rights will remain suspended. Of course, this need does not dictate the precise length of time at which the limit is to be set, beyond requiring that it should be a substantial period. Settling the number of years at seven rather than six or eight contains an element of arbitrariness, but this is true of any time-limit upon the exercise of rights.[34] As long as the reasons for having a limit are cogent, and as long as the limit chosen is consistent with these reasons, the charge of artificiality is misconceived.

A further illustration of the confusion between probative significance and considerations of policy is provided by the treatment of the difference between the presumption of formal

---

[33] *Phipson on Evidence*, 13th edn. (1982), 1052.

[34] It is as true of the minimum age of criminal responsibility of ten years of age or of the limitation period in respect of real property of twelve years.

validity of marriage and the presumption of essential validity. Both have the same basic fact: the celebration of a marriage ceremony. However, while the presumed fact under the first is that the formal requirements were complied with, the presumed fact under the second is that the parties had the capacity to marry (i.e. were not within the groups of forbidden relations, were not already married, etc.). The presumption of formal validity places the probative burden on the opponent, and requires for its discharge strong and convincing evidence, while the presumption of essential validity (or of capacity to marry) places only an evidential burden on the opponent, requiring him merely to adduce evidence capable of supporting an inference as to the absence of capacity to marry.[35] The justification that Professor Cross advanced for the distinction is that the registrar of marriages is under a duty to satisfy himself of the fulfilment of the formal requirements, whereas he has no duty to inquire into the fulfilment of the essential requirements.[36] This explanation presupposes that these presumptions represent the probabilities of the formal or essential requirements having been, respectively, fulfilled. As already explained, this could hardly be the case. The difference between the presumptions goes far deeper. It arises from the different significance which the substantive law attaches to formal and substantive conditions for marriage. As formal requirements are of lesser importance, the law makes it harder to deprive a person of the status of marriage merely because of failure to observe the formalities. By contrast, since absence of capacity constitutes a stronger justification for denying a person the rights arising from matrimonial status, the law loads the scales against persons who might have lacked such capacity.

The confusion between the legal effect of presumptions and the probative force of their basic facts may assume another form. Suppose that we have a presumption which, on proof of the basic facts, casts the burden of persuasion on the opponent, and suppose the opponent has adduced evidence in rebuttal of the presumed fact. It is sometimes said that when the court considers whether the opponent has succeeded, it must place on the one side of the scale the probative force of the presumption

---

[35] The difference is discussed in *Cross on Evidence*, 5th edn. (1979), 136–7.
[36] Ibid. 137.

and on the other the probative force of the opponent's evidence.[37] This view is untenable. The rule of the presumption only indicates who should prove what and who should lose if the court fails to be persuaded of the truth of a proposition. It has, therefore, no part to play in the weighing of the evidence. Of course, the basic fact may possess some probative force, but this will not be on account of the rule of the presumption but on account of its actual probative significance in the circumstances of the case. To illustrate this point we may refer again to the presumption of legitimacy. The fact of birth during lawful wedlock may well have a strong probative force, but such force would depend on the circumstances of the husband and wife in question and not on the presumption. The couple may, for instance, have been on bad terms and living apart, in which case the presumption of birth in lawful wedlock would have very little force.

Rules of presumption are not a direct extension of probative force but are the result of various policies of the substantive law.[38] In some cases they protect certain social institutions; for example, the presumption of legitimacy upholds family relationships where a formal status of marriage exists. In others they are designed to avoid uncertainty, as is the case with the presumption of death.[39] Some presumptions are designed to ensure that one party does not have an unfair advantage over the other in relation to the facility with which they can prove certain facts. The presumption of sanity in criminal cases, for instance, is intended to prevent the accused from taking unjustified refuge in a plea of insanity.[40] The reasons for the making of presumptions are as numerous and as open-ended as are the rules of substantive law and cannot be fully accounted for within the confines of the law of evidence.

---

[37] See the difference of opinion between Lord Denning MR and Buckley LJ in *Stupple* v. *Royal Insurance Co* [1970] 3 All ER 230.

[38] A presumption could reflect the perceived probative significance of the basic fact but its existence has to find justification in other directions; there has to be a reason for wishing to give legal support to the inferences but would in any event follow from the probative force of the basic fact.

[39] Another example is provided by s. 184 of the Law of Property Act 1925, which provides that where two or more persons have died in circumstances rendering it uncertain which survived the other, it shall be assumed that they died in order of seniority.

[40] Though it is questionable whether it is justified to impose a burden of persuasion on an accused person to prove his lack of sanity.

9

Proof beyond Reasonable Doubt: The Law's Commitment to the Innocent

INTRODUCTION

A guilty verdict may be mistaken in two different senses. A verdict is mistaken in the first sense if it does not logically follow from the evidence. In the second sense a verdict is mistaken, notwithstanding that it may logically be supported by the evidence, when it fails to conform with the facts. A mistake in the first sense will occur if I reason that a person seen running away from a burning house was therefore guilty of arson.[1] A mistake of the second kind occurs where, although my conclusion is warranted by the evidence, it is still at variance with the fact of the matter. This will happen, for instance, where I infer that the accused was the arsonist having heard the reports of honest and ostensibly reliable eyewitnesses, who turn out to have been mistaken. We may refer to the first kind of mistake as a mistake of reasoning. An inference that fails to conform to the facts as they really happened may be referred to as a mistake of fact.

To avoid conviction of the innocent safeguards have to be created against both kinds of mistakes. By taking great care we could, in principle, eliminate errors of reasoning. Several rules of evidence single out certain types of evidence for special treatment with a view to minimizing the risk of such errors. The corroboration and hearsay rules, for instance, are designed to prevent unwarranted reliance on unreliable testimony. However, no matter what we do we cannot completely eliminate mistakes of fact. This is an inescapable feature of inductive reasoning: inferences can only be reached as a matter of probabil-

---

[1] It can happen that a conclusion which is not supported by the evidence is in fact correct.

ity and not as a matter of certainty. This chapter deals with the measures taken to safeguard against errors of fact.

In ordinary affairs we deal with the risk of factual mistake by balancing the likelihood that our inference will be factually erroneous against the magnitude of the harm that we will suffer if it turns out to be so. For instance, before setting out on a long walk I will listen to the weather forecast. If I hear that there is only a small chance of rain, I will take the risk and embark on my walk. If, however, I am certain to contract pneumonia as a result of any rain I experience, I will not take the risk. The greater the harm that an event carries with it the less we are inclined to run the risk of its occurrence.

In this example our factual inference relates to future events and it is therefore verifiable. If we look out on the day in question we will see whether it is raining. By contrast, most factual issues in the courts concern past events, notably the past conduct of the accused, and their occurrence remains forever a matter of inference rather than observation. Decisions about the occurrence of past events are, however, governed by the same risk-avoidance principle. The higher the probability that we require for the proof of past events the less likely it is that our conclusions will be at variance with reality.[2]

The importance that the legal system attaches to avoiding the conviction of an innocent person is reflected in the rule that no person may be convicted unless the prosecution has proved his guilt beyond reasonable doubt. This principle found expression in Viscount Sankey LC's famous dictum in *Woolmington* v. *DPP*.[3]

Throughout the web of the English Criminal Law one golden thread is always to be seen, that it is the duty of the prosecution to prove the prisoner's guilt subject . . . to the defence of insanity and subject also to any statutory exception. If, at the end of and on the whole of the case, there is a reasonable doubt, created by the evidence given by either the

---

[2] Ball, 'The moment of truth: probability theory and standards of proof', 14 Vand L Rev 807, 813–14 (1961). This observation holds good only when a mistake about an occurrence of an event has a different disutility or disadvantage value from that attendant upon a mistake concerning its non-occurrence. This is the case in the present context: the conviction of an innocent person is much more harmful that the acquittal of a guilty person.

[3] [1935] AC 462, 481–2.

prosecution or the prisoner, as to whether the prisoner killed the deceased with malicious intention, the prosecution has not made out the case and the prisoner is entitled to an acquittal. No matter what the charge or where the trial, the principle that the prosecution must prove the guilt of the prisoner is part of the common law of England and no attempt to whittle it down can be entertained.[4]

The American Constitution does not expressly refer to the burden of proof but the Supreme Court has held that the requirement of proof beyond reasonable doubt is part and parcel of the Fourteenth Amendment due process provision. Justice Brennan said that

The reasonable-doubt standard plays a vital role in the American scheme of criminal procedure. It is the prime instrument for reducing the risk of convictions resting on factual error. The standard provides concrete substance for the presumption of innocence—that bedrock 'axiomatic and elementary' principle whose 'enforcement lies at the foundation of the administration of our criminal law'.[5]

Although in England we do not have a written constitution it is clear that here too the right of the innocent not to suffer conviction and punishment is an important constitutional right. English law is, however, no different from its American counterpart in making only indirect reference to this principle either by stressing the presumption of innocence or by invoking the requirement of proof beyond reasonable doubt.[6]

---

[4] For a historical discussion of the notion of proof beyond reasonable doubt see: T. Waldman, 'Origins of the legal doctrine of reasonable doubt', 20 Journal of the History of Ideas 299 (1959); B. Shapiro, '"To a moral certainty": theories of knowledge and Anglo-American juries 1600–1850' 38 Hastings L J 153 (1986). It is to be noted that it is the prosecution's duty to prove the accused's guilt beyond reasonable doubt. The implications of this duty will become clear when we consider the exceptions to the general rule later on.

[5] *In re Winship* 397 US 358, 363 (1970). The quotations in this dictum are from *Coffin* v. *US* 156 US 432, 453 (1896). See R. J. Y. Allen, 'Structuring jury decision-making in criminal case . . .', 94 Harv L Rev 321, (1980).

[6] To say that one is presumed innocent means little unless this statement carries some implication as to who has to prove guilt and to what standard of proof it has to be established. The 'presumption of innocence' is at times shorthand reference to the duty of the state to prove the accused's guilt beyond reasonable doubt. At other times it means that the trier of fact must approach the charge without any predisposition towards a finding of guilt.

THE COMMITMENT TO PROTECTING THE INNOCENT

The protection of the innocent from conviction is a central theme of the law of criminal evidence. Its pivotal position is explicable by the fact that the system of criminal justice as a whole is aimed at preventing harm to the individual. If the legal system could not protect the law-abiding citizen from its own mistakes, so as to avoid the possibility that—in Romilly's words—each wretch that goes to the scaffold may be an innocent victim',[7] the justification for its own existence would be called into question.[8]

The importance of protecting the innocent from conviction is not justified only on the basis that it will produce the best social results.[9] Punishing persons whose guilt was probable, though by no means certain, might provide better protection from crime but, even so, this does not justify the punishment of an individual whose guilt is in doubt.[10] To deprive a person of his liberty or his property or to inflict humiliation upon him in the knowledge that he is or might be innocent is as grave a matter when carried out under the cloak of legal process as when the same happens without the law's authority. Our starting-point must therefore be that an innocent person has a right not to be convicted and punished. If the law is to respect this right, it

---

[7] Romilly, *Observations on the Criminal Law of England* (1810), Note D, quoted in Howell, 7 State Trials (32 Charles II, 1680), 1529 n.

[8] Justice Brennan made this point when he said that the 'use of the reasonable doubt standard is indispensable to command the respect and the confidence of the community in its applications of the criminal law. It is critical that the moral force of the criminal law not be diluted by a standard of proof that leaves people in doubt whether innocent men are being condemned.' *In re Winship* 397 US 358, 364 (1970).

[9] For a discussion of Bentham's purely utilitarian views see Twining, *Theories of Evidence: Bentham and Wigmore* (1985), 95 and Postema, *Bentham and the Common Law Tradition* (1986), 343–4.

[10] Prof. Dworkin maintains that the moral claim of the innocent not to be punished is such as to disentitle us from making utilitarian calculations about it. We are not to reason that it is permissible to single out one innocent individual and punish him in order to secure a benefit, however great, for the rest of us. *A Matter of Principle* (1985), 72. For a critique of the utilitarian justification for punishing the innocent see: Ten, *Crime, Guilt and Punishment* (1987), 13. The arguments for lowering the standard of proof in order to increase protection from crime are discussed below. For an economic analysis of the cost of error in criminal cases see Posner, 'An economic approach to legal procedure and judicial administration', 2 Journal of Legal Studies 399, 410 (1973).

must erect an adequate standard of proof as a safeguard against its violation.[11]

In the discussion of the criminal standard of proof it is not uncommon to come across numerical descriptions of the requirement of proof beyond reasonable doubt. These take the form 'it is better to acquit ten guilty persons rather than convict one innocent'.[12] Fortescue, writing in the fifteenth century, had a preference for a twenty-to-one ratio,[13] while Lord Stafford preferred a thousand-to-one.[14] Since the courts do not deal with statistical data capable of generating such measurable ratios, expressions of this are no more than rough descriptions of the preferred ratio of acquittal of the guilty to conviction of the innocent. Implied in these expressions is the view that it is justifiable to trade off the conviction of an innocent person in the interest of some social benefit. Once the trading-off principle is conceded, any number of permutations in the desirable ratio is possible. Bishop Paley thought that judges should not be averse to convicting the innocent for the common good and explained that

When certain rules of adjudication must be pursued, when certain degress of credibility must be accepted, in order to reach the crimes with which the public are infested, courts of justice should not be deterred from the application of these rules by *every* suspicion of danger, or by the mere possibility of confounding the innocent with the guilty. They ought rather to reflect, that he who falls by a mistaken sentence may be considered as falling for his country.[15]

This view was strongly criticized by Romilly[16] but the idea that the right of the innocent is relative was not put to rest. It is reflected in Stepehen's comment that

[11] Fletcher, 'Two kinds of legal rules: a comparative legal study of burden of persuasion practices in criminal cases', 77 Yale L J 880 (1968).

[12] Attributed to Sir Edward Seymour; see Glanville Williams, *The Proof of Guilt*, 3rd edn. (1963), 186–7.

[13] *De Laudibus Legum Angliae*, ch. 27.

[14] Howell, 7 *State Trials* (32 Charles II, 1680), 1529; also Blackstone, *Commentaries*, Bk. 4, ch. 27, vol. 4, p. 358. See also Holdsworth, *A History of English Law*, vol. 3, p. 620.

[15] *Principles of Moral and Political Philosophy* (1817), vol. 6, ch. 9, p. 428. A similar view is attributed to Lenin; Damaska, *The Faces of Justice and State Authority* (1986), 121 n. 41. See also Glanville Williams, *The Proof of Guilt*, 3rd edn. (1963), 187.

[16] Romilly, *Observations on the Criminal Law of England* (1810), Note D, quoted in Howell, 7 *State Trials* (32 Charles II, 1680), 1529 n. See discussion by Twining in *Theories of Evidence: Bentham and Wigmore* (1985), 96.

... it is by no means true that under all circumstances it is better that ten guilty men should escape than that one innocent man should suffer. Everything depends on what the guilty men have been doing, and something depends on the way in which the innocent man came to be suspected.[17]

It is possible that Stephen was explaining the necessity for a flexible standard of proof rather than arguing for a lower ratio across the board. Indeed, modern judicial dicta give some support to the notion that the requirement of proof beyond reasonable doubt is not rigid. In one case Denning LJ said:

It is true that by our law there is a higher standard of proof in criminal cases than in civil cases, but this is subject to the qualification that there is no absolute standard in either case. In criminal cases the charge must be proved beyond reasonable doubt, but there may be degrees of proof within that standard. Many great judges have said that, in proportion as the crime is enormous, so ought the proof to be clear.[18]

This view suggests that there are a number of sub-standards within the standard of proof beyond reasonable doubt. It is clear which sub-standard is to be found at the top: proof that leaves no doubt whatever of the accused's guilt. The remaining sub-standards represent less stringent requirements of proof although we are not informed what is the minimum requirement at the lower end of this scale. As these intermediate standards authorize conviction on the basis of proof that falls short of the highest degree of proof we need to examine what justification there might be for the conviction of a person about whose guilt there is some doubt, albeit small.

The aim of the criminal process is to protect the community from crime as well as to protect the innocent from conviction. It might therefore be suggested that in determining the standard

---

[17] *History of the Criminal Law of England* (1883), vol. 1, p. 438. It might, conceivably, be justified to harm some innocent people for the greater good under conditions of complete breakdown in the rule of law, as where civil disorder has broken out and a policy of shooting curfew-breakers on sight is necessary for the purpose of restoring order. But it is inconceivable that a society in which the rule of law obtains should subscribe to a policy of inflicting harm on the innocent for the greater good of others.

[18] *Bater* v. *Bater* [1950] 2 All ER 458, 459. This view has now been endorsed by the House of Lords in *Khawaja* v. *Secretary of State for the Home Office* [1983] 1 All ER 765. See comment on this case in text corresponding to n. 38 below.

of proof we ought to strike an acceptable balance between these two aims. We need therefore to consider how, if at all, the need to protect the community from crime may require us to increase the risk of punishing the innocent.

One might appeal here to the need for deterrence.[19] It might be said that the deterrent efficacy of punishment is in part a function of the extent to which we manage to apprehend and punish offenders. It might be argued that to the extent that we increase the requirement of proof for conviction, we increase the likelihood that guilty people will go free and we accordingly weaken the deterrent force of punishment. But a number of considerations militate against the argument that a lowering of the standard of proof is needed to increase deterrence. Deterrence hinges in the first place on the identification and apprehension of offenders; offenders who have not been caught cannot be punished. Only in the second place does it depend on the rate of convictions of those who have been apprehended and charged. Increased resources in the detection of crime could go a long way towards maintaining deterrence without having to place the innocent at risk.[20]

There is a more sophisticated version of the deterrence theory which argues that the most important aspect of punishment is to educate the public by strengthening the citizen's instinct to obey the law.[21] However, the reinforcement of the public's moral instinct can take place only where the punishment is perceived as just; that is, as being inflicted on the true offender and not on an innocent person. If accused persons are convicted on evidence that falls short of proof beyond reasonable doubt, it means that there is an appreciable chance that they are in fact innocent. The more the standard of proof falls below the highest level the greater the probability that convicted persons will later

---

[19] For useful discussions of this theory see Ten, *Crime, Guilt, and Punishment* (1987); N. Lacey, *State Punishment* (1988), ch. 2.

[20] Further, if effectively deployed, the investment of greater resources in investigation would probably yield superior evidence of crime which, in turn, will be capable of maintaining higher standards of proof.

[21] Gardiner, 'The purposes of the criminal punishment', (1958) 21 MLR 117; Andenaes, 'General prevention: illusion and reality', 43 Crim L & Criminology 176 (1952); id., 'The general preventive effects of punishment', 114 University of Pennsylvania L Rev 949 (1966).

be shown to have been innocent (or will have doubt cast on their conviction) and the less confidence will convictions inspire. Doubt about guilt is immediately translatable into doubt about the justice of punishment and is liable to eat away at the confidence in the criminal system and harm the very basis upon which it stands. Nesson suggests that guilty verdicts that signify merely a degree of probability will be perceived by the public as passing judgment not about what the facts were in reality but about the state of the proof and thus 'transform the substantive message [of the criminal law] from one of morality ("feel guilty if you do wrong") to one of crude risk-calculation ("estimate what you can do without getting caught")'.[22] One does not have to postulate a public perusing the law reports in order to accept that there is a connection between the popular support for, and confidence in, the system of criminal justice and the measures taken to protect the innocent.

A lowering of the standard of proof will also undermine the second major justification for punishment: the retributive theory. According to this theory the purpose of punishment is to render to the offender his just deserts.[23] Retribution, like the sophisticated version of deterrence, relies on the moral force of punishment. Yet the moral justification works only in respect of the guilty and can hardly justify the conviction of an innocent person.[24]

The lowering of the standard of proof might perhaps be justified in a different way. It might be said that when it has been shown that it is very probable (albeit subject to some doubt) that a person has committed an offence, a sufficient potential of danger has been identified to justify measures of protecting the community from committing further offences in the future. However, it is not difficult to imagine why no legal system has developed a two-tier strategy of punishment and

---

[22] 'The evidence or the event? On judicial proof and the acceptability of verdicts', 98 Harv L Rev 1357, 1362 (1985). For criticism of this position see Allen, 'Rationality, mythology, and the "acceptability of verdicts" thesis', 66 Boston University L Rev 541 (1986).

[23] See Finnis, *Natural Law and Natural Rights* (1980), 265.

[24] Pointing out that as a consequence of the lowering of the standard many more guilty persons have been convicted could hardly assuage moral outrage at the conviction of an innocent person.

prevention.[25] Where one compounds the uncertainty that the suspect committed the offence charged in the past by the uncertainty that he will commit future offences, hardly any justification is left even for preventive measures.[26]

The notion that the criminal standard of proof represents a degree of probability falling short of the highest degree seems to have acquired a foothold in our law. In another oft-quoted dictum, Denning LJ explained the requirement of proof beyond reasonable doubt as follows:

It need not reach certainty, but it must carry a high degree of probability. Proof beyond reasonable doubt does not mean proof beyond the shadow of doubt. The law would fail to protect the community if it admitted fanciful possibilities to deflect the course of justice. If the evidence is so strong against a man as to leave only a remote possibility in his favour which can be dismissed with the sentence 'of course it is possible, but not in the least probable', the case is proved beyond reasonable doubt, but nothing short of that will suffice.[27]

In one case the jury were told that a reasonable doubt was one which would make them hesitate in their own affairs.[28] In another case the Court of Appeal endorsed the explanation that a reasonable doubt must 'be the sort of doubt which may affect the mind of a person in the conduct of important affairs'.[29] But it is unsatisfactory to define 'reasonable doubt' by reference to risk-taking practices in other contexts when different people have different risk-taking habits and clearly there are no uniform standards to be found.

Despairing of definitions Lord Goddard CJ was driven to say that

When once a judge begins to use the words 'reasonable doubt' and to try to explain what is reasonable doubt and what is not, he is much

---

[25] Though there is an element of prevention in the treatment of the mentally ill; see, for example, the Mental Health Act 1959, ss. 72, 73. See also Ten, *Crime, Guilt, and Punishment* (1987), 134. For discussion of preventive detention on the grounds of dangerousness see Floud, 'Dangerousness and criminal justice', (1982) 22 British Journal of Criminology 213.

[26] This helps to explains why in a community beset by crime heavier punishments than customary are thought appropriate but not the lowering of the standard of proof.

[27] *Miller* v. *Minister of Pensions* [1947] 2 All ER 372, 373–4.

[28] *Hepworth and Fearnly* [1955] 2 All ER 918, 919.

[29] *Gray* (1974) 58 Cr App R 177.

more likely to confuse the jury then if he tells them in plain language: 'It is the duty of the prosecution to satisfy you of the man's guilt.'[30]

Telling the jury that they must be satisfied is not wholly instructive either and the Lord Chief Justice soon elaborated his view by writing that

If a jury is told that it is their duty to regard the evidence and see that it satisfies them so that they can feel sure when they return a verdict of Guilty, that is much better than using the expression 'reasonable doubt' and I hope in future that will be done.[31]

This suggestion has not been met with unqualified approval and Lawton LJ observed that 'if judges stopped trying to define that which is almost impossible to define there would be fewer appeals'.[32] Judges are now exhorted 'not to volunteer an explanation of this expression'[33] but to satisfy themselves with the 'time-honoured formula'[34] of proof beyond reasonable doubt.

It is far from obvious that an articulation of the criminal standard of proof is superfluous. It is difficult to believe that the expression 'beyond reasonable doubt' is self-explanatory in our pluralist society. It can hardly be assumed that all jurors will have the same instinctive comprehension of the meaning of this expression.[35] Moreover, it is not only for the sake of juries that we need authoritative elaboration of the criminal standard of proof but also in order to remove dangerous misconceptions from the judiciary itself. In *Khawaja* v. *Secretary of State for the Home Office*[36] the House of Lords was faced with the need to

---

[30] *Kritz* [1949] 2 All ER 406, 410.

[31] *Summers* [1952] 1 All ER 1059. Lord Goddard also disapproved of a direction telling the jury that they must be persuaded to 'a high degree of certainty'; *Onufrejczyk* [1955] 1 All ER 247. A direction that to the jury that they must 'feel sure' was approved in *Walters* v. *R.* [1969] 2 AC 26; *Ferguson* v. *R.* [1979] 1 All ER 877; *Bracewell* (1979) 68 Cr App R 44.

[32] *Yap Chuan Ching* (1976) 63 Cr App R 7, 11.

[33] *Archbold's Pleading, Evidence and Practice in Criminal Cases* 42nd edn. (1985), 492.

[34] As Dixon J referred to it in *Dewson* v. *R.* (1961) 106 CLR 192.

[35] If evidence is required for this proposition, it may be found in cases such as *Gibson* (1983) 77 Cr App R 151. It is therefore difficult to share Lord Diplock's optimism that although due to 'differences of temperament or experience some jurors will take more convincing than others', nevertheless 'there is safety in numbers. And shared responsibility and the opportunity for discussion after retiring serves to counteract individual idiosyncrasies'; *Walters* v. *R.* [1969] 2 AC 26.

[36] [1983] 1 All ER 765.

choose between the standard of proof beyond reasonable doubt and the standard of proof on the balance of probabilities in habeas corpus cases. Lord Scarman said: 'My Lords, I have come to the conclusion that the choice between the two standards is not one of any great moment. It is largely a matter of words.'[37]

According to Lord Scarman the graver the matter in hand the more cogent must be the proof.[38] However, if juries are given to understand that the standard of proof is a flexible one they will not necessarily conclude that graver offences require stiffer standards. A jury may reason, for example, that although the accused's guilt has not been proved beyond reasonable doubt it is justified to punish where the offence has been serious in order to spare the public the risk that the accused will repeat his hideous deed.[39]

This brings us to a practical reason against having a standard of proof which is less than the highest or suggesting that there is an intermediate standard between proof on the balance of probabilities and proof beyond reasonable doubt. So far we have been assuming that the choice of the standard of proof in criminal trials is wide open; that we could set the standard at 95 per cent or at 99 per cent or at some such level. In practice this is not the position because in ordinary reasoning we almost never have sufficient statistical data to enable us to make a precise calculation of the probability of guilt. Our inferences stem from broad generalizations with the result that our conclusions are only rough assessments, inexpressible in exact percentages. It follows that for the purpose of fact-finding in the courts we can only define the standard of proof in wide terms.

Apart from proof beyond reasonable doubt there is only one other widely used standard in the law: that of proof on the

---

[37] Ibid. 783. Lord Goddard CJ too was unable to understand the difference between the two standards: *Hepworth and Fearnly* [1955] 2 All ER 918. Other comments by Lord Scarman suggest that he regards the criminal standard as an inflexible technicality of the law of evidence, thereby relegating the golden thread of the criminal law to a mere nuisance; [1983] 1 All ER 794.

[38] See my comment on the subsequent development of the Scarman philosophy in [1985] All ER Rev 156.

[39] Cf. Kaplan, 'Decision theory and fact finding process', 20 Stan L Rev 1065, 1074 (1968). Cf. Kalven and Zeisel, *The American Jury*, ch. 14.

balance of probabilities, according to which propositions must be proved as being more likely than not to be true. Suppose we felt that proof beyond reasonable doubt was too high a standard for the proof of guilt and that we were also convinced that proof on the balance of probabilities was unacceptably low. How would we go about devising an intermediate standard? A percentage figure, such as 90 or 95 per cent, is out of the question. Consequently an intermediate standard will have to be at some rough point between the two common standards. Attempts to devise a midway standard have been made in the United States in relation to civil cases involving fraud, lost wills, and rectification of contracts. This intermediate standard has been variously described as proof 'by clear and convincing evidence', 'clear, cogent and convincing proof', 'clear, unequivocal, satisfactory and convincing proof', and the like.[40] In England too there have been suggestions of a similar intermediate standard requiring 'strong, irrefragable evidence', 'strong, distinct and satisfactory evidence', or that the issue be 'clearly and unequivocally proved'.[41]

Expressions of this kind suggest a wide range of proof. For the purpose of conviction and punishment such a range is clearly too wide because at its lower end it could well suggest a degree of probability which is only a little higher than a mere preponderance of probabilities. It is one thing to say that we need not insist on proof beyond reasonable doubt, it is quite another to authorize conviction when the proof is that the accused is a little more likely than not to have committed the offence, leaving a very wide margin for the possibility that the accused is in fact innocent. It is not suggested that the expressions just mentioned are inherently more vague than the term 'beyond reasonable doubt' but, rather, that the theory that these standards represent allows for a wider range of choice than the theory of proof beyond reasonable doubt which is outlined in the next section.

It would appear therefore that there is neither a justification

---

[40] *McCormick on Evidence*, 3rd edn. (1984), 959.

[41] *Cross on Evidence*, 5th edn. 118–19. However, recent judicial pronouncements do not favour an intermediate standard; *Re Cleaver, Cleaver* v. *Insley* [1981] 2 All ER 1018, 1024.

from principle for accepting a standard lower than the highest attainable standard for the proof of guilt nor is there a practical way of devising a lower standard which is not, at the same time, too lax for the purpose of administering justice. The standard of proof beyond reasonable doubt is the law's expression of its commitment to the protection of the innocent citizen from conviction. Unless properly elaborated to reflect this commitment, proof beyond reasonable doubt could degenerate as an instrument for the protection of the innocent and give way to *ad hoc* considerations of social advantage.

THE CRIMINAL STANDARD OF PROOF: A PROCEDURE FOR ELIMINATING DOUBT

The proper direction to a jury is one that stresses the function of the test and explains that in considering the evidence the jury have to follow a mental procedure of progressive elimination of explanations consistent with innocence. In a murder trial which turned on circumstantial evidence Alderson B instructed a jury that before finding the accused guilty they must be satisfied not only that the proved 'circumstances were consistent with his having committed the act, but they must also be satisfied that the facts were such as to be inconsistent with any other rational conclusion than that the prisoner was the guilty person'.[42] This spells out that which the requirement of proof beyond reasonable doubt merely hints at: that the jury may convict only when all explanations of the evidence that are consistent with innocence have been dismissed as having no force. On this view juries are not asked to gauge their beliefs or assess how near they are to certainty. Instead juries are asked to follow a process of reasoning.

Suppose that a person is charged with theft and the only evidence against him is the testimony of a witness who says that he saw the accused snatch a wallet. In order to infer the accused's guilt beyond reasonable doubt we have to dismiss all hypotheses that permit us to assume that the accused might be

---

[42] *Hodge* (1838) 2 Lew CC 227, 228. Cf. *Bracewell* (1979) 68 Cr App R 44, 49.

innocent. We have to exclude the possibility that the witness
made a mistake in identifying the accused, that he deliberately
lied, and all other similar explanations. The same procedure
has to be followed in relation to circumstantial evidence. Suppose that a witness testifies that immediately after a mugging
incident he saw the accused running away from the scene. A
policeman testifies that he found the stolen wallet in the accused's house. The defence accounts for the accused's conduct
by saying that he was in a hurry to catch a train and maintains
that the accused was unaware of the presence of the wallet in
his house. All reasonable doubt about the accused's guilt will
have been eliminated only when, in the words of Jonathan
Cohen, 'every let-out of this nature is eliminated, either by oral,
documentary, or other evidence, or by reference to facts that the
defence admits or the court is prepared to notice'.[43] But when
may we consider a let-out to have been eliminated or, put
differently, when is doubt unreasonable?

Since certainty is in principle unattainable, the highest
attainable standard is one that so approximates to certainty as
to make no difference.[44] In the absence of absolute certainty it is
always possible that a factual hypothesis will turn out to be
false. While allowing for the theoretical possibility that it may
turn out to be false, we may have no reason whatever to doubt
the truth of a hypothesis. The possibility that our hypothesis is
false cannot therefore figure in our practical considerations because the doubt about the truth of the hypothesis is imperceptible in this context. Thus in ordinary reasoning all doubt about
the occurrence of fact X is dispelled when the possibility that X
did not occur is imperceptible. The hypothesis that X did not
occur is imperceptible when we cannot assign to it any probative value. When this is the case, the hypothesis that X did not
occur can no longer figure in our calculations and no scope for
doubt is left regarding the occurrence of X. To revert to our
earlier example, if the prosecution proves that there were no
trains at the time at which, according to the defence, the accused was running to his train, and if it proves that the accused

[43] *The Probable and the Provable* (1977), 249.
[44] Jonathan Cohen describes proof that reaches the highest degree of strength as
'full proof'; ibid. 247.

had been using the wallet no doubt will be left concerning the accused's guilt. Of course it is possible that, contrary to the true state of affairs, the accused believed, when he was running, that there was going to be a train, and it is possible that he used the wallet without knowing that he was doing so. But, in the absence of some special circumstances, such as evidence of the accused's belief that there was a train and evidence of absent-mindedness, these are possibilities that carry no perceptible probability and to entertain doubt at this stage will be unreasonable.

By telling the jury that doubt is dispelled when, and only when, the probability of innocence is imperceptible the law reinforces the message that a person must be taken to be innocent unless his guilt is proved to the highest degree. The judge's instruction is not merely designed to set some theoretical level of proof but also to counteract the factors that militate against the presumption of innocence. Darling J was not painting a fanciful picture when he wrote:

The truth is that, although the law pays a prisoner the compliment of supposing him wrongly accused, it nevertheless knows that the probabilities are in favour of the prosecutor's accusation being well founded . . . No [civil] defendant is brought through a hole in the floor; he is not surrounded by a barrier, nor guarded by a keeper of thieves; he is not made to stand up alone while his actions are being judged; and his latest address is not presumably the jail of his county.[45]

To neutralize the adverse impressions caused by the very fact of being an accused it is imperative that juries should be encouraged to give the possibility of innocence full weight. It is neither possible nor desirable to hide from the jury that the final step in the assessment of evidence is subjective. Naturally, this element of subjectivity leaves room for flexibility but the jury must understand that they must be fully convinced, in their own minds, of the accused's guilt to the exclusion of all doubt. The clearer the jury's understanding of the moral, as well as legal, duty owed to the accused the less scope there will be for variation in the standard.

The notion of imperceptible doubt helps to solve a puzzle

---

[45] Scintillae Juris (1914), 28. See also D. J. McBarnet, *Conviction* (1981).

which originates in Jonathan Cohen's attack on the mathematical interpretation of proof.[46] A policeman enters a pub in which twenty persons are sitting. According to uncontroverted evidence nineteen of them set upon the policeman and beat him to death whereas the remaining person tried to save the policeman. Suppose now that one of the twenty is caught and prosecuted for the murder. Are these facts, without more, sufficient to justify a verdict of guilty?

When faced with this example lawyers will instinctively answer in the negative. The reason for this is not that one in twenty (or 5 per cent) is a sufficiently high probability of innocence to constitute reasonable doubt. If the objection were merely to the size of the doubt, the answer would change if the ratio of guilt to innocence changed sufficiently. Yet even if we altered the proportion and said that out of a hundred or even out of one thousand persons only one person tried to save the policeman while the rest participated in his murder, we would still meet the same instinctive aversion to conviction.

This intuitive aversion stems from our inability to judge whether the accused is one of the multitude that killed the policeman or is his lone defender. If we were to convict on this kind of evidence, we would be committing ourselves to convicting all of the one hundred persons present, including the one innocent person. What makes this kind of evidence fall short of proof beyond reasonable doubt is the fact that there is a definite possibility, which cannot be dismissed as unfounded, that the accused is innocent. Thus as long as the evidence in the case leaves room for a perceptible possibility of innocence, however small, we cannot convict.

A residual statistical probability of innocence, of the kind we have been discussing, may be removed by other evidence. In *Abadom*[47] the accused was charged with robbery. According to the evidence four masked men broke into an office, smashed an internal window, and robbed the occupants. The prosecution alleged that the accused was the robber who broke the window. It showed that fragments of glass were found in the accused's

---

[46] *The Probable and the Provable*, (1977), 75.
[47] [1983] 1 All ER 364.

shoes and in order to prove that they came from the window broken by the robbers, the prosecution called expert evidence which established two things. First, that the refractive index of the glass in the shoes and the glass from the broken window was the same. Second, that only 4 per cent of the glass used in the country had that particular index. In this way it was shown to be highly likely that the glass in the shoes came from the broken window.

By itself this evidence would have been insufficient because 4 per cent of the glass in use (representing 20,000 to 40,000 tons) leaves room for very considerable doubt; there would have been nothing in the evidence to exclude the possibility that the fragments became attached to the accused's shoes not because he broke the window in question but for some other reason. To exclude this hypothesis the prosecution showed that some of the fragments were found in the upper part of the shoes, some inside them, while others were embedded in the soles. This suggested that the fragments had fallen from above in the accused's presence and he then trod on them, which was consistent with the prosecution's version of the events. The accused was convicted. However, even when we add all this together reasonable doubt still remains because there is still a considerable chance that the glass in the accused's shoes did not originate from the robbery. It may be difficult to put a figure on the incidence of breakage in the glass of the relevant refractive index and of the likelihood of it appearing in a man's shoes in that position, but we cannot dismiss it as insignificant or imperceptible. It is, after all, not a rarity for glass to break near people and, when it does, it is likely to embed itself in their shoes in the position in which it was found in Abadom's shoes.

The reason why the jury was able to dismiss this last possibility was, presumably, determined by three further, though implicit, considerations: first, the low probability of the discovery of that type of glass in the shoes of a man picked at random; secondly, the absence at the trial of evidence of any other known instance of glass being found in a man's shoes in the same way; and, thirdly, the absence of evidence explaining the presence of the glass in the accused's shoes.

In dismissing the possibility of there being another person with the same glass in his shoes the jury reasoned that had there been an innocent explanation of the presence of the glass in the accused's shoes it would have been forthcoming.[48] This too helps distinguish between the pub example and the instant case. In the pub example we knew from the start that there was an innocent person who may have been mistaken for guilty.[49] Here we do not have any reason to think the same[50] and the lack of an explanation from the accused further diminishes the possibility of there being such reason because we assume that on the whole innocent people come forward with the available exculpatory explanation.[51]

It might be said that this reasoning is inconsistent with the presumption of innocence. However, the presumption of innocence is a normative rule and not a rule about factual inferences.[52] The rule requires that the accused be treated as innocent until proved guilty and that the jury approach its task without any assumption that the accused is other than innocent, it does not require that the jury ignore the common-sense implications of the evidence.[53]

The explanation of the standard of proof outlined here reflects the existing law. It spells out that which is implicit in the test of proof beyond reasonable doubt by drawing attention to the need to consider every explanation of the evidence that is consistent with innocence and by insisting that only explana-

---

[48] As the report is silent on the point it is assumed that no explanation was given.

[49] Conviction in such circumstances would give rise to the feeling that to hold the defendant liable would be tantamount to holding him liable by association and not because he committed the offence.

[50] Although the report is silent on the point, we may suppose that the jury had no reason to assume that the accused had been picked at random. Had it been thought that the police conducted random checks and prosecuted the first person to be found with that type of glass in his shoes, it would have been more difficult to dismiss the possibility of there being another person with the same evidence about him.

[51] For the bearing of the accused's right not to account for himself on the present point see Ch. 15.

[52] Tribe, 'Trial by mathematics', 84 Harv L Rev 1329, 1371 (1971).

[53] As will emerge in Ch. 12, it is the policy of the law to suppress information about the accused's criminal record. But such suppression is not absolute and information about the accused's criminal record is allowed to emerge if it is of sufficient probative significance. In the *Abadom* case there was only one way of preventing the jury from drawing the inevitable conclusion from the finding of the glass in the accused's shoes: by excluding the evidence of the finding altogether, which would have been unjustified.

tions which carry no probative significance whatever should be rejected. The absence of any probative significance in an explanation is not just a matter of subjective feeling but one for which a rational explanation can be given.[54]

At the same time we have to recognize the limitation of any definition or explanation. The court can only advise a jury about the correct test. It cannot make absolutely certain that the jury will follow its instruction. Having said that, a direction can be more or less consonant with principle and more or less conducive to jury understanding and co-operation. A direction of the sort given by Alderson B[55] which, essentially, requires the jury to exclude every rational explanation consistent with innocence or, in other words, every perceptible doubt, is best suited to convey the idea behind criminal standard of proof and to explain the process of achieving it.

BURDEN OF PROOF AND BURDEN OF ADDUCING EVIDENCE

There is a further consideration that affects the prosecution's burden. The accused has no duty to account for himself, he is entitled to insist that the prosecution prove its case against him without any cooperation on his part.[56] It follows that in addition to the probative burden the prosecution also bears the burden of adducing evidence in respect of the elements of the offence charged. Unless it discharges it by adducing evidence from which a reasonable jury could infer guilt beyond reasonable doubt, the prosecution will have failed to make a prima-facie case and the accused will be acquitted without being called upon to present his defence.[57] However, the rule that the

---

[54] In *Stafford and Luvaglio* [1968] 3 All ER 752 O'Connor J told a jury to 'remember that a reasonable doubt is one for which you could give reason if you were asked'. A doubt for which one cannot give a reason can hardly amount to reasonable doubt but this is not to say that all reasons are easily expressible. A sense of doubt engendered by the testimony of a prosecution witness cannot always be fully accounted for; see Jerome Frank, *Courts on Trial* (1949), 170. But to say 'I am unable fully to believe this witness' is sufficient explanation for doubt.

[55] See text corresponding to n. 42 above.

[56] This aspect will be fully discussed in Ch. 15.

[57] See discussion of this in Ch. 7.

prosecution bears the burden of adducing evidence on all elements relevant to the accused's liability is not absolute.

Generally speaking, this rule applies to conditions of liability which appear on the indictment but the indictment does not have to set out all the substantive law elements that are pertinent to liability. In a murder prosecution, for instance, the indictment will state that the accused killed the victim with malice aforethought and the prosecution will have to adduce evidence in respect of the killing and of the accused's mental state. However, the indictment does not have to state, for instance, that the accused did not act in self-defence or under provocation and hence the prosecution does not have, in the first instance, to adduce evidence on these points.[58]

If the prosecution had to call evidence in order to rebut every possible exculpatory argument which might conceivably be relied upon by the accused, much time and expense would be wasted in proving matters which were not in real dispute.[59] The purpose of imposing an evidential burden on the accused is to avoid such a wasteful course. To know which are the issues in relation to which the accused bears an evidential burden we have to consult precedent.[60]

It is often said that the accused bears the burden of adducing evidence in respect of such issues. This is not altogether accurate. Although the accused has to raise these issues he need not necessarily call evidence for this purpose. In order to raise an issue it is enough for the accused to point to evidence that the prosecution has presented from which a jury might infer the exculpatory facts in question, or at least be left in reasonable doubt about their occurrence.[61] Once the accused has raised an issue of this kind it is then the duty of the prosecution to prove

---

[58] These are referred to as defences and it is said that the indictment does not have to negative defences; see discussion in text corresponding to n. 67 below.

[59] See Adams, *Criminal Onus and Exculpations* (1968), para. 3, and Glanville Williams, 'The evidential burden: some common misapprehensions', 127 NLJ 156.

[60] In addition to self-defence and provocation an evidential burden has been imposed on the accused where, for instance, he pleads automatism or drunkenness: *Bratty* v. *A-G for Northern Ireland* [1961] 3 All ER 523; necessity: *Trim* [1943] VLR 109; mechanical defect on a charge of dangerous driving: *Spurge* [1961] 2 All ER 688.

[61] *Hamand* (1986) 82 Cr App R 65.

beyond reasonable doubt that the accused did not act in self-defence, under provocation, or the like.[62] If an accused fails to raise an issue by either pointing to such evidence in the prosecution's case or adducing it himself, the judge must instruct the jury not to consider the possibility of the defence in question.

EXCEPTIONS TO THE GENERAL PRINCIPLE

'Exemption, Exception, Proviso, Excuse of Qualification'

The common law recognizes only one exception to the principle that the prosecution must prove the accused's guilt beyond reasonable doubt. If the accused pleads insanity, he has to prove it on the balance of probabilities.[63] This exception is of little practical importance because, due to the grave consequences of the success of such a plea, accused persons hardly ever raise the defence of insanity.[64]

Of far greater importance are statutory exceptions. Some of these exceptions have been expressly created by Parliament. Others are the outcome of judicial interpretation of statutes that do not make an express provision to this effect. A considerable number of statutes have been held to impose a burden on the accused to disprove an element of the offence, or prove a defence, in order to escape liability.[65] Although it is contrary to principle to do so Parliament does have the power to lay down that a person shall be convicted of a criminal offence unless he proves his innocence. The courts are free, in their interpretive role, to refuse to countenance deviation from the general principle of proof unless a statute expressly requires otherwise, but they have not exercised this freedom. On the contrary, the courts have been prepared to infer a reversal of the general rule even where the words of the statute contained no hint of a

---

[62] *Lobell* [1957] 1 All ER 734; *Gill* [1963] 2 All ER 688.

[63] See *Woolmington* v. *DPP* [1935] AC 462, 481–2 and the quotation referred to in n. 3 above.

[64] It seems to be more common for the prosecution to raise the issue of insanity. When it is allowed to do so under the Criminal Procedure (Insanity) Act 1964, s. 6, the prosecution bears the burden of proving insanity beyond reasonable doubt; *Grant* [1960] Crim L Rev 424.

[65] For a list of such provisions see *Phipson on Evidence*, 13th edn., 51 ff.

legislative purpose to this effect. As a result, the courts bear a considerable responsibility for weakening the protection of the innocent.

Two separate questions arise in this connection. First, in what circumstances does the burden of proof lie on an accused? Second, when the accused bears the burden of proof, does he bear merely an evidential burden or does he also carry the burden of persuasion? Although these are distinct questions, the considerations pertinent to both are so closely related that they may be discussed together.

In 1974 the Court of Appeal enunciated a doctrine designed to relieve the courts of any strenuous interpretive effort in determining whether a statute imposed a burden of proof on the accused. It was held in *Edwards*[66] that the common law recognized, in addition to insanity and express statutory exceptions, a further exception comparable in effect to section 81 of the Magistrates' Courts Act 1952, now section 101 of the Magistrates' Courts Act 1980, which provides:

Where the defendant to an information or complaint relies for his defence on any exception, exemption, proviso, excuse or qualification, whether or not it accompanies the description of the offence or matter of complaint in the enactment creating the offence on which the complaint is founded, the burden of proving the exemption, exception, proviso, excuse or qualification shall be on him; and this notwithstanding that the information or complaint contains an allegation negativing the exception, exemption, proviso, excuse or qualification.

According to *Edwards*, this exception concerns statutory offences which prohibit the doing of an act save in specified circumstances or by persons of specified classes or with specific qualifications or with the licence or permission of specified authorities by using terms such as 'exemption', 'exception', 'proviso', and the like. In such cases it is for the accused to prove that he comes within the exemption, exception, proviso, and the like. As an exception to the *Woolmington* principle, the *Edwards* rule suffered from an inherent flaw: there is no distinction of substance between an element forming part of the definition of the offence and an element forming an exemption, exception, or proviso to such definition. Fundamentally, there is

---

[66] [1974] 2 All ER 1085.

no difference between a provision saying: 'It is forbidden for any person to drive without a driving licence', and a provision saying: 'It is forbidden for any person to drive, except where such person holds a driving licence'.

This is not to deny that we sometimes regard certain elements of liability as exemptions or exceptions for certain purposes. For instance, from the point of view of the substantive criminal law, self-defence offers an escape from liability (though in a different sense from the sense in which the existence of a driving licence is an answer to a charge of driving without such licence). It clearly does not follow from this that self-defence is to be regarded as a defence or exemption for all purposes. We may wish to regard it as a defence for the purpose of the rules of pleading and, as we have seen, to relieve the prosecution from the need to state in the indictment that the accused did not act in self-defence and to impose the evidential burden on the accused in respect of self-defence. Clearly, it does not follow from the fact that we regard self-defence as a defence for the purposes of pleading that it is to be considered as an exception or exemption for the purpose of allocating the burden of persuasion to the accused. The important thing to realize here is that the prosecution is not relieved from pleading that the accused did not act in self-defence because self-defence is a defence or an exception in some context. Rather it is the other way around: because we wish to relieve the prosecution of liability we call self-defence an exception in this respect. Thus, for the purpose of allocating the burden of persuasion, exceptions cannot be identified by reference to pre-existing defintions.[67]

In the absence of a distinction of substance the rule enunciated in *Edwards* could depend on a terminological distinction adopted for the purpose of allocating the burden of proof.

---

[67] Mr A. Stein has drawn to my attention a substantive law distinction between justifications and excuses for determining the occasions on which the probative burden may be imposed on the accused. A justification is a factor that makes the conduct in question unblameworthy, such as self-defence. An excuse is a factor that while not removing the blameworthiness of the conduct provides a reason for leniency, such as the factor of lactation in relation to infanticide under s. 1 of the Infanticide Act 1938. He argues that the probative burden should be allowed to rest on the accused in respect of excuses only. Cf. Glanville Williams, 'Offences and defences', (1982) 2 Legal Studies 233; and his more recent article: 'The logic of exceptions', (1988) 47 Cambridge L J 261, 295.

In this case the words 'exception', 'exemption', and 'proviso' would be shorthand expressions meaning 'the burden of proof shall rest on the accused', and the rule would fulfil a word-saving function. Like all terminological conventions, however, this rule has to be confirmed by the test of usage; it has to be shown to have been adopted by the legislature for the purpose of allocating the burden of proof. Such a rule has not been adopted.[68] Since the *Edwards* ruling was supported neither by a substantive distinction nor by terminological usage it could not provide a meaningful definition of an exception.

Although flawed, the decision in *Edwards* set a dangerous precedent. It gave licence to the courts to demand that an accused person prove his innocence merely because an element of the offence happened to be contained in a sub-clause which started with words such as 'provided', 'except', or the like. The risk to the innocent was intensified by the ruling in *Edwards* that the burden cast on the accused under the exception was a probative burden that had to be discharged on the balance of probabilities. Fortunately, the House of Lords has now decided in *Hunt* that the *Edwards* principle is at best a guide to statutory interpretation and that the presence in a statute of terms such as 'exceptions', 'provisos', 'exemptions' is not conclusive.[69] It follows that section 101 of the Magistrates' Courts Act 1980 is similarly inconclusive as a guide to exceptions. By taking this line the House of Lords has cut down the scope for departures, in both summary proceedings and trial on indictment, from the rule that the burden in criminal cases is on the prosecution. It no longer automatically follows that the burden rests on the accused merely because the statute creating the offence happens to use the word 'exemption', 'exception', 'proviso' or the like.[70]

---

[68] As I explained in 'The third exception to the *Woolmington* rule', (1976) 92 LQR 402.

[69] [1987] 1 All ER 1, 11 per Lord Griffiths.

[70] There have been suggestions that *Hunt* has preserved the distinction between the definition of an offence and an exception or a defence to it (or between essential and inessential elements) as a guide to interpretation; J. C. Smith, 'The presumption of innocence', (1987) 38 NILQ 223; D. J. Birch, 'Hunting the snark: the elusive statutory exception', [1988] Crim L Rev 221. However, for the reasons discussed in text corresponding to n. 67 above, such a distinction cannot provide a reason for the imposition of a burden on the accused but, on the contrary, is the outcome of such imposition which has to be decided as a matter of policy.

The House of Lords was urged by counsel to take matters further and rule that statutory exceptions are limited to provisions that expressly, and not just by implication, impose the burden of proof on the accused. However, there was no strong authority for this proposition.[71] Indeed, a number of previous decisions had already interpreted non-express statutory provisions as imposing a burden on the accused. As a result, counsel's submission was rejected.[72]

The House was also urged to place another limitation on deviation from the general rule by holding that whenever the burden rests on the accused he bears only an evidential burden. It was suggested that in such situations the accused need only adduce sufficient evidence from which a reasonable jury might be able to infer the relevant facts but that, at the end of the day, it is upon the prosecution to prove beyond reasonable doubt that the accused did not come within the exemption.[73] The House of Lords declined this suggestion and decided that when a statute imposes a burden on the accused it is a burden of proving the element in question on the balance of probabilities.

There are two objections to this ruling. First, to hold that despite reasonable doubt concerning the commission of the offence an accused may be convicted weakens the law's commit-

---

[71] Apart from the statement in *Woolmington*, there is a dictum in *Mancini* v. *DPP* [1941] 3 All ER 272, 279, where Viscount Simon LC referred to *Woolmington* and said: 'the rule is of general application in all charges under the criminal law. (The only exceptions arise, as explained in *Woolmington's* case, in the defence of insanity and in offences where the onus of proof is specially dealt with by statute.)'; and a dictum in *Jayasena* v. *R.* [1970] 1 All ER 219, 221. However, none of these dicta addresses itself directly to the point in issue.

[72] Moreover, had the House decided that the common law recognized no statutory exceptions other than express ones, the burden in trials on indictment would have been at variance with that dictated by s. 101 for summary proceeding. As Lord Griffiths explained, the 'law would have developed on absurd lines if in respect of the same offence the burden of proof... differed according to whether the case was heard by magistrates or on indictment'; [1987] 1 All ER 9. This might not have been wholly objectionable if the jurisdiction of magistrates and of the Crown Court was mutually exclusive. In fact many serious offences, of which possession of prohibited drugs is one, are triable both summarily and on indictment.

[73] This was also the recommendation of the Criminal Law Revision Committee, 11th Report, cmnd. 4991, paras. 137–42. And see Rupert Cross, 'The golden thread of the English criminal law', Rede Lecture (1976).

ment to the protection of the innocent from conviction.[74] Second, if the court must determine in relation to each individual provision whether the legislature intended to place any burden on the accused, why should not the court also try to ascertain whether the legislature's intention was to impose the lighter evidential burden rather than the heavier probative burden?

Had the House of Lords decided that, short of an unambiguous statutory provision to that effect, the probative burden always rests on the prosecution, the decision of whether to require an accused person to disprove guilt would have been placed fairly and squarely on Parliament. This would have obliged Parliament, if it wished to provide that a person may be convicted notwithstanding that one of the elements of the offence charged has not been proved, to state so clearly and publicly.[75] As it is, the courts seem only too willing to spell out that which Parliament would rather not declare with the result that we probably now have more provisions which impose a burden on the accused than the Government would have been prepared to brave in Parliament.

It has to be said, however, that the House of Lords was conscious of the responsibility that it had assumed and it articulated an important principle to limit the scope for deviation.[76] Lord Griffiths stated that

Parliament can never lightly be taken to have intended to impose an onerous duty on a defendant to prove his innocence in a criminal case, and a court should be very slow to draw such inference from the language of the statute.[77]

---

[74] Much of the criticism levelled against *Hunt* stems from the view that the House of Lords showed insufficient enthusiasm for the golden rule: Glanville Williams, 'The logic of exceptions', (1988) 47 Cambridge L J 261, where *Hunt* is said to undermine the principle of legality; J. C. Smith, 'The presumption of innocence', (1987) 38 NILQ 223; Healy, 'Proof and policy, no golden threads', [1987] Crim L Rev 355; Mirfield, 'The legacy of *Hunt*', [1988] Crim L Rev 19.

[75] See Mirfield, *op. cit.* [1988] Crim L Rev 19.

[76] For an illuminating account see Birch, 'Hunting the snark: the elusive statutory exception', [1988] Crim L Rev 221. For a different reading of the judgment see: Mirfield, 'The legacy of *Hunt*', [1988] Crim L Rev 19.

[77] [1987] 1 All ER 11. It seems that Lord Ackner too was alive to need for restraint when he described the placing of the burden on the accused as 'necessary implication' from the words of the statute; see Ibid. 15, 19.

Indeed, the House practised what it preached. Hunt was charged with unlawful possession of morphine contrary to section 5(2) of the Misuse of Drugs Act 1971. Under the Misuse of Drugs Regulations 1973 preparations containing 0.2 per cent or less morphine were exempted from the prohibition. At the trial the prosecution proved that the substance found in the accused's possession contained morphine but it did not prove its proportion in the preparation. The House of Lords held that since proving the proportion of morphine in the preparation was not an easy matter, the burden of persuasion rested on the prosecution to prove that it exceeded the legal limit.[78]

Notwithstanding that an important opportunity was missed to reassert the law's commitment to the principle of protecting the innocent, *Hunt* is a progressive decision. Broadly speaking, it establishes that a statutory interpretation imposing a burden on the accused is justified only where, first, the statute prohibits an act generally but goes on to allow it to be performed by specified classes of persons or by persons with special permits, and, secondly, it is easy for the accused to prove that he belongs to the designated class or that he possesses the requisite permit. From a practical point of view the imposition of such a burden on an accused is of limited consequence. Suppose that an activity is prohibited in the absence of a licence to engage in it. Suppose also that, contrary to *Hunt*, the law imposed the burden of proving the absence of a licence entirely on the prosecution rather than on the accused. To discharge its burden, it would usually be sufficient for the prosecution to call evidence that the accused had been asked to produce his licence and had declined to do so. If at his trial the accused still fails to come forward with a licence or any credible explanation for its absence, the prosecution will have gone a long way towards discharging its burden of persuasion on this point.[79] Consequently, to say, as *Hunt* does, that it is upon the accused, rather than the prosecution, to prove the licence does not make much practical difference. The accused has to do much the same as he would

---

[78] For discussion see Bennion, 'Statutory exceptions: a third knot in the golden thread?' [1988] Crim L Rev 31.

[79] *Westminster City Council* v. *Croyalgrange Ltd* [1986] 2 All ER 353, 358 per Lord Bridge.

have had to do had the burden rested on the prosecution: to produce his licence or a credible explanation for its absence.[80]

The 'Criminality' of an Offence and Exceptions to the General Rule

It is necessary to mention briefly two points that have a bearing on the subject of exceptions.

Section 101 of the Magistrates' Courts Act 1980 is not an altogether arbitrary derogation from the principle that no one should be convicted unless his guilt has been established beyond reasonable doubt. Many statutory provisions with which this rule of construction is concerned establish minor offences which carry relatively light fines or the withdrawal of a permission or some similar sanction. Conviction under such provisions carries little moral stigma; such provisions are therefore more in the nature of regulatory rules than criminal prohibitions. It is principally for this reason that Parliament and the courts find it acceptable to depart from the requirement that the prosecution prove beyond reasonable doubt each and every element of liability.

Unfortunately our law does not differentiate adequately between the imposition of a burden on an accused in relation to regulatory provisions and the imposition of a burden in respect of criminal offences. In order to facilitate proper differentiation we should consider the decriminalization of purely regulatory provisions. Minor offences which do not carry the kind of stigma and the type of punishment typically associated with criminality should be placed outside the criminal process altogether, where considerations of policy will then be allowed to dictate the imposition of a burden on the defendant.[81] The criminal process will be left to concern itself with truly criminal conduct, in relation to which deviation from the principle that guilt must be proved by the prosecution will not be allowed.

The claim of the innocent to be protected from criminal sanction has implications beyond the burden of proof. We have seen that in the United States the requirement of proof beyond

---

[80] Cf. *Oxford* v. *Lincoln*, *The Times* (1 Mar. 1982).
[81] The absence of stigma is already considered as a consideration in favour of disposing with the requirement of *mens rea: Denham* v. *Scott* (1983) 77 Cr App R 210.

reasonable doubt arises from the constitutional provision of due process. As a result it is unconstitutional to impose on accused persons a probative burden in respect of an element of a criminal offence. This prohibition has created the paradoxical situation that while the legislature cannot impose on the accused a probative burden in respect of a defence, it can deny him the defence altogether.[82] For instance, the legislature is free to lay down that sexual intercourse with a girl under sixteen constitutes an offence regardless of whether the accused was aware of the girl's age. But the due-process provision prevents the legislature from making mistake as to age a defence to the charge and, at the same time, requiring the accused to prove it. The legislature is thus left with the alternative of either making *mens rea* an element of the offence and requiring the prosecution to prove it, or else doing away with *mens rea* altogether.[83]

Since in England Parliament is not subject to a similar constitutional constraint a half-way solution is available. By adopting this option and introducing a defence coupled with a burden on the accused to prove it, the legislature has managed to give the impression of acting generously.[84] This appearance of generosity has distracted attention from the question of whether the legislature should create offences that do not contain an element of moral blame, such as intention or recklessness. Commenting on this problem Jeffries and Stephen wrote:

A constitutional policy to minimise the risk of convicting the 'innocent' must be grounded in a constitutional concern of what may constitute

---

[82] Underwood, 'The thumb on the scales of justice . . .', 86 Yale L J 1299 (1977); Ashford and Risinger, 'Presumptions, assumptions and due process in criminal cases . . .', 79 Yale L J 165 (1969); J. C. Jeffries and P. B. Stephan, 'Defences, presumptions and the burden of proof in criminal cases', 88 Yale L J 1325 (1979); Allen, 'Structuring jury decision-making in criminal cases . . .', 94 Harv L Rev 321, 1798 (1980), criticism by Nesson in 94 Harv L Rev 1574 (1980) and reply, ibid. 1795.

[83] This stark alternative has created considerable difficulty and much effort has been invested in ameliorating its effects; see materials referred to in the previous footnote. Cf. Wasik, 'Shifting the burden of strict liability', [1982] Crim L Rev 567; Birch, 'Hunting the snark: the elusive statutory exception', [1988] Crim L Rev 221.

[84] For instance, possession of dangerous drugs was at one time an offence irrespective of the accused's knowledge that the drug was a proscribed drug. This harshness was ameliorated by s. 5(2) of the Misuse of Drugs Act 1971 which provides that 'it shall be a defence for the accused to prove that he neither knew nor suspected nor had reason to suspect the existence' of the proscribed drug.

'guilt'. Otherwise 'guilt' would have to be proved with certainty, but the legislature could define 'guilt' as it pleased, and the grand ideal of individual liberty would be reduced to an empty promise.[85]

Proof of Previous Convictions

The Police and Criminal Evidence Act 1984, section 74(1) provides

> In any proceedings the fact that a person other than the accused has been convicted of an offence by or before any court ... shall be admissible in evidence for the purpose of proving, where to do so is relevant to any issue in those proceedings, that that person committed that offence...

As Professor J. C. Smith has pointed out, this constitutes a reversal of the criminal burden of proof and imposes on the accused the heavy task of proving that a conviction to which he was not a party was in fact wrong.[86] According to section 74(2), once a third party's conviction is proved at the accused's trial, the third party 'shall be taken to have committed that offence unless the contrary is proved' by the accused. As the accused will have been a stranger to the events leading to that conviction, he will in all probability be badly placed to discharge this burden.[87]

In *Robertson and Golder*[88] it was argued that section 74 should be confined to cases where the commission of an offence by a third party was an essential ingredient of the offence with which the accused is charged.[89] The Court of Appeal rejected this argument and held that the wording of the section does not

---

[85] 'Defences, presumptions and the burden of proof in the criminal law', 88 Yale L J 1325, 1347 (1979).

[86] Commentary on *O'Connor* (1987) 85 Cr App R 298, in [1987] Crim L Rev 260.

[87] Suppose that *A* is charged with receiving stolen goods. The prosecution adduces *B*'s conviction for the theft of the goods. *A* who, let us suppose, did not receive the goods from *B*, may lack all means of challenging the conviction of a total stranger to whose trial he was not privy. If *A* does find evidence that contradicts the findings in the third party's conviction and adduces it at his own trial, the jury must be directed that if at the end of the day they think that it is as likely as not that *B* was innocent, they must nevertheless convict the accused.

[88] [1987] 3 All ER 231. See also *Bennett* [1988] Crim L Rev 686.

[89] On a charge of receiving, for instance, it is essential to prove theft by another.

justify such a restriction. Moreover, the court decided that a
conviction resulting from a plea of guilty has the same effect as
one that follows from a trial. This is particularly unjust, first,
because a plea of guilty in the previous case may not amount to
a genuine admission of guilt; it is known that persons plead
guilty for all sorts of reasons, including plea-bargaining.[90]
Second, where a conviction has not resulted from a trial, the
accused in the subsequent case will not normally have access to
the evidence which led to a plea of guilty and will therefore be
poorly placed to prove that the earlier conviction was mistaken.

It might happen that the previous conviction of a third party
fully proves the accused's offence as was the position in
O'Connor.[91] The accused was charged alongside *B* with conspiracy. *B* pleaded guilty and his conviction was held admissible at
the accused's trial. Since *B*'s conviction of conspiracy with the
accused imposed on the accused the burden of proving the
contrary, the effect was that from the start the accused had to
prove that he was not guilty. Lord Denning MR described the
task involved in discharging this burden when he commented
on the comparable provision in section 11 of the Civil Evidence
Act 1968:

> How is a convicted man to prove 'the contrary'? That is, how is he to
> prove that he did not commit the offence? How is he to prove that he
> was innocent? Only, I suggest, by proving that the conviction was
> obtained by fraud or collusion, or by adducing fresh evidence. If the
> fresh evidence is inconclusive, he does not prove his innocence. It
> must be decisive, it must be conclusive, before he can be declared
> innocent.[92]

A burden as heavy as this can hardly be consistent with the
golden thread.

---

[90] See McBarnet, 'Pre-trial procedures and the construction of convictions', P.
Carlen (ed.), in *The Sociology of Law* (1976), 172, 179.

[91] [1987] Crim L Rev 260.

[92] *McIlkenny* v. *Chief Constable of West Midlands* [1980] 2 All ER 277, 237. However, while accepting that a person challenging a conviction must disprove the
commission of the offence, Lord Diplock has disapproved Lord Denning's restrictions: *Hunter* v. *Chief Constable of West Midlands* [1981] 3 All ER 727, 735–6. For the
means of challenging the effect of a previous conviction see my note in (1971) 87
LQR 21.

In *Robertson and Golder*[93] the Court of Appeal accepted that trial judges have a discretion, under section 78 of the Police and Criminal Evidence Act 1984, to exclude a conviction where its admission 'would have such an adverse effect on the fairness of the proceedings that the court ought not to admit it'. But Lord Lane CJ confined the discretion to cases where the effect of the previous conviction 'is likely to be so slight that it will be wiser not to adduce it'.[94] However, the most pressing need for exclusion is where a previous conviction is likely to have a considerable effect on the accused's case and not the other way around. Unfortunately, it is unlikely that the courts would use the discretion under section 78 for the purpose of wholesale exclusion of that which is made admissible by section 74. Consequently the matter requires legislative intervention and the correct solution is to provide that proof of a previous conviction imposes on the accused only a burden of adducing evidence and not a probative burden.[95]

---

[93] [1987] 3 All ER 231.   [94] Ibid. 237.
[95] Whether a similar modification of s. 74(3), which deals with the accused's own previous conviction, is required is a different matter.

10

Corroboration

INTRODUCTION

As a general rule, a conviction may rest upon the uncorroborated testimony of one witness. There are, however, many instances in which we may feel that the testimony of one witness is not sufficiently weighty to produce belief beyond reasonable doubt. The witness's mode of speaking may be unconvincing, the facts to which he deposes may be improbable, we may find his account confused or entertain suspicion because he has a motive for lying, we mistrust his intellectual faculties, and so on. In such situations we have grounds for doubting the witness's account and for seeking independent confirmation before accepting it. Legal rules of corroboration take the matter further and attempt to forestall unwarranted reliance on testimony by formal means.[1]

Basically, English law employs two methods of seeking confirmation for potentially unreliable witnesses.[2] The statutory method consists in providing that a conviction cannot be supported in the absence of the prescribed support. With on exception the existing statutory requirements are of marginal significance.[3] Of far greater importance are the common-law rules which require the trial judge to warn the jury that it is dangerous to rely on certain kinds of evidence, though the judge must also state that the jury is free to rely on the suspect evidence if satisfied that it is reliable.

On the face of it the common-law rules stipulate that which

---

[1] See excellent discussion of the corroboration rules in Dennis, 'Corroboration requirements reconsidered', [1984] Crim L Rev 316.
[2] Ibid.
[3] They are set out in the concluding section of the present Chapter.

common sense dictates: a search for confirmation. However, these rules have degenerated into a web of technicalities which often impede justice. They require the judge to give a direction which is frequently likely to confuse the jury and distract attention from the need to treat the suspect evidence with circumspection. Moreover, the rules are so complex that judges can easily overlook their consequences and place even sound convictions at the risk of being overturned on appeal.

CORROBORATION FOR ACCOMPLICES

If a witness admits to being an accomplice, or has been convicted of complicity, the judge has to administer a warning as laid down in the case of *Davies* v. *DPP*:

In a criminal trial where a person who is an accomplice gives evidence on behalf of the prosecution, it is the duty of the judge to warn the jury that, although they may convict upon his evidence, it is dangerous to do so unless it is corroborated. This rule, although a rule of practice, now has the force of a rule of law. Where the judge fails to warn the jury in accordance with this rule, the conviction will be quashed, even if, in fact, there be ample of the evidence of the accomplice, unless the appellate court can apply the proviso to s 4(1) of the Criminal Appeal Act 1907.[4]

The House of Lords singled out three classes of witnesses for the purpose of the warning rule: first, accessories to the crime who are charged as principals, accessories before or after the commission of felonies, and persons committing, procuring, aiding, or abetting misdemeanours;[5] secondly, a receiver of stolen goods who gives evidence against an accused charged with the theft of the goods; and, thirdly, parties to other crimes commit-

---

[4] [1954] 1 All ER 507, 513; s. 4(1) of the 1907 Act has been superseded by s. 2(1) of the Criminal Appeal Act 1968. It has been held that the wife of one accomplice can corroborate her husband's evidence against the accused as well as the testimony of another accomplice; *Willis* [1916] 1 KB 933; *Evans* [1964] 3 All ER 401.

[5] The distinction between felonies and misdemeanours was abolished by s. 1 of Criminal Law Act 1967. According to Prof. Cross a warning is still necessary in the case of witnesses who have impeded the apprehension of someone charged with an arrestable offence; *Cross on Evidence*, 5th edn. (1979), 197.

ted by the accused (when such crimes are admissible proof of the offence charged).[6]

If the witness denies complicity, a conditional warning is called for.[7] The jury must be advised first to consider whether the witness is an accomplice (in the special sense of the law of evidence), and, secondly, to look for corroboration (the meaning of which is also technical, as we shall shortly see) if they consider the witness to be an accomplice. At the same time the judge has to inform the jury that they have the option to convict even in the absence of corroboration, if the witness satisfies the jury. This hardly amounts to a prescription for clarity of thought.

A further complication concerns the burden of proving that the witness in question is an accomplice. Wigmore thought that the burden should lie on whoever alleges that the witness is an accomplice.[8] Professor Glanville Williams believes that as the Crown has to prove guilt beyond reasonable doubt it should also prove beyond reasonable doubt that its witness is free of the taint of complicity.[9] The latter view is preferable in principle. However, telling the jury that if they are not convinced beyond reasonable doubt that the witness is not an accomplice they should look for corroboration, but that they may convict even in the absence of corroboration, is calculated to perplex.

Such reasons as may conceivably be advanced for treating accomplices as a special case have been collected by Professor Heydon.[10] An accomplice may wish to exculpate himself or to purchase leniency by helping the prosecution obtain the conviction of other participants in the crime and in doing so may be tempted to exaggerate their culpability or even to blame innocent people. An accomplice may inculpate another out of spite

---

[6] A warning has to be given when an accomplice gives evidence for the prosecution but not when an accomplice is charged together with the accused and testifies against the latter in his own defence; *Bagley* [1980] Crim L Rev 572; *Loveridge* (1983) 76 Cr App R 125. Cf. *Beck* [1982] 1 All ER 807, 812. If the judge were to tell the jury that they must treat a co-accused with suspicion, he would thereby be urging the jury to form a prejudice against the co-accused who is entitled to be presumed innocent.

[7] *Davies* v. *DPP* [1954] 1 All ER 507, 514.

[8] *Wigmore on Evidence*, Chad Rev, vol. 7, 2060, p. 449.

[9] 'Corroboration: accomplices', [1962] Crim L Rev 588, 595.

[10] 'The Corroboration of Accomplices', [1973] Crim L Rev 264.

or revenge. As the accomplice is familiar with the facts of the crime he can easily concoct a false account of another's involvement which would be difficult to discredit. Lastly, accomplices should be treated with suspicion because they are confessed criminals. Even if these reasons are sufficient to support an obligatory corroboration warning,[11] they do not support the rule in its present form.[12]

The principal assumption behind the accomplice rule is that the testimony of a person who has a strong motive to blame another is suspect; but there are many other situations where other types of witnesses may have similar motives. *Davies* v. *DPP* itself provides an illustration. The accused was on trial for murder by stabbing during an affray and another participant in the affray testified for the prosecution. The House decided that no warning was necessary because there was no evidence that the witness contemplated an attack with a knife. Clearly, the witness had the strongest motive to deny such contemplation in order to avoid being himself liable for murder. To take another illustration, where an offence could have been committed by only one of two persons and the accused claims that the perpetrator was in fact the prosecution's witness, the danger of perjury is every bit as great as it would be if the witness were an accomplice.[13] To exclude the obligatory warning from these situations seems devoid of good sense.[14] The accomplice rule is not only too narrow; in some respects it is also too wide. There is little justification for insisting on a warning when a witness is an accessory after the fact (i.e., a

[11] Their adequacy is discussed below.

[12] See Glanville Williams, 'Corroboration: accomplices', [1962] Crim L Rev 588; Heydon, 'The corroboration of accomplices', [1973] Crim L Rev 264; Criminal Law Revision Committee, 11th Report, cmnd. 4991, para. 183. Cf. Harnon, 'The need for corroboration of accomplice testimony and the need for "something additional" to the testimony of someone involved', 6 Israel L Rev 81 (1976).

[13] Cf. *Whitaker* (1976) 63 Cr App R 193.

[14] *Sneddon* v. *Stevenson* [1967] 2 All ER 1277, 1280, decided that 'though a police officer acting as a spy may be said in a general sense to be an accomplice in the offence, yet if he is merely partaking in the offence for the purpose of getting evidence he is not an accomplice who requires corroboration'. However, such a person may be motivated by a desire to curry favour with his superiors, or may have financial interest, so that his evidence could well be tainted with all the defects of an accomplice.

person who helped the escape of the offender) because the witness's natural motive is not to inculpate but rather to exculpate the accused and thereby exculpate himself.

The shortcomings of relying on the definition of accomplice to capture all or even most situations in which witnesses have strong motives to implicate an innocent person are hardly surprising when one considers that the notion of 'accomplice' has little to do with the risk of unreliability. The notion has evolved in order to allocate criminal liability and not for the purpose of identifying mendacity.[15]

In fact the substantive law definition is not accepted as a final arbiter as to whether an accomplice warning is necessary. Professor Heydon has gathered together a good deal of case law devoted to questions such as: Should a prostitute be considered the accomplice of a person charged with living off her immoral earnings? When the witness cannot commit the offence as a principal, can he be an accomplice? Or, should a witness who had offered a bribe be regarded as the accomplice of the acceptor of the bribe? Should a girl under sixteen be regarded as the accomplice of a man charged with having had intercourse with her?[16] Since the substantive law characterization does not address the question of reliability, the preoccupation with the subtleties of the law of accomplices merely furnishes a distraction. The real issue is whether special measures need be taken to counteract the risks of unreliability in a particular class of witnesses.[17]

Even if the warning-rule did encompass all suspect categories, we would still have to consider the desirability of insisting on a warning where there is no reason to suppose that the complicity of a particular witness in the crime makes him unreliable. For example, a particular accomplice may have no

---

[15] This was implicitly recognized by the House of Lords in *Davies* when it extended the definition of accomplice to include two classes that are not accomplices for the purpose of liability: that of the receiver who testifies against the thief and of participants in crimes other than the crime charged.

[16] Heydon, [1973] Crim L Rev 264, 270–6.

[17] Wigmore wrote: 'From the point of view of safeguarding the accused against false tales of an associate, and of estimating the credit to be given to such testimony, all the foregoing rulings are a sheer waste of time, as generalities. It is difficult enough to determine who is lying; but we do not find it out by any of these technical niceties.' *Wigmore on Evidence*, Chad Rev, vol. 7, s. 2060, p. 451.

reason for wishing to curry favour with the authorities, no scope for diminishing his own role, no motive for revenge, and so on. In defence of the present rule it might be said that neither the narrow scope of the category of 'accomplice' nor the indiscriminate warning made about witnesses in this category matter very much. Where the rule does not require a warning, a warning may still be given as a matter of discretion. Conversely, where the rule forces a warning in the absence of a real risk, no mischief can be brought about by being careful.

This argument would be persuasive if the obligatory warning resulted in encouraging extra care without, at the same time, producing an increase in acquittals on technical and insubstantial grounds. However, this is not the case.

CORROBORATION OF VICTIMS OF SEXUAL OFFENCES[18]

The Traditional Fears

The second category of witnesses requiring corroboration consists of victims of sexual offences.[19] In trials for sexual offences, committed against men or women, the judge must warn the jury that it is unsafe to convict on the uncorroborated testimony of the complainant; but he has to point out that it is open to the jury to convict in the absence of corroboration, if satisfied that the testimony is true. This rule is based on two assumptions: first, that there is a substantial risk that the complainant may have made a false accusation due to neurotic fantasy, to spite, or to shame at having consented to the accused's advances;[20] secondly, that it is difficult for a jury to assess the seriousness of this risk because the complainant may appear sincere and plausible and because the circumstances of the alleged offence, especially when children are involved, may create strong prejudice against the accused.

If the risk of undetected mendacity is real, the present rule achieves next to nothing in reducing it. The judge informs the

---

[18] See Temkin, *Rape and the Legal Process* (1987).
[19] See Dennis, 'Corroboration requirements reconsidered', [1984] Crim L Rev 316.
[20] See Criminal Law Revision Committee, 11th Report, cmnd. 4991, para. 186.

jury that they may convict in the absence of corroboration if
they feel confident that the complainant is telling the truth.
Juries that remain unaware of the complainant's mendacity,
which *ex hypothesi* is often undetectable, will give credence to the
testimony and convict the accused. Considerations of this kind
led Wigmore to advocate the subjection of complainants to
psychological tests.[21] Professor Glanville Williams has pointed
out that the effectiveness of such tests is doubtful and that,
furthermore, the subjection of complainants to these tests involves unacceptable indignity.[22]

Professor Glanville Williams advocated the imposition of a
strict corroboration requirement so that a person may not be
convicted in the absence of corroboration.[23] There are two
objections to the imposition of such a rule. First, sexual offences
are difficult enough to prove as it is. There are rarely independent witnesses and, unless violence is involved, little physical
evidence is available. Secondly, and more importantly, before
we take an extreme measure of this kind, we must consider how
serious is the risk of false accusations. Changes in sexual morality during the last few decades have removed much of the
odium from admissions of sexual behaviour with the result that,
by and large, many of the anxieties associated with testimonial
unreliability no longer obtain. Although some risk of false
accusation will always be present[24] there is no reason to suppose
it is widespread, as Temkin shows in her recent book *Rape and
the Legal Process*.[25] However, it is possible that the rule reflected
prejudice about rape victims, rather than a well-founded

---

[21] *Wigmore on Evidence*, Chad Rev, vol. 3A, s. 924a.

[22] 'Corroboration: sexual cases', [1962] Crim L Rev 662, 663. Public opinion is
likely to be opposed also to the use of lie-detectors, which Prof. Williams suggested
as an alternative. Sympathy for rape victims has received legislative expression in
the Sexual Offences (Amendment) Act 1976, which imposes constraints on the
freedom of cross-examining the complainant on her sexual experiences, other than
those involving the accused.

[23] Ibid.

[24] See the curious case of *People* v. *Dotson* 424 NE 2d 1319 and comment: S. Cobb,
'Gary Dotson as a victim: the legal response to recanting testimony', 35 Emory L J
969 (1986); E. Black, 'Why Judge Samuels sent Gary Dotson back to prison', 71
ABAJ 56 (1985).

[25] Ch. 3.

assumption about their probative inferiority.[26] If this is the case, the continued existence of the present rule is not only unnecessary but also morally objectionable.[27]

It may perhaps be said that while the corroboration warning is based on an excess of caution, it is still preferable to err in favour of the accused. This reasoning would be supportable if, first, the rule reflected some well-founded doubt about the reliability of complainants, and, secondly, it did not create confusion and lead to unnecessary acquittals on technical grounds. The first assumption is doubtful and the second is false, as we shall shortly see. The Court of Appeal has now recognized the limitations of an indiscriminate warning strategy in rape cases, accepting that if the trial judge

is required to apply rigid rules, there will inevitably be occasions when the direction will be inappropriate to the facts. Juries are quick to spot such anomalies, and will understandably view the anomaly, and often (as a result) the rest of the directions, with suspicion, thus undermining the judge's purpose.[28]

It was decided: (*a*) that there was no need for a warning in respect of identification where there was no real dispute that the accused was at the material time with the complainant; (*b*) that there was no need to advise the jury to seek corroboration that the complainant had been raped where there was no real dispute that she was raped by somebody; (*c*) that where identification was in issue and there was no reason to think that the sexual nature of the offence distorted the complainant's identification, there was no need for formal warning. This reduces very

---

[26] Wigmore wrote that '[t]he unchaste (let us call it) mentality finds incidental but direct expression in the narration of imaginary sex-incidents of which the narrator is the heroine or the victim. On the surface the narration is straightforward and convincing. The real victim, however, too often in such cases is the innocent man; for the respect and sympathy naturally felt by any tribunal for a wronged female helps to give easy credit to such a plausible tale.' *Wigmore on Evidence*, Chad Rev, vol. 3A, s. 924*a*, p. 736. A similar sentiment was expressed, though in more moderate language, by Salmon LJ in *Henry and Manning* (1968) 53 Cr App R 150, 153; see also *Mandley* [1988] Crim L Rev 688.

[27] See Temkin, *Rape and the Legal Process*; Estrich, 'Rape', 95 Yale L J 1087 (1986).

[28] *Chance* [1988] 3 All ER 225, 231. See also *Atkinson* (1988) 86 Cr App R 359, Cf *Mandley* [1988] Crim L Rev 688.

considerably the occasions when a judge has to treat the jury to technical explanations about corroboration. However, the warning requirement still obtains in situations where the issue is whether a rape has been committed and to this extent the law remains unsatisfactory.

The Victim's Complaint: A Perplexing Spectacle

We saw in Chapter 7 that the previous consistent statement of a witness is generally inadmissible on the grounds of insufficient probative weight. However, it can hardly be maintained that a prompt complaint made by the victim of a sexual assault is generally of no probative weight. Hence such complaints are admissible,[29] but trial judges have performed peculiar logical feats when explaining to juries the evidential significance of a complaint.

The hearsay rule dictates an instruction that the contents of a complaint must not be taken as evidence of the facts asserted therein.[30] What is then, we may ask, the purpose of proving a complaint? The law's answer is that a complaint may be used as 'evidence of the consistency of the conduct of the prosecutrix with the story told by her in the witness box, and as being inconsistent with her consent to that of which she complains'.[31] It follows that since the complainant denies consent it cannot be said that the complaint is not admitted as evidence of facts stated therein.

Furthermore, due to the rule (to be discussed later) that corroboration must come from an independent source, a complaint cannot amount in law to corroboration of the complainant's testimony.[32] Thus the judge has to tell the jury that although they are entitled to regard the complaint as streng-

---

[29] *Osborne* [1905] 1 KB 551. This applies to both female and male victims; *Camelleri* [1922] 2 KB 122.

[30] *Lillyman* [1896] 2 QB 167, 170. At times a complaint will be admissible under the *res gestae* doctrine; see Ch. 11.

[31] Ibid. According to Prof. Cross a complaint may be used to rebut the 'factual presumption of consent which might otherwise arise'. *Cross on Evidence*, 5th edn. (1979), 242.

[32] *Lovell* (1923) 17 Cr App R 163; *Evans* (1924) 18 Cr App R 123; *Askew* [1981] Crim L Rev 398.

thening the complainant's testimony they may not regard it as corroboration of that testimony. This is hardly illuminating.[33] *Redpath*[34] is a case in point. The accused was charged with indecent assault on a young girl. The girl's mother testified that the girl returned home very distressed and immediately complained. The court held:

If the girl goes in a distressed condition to her mother and makes a complaint, while the mother's evidence as to the girl's distressed condition may in law be capable of amounting to corroboration, quite clearly the jury should be told that they should attach little, if any, weight to that evidence because it is all part and parcel of the complaint. The girl making the complaint might well put on an act and simulate distress.[35]

This suggests that the judge must inform the jury that it is dangerous to rely on the girl's evidence in the absence of corroboration, that her distressed condition when she complained to her mother might in law amount to corroboration but that it is dangerous to rely on this corroboration because it is connected with the complaint; that the complaint is relevant to the girl's credibility but it is neither corroboration of her story nor proof of the facts stated therein. Finally, the judge has to inform the jury of the possibility of conviction even in the absence of corroboration, thus almost inviting them to ignore his previous directions. It would be better to abandon these tortuous directions, explain where the dangers lie, and impress the jury with the need to adopt a cautious and sceptical attitude. The judge may then draw attention to the factors that may enhance or undermine the probative force of a complaint.

It is important to realize that rules of the kind just discussed arise not so much from mistaken decisions as from a desire to turn reasonable rulings on points of fact into general rules of law. A case sometimes cited as authority for the rule under

---

[33] If the witness's credibility is enhanced by an immediate complaint because, in the circumstances, there was not time to concoct a false accusation, our doubts about the victim's veracity will have been removed; Glanville Williams, 'Corroboration: sexual cases', [1962] Crim L Rev 662, 664. This is now the position in Canada: *Vetrovec* v. *R.* (1982) 136 DLR (3d) 89, 102–3.

[34] (1962) 46 Cr App R 319.

[35] Ibid. 321–2. See also *Wilson* (1973) 58 Cr App R 304.

consideration is *Whitehead*,[36] where the accused was charged with unlawful intercourse with a girl under sixteen. The girl mentioned the incident for the first time weeks later, when she told her mother that she was pregnant. Lord Hewart CJ rejected the argument that her conversation with the mother could amount to corroboration saying: 'the girl cannot corroborate herself, otherwise it is only necessary for her to repeat her story some twenty-five times in order to get twenty-five corroborations of it.'[37] This decision was sensible because the lapse of time and the girl's need to account for her pregnancy robbed her complaint of confirmatory value. But the same may not obtain in other cases and no general rule should have been derived from Lord Hewart's dictum.[38]

SWORN AND UNSWORN EVIDENCE OF CHILDREN

The next requirement of corroboration concerns children. A number of factors are singled out as making children's evidence less credible than that of adults. Children's powers of observation and recollection, it is assumed (though by no means justly), are less reliable than those of adults and their tendency to imagine or distort observations is greater, as is their susceptibility to suggestion and manipulation. Perhaps a more significant consideration arises from the fact that adults have limited experience in assessing the veracity and reliability of children.[39] Moreover, the usual testing tool, cross-examination, is a blunt instrument when applied to children. Consideration for the child's welfare, especially when the child has been the victim of, or the witness to, a gruesome crime, often demands such restraint on the part of the cross-examiner as to reduce the

---

[36] [1929] 1 KB 99.
[37] Ibid. 102.
[38] For example, in *Christie* [1914] AC 545, a young boy went up to the accused shortly after the alleged incident, in the presence of his mother and a policeman, touched the accused saying, 'That is the man', and proceeded to describe the assault. To dismiss the significance of this by saying that the boy could not be his own corroborator is to turn one's back on weighty and telling evidence.
[39] We mostly encounter children within family circles where our observations may well be distorted by the relationship.

effectiveness of the examination.[40] However, the present law does not seem to meet these difficulties satisfactorily.

Two separate rules used to govern the subject. One was to be found in section 38 of the Children and Young Persons Act 1933, which empowers the court to accept the unsworn testimony of a child of tender years who does not understand the nature of the oath if 'he is possessed of sufficient intelligence to justify the reception of the evidence, and understands the duty of speaking the truth'. The section went on to provide 'that where evidence by virtue of this section is given on behalf of the prosecution the accused shall not be liable to be convicted of the offence unless that evidence is corroborated by some other material evidence in support thereof implicating him'. Side by side with this section there is a common-law rule whereby the trial judge must warn the jury that it is dangerous to act on the uncorroborated evidence of young children, unless the jury is convinced that the child in question is reliable. This rule obtains where children give sworn evidence.[41] However, the corroboration warning and its attendant rules, especially the legal definition of corroboration, divert attention from the real risks of unreliability. The Criminal Justice Act 1988 greatly simplifies the position regarding children. Section 34(1) abolishes the corroboration requirement of section 38 of the Children and Young Persons Act 1933. Section 34(2) removes the

---

[40] Concern for child welfare prompted the legislature to establish special procedures for taking children's evidence out of court: ss. 42, 43 of the Children and Young Persons Act 1933. It has also given rise to the recent debate about videotaping of children's evidence rather than examining them at the trial; Glanville Williams, 'Child witnesses', in P. Smith (ed.), *Criminal Law: Essays in Honour of J. C. Smith* (1987); Spencer, 'Child witnesses, video-technology and the law of evidence', [1987] Crim L Rev 76; id., 'Child witnesses, corroboration and expert evidence' [1987] Crim L Rev 239; Harnon, 'Examination of children in sexual offences: the Israeli law and practice', [1988] Crim L Rev 263. Section 32 of the Criminal Justice Act 1988 will enable children to testify through a live television link.

[41] A child may testify, whether or not under oath, only if the child understands the duty of speaking the truth. The differentiation between children on the basis of whether they understand the oath is without justification. The Criminal Law Revision Committee recommended that children under fourteen should never give evidence on oath, while children over that age should always be sworn, and that corroboration should be mandatory only when a child gives evidence as the victim of a sexual offence; for the rest it recommended the abolition of both the mandatory corroboration rule and the warning requirement. 11th Report, cmnd. 4991, para. 208.

need for a formal warning about child evidence and section 34(3) lays down that unsworn evidence admitted by virtue of section 38 of the 1933 Act may corroborate evidence (sworn or unsworn) given by any other person.

THE LEGAL MEANING OF 'CORROBORATION'

The most perplexing legal technicalities have grown around the definition of 'corroboration'. This definition places a limit on that which the trial judge may identify as corroboration on the occasions that a corroboration warning has to be administered or whenever corroboration is required as a matter of statute.

The courts have always recognized that corroboration need not confirm the witness's account in every single respect,[42] but before 1916 two theories concerning the requirement of confirmation competed for recognition.[43] According to the first, corroboration consisted in independent evidence that verified any part of the witness's evidence. A second view insisted on confirmatory evidence which went further and implicated the accused in the commission of the crime. The second view won the day in *Baskerville*:

evidence in corroboration must be independent testimony which affects the accused by connecting or tending to connect him with the crime, . . . it must be evidence which implicates him, that is, which confirms in some material particulars not only the evidence that the crime has been committed, but also that the prisoner committed it.[44]

The first view was rejected because it was felt that confirmation that an offence has been committed does not help to overcome the principal doubt of whether the witness has implicated an innocent person.[45] It is true that evidence which merely shows that the offence has been committed would not necessarily make it safe to rely on an accomplice's testimony that the accused was its perpetrator. But there is no reason to adopt this

---

[42] If confirmation were required on every aspect, the witness's testimony would often become redundant.

[43] *Wigmore on Evidence*, Chad Rev, vol. 7, s. 2059.

[44] [1916] 2 KB 658, 667, per Lord Reading CJ.

[45] *Farler* (1837) 8 Car and P 106; *Birkett* (1839) 8 Car and P 732; *Tumahole Bereng* v. *R.* [1949] AC 253, 265.

precaution in respect of witnesses, such as children, who cannot be supposed to have 'inside information' which they may use to implicate an innocent person. More fundamentally, it by no means follows that *only* independent evidence which implicates the accused could have sufficient confirmatory value. The fallacy involved here was exposed by Joy CB almost a century and a half ago[46] and reiterated by Wigmore:

> We are assuming that the accomplice is not to be trusted in the case in hand; his credit is an entire thing, not a separate one; therefore, whatever restores our trust in him personally restores it as a whole; if we find that he is desiring and intending to tell the true story, we shall believe one part of his story as well as another; whenever, then, by any means, that trust is restored, our object is accomplished, and it cannot matter whether the efficient circumstance related to the accused's identity or any other matter. The important thing is, not *how* our trust is restored, but whether it *is* restored at all.[47]

It is not altogether clear to what extent the law still insists that only evidence which is independent of the suspect witness may constitute corroboration of his testimony. On the one hand it has been held that the reaction of an accomplice on first hearing complaints about the crime could amount to corroboration,[48] but on the other hand it has been decided that to count as corroboration it is not enough that a piece of evidence supports the witness's own credibility, however convincingly and independently.[49]

Another complication concerns mutual corroboration. Until the decision in *DPP* v. *Hester*[50] there prevailed a rule that the testimony of a witness who required corroboration could not itself supply corroboration.[51] Although the House of Lords dismissed the rule as illogical, common sense was only partially vindicated by that decision.[52]

---

[46] Chief Baron Joy, *Evidence of Accomplices* (1844).
[47] *Wigmore on Evidence*, Chad Rev, vol. 7, s. 2059, p. 424.
[48] *Beck* [1982] 1 All ER 807, 816.
[49] *Donat* (1986) 82 Cr App R 173, 178. See also *Hills* (1988) 86 Cr App R 26.
[50] [1972] 3 All ER 1056.   [51] *Manser* (1937) 25 Cr App R 18.
[52] In *Hester* the House of Lords decided that, on the true interpretation of s. 38 of the Children and Young Persons Act 1933, an unsworn child could not corroborate a sworn child and vice versa. This has now been overruled by s. 34 of the Criminal Justice Act 1988. See also Tapper, 'Corroboration from an independent source', (1973) 36 MLR 541.

The discredited notion that one who requires corroboration cannot offer corroboration lingers on in another respect. As early as 1832 it was decided that accomplices cannot, as a matter of law, corroborate each other.[53] Shortly after the decision in *Hester* the House of Lords had occasion to consider this point in *DPP* v. *Kilbourne*[54] where the accused was charged with a number of offences of buggery and indecent assault on seven young boys, all of whom gave sworn evidence. The boys fell into two groups; the offences in respect of one group took place in 1970 and in respect of the other in 1971. A corroboration warning was required on three independent grounds: the youth of the boys, the sexual nature of the offence, and because there was a possibility that the boys were accomplices.[55] The trial judge directed the jury that the testimony of the boys in the 1970 group could corroborate that of the boys in the 1971 group and vice versa but that the testimony of boys within one group could not amount in law to corroboration of other boys in the same group, because of the risk that within each group the boys, who knew each other, could have concocted the story or been influenced by one another. The House of Lords upheld the judge's direction. Lord Hailsham said:

The word 'corroboration' by itself means no more than evidence tending to confirm other evidence. In my opinion, evidence which is (a) admissible and (b) relevant to the evidence requiring corroboration, and, if believed, confirming it in the required particulars, is capable of being corroboration of that evidence and, when believed, is in fact such corroboration.[56]

Unfortunately it remains unclear whether accomplices to the same crime may corroborate each other because Lord Hailsham went on to hold that the

reason why accomplice evidence requires corroboration is the danger of a concocted story designed to throw the blame on the accused. The danger is not less, but may be greater, in the case of fellow accom-

---

[53] *Noakes* (1832) 5 Car and P 326, 328. See also *Gay* (1909) 2 Cr App R 327; *Baskerville* [1916] 2 KB 658, 664.
[54] [1973] 1 All ER 440.
[55] They fell into the third *Davies* category, i.e. accomplices to offences other than those charged.
[56] [1973] 1 All ER 453.

plices. Their joint evidence is not 'independent' . . . and a jury must be warned not to treat it as corroboration.[57]

To hold that accomplices to the same offence may never corroborate each other does not make sense. Suppose that *A* sets out to rob a bank. He hires *X* to transport breaking-in equipment and leave the scene. He hires *Y* to come later and drive him away with the booty. To protect himself *A* makes sure that *X* and *Y* are unknown to each other. Telling a jury that *X* and *Y* cannot corroborate each other's story is to commit the solecism which both *Hester* and *Kilbourne* meant to put to rest.[58]

It is possible that the only general principle that should be derived from *Kilbourne* is that, as both Lords Reid and Hailsham emphasized, there is nothing technical in the idea of corroboration.[59]

The exercise of laying down as a matter of binding precedent a definition of corroboration has often produced poor results. In one case Lord Morris of Borth-y-Gest said:

The purpose of corroboration is not to give validity or credence to evidence which is deficient or suspect or incredible but only to confirm

---

[57] Ibid. Though he qualified this by saying that the same does not apply to accomplices in the third class, unless there is a danger that they have conspired to commit perjury. Lords Morris and Simon agreed with Lord Hailsham's view. Lord Reid observed that in most cases concerning accomplices they have been accomplices to the same offence so that there was a danger of collaboration to concoct a story, but he did not express a view on whether there should be a 'universal rule' that accomplices could not corroborate each other; [1973] 1 All ER 456.

[58] In *Turner* [1980] Crim L Rev 305, the Court of Appeal held that the fact that accomplices could not have influenced each other may be taken into account in determining their credibility, but they remained incapable of corroborating one another.

[59] To go further and infer a rule forbidding mutual corroboration by accomplices would be to ignore Wigmore's wise caution that 'the requirement of corroboration leads to many rulings as to sufficiency, based wholly upon the evidence in each case; from these no additional development of principle can profitably be gathered. As recorded precedents of supreme courts, they are mere useless chaff, ground out by the vain labor of able minds mistaking the true material for their energies.' *Wigmore on Evidence*, Chad Rev, vol. 7, s. 2059, pp. 439–40. However, English courts find it difficult to shake off the inclination condemned by Wigmore. In *Lucas* [1981] 2 All ER 1008, the Court of Appeal decided that the accused's lies in court may constitute corroboration of an accomplice's testimony, provided that they were proved to be lies other than by the accomplice's testimony. This is, of course, perfectly sensible. But the court felt compelled to hedge its decision with so many qualifications future courts could well be misled into thinking that the case is not only a record of common sense but also generally prescriptive.

and support that which as evidence is sufficient and satisfactory and credible; and corroborative evidence will only fill its role if it itself is completely credible.[60]

This dictum was interpreted as meaning that 'the jury should be directed first to consider whether the complainant's evidence is . . . credible, if it is not no amount of corroboration will cure it, unless the tendered corroboration is sufficient by itself to establish guilt.'[61] It took authority at high level to do away with this rule. In *A-G of Hong Kong* v. *Wong Muk-ping*[62] Lord Bridge explained that a witness's credibility can be meaningfully assessed only by considering how well it fits in with the circumstances of the case and that 'it is dangerous to assess the credibility of the evidence given by any witness in isolation from other evidence in the case which is capable of throwing light on its reliability.'[63] He concluded that if

the presence or absence of corroborative evidence may assist a jury to resolve, one way or the other, their doubts as to whether or not to believe the evidence of a suspect witness, it must . . . be wrong to direct [the jury] to approach the question of credibility in two stages as suggested [by the accused's counsel.][64]

Still more important is the Privy Council's reiteration of Lord Reid's view that there

is nothing technical in the idea of corroboration. When in the ordinary affairs of life one is doubtful whether or not to believe a particular statement one naturally looks to see whether it fits in with other statements or circumstances relating to the particular matter; the better it fits in, the more one is inclined to believe it. The doubted statement is corroborated to a greater or lesser extent by the other statements or circumstances with which it fits in.[65]

The reason why counsel for the accused in *A-G of Hong Kong* v. *Wong Muk-ping* was able to pursue a different view all the way up to the Privy Council lies in the theory that corroboration is

---

[60] *DPP* v. *Hester* [1972] 3 All ER 1056, 1065. See also *DPP* v. *Kilbourne* [1973] 1 All ER 440, 452.

[61] *Turner* v. *Blunden* [1986] 2 All ER 75, 78.

[62] [1987] 2 All ER 488.   [63] Ibid. 492.   [64] Ibid. 494.

[65] *DPP* v. *Kilbourne* [1973] 1 All ER 440, 456; see also *R* v. *Turner* (1975) 61 Cr App R 67, 83 per James LJ; *Spencer* [1986] 2 All ER 928, 931–2.

not merely a matter of common sense but one regulated by binding precedent. As long as this theory has any life left in it, our courts will continue to have to address themselves to the kind of counter-intuitive argument with which this case was concerned. For example, in *Hills*[66] the Lord Chief Justice gave the following explanation for quashing a conviction for a serious drugs offence:

No doubt many of the 13 items listed by the judge were evidence of circumstances which served to cast grave doubt upon the case being put forward on behalf of the appellant. If the judge had made use of that evidence in that way rather than erecting it into potentially corroborative material, no complaint could legitimately have been made. It may very well have been that had that happened the jury would still have convicted.

It is difficult to see why, in common sense, evidence that casts 'grave doubt' on the accused's defence is not to be regarded as corroboration.

STATUTORY REQUIREMENTS

There are very few statutory requirements for corroboration in English law. Some of these are antiquated in form. Section 1 of the Treason Act 1795 and section 146(5) of the Representation of People Act 1949 require a minimum of two witnesses as a condition for conviction. The method of stipulating a minimum number of witnesses was favoured by the ancients.[67] To its credit, English law has not sought safety in numbers to any significant extent.[68]

Section 13 of the Perjury Act 1911 lays down that no person shall be convicted for perjury 'upon the evidence of one wit-

---

[66] (1988) 86 Cr App R 26, 31.

[67] For biblical authority see Deut. 19: 15. It was criticized by Bentham: 'In the multitude of counselors, says the proverb, there is safety; in the multitude of witnesses there may be some sort of safety, but nothing more, it is by weight, full as much as by tale, that witnesses are to be judged.' *Rationale of Judicial Evidence* (1827), vol. 5, p. 467.

[68] *Wigmore on Evidence*, Chad Rev, vol. 7, s. 2032. The repeal of the above provisions has been recommended by the Criminal Law Revision Committee, 11th Report, cmnd. 4991, para. 195.

ness'. The idea is that a person should not be convicted when it is only a matter of oath against oath. If taken seriously, this argument proves too much, for it would follow that no accused who denies his guilt on oath should be convicted on the strength of only one witness. Another explanation is that if prosecution for perjury were easy, witnesses might be deterred from giving evidence.[69] However, if the legislature wishes to safeguard against intimidatory prosecutions it need only require the consent of the Director of Public Prosecutions for bringing a charge.[70]

The Sexual Offences Act 1956 provides that persons charged with certain offences under the act cannot be convicted 'on the evidence of one witness only, unless the witness is corroborated in some material particular by evidence implicating the accused'. These offences include procurement by threats or by false pretences of a woman for sexual intercourse, administering drugs to facilitate intercourse, and procuring girls under twenty-one.[71] The justification for these provisions is doubtful[72] and their abolition has been recommended by the Criminal Law Revision Committee.[73]

Lastly, section 79(2) of the Road Traffic Regulation Act 1984, provides that a person charged with exceeding the speed limit 'shall not be liable to be convicted solely on the evidence of one witness to the effect that, in the opinion of the witness, the person prosecuted was driving the vehicle at a speed exceeding a specified limit.' It has been decided that the section requires corroboration only for the testimony a witness who depose on the basis of his own visual impression of speed and not to an expert witness who bases his opinion on indications found at the

---

[69] Criminal Law Revision Committee, 11th Report, cmnd. 4991, para. 190.

[70] As the Criminal Law Revision Committee recommended, 11th Report, cmnd. 4991, para. 221.

[71] Sections 2(2), 3(2), 4(2), 22(2), and 23(2) of the Act.

[72] It can hardly be said that whatever their connection with the offence in question witnesses tend to make mistakes or lie when giving evidence about these offences. Nor is there any special reason why juries cannot be trusted to assess the reliability of witnesses to these offences. It may, conceivably, be argued that the woman, in relation to whom an offence has been committed, is unreliable. However, there is no reason to believe that charges of procuring are, to any serious extent, maliciously levelled against innocent persons.

[73] 11th Report, cmnd. 4991, 188.

scene of an accident, the condition of the car in question and experiments conducted with the car.[73a]

THE RETREAT OF FORMALISM

It is in the nature of legal rules that their non-observance can bring about a sanction. Failure to deliver a corroboration warning can result in the quashing of a conviction, even if there was in fact ample corroborative evidence in the case.[74] If omissions on the part of trial judges were primarily due to inexcusable oversight, the problem would not be very serious. However, omissions are often caused by the complexity of the rules.[75]

In the United States, corroboration rules have never taken root. In the Commonwealth, where the common-law rules were followed, the recent trend has been either to abrogate the rules altogether, as in Canada,[76] or avoid drastic consequences in the event of non-observance of technicalities. Thus in Australia failure to administer a warning no longer leads to the quashing of convictions if the suspect evidence was in fact corroborated.[77] English courts too have been moving slowly in this direction. Trial judges are no longer bound to utter slavishly any particular form of warning.[78] Where the trial judge has failed to give the accomplice warning, it has been held, a conviction would be

---

[73a] *Crossland* v. *DPP* [1988] 3 All ER 712.

[74] In *Trigg* [1963] 1 All ER 490, the accused was confidently identified by the victim and by two other independent witnesses but the conviction was quashed due to a failure to administer a warning. It was held that '[i]n principle . . . cases where no warning as to corroboration is given where it should have been given, should, broadly speaking, not be made the subject of the proviso to s. 4(1) of the Criminal Appeal Act 1907'; at p. 492. Cf. *Riley* (1980) 70 Cr App R 1; *Birchall* (1986) 82 Cr App R 208, and n. 100 below.

[75] Wigmore observed that 'the rule thus tends to become in practice merely a means of securing from the trial judge the utterance of a form of words which may chance to be erroneous and lay the foundation for a new trial'. *Wigmore on Evidence*, Chad Rev, vol. 7, s. 2081, p. 464.

[76] *Vetrovec* v. *R.* 136 DLR (3d) 89.

[77] *Kelleher* (1974) 131 CLR 534. See also *Warkentin* (1976) 9 National Reporter (Canada) 301; *Murphy* (1976) 9 NR 329 and Clarke, 'Corroboration in sexual cases', [1980] Crim L Rev 362.

[78] *Nembhard* v. *R.* [1982] 1 All ER 183, 186; *Spencer* [1986] 2 All ER 928, 937–8. For an illustration of an insufficient warning see *Stewart* (1986) 83 Cr App R 327.

quashed only if the evidence was on the whole unsafe and unsatisfactory.[79]

An inclination to discourage formalism may be observed in the steadfast refusal to extend the present corroboration rules into new areas. As we have seen, there are situations falling outside the 'accomplice' definition in which a witness may have the strongest motive for laying the blame falsely on the accused. It was, therefore, consistent for Edmund Davies J to hold in *Prater* that 'in practice it is desirable that a warning should be given that the witness, whether he comes from the dock, as in this case, or whether he be Crown witness, may be a witness with some purpose of his own to serve.'[80] Five years later the Court of Appeal was at pains to stress that the above dictum was 'no more than an expression of what is desirable and what, it is to be hoped, will more usually than not be adopted, ... where it seems to be appropriate to the learned judge.'[81] The court refused to accept that the *Prater* decision extended the warning categories not because it believed that the danger from witnesses falling outside the traditional categories is invariably of lesser magnitude,[82] but because it did not like the consequences of the present rules. As Ackner LJ put it in *Beck*:

the burden upon the trial judge of the summing up is a heavy one. It would be a totally unjustifiable addition to require him, not only fairly to put before the jury the defence's contention that a witness was suspect, but also ... to give an accomplice warning with the appro-

---

[79] *Jenkins* (1981) 72 Cr App R 354, 358. See also *Zielinski* (1950) 34 Cr App R 193. Though it remains to be seen whether the same will apply where the trial judge intimated to the jury that something may be regarded as corroboration where, on authority, this is not the case. In such cases convictions have been quashed regardless of whether there was reason to suppose that they were unsafe; *Christie*, [1914] AC 545; *Rudge* (1923) 17 Cr App R 113. But see *Chauhan* (1981) 73 Cr App R 232. In Australia the jury is free to find support for the victim's account in any evidence which is capable of affording such support; see Clarke, [1980] Crim L Rev 362.

[80] [1960] 1 All ER 298, 299. This was approved by the House of Lords in *DPP* v. *Kilbourne* [1973] 1 All ER 440, 447.

[81] *Stannard* [1964] 1 All ER 34, 40. See also *Whitaker* (1976) 63 Cr App R 193, 196; *Knowlnden* (1983) 77 Cr App R 94. This line has been confirmed in *Beck* [1982] 1 All ER 807.

[82] The facts of *Whitaker* (1976) 63 Cr App R 193, and *Beck* [1982] 1 All ER 807, put paid to any such notion.

priate direction as to the meaning of corroboration together with identification of the potential corroborative material.[83]

This line of reasoning has culminated in *Spencer*.[84] The accused, male nurses in an institution for mentally disturbed prisoners, were charged with the mistreatment of inmates. The case against them rested entirely on the testimony of these inmates. In his summing up the trial judge warned the jury to approach the complainants' evidence with great care because the complainants were persons of criminal character, they were mentally disturbed, and had grudges against the accused. The judge also emphasized the absence of independent corroboration. The accused appealed against their conviction on the grounds that the judge had failed to use the word 'dangerous' in his summing up.[85] The House of Lords held that 'the obligation to warn the jury does not involve some legalistic ritual to be automatically recited by the judge, in the absence of which recital the conviction will be quashed'.[86] Instead of reciting a pre-set formula trial judges have to adapt their directions to the circumstances of the case so as to appraise the jury of the difficulties that the testimony creates.

These developments indicate that our courts are losing faith in the powers of the corroboration rules and are diverting their energy to a logical analysis of evidence.[87] This process is, however, far from complete. The existing categories of common-law corroboration continue to subsist: a warning, albeit informal, is mandatory (regardless of its value) whenever a witness for the prosecution is a complainant of sexual assault or an accomplice. Failure to administer it can still result in the quashing of sound convictions. Furthermore, the technical, and frequently counterproductive, rules about the nature of corroboration continue to apply within the traditional corroboration categories.

---

[83] [1982] 1 All ER 807, 812.   [84] [1986] 2 All ER 928.

[85] [1985] 1 All ER 673.

[86] [1986] All ER 928, 937, per Lord Ackner. See also *Chance* [1988] 3 All ER 225, 231, and discussion corresponding to n. 28 above.

[87] Of particular significance in this respect is the refusal of the courts to introduce a formal corroboration requirement for visual identification even though visual identification has been shown to be unreliable and its reliability is difficult to assess; see discussion below.

Whether or not legal rules of corroboration survive, the reliability of certain types of evidence will continue to cause difficulty. This is true, for instance, of evidence of children and of evidence of visual identification.[88] A judicial direction, however careful and detailed, may not always be enough to overcome the tendency of juries to overestimate the value of some particular type of evidence. To safeguard against overestimation we have a choice between two options. First we may pass a law forbidding conviction on the basis of uncorroborated evidence emanating from these sources. This course has the disadvantage of making convictions impossible irrespective of the reliability of the evidence in question. The alternative is greater judicial scrutiny of the soundness of convictions.

To this end appellate courts need to overcome their reluctance to review decisions on points of fact. It would be the duty of the trial judge, first, to outline to the jury the weaknesses and strengths of the evidence, and, secondly, to ensure, by careful exercise of the power to withdraw the case from the jury, that no one is convicted on doubtful evidence. Where a trial judge has failed to do so and it emerges on appeal that the jury must have proceeded on unsatisfactory evidence, the conviction should be quashed.[89] An active exercise of the 'safe or satisfactory' test if vigorously applied could go far towards overcoming the risks involved in unreliable sources.[90] By applying this test to the evidence as a whole, trial judges and appellate courts will be able to examine whether the danger of unreliability has been dispelled in the circumstances of each individual case.

VISUAL IDENTIFICATION

Evidence of visual identification is notoriously unreliable.[91] The Devlin Committee found that misidentification is common, dif-

---

[88] See discussion of concerning visual identification below.

[89] It is a pity that in *Spencer* [1986] 2 All ER 928, the House of Lords did not consider the possibility that despite the trial judge's flawless direction the conviction remained unsafe as a result of the questionable character of the prosecution witnesses.

[90] See discussion of the test in Ch. 7.

[91] See Note, 'Did your eyes deceive you?', 29 Stanford L Rev 969 (1977); Mendez, 'Memory, that strange deceiver', 32 Stan L Rev 445 (1980).

ficult to detect, and that a number of honest and independent witnesses may misidentify the same person even after considerable opportunities of observation.[92] Furthermore, since witnesses may be genuinely convinced of their identification, they can inspire juries with an unwarranted sense of security. For these reasons the committee recommended that convictions should not rest solely on visual identification, even if the identification is by more than one witness. The committee accepted the need for limited exceptions; for example, in cases where the accused has offered no explanation, and where he has admitted belonging to a small group of people one of whom committed the crime.

The legislature has not adopted these recommendations and the Court of Appeal has expressed the reservation that a rule requiring corroboration which was, at the same time, subject to exceptions would be likely to produce unnecessary complications.[93] Instead, the court held that trial judges should caution juries of the weakness of identification evidence, explain that the most honourable and confident testimony can be mistaken, and point out particular factors which enhance or diminish the value of the identification.[94] The emphasis that a trial judge has to place on the danger of misidentification is a function of the seriousness of the danger in the case.[95] Where a warning is found insufficient by the appellate court, the conviction may be quashed.[96]

The Court of Appeal was probably right in its view that a strict legal requirement of corroboration could lead to unacceptable instances of acquittal. But the strategy it adopted does not solve the main problem. As the Devlin Committee showed, it is almost impossible to tell when a confident and honest witness is mistaken.[97] Hence no amount of exhortation can effectively

[92] Report on Evidence of Identification in Criminal Cases, 1976. See also Criminal Law Revision Committee, 11th Report, cmnd. 4991, paras. 198–203. Lloyd-Bostock and Clifford (eds.), *Evaluating Witness Evidence* (1983).

[93] *Turnbull* [1976] 3 All ER 549.

[94] See also *Weeder* (1980) 71 Cr App R 228.

[95] See *Oakwell* [1978] 1 All ER 1223; *Keeble* [1983] Crim L Rev 737.

[96] *Hunjan* (1978) 68 Cr App R 99; *Reid* v. *R.* [1979] 2 All ER 904.

[97] This is borne out by research; see Gross, 'Loss of innocence: eyewitness identification and proof of guilt', 16 Journal of Legal Studies 395 (1987).

safeguard against mistake because no amount of care can discern a mistake.

As the trial procedure cannot provide altogether adequate safeguards against mistaken identification, more needs to be done during the pre-trial stages. It may be possible to improve the techniques of identification,[98] but there will be cases where the identification is not a product of investigative procedures. Where the evidence consists of a bare account of what a witness saw, prosecution authorities should refrain from adducing the evidence unless it is of sufficient quality.[99] Greater pre-trial quality control will improve the present position where everything depends on a judicial direction and the jury's ability to follow it.[100]

---

[98] Ibid.

[99] Prof. Gross accepts that it 'cuts against the grain to argue that prosecutors and police officers should have primary responsibility for protecting innocent defendants', ibid. 449, but sees no better way towards a solution. Cf. Twining, 'Identification and misidentification in legal process: redefining the problem', in Lloyd-Bostock and Clifford (eds.), *Evaluating Witness Evidence* (1983).

[100] See Code of Practice for the Identification of Persons by Police Officers, issued by the Home Secretary under the Police and Criminal Evidence Act 1984, s. 66, 1985.

I I

Hearsay

INTRODUCTION

Of the great exclusionary rules which once formed the backbone of the law of evidence only the rule against hearsay has retained its vigour. According to Professor Cross's well-known formulation of the rule, 'a statement other than one made by a person while giving oral evidence in the proceedings is inadmissible *as evidence of any fact stated.*'[1] In its most straightforward application the rule forbids Jones to testify that Smith had told him that he, Smith, had seen the accused strike the fatal blow, when Jones's testimony is adduced to prove that the accused struck the blow.

A rule can exclude evidence for one of two reasons: for lack of probative value or on grounds of policy independent of probative value.[2] Hearsay it may be assumed is excluded because of the risk of error. However, in ordinary affairs we may regard hearsay with suspicion but we hardly ever decline to consider it. Indeed, hearsay is, broadly speaking, admissible in civil proceedings.[3] Its retention in criminal trials can hardly have been accidental. Criminal trials are dominated by the need to protect the innocent from conviction. Hearsay is thought to be unreliable; hence its exclusion is felt to be necessary for maintaining high standards of accuracy in findings of guilt and averting conviction of the innocent. Independent policy reasons have also been advanced for the exclusionary rule. These are often 'subtle and procedurally complex',[4] and involve theories

[1] Cross *On Evidence*, 5th edn. 6, 462. This definition has been embraced in England but other definitions have been advocated in the United States; see Park, '*McCormick on Evidence* and the concept of hearsay', 65 Minn L Rev 423 (1980).

[2] For discussion of the distinction see: Galligan, 'More scepticism about scepticism', (1988) 8 Oxford Journal of Legal Studies 249, 255.

[3] The Civil Evidence Act 1968 replaced the prohibition on hearsay with procedural safeguards against surprise and abuse.

[4] Park, 'A subject matter approach to hearsay reform', 86 Mich L Rev 51, 55 (1987); where an excellent analysis will be found.

about inherent procedural values.[5] The principal independent justification is that the admission of hearsay statements would deny the accused an opportunity to participate effectively in the proceedings instituted against him by preventing him from cross-examining the maker of the statement. It is said that it is wrong to deny the accused such an opportunity even when cross-examination is unlikely to provide a useful test of reliability.[6] The present discussion will, however, proceed on the assumption that in the main the hearsay rule rests on consideration of probative value.[7]

A hearsay statement may be flawed in four principal respects. First, the person whose statement is reported, the declarant, may have wrongly perceived the event in question. This can occur because of some defect in the declarant's senses of perception or for some other reason. Secondly, the declarant's memory may have been faulty or inaccurate when he made the statement. Thirdly, he may have lied or deliberately distorted the event.. Fourthly, the declarant's statement may have been misunderstood by the witness now reporting it. Since meaning is so dependent on context, nuance, and shared cultural background, the scope for misunderstanding is substantial.[8]

All of these risks, save the fourth, are also present when the person who observed the facts testifies in court. There is, however, one fundamental difference: when a witness is in court, the opponent is able to cross-examine him in order to investigate his powers of perception, test his memory, and appraise his veracity, thus enabling the trier of fact to determine the probative value of the testimony according to the witness's performance in the witness-box. It is the unavailability of a hearsay declarant for cross-examination which constitutes the

[5] Nesson, 'The evidence or the event? On judicial proof and acceptability of verdicts', 98 Harv L Rev 1357, 1372 (1985), suggests that the hearsay rule enhances acceptability of verdicts by protecting them from attack.
[6] Cf. Westen, 'Confrontation and compulsory process: a unified theory of evidence for criminal cases', 91 Harv L Rev 267 (1978); id., 'The future of confrontation', 77 Mich L Rev 1185 (1979); Lempert and Saltzburg, *A Modern Approach to Evidence*, 2nd edn. (1982), 520.
[7] English case law proceeds on this assumption: *Sharp* [1988] 1 All ER 65, 68.
[8] Swift, 'Abolishing the hearsay rule', 75 Calif L Rev 495, 504, (1987).

central reason for the exclusion of hearsay statements.[9] It is said that in the absence of cross-examination of the declarant jurors are likely to overestimate the probative significance of his hearsay statement.[10]

This argument cannot be dismissed altogether. On introspection most of us will admit to undue susceptibility to hearsay, especially when the hearsay appears to confirm a belief we already hold or a prejudice to which we are predisposed. It is also probably the case that free admissibility of hearsay is likely to disadvantage the accused more than the prosecution because the number of cases in which the prosecution relies on hearsay is far greater than the number of cases in which the accused relies on hearsay.[11]

A further aspect to be remembered is that hearsay is associated with unsubstantiated beliefs based on rumour, gossip, and specious word of mouth. Hence our belief that the accused should be judged on the evidence produced against him in court and not on the basis of public preconceptions explains the intuitive antagonism to hearsay.[12] The right to confrontation in the Sixth Amendment of United States constitution is, to some extent, an expression of this antagonism. This provision accords to an accused in a criminal trial the right 'to be confronted with

---

[9] *Wigmore on Evidence*, Chad Rev, vol. 5, para. 1362. A number of other reasons are commonly marshalled in favour of the exclusionary rule, of which only the more important ones need be mentioned here. It is said that the introduction of hearsay would require adjournments in order to allow the party affected to investigate the reliability of the hearsay. This inconvenience may, however, be avoided by introducing preliminary proceedings into our system. It is objected that admissibility of hearsay would tempt the police to rely on secondary and, therefore, less reliable evidence. Lastly, it is sometimes said that if hearsay were admissible, desperate accused might fabricate exculpatory hearsay statements which would be difficult to discredit totally. While this risk cannot be completely dismissed, it is not terribly serious since exculpatory hearsay is bound to be treated with suspicion. For full discussion of these reasons see Criminal Law Revision Committee, 11th Report, 132.

[10] Weinstein, 'The probative force of hearsay', 46 Iowa L Rev 331 (1961).

[11] As Lempert and Saltzburg observe, *A Modern Approach to Evidence*, 2nd edn. (1982), 493–4.

[12] See Stein, 'Bentham, Wigmore and freedom of proof', 22 Israel L Rev 243, 266 (1987); and ref. in n. 6 above.

the witnesses against him'.[13] While there is no complete overlap between the right to confrontation and the hearsay rule it is clear that there is considerable similarity in the concerns behind these two measures.[14] A further justification of the American right to confrontation is said to be 'its psychic value to litigants, who feel that those giving evidence against them should do it publicly and face to face'.[15] These aims are clearly desirable but, as we shall see, the English rule against hearsay is a very crude and inefficient instrument for securing them.

The principal criticism of the hearsay rule is that it is wider than its rationale requires. Exclusion may be justified if hearsay is evidentially inferior, but the rule excludes hearsay even when it is by no means inferior and even when it represents the best available source of information.[16] There are situations in which hearsay, far from being inferior to direct oral testimony, is superior to it, but the rule excludes evidence irrespective of its probative superiority.[17] Thus a witness is allowed to state his present recollection of a car registration number he fleetingly observed many months before, but he is not allowed to produce as independent evidence a note of the number he made soon after the observation.

The fact that the rule results in the exclusion of much useful evidence is not necessarily a conclusive argument against its value. Some disadvantage is almost always attendant on the operation of any rule. What we have to consider is whether a rule that excludes both good and bad evidence offers a better strategy for avoiding mistake than a strategy that attempts to discriminate between good and bad on a case-by-case basis.

---

[13] This right is one of several granted by the 6th Amendment in order to provide for a fair and unbiased trial. Others are: the right to a speedy public trial, the right to an impartial jury, the right to be informed of the nature of the accusation, the right to secure favourable evidence, and the right to representation by counsel.

[14] *Wigmore on Evidence*, Chad Rev, vol. 5, ch. 47.

[15] Weinstein, 'Some difficulties in devising rules for determining truth in judicial trials', 66 Co L Rev 223, 245 (1966). See also Note, 'Preserving the right to confrontation: a new approach to hearsay evidence in criminal trials', 113 University of Pennsylvania L Rev 741 (1965).

[16] For subsidiary objections to hearsay see: Criminal Law Revision Committee, 11th Report, para. 232.

[17] The rule applies equally to the out-of-court statements of witnesses testifying in court and to the statements of declarants not produced as witnesses.

Some would argue that ordinary discretionary safeguards are insufficient for dealing with the shortcomings of hearsay evidence and that, furthermore, a rigid exclusionary rule saves time and prevents uncertainty. Such arguments would be powerful if two conditions were fulfilled: first, if the rule produced results which broadly conform with common sense, and, secondly, if the rule could be shown to be clear and certain in its application. If the first condition is not fulfilled, then the benefits of exclusion would be outweighed by too great a loss of valuable evidence and by too many factually mistaken verdicts. If the second condition is not fulfilled the benefits of clarity and ease of application will disappear and the rule, to the extent that it might still be said to exist, will not offer an advantage over discretion.

The hearsay rule fulfils neither of these conditions, as the following discussion will show. The rule is at odds with common sense and as a result our judges have had to resort to numerous ploys to arrest the more extreme excesses of its operation. These efforts have made the rule more flexible and have rightly made admissibility more dependent on probative force than on conformity to a legal definition, but this only helps, in turn, to call into question the benefits to be gained from the continued existence of the rule.

THE EXTENT TO WHICH THE RULE DEVIATES FROM COMMON SENSE

Exclusion of Evidence of Innocence

The first respect in which the hearsay rule deviates from common sense concerns its exclusion of evidence of innocence.

In *Sparks* v. *R*[18] a white man was convicted of indecent assault on a four-year-old girl. The defence wished to ask the victim's mother whether her daughter, who was not called as a witness, had said to her shortly after the incident that 'it was a coloured boy' who perpetrated the assault. The trial judge refused to allow the question on the ground that it called for hearsay, and

---

[18] [1964] 1 All ER 727.

his ruling was upheld by the Privy Council, though the conviction was quashed on other grounds.

In *Blastland*[19] the accused was charged with buggering and then murdering a twelve-year-old boy. His defence was that he had engaged in an act of intercourse with the boy's consent and then left him unharmed, and that the boy was later killed by another person, *M*, whom the accused described. The House of Lords assumed that the admission of *M*'s statement confessing to murdering the boy would have been inadmissible hearsay.[20] This attitude gives insufficient weight to the protection of innocence and seems inconsistent with the priority given to this principle in other contexts.[21]

It is possible that in practice the exclusion of third-party admissions has not been a major obstacle to justice because few accused have had to rely on hearsay to support their innocence. Where the accused has relied on hearsay, either its significance was flimsy[22] or the court found some other way of doing justice.[23] It is also probably true that the rule discourages defendants from fabricating spurious hearsay in their defence.[24] However, the fact remains that the present rule may prevent an accused from adducing exculpating evidence and this is contrary to the policy of protecting the innocent.

---

[19] [1985] 2 All ER 1095.

[20] See also *Turner* (1975) 61 Cr App R 67; *Thompson* [1912] 3 KB 19; *Malcherek and Steel* (1981) 73 Cr App R 173, 185–6.

[21] In *Barton* [1972] 2 All ER 1192, 1194, it was decided that the need to prove innocence overrides legal professional privilege and Caulfield J said: 'I cannot conceive that our law would permit a solicitor or other person to screen from a jury information which . . . would perhaps enable a man either to establish his innocence or to resist the allegations made by the Crown.' American courts have decided that the hearsay rule must not be allowed to stand in the way of an accused person wishing to prove his innocence; *Chambers* v. *Mississippi* 410 US 284, 301 (1973), where Justice Powell said that 'where constitutional rights directly affecting the ascertainment of guilt are implicated, the hearsay rule may not be applied mechanistically to defeat the ends of justice.'

[22] As in *Turner*, above, and possibly in *Blastland* too.

[23] As in *Sparks*, above.

[24] The fear of fabrication is expressed in Lord Bridge's speech in *Blastland* [1985] 2 All ER 1098. It must also explain a distinction that has now developed: an exculpatory out-of-court statement by an accused person is admissible as evidence of facts stated therein, if it forms part of an admission adduced by the prosecution but not otherwise; *Sharp* [1988] 1 All ER 65.

Instances of Exclusion of Rationally Superior Evidence

The hearsay definition comprises large classes of evidence which suffer from none of the weaknesses associated with hearsay. There have been many instances of exclusion of evidentially superior evidence of which the most prominent is the case of *Myers* v. *DPP*.[25] Although the type of evidence excluded in that case is now admissible it is important to discuss it in some detail because it still exerts considerable influence on the attitude of the courts to the hearsay rule. The accused was charged with the theft of a number of motor cars. It was alleged that he operated a system of buying accident-wrecked cars, then stealing cars of a similar description, disguising them so as to correspond to the wrecked cars, and finally selling the stolen cars by presenting them as restored cars. The wrecked cars were bought with their log books which included the engine and chassis number of each car. To make the stolen cars correspond to the log books of the wrecked cars the accused, it was alleged, transferred the plates recording these numbers from the wrecked cars to the stolen ones.

Each engine bore an additional number, referred to as the block number, which was indelibly stamped inside the engine. To make out the charge against the accused the prosecution wished to show that the block numbers of the cars sold corresponded to those of the stolen cars and not to those of the wrecked ones. For this purpose the prosecution proposed to give in evidence the factory records concerning both the stolen and the wrecked cars. These records were compiled from entries made by employees who examined the cars on the assembly line. The House of Lords held that they were inadmissible hearsay on the grounds that the entries amounted to assertions by unidentifiable employees stating that they had seen the relevant numbers and entered them in the records.[26] It was said that the prosecution should have proved the records by calling

---

[25] [1964] 2 All ER 881.
[26] Lord Pearce dissenting. The conviction was nevertheless affirmed by application of the proviso to s. 4(1) of the Criminal Appeal Act 1907, then in force. One wonders whether the ruling on hearsay would have been the same had it necessitated acquittal of these clearly guilty defendants.

the employees who saw the numbers and entered them into the cards. Had the employees been unable to remember the numbers, it was held, they would have been allowed to refresh their memory from the records.

This approach seems both irrational and fictitious; irrational because the records of the numbers were vastly superior in probative force to any testimony the employees could give from memory, and fictitious because an inspection of the records could not have produced a genuine recollection in the employees' minds. The majority in *Myers* was not unaware of the absurdity of its ruling but it was motivated by two considerations. First, that the hearsay rule was a strict rule of law demanding adherence no matter how irrational exclusion might be,[27] and, secondly, that the reform of the rule, either through complete overhauling or through the creation of new exceptions, was best left to the legislature. Parliament acted with unfamiliar alacrity and enacted the Criminal Evidence Act 1965 which made admissible statements contained in business records of the kind adduced in that case.[28] However, the principle established in *Myers* has been allowed to stand and large areas of exclusion still remain.

The premise that the hearsay rule is fixed and immune from *ad hoc* judicial invention of exceptions receives periodic reaffirmation. In *Blastland*[29] the House of Lords was exhorted to recognize an exception allowing an accused to prove that a third party admitted the commission of the offence with which he stands charged. Refusing to create an exception Lord Bridge referred to *Myers* v. *DPP*[30] and explained that the case 'established the principle, never since challenged, that it is for the legislature, not the judiciary, to create new exceptions to the hearsay rule'.[31] The declared loyalty to *Myers* is, however, difficult to understand. *Myers* was decided in the express hope that the legislature would be thereby prompted into action, but

---

[27] As Lord Reid put it, '[t]his is a highly technical point, but the law regarding hearsay is technical, and I would say absurdly technical.' [1965] AC 1019.

[28] The provisions of this Act were replaced by s. 68 to 72 of the Police and Criminal Evidence Act 1984. Section 68 of the 1984 Act has been repealed by the Criminal Justice Act 1988, s. 24 of which now deals with documentary records. Cf. *Martin* [1988] 1 WLR 655.

[29] [1985] 2 All ER 1095.

[30] [1964] 2 All ER 881.   [31] [1985] 2 All ER 1098.

apart from introducing some limited exceptions Parliament has shown little inclination to overhaul the hearsay rule in criminal cases. In fact the courts have not been unfailingly faithful to the *Myers* decision.[32] On the contrary, with increasing frequency in recent years the courts have found it desirable to side-step the *Myers* decision by a variety of devices.

ARTIFICIAL METHODS OF ESCAPING THE HEARSAY RULE[33]

Refreshing Memory

A witness testifying at the trial may refresh his memory from documents presented to him in the witness box, as we have seen in Chapter 7. If the document produces in the witness's mind a recollection of the event recorded in the document, then the witness can speak from his memory and any inference drawn from his testimony rests on the witness's present recollection of his original perception. There is no difference between being reminded of, say, an opera performance I saw the month before by reading an entry to this effect in my diary and remembering the same on being asked about it. In both cases the performance might have completely gone out of my mind until my memory was stimulated in one of these ways. If I now describe the performance, the data for what happened is my present recollection.

If memory were always revived in this way, we would not need rules stipulating the types of documents that may be used for the purpose of refreshing memory. Quite frequently, however, no recollection comes to mind on reading a document containing information which the witness once knew. On being told a telephone number I may remember it long enough to enter it in my address-book, but if I am asked about it a few days later I would be quite unable to remember it, nor would

---

[32] *Andrews* [1987] 1 ALL ER 513, is of particular significance in this respect; see text relating to n. 147 below.

[33] For a survey of these methods see: Ashworth and Pattenden, 'Reliability, hearsay evidence and the English criminal trial', (1986) 102 LQR 292; D. J. Birch, 'Hearsay logic and hearsay fiddles: *Blastland* revisited', in P. Smith (ed.), *Criminal Law: Essays in Honour of J. C. Smith* (1987), 24.

my memory be usually helped by looking up the number in my
book. All I would be able to say truthfully on seeing the entry
would be that it was made by me and that it must therefore
represent the number I remembered. If the number is in issue
in litigation, and I am allowed to inspect my address-book, then
the real evidence for the number will be not my present recollection of the number but the entry in my book in conjunction
with my testimony authenticating the entry. Consequently, we
have reason to be careful about which documents we allow a
witness to consult so that witnesses are not used as a medium
for insinuating evidence which does not emanate from their
perceptions and for the accuracy or provenance of which they
are unable to vouch.

The hearsay rule insists on the fiction that a document used
for the purpose of refreshing memory is not itself evidence for
anything, even when authenticated by its maker. However, no
matter what the rule says, in common sense the trier of fact is
bound to give due weight to the original account in the document. How can this be squared with the rule against hearsay
which renders inadmissible all out-of-court statements adduced
as proof of facts stated therein? Reconciliation is achieved by
the pretence that a document is used merely to refresh memory
and that, far from being hearsay evidence, is not evidence at
all.[34] This idea might have possessed some semblance of sense if
the witness, having examined the document and refreshed his
memory, then proceeded to testify without further reference to
it. But witnesses are allowed to have continual recourse to such
documents and even to quote from them verbatim.[35]

Despite protestations that such documents do not involve
hearsay infringements, the very structure of the rules governing
their use reveals an underlying assumption that the documents
may well constitute evidence of the facts they proclaim. Why
otherwise is it required that the document should have been

---

[34] *Senat* v. *Senat* [1965] 2 All ER 505. '"The rule against hearsay" consists in
truth of two separate rules: (a) the rule requiring evidence to be first hand, and (b)
the rule requiring it to be given orally in court'; Glanville Williams, [1973] Crim L
Rev 139, 140.
[35] Policemen testifying about interviews with suspects or about observations they
had made normally read out of their notebooks word for word.

made at the time of the reported event or soon afterwards?[36] Why else must the document have been made by the witness himself or under his supervision?[37] Why must either the original of the witness's record, or a verified copy of it, be produced?[38] If there is no special significance in the witness consulting the document in the witness-box, why should not all these rules apply equally where the witness has consulted the documents just before entering the box?[39] These requirements make sense only if the document itself, quite apart from the witness's recollection, plays a central role in the inference to the fact in issue. Only then is there a reason for having safeguards concerning the provenance of the document.

Seeing that the claim that documents used to refresh memory are not evidence is so blatantly spurious, some judges have been prepared to make some concession to reality. Referring to the status of such documents Geoffrey Lane LJ said:

At the highest they showed a degree of consistency in [the witness refreshing his memory from them] which otherwise might have been lacking, just as a complaint by the victim of a sexual assault . . . may show a degree of consistency in his or her evidence . . .[40]

The assumption that there is more to the document than just stimulation to memory receives support from another rule. When the cross-examiner does not confine his examination to the passages to which the witness referred to refresh his memory but questions the witness about other parts of the document[41]

---

[36] *A-G's Reference No 3 of 1979* (1979) 69 Cr App R 411. Indeed, as Newark and Samuel point out, the less the witness could be expected to remember the greater the insistence on contemporaneity: [1978] Crim L Rev 408–9.

[37] *Mills and Rose* (1962) 46 Cr App R 336.

[38] *Kwol Si Cheng* (1976) 63 Cr App R 20; *Phipson on Evidence*, 13th edn. (1982) 780.

[39] Why is it, as the court said in *Richardson* (1971) 55 Cr App R 244, that a 'line is drawn at the moment when a witness enters the witness-box'? Cf. *Owen* v. *Edwards* (1983) 77 Cr App R 191.

[40] *Virgo* (1978) 67 Cr App R 323, 329. See also *Britton* [1987] 2 All ER 412. There is here an appeal to the ever-convenient but vacuous distinction between relevance to credit and relevance to the issue, discussed in Ch. 7. Moreover, the view that the document shows consistency is untenable where the statement in court is not independent of the document but simply a repetition of its contents.

[41] Documents used for refreshing memory must be made available to the opponent, who may cross-examine by reference to them, and to the trier of fact.

then, it is said, the document becomes evidence in the case.[42]
Yet if the document is to be considered as evidence at all, it
must be evidence of facts stated therein.[43]

The importance of a document used for the purpose of refreshing memory may be observed in *Kelsey*.[44] The prosecution's
case was that the accused's car was at the scene of the burglary
with which he was charged. To support this claim it called a
witness who testified that he made a mental note of the registration number of a car he saw at the scene of the crime, that
twenty minutes later he dictated the number to a policeman
who read it out as he took it down, but that he could no longer
remember it. The Court of Appeal held that the witness was
allowed to refresh his memory from the policeman's note. There
is of course a possibility, though a very remote one, that, at the
sight of the note, the witness might really have recollected his
original perception. But it would be wrong to suppose that the
courts are concerned to verify the true state of the witness's
recollection. Had the court in *Kelsey* been minded to ascertain
whether the witness really remembered the number, it should
have insisted that the witness be asked to pick out the correct
number from amongst several numbers presented to him, as
is done in identification parades. The truth is that our courts
are not concerned with the accuracy of memory but with the
accuracy of documents.

The practice of paying lip-service to the hearsay rule produces some odd results. In *McLean*[45] the facts were similar to
those of *Kelsey*. A witness dictated a car registration number to
one Cope but did not inspect what Cope wrote down. By the
time of the trial he had forgotten the number. The Court of
Appeal quashed the conviction because the number was proved
by Cope who produced the record and repeated its content.[46]

---

[42] *Britton* [1987] 2 All ER 412; Newark and Samuels, [1978] Crim L Rev 408,
411.

[43] The fiction that the document is merely evidence of a witness's consistency
cannot be maintained here since the witness did not repeat the passages in question
in the course of his testimony.

[44] (1982) 74 Cr App R 213.   [45] (1968) 52 Cr App R 80.

[46] In so doing the court was following similar decisions in *Grew* v. *Cubitt* [1951]
TLR 305, and in *Jones* v. *Metcalfe* [1967] 3 All ER 205, all of which are discussed by
Prof. Cross in 'The periphery of hearsay', (1969) 7 Melbourne Univ L Rev 1.

This case was distinguished in *Kelsey* on the ground that in *McLean* the number was not proved by the witness who perceived it but by the scribe who took it down. This distinction is unconvincing because in both cases the evidence consisted in the record rather than in what the witness could say in court.[47]

This kind of distinction is the price paid for maintaining the untenable view that the document is not evidence in the case, a price which not only seems offensive to common sense but also results in unnecessary acquittals on appeal.[48]

Section 24(b)(iii) of the Criminal Justice Act 1988, removes some of the need for this distinction. A document that has been created or received by a person in the course of trade, business, profession, or other occupation will now be admissible as evidence of facts stated therein if 'the person who made the statement cannot reasonably be expected ... to have any recollection of the matters dealt with in the statement'. This provision applies only to statements prepared for criminal proceeding and investigations. It will thus be no longer necessary to maintain the fiction that policemen merely refresh their memory from their notes. However, the condition that the maker of the statement 'cannot be reasonably expected to have any recollection' is rather strange because it excludes, for example, the contemporaneous notes of a policeman who has some recollection, albeit partial, of the events described in the notes.[49] Many instances where documents are used for the purpose of refreshing memory still remain outside the scope of the section altogether.

It is possible that the House of Lords' decision in *Sharp*[50] has set in motion a development that will put an end to all the spurious distinctions which have accompanied the use of out-of-court statements in this and other contexts. The prosecution in this case adduced a statement made by the accused to the police which was partly inculpatory and partly exculpatory. Following tradition the trial judge instructed the jury that the inculpatory part was to be taken as evidence of facts stated but warned that

---

[47] It may be that the record of the number in *Kelsey* was more reliable by virtue of it having been repeated aloud by the scribe while taking it down, but this is not the ground on which the court chose to distinguish the case.

[48] Cf. *Virgo* (1978) 67 Cr App R 323.

[49] Cf. *Cross on Evidence*, 6th edn. (1985), 254.

[50] [1988] 1 All ER 65.

the exculpatory part was not to be so regarded. Disapproving of the direction Lord Havers said:

How can the jury fairly evaluate the facts in the admission unless they can evaluate the facts in the excuse or explanation? It is only if the jury think that the facts set out by way of excuse or explanation might be true that any doubt is cast on the admission, and it is surely only because the excuse or explanation might be true that it is thought fair that it should be considered by the jury.... a jury will make little of a direction that attempts to draw a distinction between evidence which is evidence of facts and evidence in the same statement which whilst not being evidence of facts is nevertheless evidentiary material of which they may make use in evaluating evidence which is evidence of facts. One has to write out the foregoing sentence to see the confusion it engenders.[51]

The importance of this decision lies in the recognition that once a statement is put before a jury, it makes little sense to ask a jury not to regard it as evidence when its content is clearly relevant to an issue in the case. In consistency, this view ought now to affect the practice of the courts wherever an out-of-court statement is adduced on account of the information that it contains and an end should be put to the pretence that it is not evidence of the information that it provides.

Negative Inferences

We have seen that in *Myers* v. *DPP*[52] the House of Lords decided that the hearsay rule must be strictly adhered to and that the courts should refuse to create new exceptions where none existed before. In the absence of reform of the hearsay rule this decision placed a great strain on the common sense of even the most precedent-conscious judge and it was only a question of time before courts began to find ways of circumventing the strictures of the House of Lords.[53]

In a number of recent cases the courts have decided that a record adduced in order to support an inference from the non-existence of an entry in the record does not amount to an infringement of the hearsay rule. In *Shone*[54] the accused was

---

[51] Ibid. 71.   [52] [1964] 2 All ER 881.
[53] See refs. in n. 33 above.   [54] (1983) 76 Cr App R 72.

charged with the theft of three car-springs from a warehouse. The prosecution called the clerk in charge of the warehouse who adduced the stock-book and explained that had the springs been removed from the warehouse legitimately there would have been an entry to that effect in the stock-records; the records showed no such entry. Distinguishing the case of *Myers* the Court of Appeal decided that evidence was admissible because it

> was not hearsay, but evidence from which the jury were entitled to draw the inference . . . that all three springs were stolen. If there had been one spring found in the appellant's possession, which was traceable to Longs [the warehouse], the absence of a record of sale or legitimate disposal would have been evidentially relatively insignificant . . . the absence of such a record in respect of all three springs . . . was overwhelming.[55]

Strictly speaking there is no difference between drawing a negative inference from the absence of an entry in a stock-record and drawing a positive inference from the existence of an entry that the goods were sold. An inference from the absence of an entry presupposes that the entries that have been made are complete, i.e. that the record does not lie when it is silent.[56] If the duty of reporting facts fit for entry in the record rests on persons not called as witnesses, the inference must run through their express or implied statement (or undertaking) that they have made true and complete reports.[57]

The distinction between entries and absence of entries does not arise from some internal logic of the hearsay rule but from

---

[55] Ibid. 76. See also *Patel* [1981] 3 All ER 94; *Muir* (1984) 79 Cr App R 153.

[56] Against this view some may argue that the inference is not drawn from the entries but from the very existence of a record in which entries would be made in appropriate cases; indeed, that a negative inference may be drawn from a completely empty record. Even so the inference could only be drawn from the express or implied statement that the record is accurate and complete. See also Graham, 'Stickperson hearsay: a simplified approach to understanding the rule against hearsay', (1982) University of Ill L Rev 887; Saltzburg, 66 Calif L Rev 1011 (1978).

[57] Otherwise *Myers* itself could have been decided differently on the grounds that the factory records contained no entries that reflected the combination of numbers on the cars in question.

the undesirability of excluding the best evidence available.[58]
This amounts to a withdrawal of the hearsay rule from an area
where there is no justification for its application.

Real Evidence

The legal concept of 'real evidence'[59] which, like other vintage
concepts, appeared to have lost any practical significance has
recently surfaced to explain the limits of the hearsay rule.

In *Castle* v. *Cross*,[60] on a charge that the accused failed to
provide a specimen of breath, the prosecution adduced a printout of an automatic breath-testing device called an Intoximeter.
The Divisional Court dismissed the objection that the printout
was hearsay[61] and decided that as 'a tool, albeit a sophisticated
tool', the printout was 'real evidence'.[62]

The machine's 'statement' is not made by a person. Its probative significance depends on the accuracy and reliability of the
machine.[63] If the reliability of the machine can be established

---

[58] It was perhaps with a view to allowing for further deviations from the rigours
of hearsay that the Court of Appeal said that 'the bounds of that decision [*Myers*]
appear still unsettled in cases of systematically compiled records where evidence
about the conclusions to be drawn from such records is adduced by witnesses who
were themselves concerned in their compilation in the ordinary course of their
duties'; *Abadom* [1983] 1 All ER 364, 367–8.

[59] For discussion of this notion see Best, *Principles of the Law of Evidence*, 12th edn.
(1922), app. A by Phipson; Noakes, 'Real evidence', (1949) 65 LQR 57.

[60] [1985] 1 All ER 87.

[61] Another panel of the same court held that the printout was a statement:
Gaimster v. *Marlow* [1985] 1 All ER 82.

[62] The provenance of the 'real-evidence' theory is suspect. Reference is often
made to *Maqsud Ali* [1965] 2 All ER 464, where a tape-recording was held admissible, but the recording contained a confession which was in any event admissible.
The same goes for *Senat and Sin* (1968) 52 Cr App R 282. These cases formed the
basis of the decision in *The Statue of Liberty* [1968] 2 All ER 195, where a radar
recording was held admissible for proving the course of ships and which did involve
a hearsay problem. The most detailed discussion is in *Wood* (1983) 76 Cr App R 23
where Lord Lane CJ described a computer used to analyse the results of chemical
tests as a 'tool' and the printout of the computer as 'real evidence' (27). However,
he ignored the problem involved in the implicit reliance on the maker of the
computer, unless of course the machine's reliability was independently proved as it
might have been in that case.

[63] A distinction has to be drawn between information stored in a machine, such
as a computer, and information generated by the machine; see Tapper, *Computer
Law*, 3rd edn. (1983), ch. 6, and J. C. Smith, 'The admissibility of statements by
computer', [1981] Crim L Rev 387.

without reference to the statements of the persons who made it, no hearsay problem arises. In *Castle* v. *Cross*[64] Stephen Brown J found a short-cut to proof of reliability by assuming that the Intoximeter was accurate on the strength of the presumption of *omnia praesumuntur rite esse acta.* However, not all machines of this kind will be so widely used as to give rise to the presumption; even if they do, the presumption may not be sufficiently weighty to exclude reasonable doubt, especially where complicated and sensitive machine operations are involved. Moreover, it is doubtful whether this presumption has any application to the reliability of machines because its function is to deal with the legal validity of official actions, not with the accuracy of machines.[65]

Operative Words: Words Relevant to an Act or an Issue

A statement is not considered to infringe the hearsay rule if it is not adduced in order to prove the truth of that which it states. Where the legal system attaches certain consequences to the very making of a statement,[66] the statement may be proved for the purpose of establishing that it was made. Thus words of a contractual offer may be proved in order to establish a contract because words of offer and acceptance result in a binding contract. It is therefore said that such statements are proved as original evidence and are not adduced as evidence of anything other than the fact that they were made.[67]

However, admissibility of such words has been extended beyond statements with independent legal consequences to cover statements that explain or qualify some act that they accompany.[68] On a charge of running an illegal betting shop it has been held, in the Commonwealth and the United States,

---

[64] [1985] 1 All ER 87.

[65] Cf. *Cross on Evidence*, 6th edn. (1985), 134.

[66] That is, the statement is a constitutive fact.

[67] Doubts have been expressed about the correctness of this view: Park, '*McCormick on Evidence* and the concept of hearsay', 65 Minn L Rev 423, 441.

[68] The fact that the statement happens to accompany some act of the declarant does not alter the fact that the court is required to infer its truth. True, the statement might be more reliable in such circumstances, but reliability is considered irrelevant by orthodoxy. The comments made in this section should be read in conjunction with the comments on implied assertions.

that it is admissible to adduce evidence that, while the police were raiding the premises, telephone calls were received in which unidentified callers tried to place bets.[69] However, decisions to admit such evidence ignore the fact that by dialling a telephone number one is addressing oneself to the intended recipient of the call. The act of dialling is a mechanical equivalent of a verbal address. There cannot be a difference between saying 'Look here, Mr Bookie, I wish to place a bet on Lucifer' and dialling Mr Bookie's number and then saying 'I wish to place a bet on Lucifer'.

The theory of operative words was taken to its logical conclusion in *Woodhouse* v. *Hall*[70] where the requirement for a mechanical act was dispensed with. The accused was charged with the management of a brothel and the police were allowed to testify that, while visiting the premises, they overheard unidentified women offering sexual services to unidentified men. If we ask ourselves how the court is to infer the fact in issue from the fact that the statements were made, the answer must be: by reasoning that, when the women made the said statements, they intended to offer themselves to clients as part of the services provided by the establishment. Yet this is the very reasoning that the hearsay rule forbids; it forbids adducing out-of-court statements as proof of facts stated therein, whether expressly or, as here, by implication.[71] Recently the Court of Appeal seems to

---

[69] *State* v. *Tolisano* 70 A2d 118 (1949); *McGregor* v. *Stokes* [1952] V L R 347; *Police* v. *Marchirus* [1977] 1 NZLR 288. In the United States this theory has even provided justification for admitting the statement of an unidentified person who said, while giving heroin to *J*, that *P* will pick it up from *J*, as evidence against *P*: *US* v. *Jackson* 588 F2d 1046, 1049 n 4 (5th Cir). According to Prof. Cross, it 'is truly said that the evidence is only relevant if it is assumed that the unknown callers believed the premises in question to be a betting-shop, but they were acting on their beliefs by attempting to place bets and not merely making assertions about their states of mind. It is therefore arguable that the receipt of the calls is proved as circumstantial evidence of the conduct and not as a set of hearsay statements of the reasons for making them.' *Cross on Evidence*, 5th edn., 10. This view receives support from *Ratten* v. *R.* [1971] 3 All ER 801, 805–6; and *Blastland* [1985] 2 All ER 1095, 1102–3.

[70] (1981) 72 Cr App R 39.

[71] It might be argued that in attempting to place a bet the caller does not explicitly state his belief that the premises are used as a betting shop and that he cannot therefore be said to have made a statement to that effect. However, a similarly inexplicit statement—'Your house is burning and you are going away'—was held inadmissible hearsay when offered to prove the identity of the person to whom it was addressed: *Teper* v. *R.* [1952] 2 All ER 447.

have accepted that an infringement of the rule is involved in these situations.[72]

The methodology just described illustrates a fairly common tendency in this area. A certain type of statement is taken to be reliable. To avoid exclusion the court searches for a convenient tag which may be given to this type of evidence so that it may pass for something other than hearsay. To fulfil its function the tag or label must be associated with admissible evidence. Hence the usefulness of notions such as 'operative words' and 'circumstantial evidence directly relevant to the issue'.[73] Once the label is attached to a piece of evidence, the inhibiting effect of the hearsay rule disappears as if by magic.

Implied Assertions

The hearsay rule excludes out-of-court statements when they are adduced as evidence of any fact stated; but what is a 'statement' and what is a 'fact stated'?[74] A statement is an utterance or a written expression intended to convey some meaning. Hence a statement of fact conveys the meaning that a fact exists or that it does not exist.[75] An utterance can suggest the existence of a fact in several ways and we have now to consider how many of these ways are caught by the hearsay rule.

An assertion of one fact might support an inference concerning the existence of another fact. A's assertion that he paid money into his bank account on a certain day could be used as evidence for the fact that the bank was open. To limit the hearsay rule to express assertions would be absurd because all the dangers involved in relying on the express assertion 'The

---

[72] *Harry* (1988) 86 Cr App R 105. The decision in the case is not only at odds with previous authority (see comment by D. J. Birch, [1987] Crim L Rev 326) but also provides a further instance of the potential of the rule to cause injustice since the evidence excluded was adduced by the accused in order to exculpate himself. See also discussion in the next section.

[73] *Blastland* [1985] 2 All ER 1103. In *Lydon* (1987) 85 Cr App R 221, 224, a piece of paper bearing the accused's name was held admissible to prove his connection with it because 'it could be regarded as no more than a statement of fact involving no assertion as to the truth of the contents of the document'.

[74] See S. Guest, 'The scope of the hearsay rule', (1985) 101 LQR 385.

[75] To state 'that X' is equivalent to asserting X.

bank was open on Monday' are equally present when we are
asked to infer the same fact from the assertion 'I paid some
money into my bank account on Monday.' It is true that the risk
that the last statement was uttered in order to mislead about
the bank opening hours is remote, but the other risks involved
in hearsay—mistaken perceptions faulty memory, and misunderstanding of utterance—are equally present. Indeed, they
are possibly greater because the declarant had no reason to be
as careful about the day of the payment as he would have been
had the day been the principal reason for his statement. Decided cases are not altogether clear on the point, but it is
probably the case that implied as well as express assertions are
excluded.[76]

In *Lloyd* v. *Powell Duffryn Steam Coal Co*[77] the issue was
whether a child was the son of the deceased. The House of
Lords held that the deceased's promise to the child's mother to
marry her, and his declarations to others that he was going to
marry the girl because she was pregnant, were admissible to
prove fatherhood. Lord Atkinson said that the significance of
the statements consisted 'in the improbability that any man
would make these statements, true or false, unless he believed
himself to be the father of the child'. On this view it would seem
that any implied assertion of sufficient probative force would be
admissible. Recently, however, the House of Lords has expressed the view that the case was decided not on the issue of
fatherhood, but on the different issue of whether the child would
have been supported by the deceased, on which statements of
intention would be admissible under an exception.[78]

---

[76] A much-discussed example is the utterance 'Hello, Mr Smith' adduced to
support a conclusion that Smith was present at the time and place where the words
were spoken. In this kind of situation the risk of misinterpretation is particularly
serious because, first, it is easier to mishear or misinterpret short exclamations than
long utterances that are made in some explanatory context, and, secondly, the
evidential value of greetings and the like depends on the degree of acquaintance
between the persons involved and on the circumstances of the greeting. In the
absence of cross-examination it is very difficult to assess these factors and to place
much reliance on such utterances. *Teper* v. *R.* [1952] 2 All ER 447, provides an
illustration. Situations are, however, likely to arise where the utterance is of such
compelling probative force that the courts would find admissibility irresistible.

[77] [1914] AC 733.   [78] *Blastland* [1985] 2 All ER 1095, 1100–1.

Equally inconclusive is the much discussed, if nebulous, decision in *Wright* v. *Doe d. Tatham*[79] which points in the direction of exclusion. There the sanity of the testator was in issue and the question arose whether it was admissible to adduce letters written to the testator by people who knew him for the purpose of showing that the style and manner of the letters indicated that the writers considered the testator sane. After the case had taken a long journey through the courts, the Exchequer Chamber decided that the letters were inadmissible.

A question also arises in relation to implications from conduct. Conduct such as pointing at a man on an identification parade clearly amounts to a verbal assertion and is caught by the hearsay rule. Yet even here the courts are known to admit evidence when they regard it important and significant.[80] When it comes to inferences from conduct not intended to be assertive the position is more complicated.

In *Wright* v. *Doe d Tatham*[81] Parke B posed a number of hypothetical questions: A wager is made by third parties as to the existence of fact X; is payment of a large sum of money under the bet admissible as evidence of X? A captain, having examined his ship, boards it with his family; is this admissible evidence of seaworthiness? Parke B was quite clear that drawing inferences from these acts would infringe the hearsay rule.[82] While it is true that, generally speaking, insincerity is less likely in this type of situation, the danger of misinterpretation is very considerable. The captain may have examined his ship for some reason other than to determine its seaworthiness. Since the inference from such conduct entails an inference about the captain's state of belief an inference has to rely on his powers of perception, judgment, and memory, as in the case of assertive

---

[79] (1837) 7 Ad & El 313. The case is complicated by an alternative ground for the decision based on the fact that the letters in question infringed the opinion rule.

[80] In *Osborne and Virtue* [1973] 1 All ER 649, a policeman was allowed to testify that a witness had pointed at the accused, by way of identification, at an identification parade. See also *Christie* [1914] AC 545. Interestingly, an exclamation of identification is admissible in the US under the exception concerning present-sense impression: Federal Rules of Evidence, Rule 803(1); *US* v. *Napier* 518 F2d 316 (1975).

[81] (1837) 7 Ad & El 313.   [82] Ibid. 386–9.

conduct. Modern support can be found for Parke B's view that implications from conduct infringe the hearsay rule.[83]

The balance of modern authority is, however, in favour of regarding non-assertive conduct, and often non-assertive statements too, as falling outside the hearsay rule. Professor Cross gave the following reason for not regarding Parke B's examples as involving hearsay: 'At no stage in the reasoning justifying its [i.e. the captain's conduct] admissibility is the court asked to assume that something said by one person to another was true.'[84]

It is difficult to follow why so much depends here on whether somebody said something to another. Professor Cross accepted that pointing at a suspect in an identification parade is hearsay despite the fact that nothing is said. He also regarded as hearsay a statement asserting X when it was adduced for proving Y by implication, even though nobody actually said that Y was the case.

The reason for the sophistry devoted to justifying inferences from non-assertive conduct lies in the undesirability of excluding evidence of clearly strong probative value. Much proof in criminal cases depends on drawing inferences from conduct which is relevant because it displays the actor's belief in the fact in issue. If the death of A is in issue it would seem absurd to exclude the evidence that, having examined A, a doctor put him in a mortuary van, to use one of Professor Cross's examples. This is reflected in the American Federal Rules of Evidence which include within the ambit of hearsay only non-verbal conduct which is intended to be assertive.[85]

Whatever the definition of hearsay, there are numerous instances where the courts of all Anglo-American jurisdications

---

[83] *Holloway* v. *McFeters* (1956) 94 CLR 470. See Baker, *The Hearsay Rule*, 6.

[84] *Cross on Evidence*, 5th edn., 473.

[85] Hearsay is defined by Rule 801(c) as 'a statement, other than one made by the declarant while testifying at the trial . . . offered in evidence to prove the truth of the matter asserted'. (Cf. *Ratten* v. *R.* [1971] 3 All ER 805: 'A question of hearsay only arises when the words are spoken "testimonially", i.e. as establishing some fact narrated by the words'.) 'Assertion' is not defined by the rules but has been said to have 'the connotation of a forceful or positive declaration'; *US* v. *Zenni* 492 F Supp 464, 468 (1980). See also Rule 801(a). See also Weinstein, Mansfield, Abrams, and Berger, *Evidence, Rules and Statutes Supplement* (1984) 95.

are prepared to draw inferences from implied assertions either by simply ignoring the problem of hearsay or else by attaching some other label to the evidence, such as the 'operative words' used in the betting-shop situation discussed above.

THE EXCEPTIONS TO THE HEARSAY RULE

Introduction

If the hearsay rule is to be considered a well-defined rule of law, the exceptions to the rule must appear equally well-defined and strict. The traditional view is that just as the rule provides a sharp and clear guide as to practice so do the exceptions.[86] However, an examination of the exceptions shows that this is not the case.

At the outset of his discussion of the exceptions to hearsay Wigmore pointed out that while the rule is based on the assumption 'that many possible sources of inaccuracy and untrustworthiness which may be underneath the bare untested assertion of a witness can best be brought to light and exposed, if they exist, by the test of cross-examination',[87] this consideration gives way on occasion to two countervailing considerations. The first is necessity, as where hearsay provides the only available information and it is felt that admitting hearsay is preferable to foregoing the information altogether. The second consideration is the probability of trustworthiness. As Wigmore put it, if 'a statement has been made under such circumstances that even a skeptical caution would look upon it as trustworthy . . . in a high degree of probability, it would be pedantic to insist on a test whose chief object is already secured.'[88]

---

[86] Lord Reid made this point when he said: 'The whole development of the exceptions to the hearsay rule is based on the determination of certain classes of evidence as admissible or inadmissible and not on the apparent credibility of particular evidence tendered. No matter how cogent particular evidence may seem to be, unless it comes within a class which is admissible, it is excluded.' [1964] 2 All ER 881, 887.

[87] *Wigmore on Evidence*, Chad Rev, vol. 5, para. 1420, p. 251.

[88] Ibid. 252.

The discussion of the exceptions will be confined to the more important ones.[89]

Statements of Deceased Persons

The various exceptions concerning statements of persons since deceased have in common the necessity of securing the information that the deceased possessed; but they are also based on considerations of trustworthiness. This is true, for example, of the exception concerning the declarations of deceased persons against their own interest.[90] Trustworthiness is thought to be enhanced by the insistence that only statements concerning matters on which the deceased had personal knowledge are admissible and by the improbability that a person would tell a lie against his own material interest.[91]

A similar combination of factors lies behind the exception concerning declarations made in the course of duty by persons since deceased. Here trustworthiness is further strengthened by the requirements that the declaration be contemporaneous with the act done in the course of duty, such as recording a fact, and that the declarant had no reason for lying.[92]

Dying Declarations as to Cause of Death

Necessity is the dominant reason for the exception whereby, as Professor Cross put it, the

---

[89] The following exceptions are omitted: statements in public documents; see *Phipson on Evidence*, 13th edn. (1982), para. 25–11 ff. and *Wigmore on Evidence*, Chad Rev, vol. 5, paras. 1632 ff.; published works of a public nature; *Phipson on Evidence*, 13th edn. (1982), ch. 26.

[90] Prof. Cross defined it as follows: 'In criminal cases the oral or written declaration by a deceased person of a fact which he knew to be against his pecuniary interest or proprietary interest when the declaration was made, is admissible as evidence of that fact . . . provided the declarant had personal knowledge of such fact.' *Cross on Evidence*, 5th edn. 551–2.

[91] Though of course it is not impossible that a person would tell such a lie, as we are reminded by *Ward* v. *H S Pitt & Co* [1913] 2 KB 130, 138. See Baker, *The Hearsay Rule*, 66–7. Even apart from the possibility of a person lying against his interest, there is the possibility that the declarant might have regarded the lie as furthering his interest for reasons which are unknown to us.

[92] *Cross on Evidence*, 5th edn. 560. Exceptions, it should be noted, also exist for declarations made by deceased persons about general rights and about pedigree.

oral or written declaration of a deceased person is admissible evidence
of the cause of his death at a trial for his murder or manslaughter
provided he was under a settled hopeless expectation of death when
the statement was made and provided he would have been a competent witness if called to give evidence at the trial.[93]

It is commonly claimed that admissibility of such statements
is justified by their reliability and reference is made to the
sombre dictum of Eyre CB where he explained that dying
declarations are admissible because

they are . . . made in extremity, when the party is at the point of death,
and when every hope of this world is gone; when every motive to
falsehood is silenced, and the mind is induced by the most powerful
considerations to speak the truth; a situation so solemn, and so awful,
is considered by the law as creating an obligation equal to that which
is imposed by positive oath administration by a Court of Justice.[94]

The suggestion of reliability is supposedly strengthened by
the courts' insistence on 'settled hopeless expectation of death'
as a condition to admissibility. It has, for instance, been held
that if the expectation of death is qualified by hope of
recovery—however small—the declaration is rendered inadmissible.[95] However, the assumption of reliability is at odds
with the limitations placed on the exception. If a declaration of
this kind is considered to be reliable, why is admissibility confined to trials for homicide? Why is the declaration only
admissible on the issue of the declarant's cause of death, and is
not admissible when the declarant has, contrary to all expectation, survived the attack? And why, above all, is such a declaration only admissible when the accused is charged with the
homicide of the declarant himself and is not admissible when he
is charged with the homicide of another person?

It seems more reasonable to suppose that the exception is a
concession to moral necessity. It would be publicly unacceptable to let a killer go free because the dying declaration of his
victim fell within the hearsay rule. This has been spelled out in

---

[93] *Cross on Evidence*, 5th edn., 564.   [94] *Woodcock* (1789) 1 Leach 500.
[95] *Phipson on Evidence* 13th edn., 489; and see in particular *Jenkins* (1869) LR 1
CCR 187.

Nembhard v. *R.*[96] where Sir Owen Woodhouse stressed the 'consideration that it is important in the interests of justice that a person implicated in a killing should be obliged to meet in court the dying accusation of the victim . . .'. Being a concession to moral sentiment the exception concedes the bare minimum, hence its limitations.

Res gestae

There is a whole host of exceptions that go under the name of *res gestae*. The term *res gestae*, or part of the matter, generally refers to matters that are contemporaneous with some event under consideration.[97] *Res gestae* overrides all exclusionary rules. The categories coming under the head of *res gestae* are so vague as to suggest that *res gestae* is a general safety valve designed to render admissible otherwise inadmissible evidence when exclusion is considered unacceptable.[98]

At one time it was thought that *res gestae* evidence was not hearsay at all and did not depend on an exception for its admissibility.[99] Nowadays this approach is frowned upon and *res gestae* statements are understood to form exceptions to the exclusionary rules.[100] The former view was not, however, without merit in that it drew attention to the inappropriateness of regarding certain statements as hearsay.[101]

It is convenient to discuss the *res gestae* rules by reference to the different situations they encompass.

Spontaneous Exclamations Statements made during, or immediately after, an event and in the excitement of involvement

---

[96] [1982] 1 All ER 183, 185.

[97] Cf. Stone, '*Res gestae reagitata*', (1939) 55 LQR 66.

[98] For historical survey see Thayer, 'Bedingfield's case: Declarations as part of the Res Gestae', 15 American Law Rev 1 (1881); *Wigmore on Evidence* Chad Rev, vol. 5, para. 1767.

[99] Baker, *The Hearsay Rule*, 160. This usage, as the cases quoted by Baker indicate, was often accompanied by a dubious claim that *res gestae* statements were not being relied upon to prove the facts asserted; a claim more understandable by its inclusionary effect than by its logic.

[100] *Cross on Evidence*, 5th edn. 575–6.

[101] Wigmore observed that 'The nature of the hearsay rule is nowhere better illustrated and emphasised than in those cases which fall outside the scope of its prohibition'. *Wigmore on Evidence*, Chad Rev, para. 1766.

in it are admissible as evidence of facts stated therein. The idea behind this rule is simple: the hearsay rule is intended to exclude unreliable statements, but contemporaneous and spontaneous exclamations are likely to be reliable and need not therefore be treated as ordinary hearsay. At one time this idea was thought to have crystallized into a strict rule of law and this gave rise to sterile conceptualism. Contemporaneity was treated as a technical requirement. In order to ascertain whether a statement was part of an event much learning was devoted to the individuation of an 'event' and to the nature of the connection between words and events.

An illustration is provided by *Bedingfield*[102] where, on a charge of murder by cutting a woman's throat, the accused's defence was that the woman committed suicide. To refute this defence the prosecution proposed to call evidence that the deceased woman rushed out of the accused's room with her throat cut, cried, 'See what Bedingfield has done to me', and immediately died. The evidence was held inadmissible because it did not form part of a relevant event. The cry, as Cockburn CJ put it, 'was something stated . . . after it was all over, whatever it was, and after the act was completed.'[103]

It is only recently that the law has shed some of the more spurious technicalities that have haunted the present topic. We owe this mainly to the Privy Council decision in *Ratten* v. *R.*[104] The accused pleaded accident to a charge of murdering his wife with a shotgun. The accused, his wife, and their children were alone at home. According to the evidence the wife was alive at 1.12 p.m. and dead by 1.20 p.m. on the day in question. A telephone operator was called by the prosecution who testified that at about 1.15 p.m. on that day she plugged into a certain number in response to a call from that telephone number, that a woman's voice, which sounded hysterical and frightened, asked for the police and immediately hung up. That number was the accused's telephone number. The defence objected to the telephonist's testimony on the ground that it amounted to hearsay. Rejecting this contention the Privy Council decided that the

---

[102] (1879) 14 Cox CC 341.
[103] Ibid. See also *Li Shu-ling* v. *R.* [1988] 3 All ER 138, 141.
[104] [1971] 3 All ER 801.

evidence did not infringe the hearsay rule because the caller's statement was admitted as a fact relevant to the issue of whether a telephone call was made from the accused's home during the critical time, and because the call tended to rebut the accused's defence of accident since the caller's voice betrayed fear.[105]

The Privy Council took matters further and held that even if the caller's statement had been adduced as proof of facts stated in it, it would still have been admissible as *res gestae*. It is on this point that the judgment makes its most important contribution, in that it settles that the test of admissibility is really a test of probative weight and not of conformity to some technical definition. As Lord Wilberforce put it:

> hearsay evidence may be admitted if the statement providing it/is made in such conditions (always being those of approximate but not exact contemporaneity) of involvement or pressure as to exclude the possibility of concoction or distortion to the advantage of the maker or disadvantage of the accused.'[106]

Lord Wilberforce was unequivocal in rejecting the previous technical approach under which, as he put it, 'concentration tends to be focused on the opaque or at least imprecise Latin phrase rather than on the basic reason for excluding the type of evidence which this group of cases is concerned with.'[107] However, matters were not allowed to rest there and *Myers* returned to haunt the House of Lords. In *Andrews*[108] counsel for the accused contended that *Ratten* amounted to an extension of the *Bedingfield* principle and was, as such, a breach of the vow in *Myers* not to create new exceptions. Fortunately, the House of Lords found the strength to put that vow behind it and to hold that admissibility depended on probative value, as the test formulated by Lord Ackner clearly suggests:

(1) The primary question which the judge must ask himself is: can the possibility of concoction or distortion be disregard? (2) To answer that

---

[105] The House of Lords in *Blastland* [1985] 2 All ER 1095, 1103, approve *Ratten* on this basis.

[106] [1971] 3 All ER 808.

[107] Ibid. 806. the involvement of the declarant in the event in question has, of course, to be proved by evidence independent of the declaration; Ibid. 808.

[108] [1987] 1 All ER 513.

question the judge must first consider the circumstances in which the particular statement was made, in order to satisfy himself that the event was so unusual or startling or dramatic as to dominate the thoughts of the victim, so that his utterance was an instinctive reaction to that event, thus giving no real opportunity for reasoned reflection . . . . [109]

Whether it is concerned with the definition of hearsay or with the scope of the *res gestae* exception, the decision in *Andrews* does more than any recent decision to shift the basis of admissibility from a fixed definition to a test of trustworthiness. Broadly speaking, hearsay statements of eyewitnesses are admissible if their reliability is secured by intense and unselfconscious involvement in an event.[110] In its generality *Andrews* makes other exceptions redundant. If, for instance, spontaneity and involvement can be proved it is unnecessary to rely on the exception of dying declarations as to the cause of death.[111]

The admissibility of spontaneous exclamations should not however, be allowed to distract the trier of fact's attention from the special dangers of unreliability created by such evidence. Weinstein described it as follows:

when the witness is not an objective spectator, but an observer involved in the event and subject to the distortion of his own heightened emotional and intellectual expectations and needs, the possibility of error in the trier of fact's reconstruction of the event is compounded by the necessity of discounting what the trier believes to be the effect of the involvement on the witness's observation, memory and relation.[112]

Statements Accompanying Relevant Acts   We saw earlier that 'operative words' or 'statements relevant to an issue' are considered to be non-hearsay evidence. The same idea appears sometimes under the guise of a *res gestae* exception. Thus a statement

---

[109] Ibid. 520. In addition to these two points his Lordship makes three more points which elaborate the first two.

[110] For illustration see *Nye and Loan* (1978) 66 Cr App R 252. *Tobi v. Nicholas* (1988) 86 Cr App R 323. The position is similar in the USA: *Wigmore on Evidence*, Chad Rev, ch. 59.

[111] See *Turnbull* (1985) 80 Cr AppR 104, and comment in *Andrews* [1987] 1 All ER 518.

[112] Weinstein, 'Some difficulties in devising rules for determining truth in judicial trials', 66 Col L Rev 223, 232 (1966).

accompanying an act and closely connected with it is admissible to explain the act. A commonly cited example is that of a wife who deposited an axe and a carving knife with a neighbour saying that she was afraid of her husband. At the husband's trial for murdering his wife the statement was held admissible to prove the wife's fear.[113] Acts of this kind would often be inexplicable unless reference is made to the statement accompanying and explaining them. Even the rule against hearsay cannot induce the courts to exclude the entire event nor to commit the absurdity of admitting an act of depositing an axe and a knife, for example, but not the words accompanying the act.

Declarations About Contemporaneous State of Mind   Statements expressing the declarant's present state of mind are admissible to prove his state of mind. The reason given for the exception is that the declarant's statement is usually the best evidence of his state of mind. If, however, admissibility is taken further and the trier of fact is allowed to infer from A's belief in fact X that X itself is true, then the rule against hearsay will have been completely overtaken by the exception because all hearsay statements involve an element of belief. Consequently, the exception is said to allow only the inference that A believed X but does not sanction the inference that X is true. Thus, A's statement that his bank account is overdrawn is admissible to prove that A believed his bank account to be overdrawn, but not to prove that the account was in fact overdrawn.

Driven by common sense our judges have been unable to resist the temptation of drawing inferences from the belief of a person to the facts with which the belief is concerned. No amount of sophistry can alter the fact that in *Ratten* v. *R.*[114] the wife's hysterical call for the police would have given rise not only to an inference that she was afraid of her husband but also to the inference that she must have had good reason for her fear, thus refuting her husband's defence of accident. In *Andrews* the House of Lords expressed the view that the statement 'I am coming for his address' made by a woman to her neighbour

---

[113] *Edwards* (1872) 12 Cox CC 230.
[114] [1971] 3 All ER 801 discussed above.

shortly after the accused had removed a clock from her house was admissible to prove that she had not consented to the removal.[115] Since the issue was whether she had consented at the time of the removal, the statement proved not only the declarant's state of mind at the time of the utterance but also the absence of consent at the earlier time of the removal of the clock.

According to *Moghal*[116] state of mind may prove subsequent facts. The accused was charged with murder in circumstances where the killing could have been done only by the accused or his mistress. The accused was allowed to give in evidence the mistress's declaration that she intended to kill the victim, in order to show that she did the killing. It is notable that when the hearsay implications were considered by the House of Lords in *Blastland*,[117] the admissibility of the statement in *Moghal* was criticized on the ground that it lacked probative value.[118]

It will be remembered that *Blastland* itself turned on a point of probative significance. There the accused, who was charged with the buggery and murder of a twelve-year-old boy, claimed that he had left the boy alive and that the boy was murdered shortly afterwards by another person, *M*, whom the accused described. The defence sought to adduce evidence that *M* had told other persons, before the discovery of the body, that he knew about the murder. According to the defence, *M*'s statements proved his state of knowledge, and this knowledge, in turn, went to show that *M* was the culprit. Lord Bridge pointed out, however, that such an inference amounted to 'mere speculation'; *M*'s knowledge may have been derived from witnessing the murder by the accused and did not necessarily support the inference proposed by the defence.[119] The principle was explained by Lord Bridge as follows:

---

[115] [1987] 1 All ER 519. This observation was made by reference to *Boyle* (1986), unreported.

[116] (1977) 65 Cr App R 56.   [117] [1985] 2 All ER 1095.

[118] Referring to the relevant dictum in *Moghal* where the mistress's statements were held admissible Lord Bridge said: 'I venture to doubt whether it [*Moghal*] was correct, precisely because I cannot see how a threat by Sadiga against Rashid's [the victim] life, made six months before the murder, however virulently the threat was expressed, was of any relevance to the issue whether Moghal was a willing accomplice or an unwilling spectator when the murder was committed.' [1985] 2 All ER 1104.

[119] Ibid. 1100.

statements made to a witness by a third party are not excluded by the hearsay rule when they are put in evidence solely to prove the state of mind either of the maker of the statement or the person to whom it was made. What a person said or heard said may well be the best and most direct evidence of that person's state of mind. This principle can only apply, however, when the state of mind evidenced by the statement is either itself directly in issue at the trial *or is of direct and immediate relevance to the issues which arises at the trial.*[120]

The underlined words refer to cases such as *Ratten* v. *R.*, and tacitly imply that when an inference as to a fact in issue may be cogently drawn from a state of mind this should be done.[121] Consequently, rather than say that there is a rule allowing a statement to prove a state of mind but disallowing the statement to form the basis for an inference as to facts implied by such state of mind, we should regard the propriety of such inferences as depending wholly on their rational cogency.[122]

The American case *Mutual Life Insurance Co* v. *Hillmon*[123] has attracted much attention in this context. In a claim on a life-insurance policy the issue was whether a body found at Crooked Creek was that of the assured, Hillmon, or of a friend of his, Walters. The insurance company's case was that the body was that of Walters who, they alleged, had been murdered by Hillmon. To prove their allegation, the defendants proposed to adduce letters from Walters sent two weeks before the body was found to his relatives saying that he intended leaving Wichita and travelling with Hillmon. The Supreme Court held that the letters were admissible to prove Walters's intention, and that such intention—if proved—made it more probable that Walters

---

[120] [1985] 2 All ER 1099, emphasis added. For comment see: Carter, 'Hearsay relevance and admissibility: declarations as to state of mind . . .', (1987) 103 LQR 106.

[121] Whether the statements in *Blastland* were indeed too weak to prove anything about the accused': innocence is not easy to judge in the absence of a fuller report on the facts. It is interesting to compare here the rejection of a statement of intention to make a social call in *Wainwright* (1875) 13 Cox CC 171 (see also *Pook* (1871) 13 Cox CC 172) with the admission in evidence of a policeman's statement of his intention to make a call in the course of his duty in *Buckley* (1873) 13 Cox CC 293.

[122] See also text relating to n. 115 above and Park, '*McCormick on Evidence* and the concept of hearsay . . .', 65 Minn L Rev 423 (1980).

[123] 145 US 285 (1892).

did go with Hillmon than if there had been no proof of such intention.[124]

Statements Concerning Physical Sensations Declarations concerning the contemporaneous physical sensations of the declarant (e.g. 'my hand is hurting') are admissible evidence of such sensations. The reasons for this are similar to the reasons justifying the last-mentioned exception.

THE WEAKNESS OF THE EXCEPTIONS RATIONALE

There is a commonly held view that all exceptions to the hearsay rule are justified by considerations of necessity and of sufficient guarantees of reliability. This view is not entirely borne out by the law.

There are situations where one particular source of unreliability stands out as the most serious obstacle to admissibility. In such situations the removal of the main source of unreliability might well justify an exception on the grounds that the rationale of the hearsay rule does not obtain. At times the most tricky problem is evaluating the degree to which the witness reporting an out-of-court statement understood correctly what the declarant said.[125] Hence many of the hearsay exceptions have developed around evidence in respect of which no further causes of unreliability remain once the danger of misunderstanding is removed. These are the common-law exceptions that deal, amongst others, with public documents[126] and published

---

[124] Prof. Cross thought that the position would be different under English law because to infer from Walters's statement that Hillmon had agreed to meet him infringes the hearsay rule; *Cross on Evidence*, 5th edn., 588. It is true that there is an infringement here but it is no different from the infringement involved in the inference of a threat from the wife's call for the police in *Ratten* v. *R*. If we are not worried by the possibility that although *A* believes himself threatened by *B*, *B* has not threatened *A*, why should we be worried by the possibility that although *Y* believes that *X* agreed to meet him, this was not the case? Besides, Walters's intention renders probative weight to the inference of a meeting with Hillmon quite apart from Hillmon's agreement; see *Buckley*, (1873) 13 Cox CC 293.

[125] Paradoxically, inferences from hearsay may be most vulnerable on the very point on which we have direct oral evidence.

[126] *Phipson on Evidence*, 13th edn. (1982), ch. 25.

works of a public nature.[127] In addition to this sort of common-law exception most of the exceptions created by statute refer to documents, such as documents made in the course of duty and computer records.[128]

However, in the case of the non-documentary exceptions the removal of one source of unreliability does not guarantee reliability.[129] For instance, spontaneous exclamations are thought reliable because they are made in circumstances which allow no time for concoction or for erosion of memory. Yet of the four sources of unreliability that characterize hearsay only two are reduced: mendacity and faulty memory. At the same time the other two sources, mistaken perception and misinterpretation by the person hearing the exclamation, remain. Frequently, to the extent that the former risks are diminished, the remaining risks are increased. The likelihood of misperception by a declarant is probably above average when he labours under pressure and excitement. The risk of misunderstanding increases because the declarant does not formulate his meaning with care and deliberation and, further, because the person who hears the exclamation might himself be emotionally affected by the event so that his own powers of understanding are reduced.

In the case of the exception concerning state of mind the declarant could not possibly mistake his own state of mind nor is there scope for forgetfulness, but the remaining two risks continue to subsist. His statement may have been misunderstood by the witness and, much more importantly, the declarant may have lied. Most lies are about one's own state of mind. We lie about our intentions, emotions, and attitudes quite frequently. Moreover, much of this lying is morally acceptable for reasons of politeness, respect for another's feelings, protecting of one's own privacy, and the like. It is therefore quite unrealistic to suppose that statements about state of mind are somehow more reliable than other forms of hearsay.

---

[127] Ibid. ch. 26.

[128] See s. 68–72 of the Police and Criminal Evidence Act 1984. In the United States, out of the twenty-three specific exceptions in Rule 803 of the Federal Rules of Evidence devoted to situations in which the availability of the declarant is immaterial, sixteen deal with records.

[129] For an excellent critique of the exceptions strategy see Tribe, 'Triangulating hearsay', 87 Harv L Rev 957 (1974).

It would appear therefore that the appeal to reliability does not provide a convincing justification for some of the more important common-law exceptions. We must therefore consider whether the argument of necessity offers a better explanation.

The first difficulty with the argument of necessity is its lack of clarity. 'Necessity' can be either relative to the rest of the evidence in the case or to the source of the information. In the former sense (which may be referred to as issue-related necessity) it means that the evidence is necessary for resolving the issue because there is no other evidence on the point.[130] This, however, is not the notion that could be said to be at the root of the present exceptions because under the existing exceptions evidence becomes admissible irrespective of whether there is the other evidence on the issue. Here we have to interpret 'necessity' as being relative to the declarant (declarant-related necessity). Accordingly, the exception concerning dying declarations is justified because without an exception the information that deceased persons possessed will be unavailable to the court. However, this kind of 'necessity' does not provide a full explanation for the exceptions because, if it did, it would equally justify admissibility in all situations where the original declarant is unavailable and not only where he is dead. It would have justified, for example, the reception of records in *Myers* v. *DPP* despite the fact that the compilers of the factory records could not be traced. Moreover, the appeal to necessity assumes that hearsay is essential for determining an issue (otherwise we would not bother to create an exception), in which case its unreliability makes it all the more dangerous as a ground for deciding the case.[131]

It cannot be said, therefore, that the exceptions exist only in situations where the hearsay dangers are removed or where there is an overriding consideration of necessity. Rather, the existence of a number of important exceptions is explicable by a desire to diminish the scope for hearsay objections. Indeed, it is not without significance that the debate has always been

---

[130] There can of course be a weaker usage in this sense, as where there is other evidence on the issue but the other evidence is inferior, incomplete, or less convenient. In this last sense a timetable is necessary for ascertaining the departure time of a train even though the information may be obtained in other ways.

[131] See Bentham, *Rationale of Judical Evidence* (1827), vol. 3, bk. vi, ch. 12, p. 564.

concerned with whether the hearsay rule should retreat even further back and not with whether it should penetrate areas from which it is excluded.

American law has seen an interesting development in relation to exceptions. The Federal Rules of Evidence list a considerable number of exceptions and conclude with a residual exception in Rule 803:

(24) *Other exceptions.* A statement not specifically covered by any of the foregoing exceptions but having equivalent circumstantial guarantees of trustworthiness, if the court determines that (A) the statement is offered as evidence of a material fact; (B) the statement is more probative on the point for which it is offered than any other evidence which the proponent can procure through reasonable efforts; and (C) the general purpose of these rules and the interests of justice will best be served by admission of the statement into evidence. However, a statement may not be admitted under this exception unless the proponent of it makes known to the adverse party sufficiently in advance of the trial or hearing to provide the advance of the trial or hearing to provide the adverse party with a fair opportunity to prepare to meet it, his intention to offer the statement and the particulars of it, including the name and address of the declarant.[132]

The residual exception throws into relief the weaknesses of the present exception strategy. The exception requires, in the first place, 'equivalent circumstantial guarantees of trustworthiness'; equivalent, presumably, to those involved in the preceding twenty-three exceptions. These twenty-three exceptions hardly have a common denominator. The residual exception requires that the statement should be 'more probative on the point . . . than any other evidence which the proponent can procure' when the other exceptions are not subject to a comparable requirement. Why should this be a condition to admissibility under the residual exception when, *ex hypothesi*, this exception can only apply where the evidence carries the similar guarantees of trustworthiness as does evidence falling under the other exceptions?[133]

---

[132] The exceptions in Rule 803 obtain irrespective of the declarant's availability. Rule 804, which lists exceptions depending on the declarant's unavailability, contains a residual exception in identical terms.

[133] It seems, however, that the exception is to be applied only in rare situations: *McCormick on Evidence*, 3rd edn. (1984), 907.

THE FUTURE OF THE HEARSAY RULE

Criticism of the hearsay rule is not new. With characteristic meticulousness and idiosyncratic terminology Bentham analysed the various weaknesses of hearsay, both written and oral.[134] He accepted that hearsay was in many cases inferior to direct oral testimony but he believed that hearsay should be excluded only when superior oral evidence was available; otherwise it should be admissible. He maintained that exclusion of hearsay that constituted the best available proof was likely to lead to more mistaken factual conclusions than would its admission. The correctness of this view about the balance of utility still forms the core of the hearsay debate.

Scholarly criticism of the hearsay rule comes down in favour of Bentham's view.[135] But the rule has its defenders too.[136] We seem to be inextricably torn between, on the one hand, our mistrust of hearsay, and, on the other, our resistance to taking the hearsay rule, which expresses this mistrust, to its logical conclusion. The rule ordains exclusion but, as we have seen, many of the exceptions and quasi-exceptions evince a judicial desire to admit a great deal of hearsay evidence, even when reliability remains vulnerable to some hearsay weakness. The inevitable outcome has been a compromise. The compromise of the Anglo-American law is to combine the hearsay prohibition with common-law exceptions, statutory exceptions, judicial inventiveness, and real or pretended ignorance of the more unpalatable consequences of the hearsay rule.

To a large extent both here and in the United States there

---

[134] Bentham, *Rationale of Judicial Evidence* (1827), vol. 3, b. VI, chs. 2, 4, 5. See Keeton and Marshall, 'Bentham's influence on the law of evidence', in *J. Bentham and the law* (1948), 79.

[135] Amongst the critics many great writers are numbered: Thayer, McCormick, Morgan, and Maguire, to mention a few. For a survey see Weinstein, 'The probative force of hearsay', 46 Iowa L Rev 331, 342 (1961).

[136] Wigmore supported the hearsay rule, though his support was conditional on reform; *Wigmore on Evidence*, 3rd edn., vol. 5, para. 1427; id., *The Principles of Judicial Proof*, 2nd edn. (1931), 970. However, as Ezra R. Thayer remarked, making sense of hearsay 'is an undertaking so Procrustean as to defy even the brilliant ingenuity of Professor Wigmore'. 'Observations on the law of evidence', 13 Mich L Rev 355, 360 (1915); for a review of academic literature see Park, 'A subject matter approach to hearsay reform', 86 Mich L Rev 51 (1987).

has for a long time been a form of judicial discretion in the admission of hearsay. It consists, as we have observed, in judicial inventiveness and in studied ignorance of the rule.

To maintain a semblance of a rule of law, the hearsay rule exacts from its faithful exponents an amount of casuistic sophistry that increases with almost every fresh decision on the subject. It might be argued that the tension between hearsay theory and hearsay practice is a healthy one in that the theory discourages the introduction of either worthless or inferior evidence while the pragmatism of the courts secures the admission of evidence that is reliable and useful. But this tension is, in fact, far from wholesome. At the level of exposition we have the rule and its exceptions but at a practical level these do not necessarily determine admissibility. Theory dictates exclusion regardless of the probative force of the hearsay in question. Practice suggests that admission is very much a function of probative force. This diversity has meant that the pragmatism of the courts has had tó remain concealed behind lip-service to the theory of hearsay.[137] Hence decisions in individual cases depend on the extent to which the judge is familiar with the inclusionary tactics. However, the subterfuge involved in these tactics has prevented their even dissemination within the judiciary. Consequently, the ameliorating effects of pragmatism have been haphazard and limited in scope and have been achieved by a process of Byzantine complexity.

This state of affairs itself suggests a solution: the legitimization of the inclusionary principle. Rather than rely on precisely defined and technically complex, and, at the same time, legally inconclusive exceptions, trial judges should have the power to admit hearsay whenever it is of sufficient probative value.[138] The inclusionary power will at once get rid of all the exceptions and their technical manifestations. Moreover, by shifting the emphasis to the evidential value of the statement, the question of whether a piece of evidence is or is not hearsay will also lose

---

[137] Ashworth and Pattenden, 'Reliability, hearsay evidence and the English criminal trial', (1986) 102 LQR 292.

[138] Cf. Glanville Williams, 'The proposals for hearsay evidence', [1973] Crim L Rev 76.

much of its practical significance. Admissibility will no longer be conclusively determined by the categorization of evidence as hearsay. Excessive judicial ingenuity has been devoted to determining whether a photofit picture amounts to hearsay or whether the reporting of what was seen in a video display infringes the hearsay rule, at the expense of a proper examination of the questionable reliability of such pieces of evidence.[139]

This proposal is far from revolutionary. It consists in taking the American strategy of a residual exception to its logical conclusion and replacing it by the kind of guidelines outlined by the House of Lords in *Andrews*.[140] In addition to sufficient probative weight the admissibility of hearsay should be subject to two further conditions. First, where the maker of the statement is available he should be called as a witness.[141] Secondly, notice should be given to the opposite side of an intention to adduce hearsay evidence so that the opponent may have the time to prepare a case against its reception.

Against inclusionary discretion it has been argued by Lempert and Saltzburg that the judiciary cannot be trusted with such discretion because some judges are of insufficient intellectual calibre to exercise it, while others are partial towards the prosecution and would tend to admit more frequently hearsay favouring its case.[142] It can hardly be disputed that judicial ability varies from judge to judge, not only in relation to fact-finding problems but also to law-finding ones. But it is difficult

---

[139] *Cook* [1987] 1 All ER 1049; *Taylor* v. *Chief Constable of Cheshire* [1987] 1 All ER 225, and my comment in [1987] All ER Rev 112. Cf. *Li Shu-ling* v. *R.* [1988] 3 All ER 138.

[140] [1987] 1 All ER 513, 520–1; see discussion relating to n. 108 above. This strategy is preferable to that advocated by the Criminal Law Revision Committee in its 11th report, cmnd. 4991, cls. 30–41 of the proposed bill. The Committee drew up detailed and intricate rules which could well give rise to as much technical complexity as exists at the moment. Earlier attempts at a far-reaching reform by the Model Code of Evidence in 1942 and by the Uniform Rules of Evidence in 1953 failed because the profession was not ready for wholesale abolition of hearsay; see Barton and Cowart, 'The enigma of hearsay', 49 Mississippi L J 31, 33 (1978).

[141] This too is no novel idea in criminal cases. In *Andrews* [1987] 1 All ER 513, 521, Lord Ackner wrote: 'I would . . . strongly deprecate any attempt in criminal prosecutions to use the doctrine [of *res gestae*] as a device to avoid calling, when he is available, the maker of the statement.'

[142] Lempert and Saltzburg, *A Modern Approach to Evidence*, 2nd edn. (1982), 523.

to see why differences in intellectual calibre are fatal to an inclusionary rule more than to any other judicial exercise.

Indeed, judges already have to exercise much discretion in admissibility; they have, for instance, to determine whether the probative force of evidence is sufficient to justify admission, they have to decide whether prejudicial effect outweighs probative force, they have to judge whether the prosecution has adduced sufficient evidence to require an answer from the accused. Even in the admissibility of hearsay there is a strong element of discretion in that enterprising judges are able to find ways around the exclusionary rule by means of technical distinctions. However, the exercise of this inclusionary discretion is conducted at present by subterfuge. The technical ground which leads a judge to decide that a piece of evidence is not really hearsay will often conceal considerations of probative value. It would be better if discretion were exercised in an open and accountable way. A judge who believes that a piece of evidence should be admitted on the grounds that its usefulness outweighs the disadvantages of its admission, should be able to say so and face the consequences of criticism on appeal and public opinion. Accountability will thus make it more difficult for judges to exclude hearsay that tends to prove innocence because they will not be able to take refuge behind rules. Doubtless, judicial ability to exercise discretion properly and correctly will improve with practice.

It has been observed that all the changes in the law, at least this century, have been in the direction of increased admissibility. Impending legislative reform will further eat away at the rule against hearsay. However, although the trend towards the abolition of formal obstacles to the admissibility of useful evidence is welcome, the structure of the proposed provisions leaves a lot to be desired.

Section 23 of the Criminal Justice Act[143] 1988 renders admissible statements in documents in certain circumstances, as where, for example, the maker of the statement is dead or unfit to attend the trial, where the maker is outside the jurisdiction and it is impractical to secure his attendance, or where, although

---

[143] Mr A. Stein drew my attention to a number of difficulties in the Criminal Justice Act 1988. See also D. J. Birch, 'The evidence provisions in the Criminal Justice Act 1988', [1989] Crim L Rev 15.

diligent steps have been taken to find him, the maker cannot be traced.[144]

A more controversial part of this section sanctions, in sub-section (3), the admissibility of a statement 'made to a police officer... [if] the person who made it does not give oral evidence through fear or because he is kept out of the way'. This provision is designed to discourage intimidation of prosecution witnesses by the accused or his henchmen, but it is too rash. It assumes that the witness is available, otherwise his statements will be admissible under the previous exceptions. But if he is available, why should he not be summoned? The licence not to summon an available witness makes it far too easy for witnesses to avoid the duty to testifying. A witness will only have to say that he is afraid to testify and the police or the prosecution will then oblige him with a dispensation by undertaking to submit his statement instead. Such dispensation should not be given unless there is evidence that the accused or somebody connected with him has attempted to intimidate witnesses.[145] Even then every effort should be made to secure their attendance in court so that the trial judge may form an impression of the genuineness of the claim.

Not only is section 23 too wide in this respect, it is also easily side-stepped. It makes an out-of-court statement admissible only when the maker of the statement 'does not give oral evidence'. An accused who is prepared to threaten witnesses will not ask them to refrain from testifying but, rather, to refrain from incriminating the accused. Once a witness appears, his statement is not, under the present exception, admissible as evidence of the truth of facts stated, notwithstanding the fact that he has been threatened.

---

[144] When statements are tendered by the prosecution under these exceptions, the court would do well to insist that the prosecution proves that it has done its utmost to obtain the attendance of the person in question; otherwise it would be only too easy for the prosecution to deny the accused the facility of cross-examination.

[145] Under s. 13(3) of the Criminal Justice Act 1925 the deposition of a person taken before examining justices may be adduced at the trial if it is proved that he is 'kept out of the way by... the accused or on his behalf...'. In view of *O'Loughlin and McLaughlin* (1987) 85 Cr App R 157, it may be that the requirement of s. 13 was too stringent but it is unjustified to do away with the need for any nexus between the accused and the witness's absence from the box. However, in the exercise of their discretion under s. 25(1) of the 1988 Act the courts may insist on a nexus.

Fairness requires that a comparable provision should be made in respect of a statement made to somebody other than a police officer by a person who is not prepared to testify for the accused because he fears the authorities.

Section 24 considerably widens the present exception regarding business records by rendering admissible 'documents created or received by a person in the course of trade, business, profession or other occupation, or as the holder of a paid or unpaid office'. This is subject to the requirement that 'the information contained in the document was supplied by a person . . . who had, or may reasonably be supposed to have had, personal knowledge of the matters dealt with'. It is unfortunate that the section does not make it a condition of admissibility that the person making the document should be acting under some duty to make a full and correct record, especially when he himself has no personal knowledge of the matters recorded.

Both sections 23 and 24 make it clear that the new arrangements are subject to the restriction that they do not render admissible 'a confession made by an accused person that would not be admissible under section 76 of the Police and Criminal Evidence Act 1984'. This is mystifying. The restriction cannot refer to the accused in whose trial the hearsay statement is adduced.[146] The restriction is not confined to confessions that have already been excluded under section 76 but to such as 'would not be admissible' under that section. It follows that when the prosecution adduces *B*'s confession in *A*'s trial, an investigation will have to be conducted into the circumstances of the interrogation that led to *B*'s confession. Since, *ex hypothesi*, *B* will not be in attendance, it is difficult to imagine how such investigation can be conducted.[147]

---

[146] The ref. in s. 23, for example, to a person outside the UK or to a person whose attendance it is impractical to secure must refer to a person other than the accused. It is possible that *Lui Mei Lin* v. *R.*, *The Times* (26 Oct. 1988), offers a way for side-stepping this provision by using the accused's own inadmissible confession not as evidence of facts admitted therein but for the purpose of cross-examining him.

[147] If *C*'s confession is not admissible against him and *D*'s confession is likewise inadmissible, may the prosecution charge only *D* and adduce *C*'s confession? Since *C* is not 'an accused', the proviso would seem not to touch this situation.

Further, the restriction speaks only of confessions that would not be admissible under section 76 but is silent about confessions that are excludable under section 78 of the Police and Criminal Evidence Act 1984. Perhaps it was thought that special reference to the latter section was unnecessary because it confers a discretion to exclude and this discretion may always be exercised.

In devising these provisions the legislature has followed the traditional path of trying to capture instances of usefully probative hearsay within legal definitions. These definitions are complex and are liable to give rise to many disputes which will consume much judicial time and ingenuity. At the end of the day, however, judges will still have to address themselves to the most crucial question: Is the hearsay safe enough to justify admission in evidence? This is because section 25 requires the court to exclude evidence that is admissible under section 23 and 24 if it 'is of the opinion that in the interests of justice a statement . . . ought not to be admitted'. The legislature would have done better to establish, as a general principle, that if the prosecution wishes to adduce hearsay evidence it must convince the court that it is of such probative weight that no injustice will be caused to the accused by being deprived of the opportunity of cross-examination. As regards hearsay adduced by the accused, the general principle should be that it will be admissible whenever exclusion would undermine the interests of justice. For the rest the matter should be left to judicial good sense. There is little doubt that before long the rule against hearsay will be reduced to these two principles and it is a pity that in the mean time valuable resources will be wasted to no good purpose.

I 2

Similar-Fact Evidence

INTRODUCTION

We have so far considered two strategies for preventing mistakes in drawing inferences: requiring suspect evidence to be corroborated and excluding unreliable evidence altogether. A third strategy, employed in relation to prejudicial evidence, is concerned with selective exclusion.[1]

Sometimes an accused's past crimes or some other discreditable conduct have a bearing on the issues arising in his trial.[2] But proof of his crimes or discreditable conduct poses serious problems. At the simplest level such proof may lead to an exaggerated estimation of the probative value of previous crimes and other deviant conduct. The trier of fact may reason that because the accused stole a bottle of whisky from a supermarket five years earlier he must also have been guilty of the theft of the car with which he is now charged.[3]

Evidence of previous crimes might not only distort the inferential process; it could also threaten two central principles of our criminal justice. The first is that in any criminal trial the accused stands to be tried, acquitted, or convicted only in respect of the offence with which he is charged. The second is that conviction must take place only if the jury are persuaded of the accused's guilt beyond all reasonable doubt. I shall refer to

---

[1] This chapter is based on the article: 'Similar fact evidence: the unobservable rule', (1987) 104 LQR 187.

[2] In England and the Commonwealth the term 'similar-fact evidence' refers to evidence of past crime and discreditable conduct. In the United States there is less uniformity; the usual terms are 'evidence of other crimes', 'bad character as evidence of crime', 'similar happenings', and the like. In line with the English practice, the term 'similar-fact evidence' will be used to refer to evidence that shows the accused in a negative light.

[3] *Wigmore on Evidence*, 3rd edn. (1940), vol. 1, s. 57.

these as the principle of confining verdicts to the charge and the principle of full proof.

On being informed that the accused has committed other crimes in the past a jury may decide that the accused deserves punishment whether or not he is guilty of the offence charged. As Wigmore put it, the 'deep tendency of human nature to punish, not because our victim is guilty this time, but because he is a bad man and may as well be condemned now that he is caught, is a tendency which cannot fail to operate with any jury, in or out of court.'[4] This could happen where there is a feeling that the accused got away on previous occasions without conviction or with unduly light punishment; or where the accused is charged with a particular act of prohibited homosexual conduct but a stigma attaches to the sexual inclination as such. In these situations—and there may be many others—there is a real possibility that the jury's verdict will reflect their judgment about the accused's character rather than their findings about the commission of the offence charged.[5]

Knowledge of the accused's criminal past could affect the criminal standard of proof by influencing the jury to be satisfied with proof of guilt that falls short of proof beyond reasonable doubt. This could happen where the jury decides not to give the accused the benefit of the doubt. A decision to convict regardless of doubt is different from a decision to convict in the mistaken belief that the evidence proves guilt beyond reasonable doubt. The former involves a judgment that the accused does not deserve to benefit from the standard of proof and therefore infringes the second principle mentioned, that of full proof.

Broadly speaking, the strategy that our courts have developed for dealing with this problem consists of taking measures to keep the jury ignorant of the accused's discreditable past. However, this strategy is flawed in two ways. First, the tests for exclusion are far too complicated and unevenly applied, and,

---

[4] Ibid.

[5] Of course the trier of fact may also exaggerate the probative force of previous offences and reason that because the accused committed, say, buggery in the past he must also have done so on the occasion in question, but this is different from reasoning: he should be punished whether or not he committed the offence charged. See: Lempert, 'Modeling relevance', 75 Mich L Rev 1021, 1035 (1975).

secondly, the measures taken to prevent undue prejudice when evidence of previous misconduct has emerged are inadequate.

THE *MAKIN* LEGACY

There are two great landmarks in this field. The first is Lord Herschell LC's opinion in *Makin* v. *Attorney-General for New South Wales*.[6] Lord Herschell laid down a two-limbed rule for dealing with similar-fact evidence. According to its exclusionary part the prosecution is forbidden

to adduce evidence tending to show that the accused has been guilty of criminal acts other than those covered by the indictment, for the purpose of leading to the conclusion that the accused is a person likely from his criminal conduct or character to have committed the offence for which he is being tried.[7]

By its inclusionary part, however, such evidence was admissible if it was 'relevant to an issue before the jury and it may be so relevant if it bears upon the question whether the acts alleged . . . were designed or accidental, or to rebut a defence which would . . . be open to the accused'.[8] Upon this theoretical distinction an entire structure of categories of permissible relevance was erected. In addition to those mentioned by Lord Herschell himself further categories were created for evidence showing system, for evidence designed to rebut the defence of innocent association, and many others besides.[9] Whenever evidence could be fitted into one of these categories it was held admissible.

Thompson v. *R.*[10] illustrates the fallacy involved in the distinction. The accused was charged with acts of indecency on two boys. The boys testified that the accused committed the acts on a certain day and made an assignation to meet them again later. At the appointed time the accused turned up but, sensing

---

[6] [1894] AC 57. The second is *Boardman* v. *DPP* [1974] 3 All ER 887, discussed in the following section.

[7] [1894] AC 65.   [8] Ibid.

[9] See *Cross on Evidence*, 4th edn. (1974), 319–38; Cowen and Carter *Essays on the Law of Evidence* (1956), 106.

[10] [1918] AC 221.

the presence of the police, he gave the boys some money and told them to go away. He was approached by the police, tried to escape, and was arrested. At his trial the accused denied any prior acquaintance with the boys whereupon the prosecution was allowed to show that, on his arrest, two powder-puffs were found in his pockets and that photographs of naked boys were recovered from his home. The House of Lords held that this evidence was admissible, notwithstanding that it showed the accused to have a disposition towards homosexuality, because it was relevant to an issue in the case. This issue was variously described as an issue of the credibility of the boys,[11] an issue of the accused's identity and intention,[12] and an issue of the accused's identifying 'hall-mark'.[13]

However, the reason why the evidence in question supported the boys' credibility had to do precisely with the accused's disposition; it made it much more likely that the boys were telling the truth than that they picked the wrong person. Similarly, the evidence tended to prove the accused's identity and intention, because a homosexual person was much more likely than heterosexual men to have made the assignation. And yet again, to describe homosexuality as a 'hall-mark' is nothing more than to attribute to the accused a propensity towards homosexual behaviour. In reality the categories of relevance were, to borrow Professor Julius Stone's metaphor, like pegs upon which the prosecution could hang the accused's dirty linen without much regard to its probative weight.[14]

THE *BOARDMAN* THEORY

The second important landmark is the case of *Boardman* v. *DPP*[15] in which the House of Lords accepted that a distinction between kinds of relevance could not form the basis of a test of admissibility. It decided that admissibility should not depend upon conformity to some definition but on judicial discretion.

---

[11] Lord Finlay LC, ibid. 225.   [12] Lord Atkinson, ibid 229–30.
[13] Lords Sumner and Parker, ibid. 235 and 231 respectively.
[14] See ref. in n. 16 below.   [15] [1974] 3 All ER 887.

Evidence of a similar-fact nature may be admitted if in the trial judge's view its probative force in relation to an issue in the trial outweighs is prejudicial effect.[16] One would have supposed that this decision would have put paid to the earlier technicalities. However, this was not to be.

The seeds for the reversion to distinctions between different uses of evidence were, however, sown in *Boardman* itself. While the essence of the Lords' speeches was the assertion of the rule that similar-fact evidence was admissible if its probative weight exceeded its prejudicial effect,[17] some of their Lordships indicated that in addition to this rule the trial judge possessed a discretion to exclude evidence if its prejudicial effect outweighed it probative value.[18] The suggestion of a difference between discretion and the rule implies that there is more to the rule than a balance of prejudice and probative force, although quite what is unclear.[19] In its own terms, the *Boardman* philosophy leaves no room for a superimposed discretion. As Hoffmann was quick to point out, judicial 'discretion' to exclude evidence when its prejudicial effect outweighed its probative force is the essence of the rule itself.[20] Alternatively the distinction might imply that in relation to evidence falling outside the rule the judge is free to decide in favour of admissibility even though he has come to the conclusion that the prejudicial effect of the evidence does exceed its probative value, which is absurd.[21]

---

[16] This solution was anticipated by Prof. Julius Stone in: 'The rule of exclusion of similar fact evidence: England', 46 Harv L Rev 954, 984 (1932). He showed that early English law determined admissibility by degree of relevance rather than by category of issue. If this is so, the pre-*Makin* law was not very different from the *Boardman* law.

[17] [1974] 3 All ER 887, 892 per Lord Morris, 896 per Lord Wilberforce, 909 per Lord Cross.

[18] [1974] 3 All ER 887, 905-6 per Lord Hailsham, 913 per Lord Salmon.

[19] This problem is explored by Mirfield, 'Similar facts: *Makin* out?', [1987] CLJ 83, 94.

[20] 'Similar facts after *Boardman*', (1975) 91 LQR 193, 204-6. For subsequent discussions see: C. R. Williams, 'The problem of similar fact evidence', (1979) 5 Dalhousie L J 281, 341; Tapper, 'Proof and prejudice', in Campbell and Waller (eds.), *Well and Truly Tried* (1982), 185-8, 208-9; Allen, n. 35 below; Mirfield, 'Similar facts: *Makin* out?', [1987] CLJ 83.

[21] In *Cross on Evidence*, 6th edn. (1985), 337-42, it is suggested that, although both rule-exclusion and discretionary-exclusion involve the same balancing test, the former is subject to greater appellate control than the latter. It is difficult to see why there should be such a difference seeing that in both cases the aim is to prevent prejudice. Nor does it make sense to formulate an appellate policy in terms that suggest a difference of substance between tests of admissibility when none exists.

Once the existence of both a rule of law and a discretionary test was hinted at, commentators set out to construct a new rule around this idea. The favourite source of inspiration has been Lord Hailsham's speech in *Boardman*. His Lordship said: 'When there is nothing to connect the accused with a particular crime except bad character or similar crimes committed in the past, the probative value of the evidence is nil and the evidence is rejected on that ground.'[22]

It is plainly false to say that evidence of bad character or previous offences never carries any probative weight in relation to guilt. As long as we believe that human behaviour is not entirely arbitrary and unpredictable but, on the contrary, that behaviour is on the whole dictated by the make-up of the subject, character will have both predictive force and probabilistic significance concerning a person's past acts or omissions.[23] Perhaps Lord Hailsham used the word 'relevant' to mean 'legally relevant', or 'sufficiently relevant'.[24] Even then, it is not the case that evidence of past crimes has never been admissible in its own right and as the sole evidence for the crime charged.[25] Lord Hailsham's false assumption about relevance led him to formulate the rule that

> ... what is *not* to be admitted is a chain of reasoning and not necessarily a state of facts. If the inadmissible chain of reasoning be the *only* purpose for which the evidence is adduced as a matter of law, the evidence itself is not admissible. If there is some other relevant, probative, purpose than the forbidden type of reasoning, the evidence is admitted, but should be made subject to a warning from the judge that the jury must eschew the forbidden reasoning.[26]

---

[22] [1974] 3 All ER 904.

[23] As Patterson J put it: 'I cannot in principle make any distinction between evidence of facts and evidence of character: the latter is equally laid before the jury as the former, as being relevant to the question of guilty or not guilty: the object of laying it before the jury is to induce them to believe, from the improbability that the person of good character should have conducted himself as alleged, that there is some mistake or misrepresentation in the evidence on the part of the prosecution, and it is strictly evidence in the case.' *Stannard* (1837) 7 C & P 673.

[24] As has been suggested by Hoffmann; n. 20 above, 204–6.

[25] In the case of *Straffen* [1952] 2 All ER 657, the entire case for the prosecution rested on the similarity between the offence charged and the offence that the accused was known to have committed earlier.

[26] [1974] 3 All ER 905–6.

This remark has already grown into 'a most important requirement' to the operation of the rule concerning similar-fact evidence, as the current edition of *Cross on Evidence* would have it.[27] We are told that before the rule excluding similar-fact evidence will bite, the evidence should be relevant by way of the 'forbidden reasoning'.[28] Accordingly, if relevance is not by way of an argument from disposition the judge does not have to consider the balance of prejudice and probative value. There are certainly situations where the evidence of previous crime is relevant in a way which has nothing to do with character, as where the accused's presence at the scene of the crime can be shown by reference to the fact that he had just escaped from prison.[29] According to this interpretation, his escape is relevant only for proving his presence, while the inference that he must be a criminal is logically neither here nor there as far as the issue in question is concerned. But it does not follow that no prejudice can arise from this last inference.

The problem is that disclosure of the accused's criminal record can create prejudice irrespective of the purpose for which the prosecution calls the evidence.[30] Consequently, fairness to the accused demands that whenever evidence of past crime is introduced it should be incumbent on the judge to consider the balance of probative force against prejudice.

Expressing a similar view Hoffmann suggested that in *Makin* itself the evidence was relevant quite apart from disposition and yet it was nevertheless felt necessary to invoke the similar-fact evidence test. The Makins were charged with the murder of a child whose care they had undertaken for reward. Their defence was that the child had died from natural causes. To rebut this defence, the prosecution was allowed to show that the corpses of a number of other children were found buried in the accused's garden. According to Hoffmann the

evidence was relevant on account of the statistical improbability that a number of children which the Makins have at various times had in

---

[27] 6th edn. 316. See also Carter, 'Forbidden reasoning permissible: similar fact evidence a decade after *Boardman*', (1985) 48 MLR 29.

[28] *Cross on Evidence*, 6th edn (1985), 316.   [29] *Straffen* [1952] 2 All ER 657.

[30] For discussion of this point see: R. B. Kuhns, 'The propensity to misunderstand the character of specific acts evidence', 66 Iowa L Rev 777 (1981).

their care would all have died of natural causes. From this it followed
that they were likely to have been murdered . . . But . . . the similar-fact
evidence was not used to show that the accused were the sort of people
likely to have committed the offence. On the contrary, any view about
the characters of the Makins is derived from a conclusion that they
were guilty and not vice versa.[31]

Despite Hoffmann's view that the test was unaffected by this
kind of distinction, the distinction has already acquired the
label of relevance by way of 'objective improbability'[32] and has
been embraced as a test for the application of the similar-fact
rule.[33]

Cross on Evidence deduces from *Boardman* that the stronger the
rest of the evidence (apart from evidence of past crime) the less
is the weight which similar-fact evidence has to carry in order to
be admissible, because the gap that has to be filled to provide
proof beyond reasonable doubt is narrower.[34] This view will be
justified in some situations but not in others. In some cases the
strength of the rest of the evidence will count for the exclusion
of similar-fact evidence rather than its admission because a
point will come at which the rest of the evidence is so strong
that any evidence of past crime can add only little weight but
much prejudice.[35]

Since the decision in *Boardman* the courts have adopted a few
catch-phrases in much the same way as they embraced the
pre-*Boardman* categories. Two phrases have gained currency.

---

[31] n. 20 above, 199.

[32] Piragoff, *Similar Fact Evidence, Probative Value and Prejudice* (1981), 44. Cf. Tapper, n. 20 above, 198.

[33] *Cross on Evidence*, 6th edn. (1985), 318–19; where it is also suggested that while this type of reasoning does not call for the application of the similar-fact rule, the trial judge should have a discretion to exclude the evidence if its prejudicial effect outweighs its probative weight, ibid. 321. As we have seen, this is the very test that we expect the judge to apply to similar-fact evidence.

[34] 6th edn. (1985), 323.

[35] In *Thompson* v. *R.* [1918] AC 221, discussed in text relating to n. 10 above, there was overwhelming evidence against the accused, both direct and corroborative, and the introduction of the powder-puffs and the nude pictures could only have created derision and animosity without contributing much to the ascertainment of guilt. Another writer has suggested that 'where the jury are permitted to reason directly from the accused's criminal disposition the evidence must attain the highest standard of cogency'; Allan, 'Similar fact evidence of disposition: law, discretion and admissibility', [1985] MLR 253, 262. This distinction is as suitable to support a rule about the burden of proof as it was appropriate to sustain an admissibility rule.

One is that 'evidence is admissible as similar-fact evidence if, and only if, it goes beyond showing a tendency to commit crimes of this kind and is positively probative in regard to the crime now charged.'[36] If this means that tendency to commit a specific crime is never sufficient to justify admissibility, it is misleading, as we have seen.[37] If it means that similar-fact evidence must be of sufficient strength to be admissible, then it is so general as to offer little guidance in assessing the balance of prejudice and probative force. The other phrase is 'unique or striking similarity'.[38] This too is misleading. Far less than striking similarity will be sufficient where the rest of the evidence renders the accused's criminal record highly telling.[39] In other situations even striking similarity would not be enough. As Tapper pointed out, to be of significance the similarity has sometimes to be dissimilar from any other person's criminal activities, and peculiar to the accused.[40] Both catch-phrases share the same fault: in an attempt to achieve generality they gloss over the crucial importance of the particular context in determining admissibility. Furthermore, there is still some hankering after the *Makin* rule. In one case the Court of Appeal held that *Boardman* was confined to proof of the accused's previous criminal acts and did not cover situations where his general inclination was relied upon.[41]

Despite the praise lavished on *Boardman*[42] it is not easy to see why so much hope was pinned on this decision when their Lordships went out of their way to deny that they were making any substantial change in the law. Lord Herschell LC's formulation in *Makin* was expressly endorsed by three of the judges in *Boardman* with no disagreement from the other members of the court. True, their Lordships criticized the post-*Makin*

[36] *Rance and Herron* (1976) 62 Cr App R 118, 121. See also: *Scarrott* [1978] 1 All ER 672, 676; *Mansfield* [1978] 1 All ER 134, 137–9.
[37] See text corresponding to n. 25 above.
[38] *Mustafa* (1977) 65 Cr App R 26, 30, 31; *Johannsen* (1977) 65 Cr App R 101, 103; *Novac* (1977) 65 Cr App R 107, 112; *Mansfield* [1978] 1 All ER 134, 137–9.
[39] As in *King* [1967] 1 All ER 379.
[40] Tapper, 'Similar facts: peculiarity and credibility', (1975) 38 MLR 206.
[41] *Lewis* (1983) 76 Cr App R 33. Cf. *Butler* (1987) 84 Cr App R 12, where the opposite view is expressed and where the various 'principles' that have grown after *Boardman* are discussed.
[42] The judgment was heralded by Hoffmann as an 'intellectual breakthrough'; 'Similar facts after *Boardman*', (1975) 91 LQR 193.

tendency to determine admissibility by reference to artificial categories,[43] but it is significant that their Lordships did not disapprove of decisions that had been arrived at under the old approach. Indeed, having considered previous authority Lord Morris was confident that 'judges can be trusted not to allow so fundamental a principle [of exclusion] to be eroded'.[44] Although the House of Lords need not have expressed any view about the correctness of previous decisions to admit or exclude particular evidence, it went out of its way to endorse a number of earlier decisions.[45] It would therefore seem to follow that decisions on admissibility are unaffected by whether the courts follow the *Makin* doctrine or the newer one. This explains, as Mirfield has shown, the recent revival of the *Makin* test.[46]

'PREJUDICE': THE INEPTNESS OF THE *BOARDMAN* RULE

Underlying the speeches in *Boardman*, and many judicial pronouncements before and since, is the assumption that the danger against which the exclusionary policy is erected is that the jury may exaggerate the probative force of the accused's previous misconduct. On this assumption the purpose of an admissibility test is to ensure that juries correctly follow the canons of inductive logic.[47] If this were so, the task of the trial judge would be relatively easy because it would be confined to ensuring that the jury's reasoning from evidence to inference was free of logical mistakes. It is true that many of us make mistakes of inference at times, but it is not the case that we insist on continuing to make the same mistakes once we have been per-

---

[43] Lord Wilberforce, for instance, warned against 'fine distinctions' that 'lend an unattractive unreality to the law'. [1974] 3 All ER 897.

[44] Ibid. 893.

[45] The balancing-test is a tool to be applied by the trial judge in the light of the special features of the individual case and the House of Lords could not have known how previous cases would have been decided had this test been used. See also text relating to n. 81 below.

[46] 'Similar facts: *Makin* out?', [1987] CLJ 83. In *Lunt* (1987) 85 Cr App R 241, the Court of Appeal seemed to imply that *Boardman* may now be considered as merely a gloss on *Makin*. The disinclination of the courts to engage in the *Boardman* weighing exercise may be observed in *Williams* (1987) 84 Cr App R 299. The issue was whether a previous threat by the accused against the victim was admissible to prove his intention. Rather than devote its attention to the probative weight of the threat the Court of Appeal surveyed previous cases going back eighty years.

[47] See Carter, n. 27 above.

suaded of the shortcomings of our reasoning. Indeed, intelligence consists, to a large extent, of the ability and willingness to make continual adjustments to the reasoning process. Trial by judge and jury is based on this assumption. The jury is supposed to be familiar with the rules of common-sense reasoning and the task of the judge is to help them along by pointing out the pitfalls.

Of equal concern, however, are the risks outlined in the introduction to this chapter. Similar-fact evidence may lead the trier of fact to convict the accused because the accused had behaved badly in the past rather than because he committed the crime charged, and thus infringe the principle of confining the verdict to the charge. Or it may lead to a decision not to give the accused the benefit of doubt and thus infringe the principle of full proof. It is the risk to these cherished principles that accounts for the passion shown by judicial pronouncements on the subject, rather than the simple risk of overestimation of probative value. According to Viscount Sankey LC the first limb of Lord Herschell LC's famous dictum expresses 'one of the most deeply rooted and jealously guarded principles of our criminal law' and is 'fundamental in the law of evidence as conceived in this country'.[48] In the United States Cardozo CJ said:

Fundamental hitherto has been the rule that character is never an issue in a criminal prosecution unless the defendant chooses to make it one. . . . In a very real sense a defendant starts his life afresh when he stands before a jury, a prisoner at the bar.[49]

The principle of confining the verdict to the charge and the principle of full proof represent social choices. Such choices are not derived from the canons of factual reasoning.[50] This factor

[48] *Maxwell* v. *DPP* [1935] AC 309, 317, 320.

[49] *People* v. *Zackowitz* 172 NE 466 (1930).

[50] The first principle is based on the belief that it is unfair that an accused should be answerable, at his trial, for anything but the offence charged (except that at the sentencing stage his record may influence his punishment). The second represents a choice about the risk of mistake that society is prepared to run in bringing about conviction of the guilty. Deviation from these principles would also amount to an infringement of the general requirement of fairness: treating like cases alike. A jury that accepts a low standard of proof in conviction or that convicts because of the accused's record regardless of his responsibility for the offence charged, treats an accused with a criminal record differently from the way it would treat an accused without a criminal record.

has important implications for our admissibility test. Since 'prejudice' means also violation of these non-inductive principles, it follows that the test of admissibility requires the balancing of incommensurable factors: the probative weight of the evidence, which is controlled by inductive reasoning, against the likely risk to the two principles of criminal justice, which represent non-factual choices.

The mere fact that admissibility depends on balancing of incommensurable factors does not of itself, however, account for the difficulty involved in determining admissibility.[51] What accounts for the difficulty is the problem of moral or non-factual 'prejudice' as distinguished from factual mistake, to which neither the *Boardman* nor the *Makin* rules address themselves.

Both rules share the strategy of keeping the jury unaware of the accused's criminal record as far as possible. This exclusive concentration on securing the jury's ignorance leaves the courts powerless to deal with the problem of prejudice in those cases where they feel obliged to admit the evidence. It does not follow that because evidence of past crime has been admitted on the basis that its probative value exceeds its prejudicial effect, it will not have a prejudicial effect in the sense of causing a departure from our two principles of criminal justice. To protect the accused from prejudice arising from evidence that has been admitted, the trial judge exhorts members of the jury to have regard only to its probative force and not to allow themselves to be influenced in other ways. However, it is the notorious ineffectiveness of this kind of injunction that is responsible for the rule in the first place. There is little protection against departure from these principles once evidence is admitted in accordance with the rule.

The present strategy has nothing to contribute when the accused's record has percolated through to the jury in other ways. For instance, a jury that has not heard evidence of the accused's good character might well assume that he has a bad

---

[51] Relevance itself, the *sine qua non* of admissibility, is not only a matter of logical probability, it is also a matter of sufficiency. Legal relevance is 'a *variable* standard, the probative value of the evidence being balanced against the disadvantages of receiving it such as taking up a lot of time or causing confusion', to borrow from Hoffmann; n. 20 above, at 205. Judges find it quite straightforward to determine sufficiency of relevance.

character.[52] To say that this does not happen very often is, again, to place too much store on a questionable strategy of ignorance. It is an unhealthy law that has to rely for its implementation on ignorance of its rules. In fact trial judges themselves sometimes undermine public ignorance in this respect. A practice has developed whereby, after the verdict, judges detain the jury when sentencing an accused with previous convictions. The aim seems to be to fortify the jury in their conclusion, when the jury has convicted, or to give them cause for regret, when the jury acquitted but the accused is convicted on other counts on which he had pleaded guilty.

It would be unjust, however, to blame the Privy Council in *Makin* or the House of Lords in *Boardman* for these failings. The roots of the problem are buried deep in our theory of criminal procedure.

'LEGITIMATE PREJUDICE'

Is it really the case that a criminal trial is strictly concerned with the question of fact: 'Did the accused do the act charged'? Does the accused really, in the words of Cardozo CJ, 'start his life afresh when he stands before a jury, a prisoner at the bar'?[53] There are a number of respects in which the accused's record, for both moral and immoral behaviour, is allowed to affect the verdict or, at any rate, is tolerated when it does so.

The Accused's Good Character

All Anglo-American systems of jurisprudence recognize the right of an accused person to give evidence of his own good character. It has been suggested that the accused's good character is not really relevant to the charge laid against him and that it is only made admissible by the law as a gesture of humanity.[54] But what is this element of 'humanity'?

---

[52] This happens where members of the jury have heard several trials and have been treated to evidence of good character in some cases but not in others.

[53] See n. 49 above.

[54] *Hurst* v. *Evans* [1917] 1 KB 352, 357; *Miller* [1952] 2 All ER 667. Humanity is also given as a reason for exclusion of discreditable evidence: *Sims* [1946] 1 All ER 697, 700.

The criminal trial determines moral guilt, as well as legal liability. It is the moral guilt, above all, which justifies the infliction of suffering on the guilty, especially when the punishment is justified by considerations of retribution. Moral standing is relevant and admissible at the sentencing stage because we believe that, amongst other considerations, punishment should be in proportion to the past behaviour, good or bad, of the accused. But a conviction is of itself a form of punishment. Its very existence could deal a fatal blow to the accused's standing in the community, to his self-respect, and to his economic prosperity. It is therefore understandable that any tribunal should wish to know not only whether the accused committed the offence charged but also whether he deserves to be convicted.

Aside from its strict probative significance, the accused's good character could, and most probably does, influence the jury's deliberation in a number of ways. It could lead the jury to decide that in view of the accused's unblemished character they will run no risk of a mistaken conclusion of guilt. Or they could come to the conclusion that although the elements of the offence have been proved it would not be right to convict such a worthy person. In either case there will be a departure from our twin principles of criminal justice.[55]

It is difficult to consider such departures as aberrations. The rule entitling the accused to give evidence of his own good character acknowledges this facet of the criminal trial or, at the very least, demonstrates tolerance for the wishes of those accused who prefer to have their guilt determined by reference to their moral standing as well as to the evidence on the indictment. When a trial judge instructs the jury to disregard the accused's criminal past he is asking them to refrain from doing something which is both natural outside the law and permissible in court when the accused's merits, rather than demerits, are put on the scales.

---

[55] The first decision departs from the principle that proof beyond reasonable doubt of the offence charged is both a necessary and sufficient condition for conviction. The second decision is at odds with the principle that the verdict should be concerned only with the accused's liability for the offence charged.

The Accused's Bad Character

Nowhere is the ineptness of the present strategy more obvious than in relation to the cross-examination of the accused on his previous convictions and bad character.[56] Such cross-examination is authorized by the notorious section 1(f) of the Criminal Evidence Act 1898 if the accused

(ii) . . . asked questions of the witnesses for the prosecution with a view to establish his own good character, or has given evidence of his good character, or the nature of the conduct of the defence is such as to involve imputations on the character of the prosecutor or the witness for the prosecution; or
(iii) he has given evidence against any other person charged in the same proceedings;

Even if he avoids calling evidence of good character, the accused retains limited control over the occasions on which he is liable to be cross-examined about his bad character. If, for example, his defence is that the Crown witness has falsely implicated him in the offence because he would not give in to the witness's blackmail, this justifies cross-examination on his criminal record. The accused need only deny that he made the confession attributed to him by the police to lay himself open to cross-examination of this kind.[57]

In these situations the accused's criminal record is disclosed not because its probative force exceeds its prejudicial effect but on what is known as the 'tit-for-tat' principle, i.e. if 'the accused is seeking to cast discredit on the prosecution, then the prosecution should be allowed to do likewise'.[58] But what exactly is the prosecution supposed to achieve by such cross-examination? As we shall see, the judge must direct the jury that they may only take the accused's criminal record into consideration in determining his credibility but not his guilt. There are a number of objections to this type of instruction.

First, it is based on the fallacy that there is a significant distinction between relevance to credit and relevance to guilt.[59] Secondly, even if there were such a distinction, it does not seem

---

[56] This matter is comprehensively discussed in the next chapter.
[57] *Britzman* [1983] 1 All ER 369.
[58] *Selvey* v. *DPP* [1968] 2 All ER 497, 521.
[59] See the discussion in Ch. 7.

to govern the practice under section 1(f)(ii) since the prosecution is not confined to cross-examining only on previous convictions that reflect on the accused's veracity as a witness. Thirdly, the inability of the jury to avoid the 'forbidden reasoning' is, as we have seen, the reason for the similar-fact rule and also for the rule that the accused is not liable, as is any other witness, to unlimited cross-examination about his character. It cannot, therefore, be assumed that a warning will be effective to prevent prejudice.

Joinder of Counts and of Accused

Under the Indictments Rules 1971, rule 9, charges regarding different offences 'may be joined in the same indictment if those charges are founded on the same facts, or form, or are part of a series of offences of the same or a similar character.' It is not a necessary condition of joinder that the evidence on one offence be admissible on the other offences charged in the same indictment. In the leading case of *Ludlow* v. *Metropolitan Police Commissioner*[60] the House of Lords approved of joinder of an offence of attempted larceny from one pub with the offence of robbery with violence in another pub some two weeks later although the evidence regarding one offence was clearly inadmissible regarding the other. It was sufficient that the offences were similar in nature and that they happened in neighbouring pubs within sixteen days. The juxtaposition of these offences was bound to create the impression that the accused was the kind of man who was inclined towards theft offences in pubs, especially after he had a few drinks. However, Lord Pearson brushed aside the risk of prejudice by saying that present-day juries 'could be relied upon in any ordinary case not to infer that, because the accused is proved to have committed one of the offences charged against him, therefore he must have committed the others as well,'[61] despite the fact that this is

---

[60] [1970] 1 All ER 567.
[61] Ibid. 575. It now seems that a jury can also be relied upon to perform extraordinary mental gymnastics. In *Lui Mei Lin* v. *R., The Times*, (26 Oct. 1988), it has been held that when a co-accused uses an inadmissible confession in cross-examining the accused, the jury must be told not only that the confession is not evidence of the facts admitted in it, but also that it may only be taken into account for judging the credibility of the accused's evidence against the co-accused and not his credibility in denying his own guilt.

the very assumption about juries that the courts have so strenuously resisted in relation to similar-fact evidence. Indeed, in *Boardman* Lord Cross drew attention to the inconsistency:

If the charges relating to different offences are tried together it is inevitable that the jurors will be influenced, consciously or unconsciously, by the fact that the accused is being charged not with a single offence against one person but with three separate offences against three persons.[62]

Despite subsequent support for Lord Cross's view,[63] his reservations have been held not to have affected the *Ludlow* principle.[64] The result is that while similar-fact evidence has to be justified by reference to special factors, the test for joinder is diametrically opposite:

The judge has no duty to direct separate trials . . . unless in his opinion there is some special feature of the case which would make a joint trial of the several counts prejudicial or embarrassing to the accused and separate trials are required in the interest of justice[65]

There are numerous instances where joinder has been struck down on the grounds of prejudice, but the fact remains that joinder is allowed where evidence relating to one offence is inadmissible regarding the other. The reason for this is that the rules of joinder are not primarily designed for increasing the factual accuracy of verdicts. Generally, joinder serves the purpose of ensuring economy of resources, but at times joinder is demanded by more important social considerations. The criminal trial is not only a forum for ascertaining the facts of offences but also a forum for giving expression to society's disapproval of crime and for reinforcing public confidence in law enforcement. Holding separate trials for offences forming part of the same perceived onslaught on the community could

---

[62] *DPP* v. *Boardman* [1974] 3 All ER 887 910–11. For discussion of this aspect see Weinberg, 'Multiple counts and similar fact evidence', in Campbell and Waller (eds.), *Well and Truly Tried* (1982), 250.

[63] *Novac* (1977) 65 Cr App R 107, 111; and possibly *Mansfield* [1978] 1 All ER 134, 137.

[64] *McGlinchey* (1984) 78 Cr App R 282, 287–8. See also *Marsh* (1986) 83 Cr App R 165.

[65] *Ludlow* v. *Metropolitan Police Commissioner* [1970] All ER 567, 575–6.

fail to satisfy the public desire to resolve the perceived threat, especially if verdicts turn out to be inconsistent. This does not mean that the purpose of joinder is to obtain conviction on all the joint counts; it simply reflects that differing verdicts are more likely to command public respect when the connected incidents have been looked at together.[66]

That the public dimension could be the predominant reason for joinder was made clear in the notorious gangland murders case of the Kray brothers. The Court of Appeal recognized that the joinder of two separate murder offences involved 'inevitable prejudice' but concluded that the fact that the murders were 'committed in cold blood and ... bore the stamp of a gang leader asserting his authority by killing in the presence of witnesses whose silence could be assured by that authority ... made it desirable *in the public interest* that these two unusual cases should be examined together'.[67]

Intended and Accidental Disclosure of the Accused's Record

There is a marked contrast between the judiciary's approach to admitting the accused's criminal record in evidence and its relaxed attitude to the consequences of jury-knowledge of a criminal record which has come about otherwise than by its formal admission in evidence.

Where it accidentally emerges during the trial that the accused has a criminal record, the trial judge has a wide discretion in the matter, with which the Court of Appeal has been

---

[66] Where the accused pleads guilty to some counts and the trial continues on others, the jury has to be kept ignorant of the guilty pleas; *Darke* (1937) 26 Cr App R 85. The fact that the jury must be kept ignorant of the guilty pleas is no indication that the joinder was incorrect *ab initio*. It indicates a desire to avoid the effect that such knowledge might have on the jury when it is anyway possible to resolve a number of counts in one trial. If the jury have been informed of the guilty plea, the conviction would not necessarily be quashed: *Lashbrooke* (1958) 43 Cr App R 86.

[67] *Kray* [1969] 3 All ER 941, 944–5, emphasis added. In *Makin* v. *A-G for New South Wales* [1894] AC 57, there was sufficiently compelling evidence to prove the murder of the baby with which the indictment was concerned, yet the prosecution called evidence of the discovery of the other bodies because, presumably, it was felt that public concern demanded that the whole enormity of the accused's enterprise be brought exposed.

very reluctant to interfere.[68] In *Coughlan and Young*[69] Coughlan stood charged of an IRA conspiracy to cause explosion. During his cross-examination a co-accused said: 'I was sentenced in Manchester with Coughlan, we got sixteen years'; the clear implication being that the Manchester verdict was also for an offence connected with the IRA. The Court of Appeal felt that this kind of casual remark tends to be forgotten by the jury and that no prejudice occurred.[70]

In one case a conviction was challenged because it subsequently became apparent that one of the jurors was familiar with the accused's criminal record and considered them to be villains. The court rejected the challenge saying:

> This court knows of no case, and none has been referred to us, in which knowledge of a prisoner's previous convictions or character by a member of a jury has been held to be . . . an automatic disqualificaton, or to prevent him from hankering to the evidence, observing the oath which he has taken, and affording the prisoner a fair trial.[71]

Similarly, there appears to be overwhelming reluctance to interfere with guilty verdicts challenged on the basis that pre-trial publicity impaired the fairness of the trial. As a result, courts are easily satisfied that the pre-trial emergence of the accused's criminal record did not influence the jury. In *Malik*[72] the Sunday Times wrote of the accused shortly before his trial for incitement to racial hatred that he was a 'brothel keeper, procurer and property racketeer'. The court found the newspaper guilty of serious contempt which was likely to prejudice the fair trial. At the same time the court held that fair trial had not been prejudiced because the accused's credibility was not in

---

[68] *Palin* [1969] 3 All ER 689; *Weaver* [1967] 1 All ER 277; *Featherstone* [1942] 2 All ER 672. See *Taylor* (1934) 25 Cr App R 46 where the conviction was quashed because a previous conviction was inadvertently elicited by the judge himself.

[69] (1976) 63 Cr App R 33.

[70] Ibid. 38. Cf. *Lamb* (1980) 71 Cr App R 198.

[71] *Box* [1963] 3 All ER 240, 242. See also *Hood* [1968] 2 All ER 56. It has been said that if the law had required that, upon such disclosure, the jury must be discharged, 'it would simply make it too easy if a trial is not going well for one co-accused to say something which would secure his co-accused the advantage . . . of a new trial'; *Sutton* (1969) 53 Cr App R 504. However, a similar approach is adopted even where there is no danger of tactical manipulation.

[72] [1968] 1 All ER 582 Note.

issue. It is true that the accused accepted uttering the words complained of, but he denied that he intended them to convey the normal meaning. Consequently, both his intention and credibility were very much in issue.

In *Savundranayagan*[73] the accused was charged with fraud offences which, at the time of their discovery, attracted much public attention, and newspapers reported the accused's unsavoury record extensively. Subsequently he was interviewed on the television, where the object was 'to establish his guilt before an audience of millions of people'; an event that the court found 'deplorable'.[74] None the less, the court refused to interfere with the conviction on two grounds: first, because the accused voluntarily submitted to the interview, and, secondly, because the trial took place eleven months after the interview and the jury were warned to put the pre-trial publicity out of their minds. It is difficult to see the force of the first reason when the court itself emphasized that the accused had not appreciated the nature of the interview.[75] The force of the second reason is undermined by the fact that its two parts cut across each other: the strong warning must have been necessary because of the real possibility that the jury's memory had not faded; if it had, it may well have been revived by the warning.

The likelihood of prejudice cannot depend on how the jury learns of the accused's criminal record. True, when the record is given in evidence by the prosecution it receives more prominent attention, but then at least the judge can try and forestall undue prejudicial effect in his summing-up, whereas on the occasions that the accused's record has been introduced accidentally this may not be possible.

'LEGITIMATE PREJUDICE' AND THE SIMILAR-FACT EVIDENCE RULE

This survey has drawn attention to a number of factors. Prejudicial information may emerge and influence the jury without

---

[73] [1968] 3 All ER 439 Note.   [74] Ibid. 441.
[75] Which was manipulated by 'a skilled interviewer whose clear object was to establish his guilt before an audience of millions of people'. Ibid.

having first passed through the judicial test of probative weight and prejudicial effect. When this happens deviation from the principles of criminal justice may go unchecked. The principle of confining the verdict to the charge is by no means absolute. The accused is allowed to choose not to start his life afresh at the bar, but to be judged on his entire moral record.

It is against this background that we must now consider the theory concerning the admissibility of similar-fact evidence. If deviation from the principle that the accused is tried only for the offence charged and nothing else is common, we cannot expect to find strict compliance with the principle when it comes to the admissibility of evidence. Looked at from this point of view Lord Herschell LC's famous dictum[76] appears in a new light. It expresses neither an antithesis between kinds of relevance nor one between degrees of relevance but a tension between an ideal and reality. The exclusionary part reflects the aspiration that the accused be tried only for the offence charged, while the inclusionary part accepts that this cannot always be achieved. Much of the dissatisfaction with the rule concerning similar-fact evidence, whether it be the *Makin* or the *Boardman* version, is caused by unduly high expectations. Judges have protested too much about the importance of the principle of exclusion and, as a consequence, their record on admissibility has been found wanting and has prompted a continual search for fresh and better rules. But when it comes to practice, admissibility is determined by the same imprecise judicial instincts about acceptable and unacceptable prejudice that determine the result in other areas, where no pretence of a rule is maintained.

In the application of the admissibility test judges too are prey to prejudice. In *Sims*[77] the accused was tried on an indictment containing seven counts. Three charged him with buggery with three men, three charged, in the alternative, with gross indecency with the same men, and one concerned indecency with a fourth man. The accused applied for severance of the counts relating to different men but was refused and subsequently convicted.[78] The Court of Appeal held that severance was right-

---

[76] *Makin v. A-G for New South Wales* [1894] AC 57, 65.
[77] [1946] 1 All ER 697.
[78] He was acquitted on the indecency charge with the fourth man. Originally the indictment also contained three counts of indecent assault on three boys, but these were severed.

ly refused since evidence relating to one complainant was admissible on the charges relating to the others. In a judgment largely prepared by Denning J, delivered by Lord Goddard LCJ, and subscribed to by three further High Court judges, the court said:

Sodomy is a crime in a special category because, as Lord Sumner said in *Thompson* v. *R* ([1918] AC 221, at p. 235): 'Persons . . . who commit the offences now under consideration seek the habitual gratification of a particular perverted lust, which not only takes them out of the class of ordinary men gone wrong, but stamps them with a hallmark of a special and extraordinary class as much as if they carried on their bodies some physical peculiarity.' On this account, in regard to this crime we think that the repetition of the acts is itself a specific feature connecting the accused with the crime and that the evidence of this kind is admissible to show the nature of the act done by the accused.[79]

Sims was reviewed in *Boardman* where the House of Lords disapproved of the idea that sodomy was in a special category. Lord Cross said:

The attitude of the ordinary man to homosexuality has changed very much even since *R* v. *Sims* was decided and what was said on that subject in 1917 by Lord Sumner in *Thompson* v. *R*—from which the view that homosexual offences form a class apart appears to stem—sounds nowadays like a voice from another world.[80]

Clearly then, Lord Cross did not disapprove of *Sims* and of *R.* v. *Thompson* because they failed to engage in the balancing process. He was prepared to support the result reached in *Sims* on the grounds, also mentioned in that case, that the acts charged in relation to the different complainant bore a 'striking similarity'.[81] There is no escaping from the fact that the 'striking similarity' in *Sims* stemmed from the court's moral view that 'The specific feature in such cases lies in the abnormal and perverted propensity which stamps the individual as if marked by a physical deformity.'[82]

---

[79] [1946] 1 All ER 701.   [80] [1974] 3 All ER 909.

[81] Lord Cross's support for the actual result in *Sims* may not have been wholehearted; [1974] 3 All ER 909–10. But Lord Hailsham leaves us in no doubt about his approval, subject to the reservation that homosexuality did not form a special category. Ibid. 903.

[82] [1946] 1 All ER 697, 700. To suppose that judges can get away from this kind of moral view when assessing probative weight has as much reality to it as the supposition that juries can put it aside when passing judgment.

The similarity in *Sims* consisted in the fact that the acts of buggery took place in the accused's home. This very combination of facts was commented upon by Bridge LJ in *Novac*[83] where he said:

We cannot think that two or more alleged offences of buggery . . . committed in bed at the residence of the alleged offender with boys to whom he had offered shelter can be said to have been committed in a uniquely or strikingly similar manner. If a man is going to commit buggery with a boy he picks up, it must surely be a commonplace feature of such an encounter that he will take the boy home with him and commit the offence in bed.[84]

These proclivities must have been as commonplace in 1946 and in 1974 as in 1977. What accounts for the difference is a change in the moral attitude to homosexuality and not a revision of the probabilistic calculation. *Sims* was decided on the *Makin* rule. The *Boardman* test, according to the judges in that case, would have made no difference to the result in *Sims*. But the *Boardman* test applied to a *Sims*-type situation in *Novac* produced different results. How, then, can we believe that it is the legal rule concerning the balance of probative weight and prejudice that accounts for these results?

ADDRESSING THE MORAL PROBLEM

As we have seen, the protection of the accused from prejudice is unsatisfactory. The belief, which still lingers in our law, that legal categorization of prejudicial evidence can help the trial judge exercise his exclusionary discretion has distracted judges from the need to combat their own prejudices, as the discussion of *Sims* has shown. By concentrating on admissibility the present strategy largely ignores the reality that disclosure of the accused's criminal record is likely to have important consequences for the principle of confining the verdict to the charge and for the principle of full proof. On the occasion where the accused's past record is either admitted under the rules or has

---

[83] (1977) 65 Cr App R 107.   [84] Ibid. 112.

transpired otherwise the protection from prejudice is inadequate.

At present the assumption is that only persons 'who have not been trained to think judicially' yield to prejudice.[85] This is simply not so. Though their threshold of susceptibility may differ somewhat, judges, in common with most other human beings, are susceptible to moral influence and prejudice. Conversely, most citizens share with the judiciary the sentiment that a conviction must reflect only the transgression in question and the belief that a conviction is not justified when guilt has not been proved beyond reasonable doubt, though popular appreciation of these principles may be less clear. than their judicial understanding. Thus to combat prejudice judges need appeal to the jury's own sense of justice. However, judges do the very reverse. When the accused's record is investigated under the section 1(f)(ii) of the 1898 Act the jury are told that in law they must consider the criminal record only in relation to the accused's credibility and not his guilt. Since in common sense a criminal record would often be relevant to guilt, such a direction suggests that there is some special legal rule to be observed here. By creating a conflict between the normal standards familiar to the jury and legal standards, judges have limited their own ability to guide the jury because juries are unlikely to defer to a legal standard which they do not understand or for which they have no sympathy.

A more effective way of combating prejudice would be to bring into the open the scope of prejudice created by evidence of past criminal record and strive to persuade juries that the principles of criminal justice, which require resisting prejudice, reflect their own perceptions of justice. If members of the jury are made to understand this, they would be better able to resist the temptation of convicting because of the accused's bad character. Commenting on the strategy of dealing with prejudice by rules of evidence Weinstein wrote:

The rules of evidence can do little, by themselves, to prevent conscious distortions by the trier. They should, however, permit all possible relevant evidence and argument to be brought to bear on the trier so

---

[85] *Bond* [1906] 2 KB 389, 395–6.

that he will at least be forced to bare his soul to himself and to consciously, though silently, justify his actions.[86]

The availability of more effective means of persuading a jury to abide by the principles of criminal justice will make the question of admissibility less important because the tools will be in place for counteracting prejudice. At the same time the judicial articulation of the nature and scope of prejudice will also help judges to resist their own prejudices when determining admissibility. Judges will still be required to practise discrimination in admissibility because we should not court moral conflict unnecessarily. However, in determining admissibility judges will be subject to less pressure and will not have to seek refuge in special rules.[87] Where prejudicial information has emerged incidentally, without passing the judicial filter, trial judges will have the instrument of persuasion for reducing its danger and will not have to do as they have felt obliged and turn their backs to it.

---

[86] Weinstein, 'Some difficulties in devising rules for determining truth in judicial trials', 66 Col L Rev 223, 238 (1966).

[87] An analogy is provided by the advice to prosecuting counsel to eschew unnecessarily emotive language which can excite sympathy for the victim or prejudice against the accused in the minds of the jury. Where the facts themselves may have this tendency, it is desirable for the prosecuting counsel in his opening speech to warn the jury that neither sympathy nor prejudice should be allowed to influence their approach to the evidence. *Archbold's Pleading, Evidence and Practice in Criminal Cases*, 42nd edn. (1985), s. 4–177, p. 328. Prosecuting counsel should regard themselves as ministers of justice: *Puddick* (1865) 4 F & F 497, 499; *Banks* (1916) 12 Cr App R 74, 76.

13

Cross-Examination of the Accused

The probative force of testimony depends on four factors: on the reliability of the witness's perception of the event to which he deposes, on his memory, on his veracity, and on the extent to which his testimony is correctly understood. When an accused person testifies in his own defence attention will naturally be focused on his veracity. This chapter discusses the problems involved in challenging an accused on this point.

Broadly speaking, the cross-examiner can employ two tactics to impugn the veracity of a witness. He can attempt to show that the witness has lied in his testimony on particular points. For instance, the cross-examiner may extract an admission from the witness that he has lied or he may call other witnesses to prove this. Alternatively he can try to undermine the witness's credibility by showing that, whether or not it can be positively proved that the witness lied on the point in question, the witness is the kind of person that cannot be believed on his oath.

We may say that this is a difference between direct and indirect proof of mendacity. Direct proof of mendacity takes place where it is shown that the witness's testimony is at variance with the facts. Indirect proof of mendacity is proof that bears not on the truth of the witness's statements in-chief but on his general record for truth-telling; the testimony of a person who is given to lying carries, naturally, less weight. However, although different tactics of undermining veracity are involved, there is no difference of principle since both tactics are directed to reducing the probative value of the testimony.[1]

---

[1] See discussion in Ch. 7 about the difference between relevance to issue and relevance to credibility.

This explanation does not convey the full potential of the difference between the two methods of challenging a witness. A cross-examiner resorting to the second method sometimes intends to do more than limit the probative value of the testimony; he may attempt to impugn the witness's entire moral standing. When a cross-examiner attacks the moral standing of a witness he often does so not only with a view to showing that the witness's word carries less truth-value but also to suggest that the morality and humanity of the witness is so inferior that no verdict can be based on his testimony.[2] We may refer to the factual probability that the witness is telling the truth as 'probative credibility' and to the tendency of a witness's moral standing to encourage or discourage reliance on him as 'moral credibility'.[3]

An instance of an attack on moral credibility is provided by the method that used to be deployed against victims of rape. Defence counsel would question the complainant about her sexual experience with a view to establishing promiscuity.[4] The purported excuse for this was that promiscuity was relevant to the issue of consent. Such relevance was very often untenable.[5] Frequently the real purpose of the cross-examination was to show the complainant to be so morally inferior as either not to deserve the court's sympathy or not to provide a suitable foun-

---

[2] For a survey see Pattenden, 'The character of victims and third parties in criminal proceedings other than rape trials', [1986] Crim L Rev 367. A useful study of the American law is to be found in Wydick, 'Character evidence: a guided tour to the grotesque structure', 21 U C Davis L R 123 (1987).

[3] This is not to say that a morally flawed person can never be relied upon in a criminal trial but rather than moral infirmity creates a suspicion towards the witness which is greater than his probative shortcomings justify.

[4] For a strong criticism of the treatment of rape victims in and out of court see Temkin, *Rape and the Legal Process* (1987), ch. 1.

[5] Thus a person who is known to be promiscuous is unlikely to resort to a false accusation of rape in order to protect her reputation. Similarly, a person of considerable sexual experience is less likely to be overcome by shame or remorse and tell lies about the nature of the intercourse. See: McNamara, 'Cross-examination of the complainant in a trial for rape', (1981) 5 Crim L J 25; Elliot, 'Rape complainants' sexual experience with third parties', [1984] Crim L Rev 4; Temkin, 'Regulating sexual evidence history: the limits of discretionary legislation' (1984) ICLQ 942; Estrich, 'Rape', 95 Yale L J 1087 (1986).

dation for punishing the accused.[6] That this method of challenging complainants was not really necessary for the factual determination of the charge was recognized by the legislature. Section 2(1) of the Sexual Offences (Amendment) Act 1976 forbids cross-examination (and, indeed, independent evidence) concerning 'any sexual experience of a complainant with a person other than' the accused. But section 2(2) goes on to provide that the trial judge should allow such questions if they are necessary for securing a fair trial. Today the sexual experience of the complainant may be gone into only when it is already relevant to the accused's guilt but not otherwise.[7]

Moral credibility has always been an important consideration in the legal process. Well into the eighteenth century non-Christians were disqualified from giving evidence in the courts.[8] Ostensibly the reason for the disqualification had to do with the oath which presupposed subscription to the Christian faith. In reality the disqualification was founded on a supposed moral inferiority. It arose, as Wigmore put it, from a 'deep-rooted instinct to distrust the alien of another nation,—much more the alien of another creed or race or color.'[9] Today our moral beliefs are more rational but it would be a mistake to suppose that this moral instinct is completely extinct. It is therefore important to limit the extent to which the moral credibility of the accused and of the witnesses can colour the judgment of the trier of fact and distract him from a correct assessment of probative credibility. We have to accept that the criminal verdict often reflects on the moral standing of the accused and, perhaps, even on that

---

[6] Jackson observed: '[o]ne's moral criteria of what makes a good, honest witness will be difficult to distinguish from one's criteria of what makes a good, honest person, and, therefore, when a fact relating to what a witness did or did not do is in issue, judgments which are made on what kind of person the witness is for the purpose of assessing his credibility, will inevitably colour one's judgment of what kind of acts he committed or did not commit.' 'Questions of fact and questions of law', in Twining (ed.), *Facts in the Law* (1983), 98. See also Weinstein, 'Some difficulties in devising rules for determining truth in judicial trials', 66 Col L Rev 223, 233 n. 40 and text (1966).

[7] See *Viola* [1982] 3 All ER 73, and discussion in Ch. 7.

[8] *Wigmore on Evidence*, 3rd edn. (1940), vol. 2, ss. 515 ff.

[9] Ibid. n. 516.

of witnesses. But we must ensure that as far as practicable moral standing is not the reason for a criminal verdict.

With this in mind we may now turn to the cross-examination of the accused. When the accused was made competent to give evidence on his own behalf in 1898 the legislature was faced with a dilemma. If, on the one hand, the accused is made liable to be cross-examined on his moral credibility as any other witness, he runs the risk of having his moral blemishes exposed. This may, in turn, create undue moral prejudice against him for the reasons discussed in the last chapter and so deter him from testyfying. On the other hand, if he is rendered immune from cross-examination, he will have an unfair advantage in that his testimony will not be subject to the usual tests of reliability; which advantage may be exploited for creating a distorted picture in the mind of the trier of fact.

Although the discussion in this chapter is concerned with the provisions of section 1 of the Criminal Evidence Act 1898, it is important to appreciate that the problems raised by the distinction between moral and probative credibility are inherent in our adversarial procedure. Even if we did not have the present provisions, we would still have to seek ways of achieving a fair balance between the prosecution's freedom to subject the accused to searching scrutiny of his credibility, which might create prejudice against him, and the accused's immunity from such scrutiny, which may distort the factual picture. Section 1 of the 1898 Act provides:

(e) A person charged and being a witness ... may be asked any question in cross-examination notwithstanding that it would tend to criminate him as to the offence charged:

(f) A person charged and called as a witness ... shall not be asked, and if asked shall not be required to answer, any question tending to show that he has committed or been convicted of or been charged with any offence other than that wherewith he is then charged, or is of bad character, unless—

(i)   the proof that he has committed or been convicted of such other offence is admissible evidence to show that he is guilty of the offence wherewith he is then charged; or

(ii)   he has personally or by his advocate asked questions of the witnesses for the prosecution with a view to establish his own good character, or has given evidence of his good character, or the nature or conduct of the defence is such as to involve imputations on the character of the prosecutor or the witnesses for the prosecution; or

(iii) he has given evidence against any other person charged in the same proceedings;

The compromise adopted by this provision is that while an accused who chooses to testify is liable to cross-examination, his examination is more limited than that of ordinary witnesses. Ever since 1898 the courts have struggled to comprehend the practical consequences of this compromise. Three factors have hampered the courts in this struggle: first, the belief that the wording of the enactment of itself constitutes a guide to practice, second, the assumption that there is a meaningful difference between kinds of evidentiary relevance, and, third, the failure to recognize the distinction between probative credibility and moral credibility in the sense explained earlier.

CROSS-EXAMINATION WITH A VIEW TO SHOWING THAT THE ACCUSED COMMITTED THE OFFENCE CHARGED

The debilitating force of the first factor emerges from *Jones* v. *DPP*,[10] the principal authority on the interpretation of subsection $1(f)(i)$. The accused was charged with the murder of a young girl. When first questioned he gave a false alibi capable of support. Later he retracted this alibi and said that he had been with a prostitute whom he was unable to identify. In his testimony he explained that he had invented a false alibi because he had been in trouble before and was afraid that the police would not believe his true but uncorroborated alibi. He went on to describe a conversation he had with his wife on returning home from his visit to the prostitute. The prosecution was allowed to put to him that he had set up a similar alibi and had recounted a similar conversation with his wife when he had been in trouble with the police on the previous occasion.[11]

---

[10] [1962] 1 All ER 569.

[11] The prosecution did not reveal that on the previous occasion too he had accosted a young Girl Guide and raped her, an offence in respect of which he was subsequently convicted. There was a suggestion that this evidence might have been relevant in-chief but the prosecution declined to call the girl out of consideration for her welfare.

A majority in the House of Lords held that had the accused himself not revealed that he had been in trouble with the police before, his cross-examination would have been improper. To understand this conclusion it is necessary to appreciate the method of statutory interpretation that led to it. Lord Reid outlined it as follows:

The question [regarding the meaning of the section] can only be answered by taking the words which Parliament has used and applying to them the ordinary methods of construction . . . It is a cardinal principle applicable to all kinds of statutes that one may not for any reason attach to a statutory provision a meaning which the words of that provision cannot reasonably bear.[12]

Possessed by this interpretive philosophy the majority in *Jones* paid scant attention to the legislative policy behind the subsections (*e*) and (*f*) and approached the problem as if it were a grammatical puzzle which could be solved independently of context. This led Lord Reid to conclude that the Act deals with three types of questions which may be put to the accused:

(1) those which would tend to criminate the accused as to the offence charged, (2) those tending to show that he has committed or been convicted of or been charged with some other offence, and (3) those tending to show that he is of bad character.[13]

He gave the following reason for believing that these classes of questions were mutually exclusive:

This raises at once the question what is the proper construction of the words in proviso (*e*) 'tend to criminate him as to the offence charged.' Those words could mean tend to convince or persuade the jury that he is guilty, or they could have the narrower meaning—tend to connect him with the commission of the offence charged. If they have the former meaning there is at once an insoluble conflict between proviso (*e*) and (*f*). No line of questioning could be relevant unless it (or answers to it) might tend to persuade the jury of the guilt of the accused. It is only permissible to bring in previous convictions or bad character if they are so relevant, so, unless proviso (*f*) is to be deprived of all content, it must prohibit some questions which would tend to criminate the accused of the offence charged if those words are

---

[12] Ibid. 574.   [13] Ibid.

used in the wider sense. But if they have the narrower meaning there is no such conflict. *So the structure of the Act shows that they must have the narrower meaning.*[14]

On this view proviso (*e*) permits cross-examination on matters that directly tend to connect the accused with the offence charged whereas proviso (*f*) forbids, subject to exceptions, cross-examination on matters that indirectly prove the commission of the offence and forbids cross-examination tending to show the accused to be of bad character. On top of the notorious distinction between relevance to the issue and relevance to credibility we now seem to have a baffling subdivision between direct and indirect relevance to the issue.[15]

The minority in *Jones*, consisting of Lord Denning and of Lord Devlin, was right to reject the majority approach and focus on the nature of the problem that faced the legislature. As we have seen, the difficulty posed by making the accused a competent witness was that disclosure of the accused's criminal antecedents could induce the jury to convict the accused because of his moral blemishes rather than because his offence was proved. Once we have realized that the section's main concern is to ensure that the jury judge the act, not the actor, we can hardly fail to notice that it is identical to the problem that we face in relation to similar-fact evidence: How to investigate the charge without exposing the accused to undue prejudice? Understood in this way subsections (*e*) and (*f*) merely subject the freshly permitted cross-examination of the accused to the established principle for dealing with a familiar conflict.

---

[14] Ibid. 575, emphasis added. Viscount Simonds and Lord Morris concurred.

[15] The majority must have accepted that to ask an accused: 'Where were you at the time of the crime?' is a 'directly relevant' question and therefore allowed under s. 1(*e*). His answer: 'I was staying with friend in a different town' must also, presumably, be 'directly relevant' because it negatives the possibility that he committed the offence. May the prosecution ask the accused whether he had beaten up his friend (who is unavailable) the day before and was therefore unlikely to have been staying with him? According to the majority such a question would presumably be only 'indirectly' relevant because, on its own it neither tends to prove nor disprove the offence. It is, however, possible that the majority had a difference of degree in mind, rather than one of kind. In this case direct relevance would indicate strong relevance and indirect relevance would refer to remote relevance. This will be sensible and, in fact, close to the minority's view.

Lord Devlin emphasized this aspect when he said in *Jones* v. *DPP*:

proviso (f) takes a natural place in the law of evidence. . . . the rule in *Makin's* case covers both evidence led against the accused and evidence sought to be obtained from him in cross-examination; proviso (f) shuts out nothing that is relevant to the issue but gives complete protection to the accused against attacks on his reputation and credit unless he throws his hat into the ring.[16]

Accordingly, subsection (*e*) makes it clear that the legislature does not wish to afford an accused who chooses to testify a refuge from answering questions the answer to which could incriminate him of the offence charged.[17] If the matter had been taken no further, the position of the accused would have been similar to that of any other witness and he would have been exposed to almost unlimited moral prejudice. Hence subsection (*f*) places a limitation on the removal of the privilege in subsection (*e*) and deals with 'any question tending to show that he has committed or been convicted of or been charged with any offence other than that wherewith he is then charged, or is of bad character'. These questions are forbidden except in three situations, the first of which, set out in (*f*)(i), is a reference back to the principle set out in (*e*). Thus, subsection (*f*)(i) allows questions directed to show that the accused 'is guilty of the offence wherewith he is then charged'.

Interpreting subsection (*f*)(i) as applying the similar-fact test means that questions are permissible if their probative significance outweighs their prejudicial potential. This interpretation has the merit of bringing to bear on the accused's cross-examination the same principle that governs evidence-in-chief

---

[16] [1962] 1 All ER 599. *Makin* v. *AG for New South Wales* [1894] AC 57, has been discussed in Ch. 12. The connection between the *Makin* principle and the accused's cross-examination is also mentioned by Viscount Sankey in *Maxwell* v. *DPP* [1935] AC 309, 317. Unfortunately, Lord Devlin's view lost much of its force due to the insistence that 'character' in provision (*f*) meant reputation and not psychological make-up. See n. 20 below and corresponding text.

[17] An accused who wanted to have his say without being cross-examined could make a statement from the dock. This facility has been abolished by s. 72 of the Criminal Justice Act 1982, but the accused's counsel may still put forward on his behalf his version of the events.

and of avoiding the opaque distinction upon which the majority view is founded.[18]

A textual complication has to be mentioned. The opening paragraph of subsection (f) forbids questions relating to: (1) the commission of another offence; (2) conviction thereof; (3) a charge in respect of another offence; and (4) bad character. Subsection (i) mentions only the first two types of question so that the impression is given that even though a question is relevant to proving the offence charged, it is still forbidden if it also relates to another charge (type 3) or if it also relates to bad character (type 4). In *Jones* Lord Devlin tried to overcome this problem by construing 'character' to mean reputation (which is generally irrelevant to the commission of the offence).[19] Considering the several references to 'character' in different parts of subsection (f) this interpretation is untenable.[20] Even if Lord Devlin were right in his interpretation of 'character' this would still leave the problem of a mere 'charge', relating to another offence, which is mentioned in the opening paragraph of subsection (f) but not in subsection (f)(i).[21]

However, the textual asymmetry does not find a neat solution in the majority view in *Jones* either. Under this interpretation

---

[18] It fulfils Viscount Simon's stricture in *Stirland* v. *DPP* [1944] 2 All ER 13, 18, that it 'is most undesirable that the rules which should govern cross-examination to credit of an accused person in the witness box should be complicated by refined distinctions involving a close study and comparison of decided cases, when in fact these rules are few and can be simply stated.'

[19] [1962] 1 All ER 569, 597 ff.

[20] Lord Devlin assumed that reputation is never relevant to the commission of an offence and thus the imbalance between the prohibition and exception (i) is removed. However, 'character' will have to have the same meaning throughout subs. (f) which would mean that an accused giving evidence of, in the words of subs. (f)(ii), 'his own good character' would be testifying about his reputation rather than about his law-abiding inclination, which is improbable. Similarly, we would have to hold, as D. J. Birch pointed out to me, that when an accused confines himself to specific examples of bad conduct on the part of a witness but ignores his reputation, the accused is not attacking the witness's character.

[21] It cannot be assumed that a previous charge (not resulting in conviction) can never be relevant to providing the offence. While in most situations the fact that the accused had in the past been charged with an offence will be insufficiently relevant to prove the offence for which he is standing trial (as in *Maxwell* v. *DPP* [1935] AC 309), there will be situations where a previous charge would be relevant (as where the previous charge informed the accused of a fact the knowledge of which he now denies).

subsection $(f)(i)$ is confined to questions that are 'indirectly' relevant. It follows that 'indirect' questions are allowed in relation to past crimes and convictions but not to charges and other discreditable acts. On this view an accused may be questioned about the grave and highly prejudicial matter of a previous murder, or conviction thereof, but not about the less-serious and less-prejudicial fact that he had been charged with murder and acquitted.[22]

The main weakness of the majority view in *Jones* is that it lays down, in the words of D. J. Birch, 'a narrower rule for cross-examination than that which is applicable to evidence adduced by the prosecutor in-chief'.[23] The interpretation advocated here has the advantage of regarding subsection $(f)(i)$ as a reference back, albeit an awkward one, to the general principle in subsection (e), so that whatever is admissible in-chief is admissible in cross-examination and we do not have to distinguish between the four categories mentioned in the opening paragraph of subsection (f). Thus the prosecution will be allowed to ask questions that tend to rebut the accused's version of the events as presented in-chief notwithstanding that the questions tend to reveal the accused's previous crimes.[24]

The practical difference between the two schools in *Jones* was, however, considerably reduced by the majority's decision that the words 'tending to show' in the opening paragraph of subsection (f) meant 'tending to make known'. Since in *Jones* the jury knew from the accused himself that he had been in trouble

---

[22] In *Cokar* [1960] 2 All ER 175, the accused was charged with burglary and testified that he did not know that it was prohibited to enter a stranger's house in order to sleep inside. The Court of Criminal Appeal held that it was wrong for the prosecution to cross-examine the accused about a previous charge, resulting in acquittal, for an offence committed in similar circumstances. It was not doubted that the question was relevant to prove the accused's knowledge, but it was thought that the absence of a reference to a charge in subs. $(f)(i)$ constituted a complete bar. The interpretation advocated by the minority would have avoided such an absurd result since the evidence was relevant to rebut a defence advanced by the accused. See Lord Devlin's comments in *Jones* v. *DPP* [1962] 1 All ER 569, 595–7.

[23] Comment on *Anderson* [1988] Crim L Rev 297, 299. By sanctioning a very loose connection between what the accused has revealed in-chief and what the prosecution may put to him in cross-examination, *Anderson* [1988] 2 All ER 549 drives a coach and horses through the majority view in *Jones*, and establishes a principle close to the position advocated by the minority in *Jones*.

[24] See *Anderson* [1988] 2 All ER 549, 555–6, *obiter*.

with the police, his cross-examination by the prosecution was upheld by the majority because it did not reveal to the jury anything that they did not already know and approved by the minority because it disproved the accused's defence.[25]

Although the debate concerning the relationship between subsection (*e*) and subsection (*f*)(i) attracted much attention, subsection (*f*)(i) is of limited practical importance. If evidence of a previous offence or other discreditable act of the accused is, in the words of the subsection, 'admissible evidence to show that he is guilty of the offence wherewith he is then charged', it would usually be admissible in-chief under the similar-fact evidence rule. Lord Lane CJ explained this in *Anderson*:

> Thus if the prosecution know that a particular defence is going to be advanced, they may (subject to the judge's discretion) call evidence to rebut it as part of their own substantive case even if that tends to show the commission of other crimes. The defendant can plainly then be cross-examined about the matter. If the prosecution do not know of the evidence in advance, then they may call evidence to rebut it and the defendant can then be recalled, if that is desired, to deal with the rebutting evidence.[26]

EVIDENCE OF GOOD CHARACTER AND IMPUTATIONS: INTRODUCTION

When a question arises in relation to (*f*)(i) or in respect of similar-fact evidence, we are concerned with the relevance of the accused's discreditable past to the offence charged. Subsection (*f*)(ii) does not deal with such relevance. It is concerned with situations in which the floodgates may be opened so that the prosecution may investigate the accused's moral record irrespective of its bearing on the commission of the offence.

---

[25] In *Jones* the fact that the accused had given an identical alibi on a previous occasion tended to undermine the current alibi whether or not the accused had revealed so in-chief and it is therefore unclear why the accused's revelation should make a difference to admissibility.

[26] [1988] 2 All ER 549, 556. See also *Jones* v. *DPP* [1962] 1 All ER 578; *Scott* (1984) 79 Cr App R 49.

The received view is that while subsection $(f)(i)$ deals with evidence that is relevant to the issue (be it 'direct' or 'indirect' relevance), subsection $(f)(ii)$ is concerned with matters relevant to credit.[27] This distinction lacks logical and practical justification, as we have seen.[28] Undermining the credibility of the accused's defence could greatly increase the probability that he committed the offence. Consequently, even if one accepts a difference between the two kinds of relevance, it cannot be said that relevance to credibility is inherently less important from the point of view of proving the offence charged and in many cases it may assume, as Munday observed, a critical importance.[29]

Not only can evidence of character affect the probability that the accused committed the offence but also, and more significantly, it can undermine the accused's moral credibility and induce the jury to deviate from the two cardinal principles of criminal justice: the principle that the accused must be tried only on the offence charged and the principle that a person may be convicted only if his guilt has been established beyond all reasonable doubt.[30] To safeguard these principles it is vital to place substantial limitations on the prosecution's freedom to cross-examine the accused on his moral antecedents. Subsection $(f)(ii)$ provides that cross-examination directed to disclose the commission of a previous offence, a conviction, a charge, or bad character is allowed if the accused:

has personally or by his advocate asked questions of the witnesses for the prosecution with a view to establish his own good character, or has given evidence of his good character, or the nature or conduct of the

---

[27] *Cross on Evidence*, 6th edn. (1985), 360–8.

[28] See discussion in Ch. 7. If the accused says in his testimony, 'At the time of the offence I was in a different place', his statement is clearly relevant to the issue because it reduces the probability that he committed the offence. To prove that the accused lied removes the negative probability and therefore increases the positive probability that he committed the offence. It is therefore misleading to say that in the latter case the evidence only goes to the accused's credit and not to the issue.

[29] R. Munday, 'Stepping beyond the bounds of credibility: the application of section $1(f)(ii)$ of the Criminal Evidence Act 1898', [1986] Crim L Rev 511, 513, where an interesting discussion of the problems involved in assessing the accused's credibility will be found.

[30] See discussion of this point in the previous chapter.

defence is such as to involve imputations on the character of the prosecutor or the witnesses for the prosecution.

Since cross-examination by the prosecution is triggered-off by something done by the defence, an interpretation of the provision must start by investigating this triggering mechanism. We should ask: What is it in the nature of the defence that justifies an otherwise prohibited cross-examination? Having answered this question, we should then confine the permissible cross-examination to the points that triggered it off in the first place.

The subsection addresses itself to two different situations: first, a case where the accused, either himself or through other witnesses, has introduced evidence of his own good character, and, second, a case where the defence has adversely commented on the character of witnesses for the prosecution, whether or not the accused has added his testimonial voice to the criticism. These will now be discussed in turn.

EVIDENCE OF GOOD CHARACTER

The Purpose of Evidence of Good Character

The first thing to investigate in interpreting the first part of subsection (f)(ii) is the purpose for which the accused introduces evidence of good character.

An accused who calls evidence of his own good character does not set his sights exclusively on increasing his credibility as a witness. He often seeks to achieve two further goals: to show that he has a law-abiding disposition and that, therefore, he is less likely to have committed the offence, and, further, to obtain the jury's sympathy and leniency and induce them to judge him on his merits and not just on the charge.[31] The first aspect of good-character evidence has not escaped judicial notice. Viscount Sankey LC observed that an accused who calls evidence of his own good character does so 'for the purpose of showing that it is unlikely that he committed the offence charged'.[32] If

---

[31] Wills, *Theory and Practice of the Law of Evidence* (1894), 56–7.
[32] *Maxwell* v. *DPP* [1935] AC 309, 319. See also: *Naudeer* (1985) 80 Cr App R 9.

the accused asks the jury to conclude that a man of his good character is unlikely to have committed the offence, is it not reasonable or just that a jury which has been persuaded that he is of bad character should conclude that the accused is, if anything, more likely to have committed the offence.[33]

The second goal of an accused who adduces evidence of good character is to invite the jury to take into account his general good character in arriving at a verdict and not to confine their deliberations to whether or not he has committed the offence charged. An accused who takes this course hopes to be judged on his moral standing; he asks the jury to judge, as it were, the person rather than the offence. Looked at from this point of view, proof of good character constitutes a plea for clemency. Once we accept the right of the accused to make such a plea, we call upon the trier of fact to engage in a moral calculus. An accused who takes this step must also accept the risk of an unfavourable outcome.

It does not follow from this, nor is it suggested, that a jury should be free to convict merely because the accused has a bad character. What does follow is that we need to develop a vocabulary for discussing the problem so that we may limit the moral prejudice likely to be generated by the revelation of the accused's discreditable past. The judge should explain in plain language the importance of confining one's considerations to judging the probative force of testimony and resisting the prejudice that might be created by the moral standing of a witness or an accused.

Suppose that on a charge of murder the defence sets out to depict the accused as a sensitive, upright, and humane person who has devoted his entire life to caring for others. The prosecution should surely be allowed to show that the accused's moral standing is the very opposite of that suggested by the defence. Upon learning of the accused's true ruthless nature, however, a fair-minded person, who has been brought to understand the unfairness of allowing moral credibility to dominate factual inference, will not reason that a conviction is justified

---

[33] This understandable reaction too has not passed unnoticed either: *Samuels* (1956) 40 Cr App R 8, 12.

regardless of the evidence concerning the accused's responsibility for the murder. Such a person will not say to himself that now that the accused has been shown to be of bad character all caution may be abandoned, but will weigh the evidence against the accused. If evidence of the accused's guilt is strong, he will find it more difficult to disbelieve it or to resolve doubts in favour of the accused. But he will not lose sight of his duty to start by considering the evidence of guilt rather than the accused's character and he will certainly not allow himself to convict where the evidence does not prove guilt.

A preoccupation with spurious distinctions has, unfortunately, distracted attention from the need to confine the scope for moral contest. For instance, Australian decisions seem to insist that juries must be instructed that when the accused has been shown in cross-examination to be of bad character, this information should be used strictly for the purpose of removing from their minds the impression that the accused has a good character.[34] When a similar proposal was made in an English case Edmund Davies LJ balked at it, saying:

> If the accused calls evidence of good character and is shown by cross-examination to have a bad character, the jury may give this fact such weight as they think fit when assessing the *general* credibility of the accused. They cannot be expected to execute the metaphysical feat of treating the evidence as relevant to credibility on one issue but irrelevant on another, and they are not required to do so.[35]

Appreciating perhaps that the Australian direction may cause some difficulty to persons guided by common sense, one commentator suggested that if juries are found incapable of following such instruction, we should abolish the jury system alto-

---

[34] *Domini* v. *R.* (1973) 47 ALJR 69, 73; *Matusevich* v. *R.* [1977] 15 ALR 117, 119; *Beech* (1978) 20 SASR 410, 420–3. But see *Woolcott Forbes* (1944) 44 SR (NSW) 333, 340, 341; *Stalder* (1981) 3 A Crim R 87, 96.

[35] *Longman and Richardson* [1968] 2 All ER 761, 768. The Privy Council was deterred from requiring just such a feat when it held, in *Lui Mei Lin* v. *R.*, *The Times* (26 Oct. 1988), that when a co-accused uses an inadmissible confession in cross-examining the accused, the jury must be told not only that the confession is not evidence of the facts admitted in it, but also that it may only be taken into account for judging the credibility of the accused's evidence against the co-accused and not his credibility in denying his own guilt.

gether.[36] This reaction exemplifies a fairly common tendency to overlook the purpose of evidence of good character with which the prosecution's cross-examination must be concerned.

Limiting Issues of Good Character

Although it is important to be able to persuade juries to resist the distraction created by evidence of moral credibility it is still preferable to suppress such evidence as much as possible, especially when it concerns the accused.

Fundamentally, character should be allowed to become an issue only where the trial judge is convinced that the accused has sought to put his character in issue.[37] To some extent this principle is already reflected in practice. In the absence of any duty on the defence to declare its intention to put the accused's character in issue, the courts have to judge for themselves whether the nature or conduct of the defence has had this result. To place his character in issue the accused has positively to solicit the evidence of his good character and it is not enough that a witness has volunteered his views about the accused.[38] Thus if the defence elicits facts solely in order to arouse the jury's sympathy, character will have been placed in issue.[39] Evidence adduced by the accused to establish innocence may on occasion have the side-effect of showing him in a morally favourable light. If such evidence were held to give rise to an issue of character, the accused would be unjustly hampered in

---

[36] Pattenden, 'The purpose of cross-examination under section 1(f) of the Criminal Evidence Act 1898', [1982] Crim L Rev 707, 713. Given that common-sense reasoning and moral sentiment influence fact-finding whether by judge or jury it is difficult to see what can be achieved by a change from lay judges to professional ones. Furthermore, if professional judges become triers of fact, the amount of prejudicial evidence will increase due to the assumption in judicial circles that professional judges are immune from prejudice and need not necessarily be kept ignorant of such evidence.

[37] It is sometimes suggested that it is inaccurate to say of an accused calling evidence of his good character that he puts his character in issue because the issues in the case are confined to the charge. If the account suggested above is correct, then the accused does very much place his character in issue.

[38] *Redd* [1923] 1 KB 104. Similarly, allusion to one conviction does not imply accused has not got others and is not evidence of good character; *Thompson* [1966] 1 All ER 505.

[39] E.g. that he regularly attends mass: *Ferguson* (1909) 2 Cr App R 250.

his defence. In these situations the courts have therefore held that the issue of character does not arise.[40]

Sometimes, an accused produces evidence of good behaviour for the specific purpose of leading to the conclusion that he is unlikely to have committed the offence. For example, an accused charged with larceny by failing to return lost property testified that on a previous occasion he had returned lost property.[41] The courts seem to regard such tactics as opening the gate to cross-examination on character.[42]

An inflexible rule whereby every time the accused adduces evidence of non-criminal disposition he is putting his character in issue is unjustified. The purpose of subsection (f)(ii) is not to punish an accused who has introduced evidence of his own good character but to enable the trier of fact to adjudicate fairly on the issue raised by the accused.[43] An accused who asks to be judged on his entire moral record has to accept an investigation into his record. But an accused may reveal some of his moral behaviour because it has an immediate bearing on an issue in the case and not because he wants to secure sympathy regardless of the truth of the accusation.[44]

An accused who gives evidence of a non-criminal propensity in order to disprove the charge is not necessarily extending the dispute beyond the charge. He may merely be countering the charge. When this is the case his cross-examination should be governed not by subsection (f)(ii) but by subsection (f)(i). The former provision should be confined to cases where the accused has placed his entire character in issue while the latter should govern cross-examination directed to rebutting a line of defence which is connected with the issues arising from the charge. For instance, an accused may call evidence of his heterosexual inclination in defence to a charge involving homosexual behaviour, or he may testify that as a rich man he is unlikely to

---

[40] *Lee* [1976] 1 All ER 570; *Ellis* [1910] 2 KB 746.

[41] *Samuel* (1956) 40 Cr App R 8.

[42] See, for instance, *Powell* [1986] 1 All ER 193.

[43] Cf. Babcock, 'Fair play: evidence favourable to an accused . . .', 34 Stan L Rev 1133, 1135 (1982).

[44] If such evidence has also the effect of arousing sympathy for the accused the judge should decide that an issue of character has arisen only if such sympathy is likely to distort the factual findings.

resort to the exploitation of prostitutes. In such situations the trial judge ought to limit the cross-examination to the accused's sexuality and wealth respectively.

We cannot expect to be able to articulate rules as to what counts as putting one's character in issue as distinguished from just raising a specific issue of disposition. These matters necessarily depend on the way in which each case has proceeded and there is hardly scope for binding precedent in this regard. There is no sense in distinguishing between rule and discretion in the matter of placing one's character in issue. When subsection $1(f)$(ii) sanctions cross-examination on the accused's bad character where he has elicited evidence 'with a view to establish his own good character', it both creates a rule and confers discretion. It settles once and for all that if the accused has put his character in issue, the prosecution is free to look into it when cross-examining the accused. But it leaves it to the judge to decide whether in the particular case before him the accused has indeed put his character in issue.

IMPUTATION AGAINST THE CHARACTER OF PROSECUTION WITNESSES

The Problem

The second, and the more problematic, part of subsection (f)(ii) provides that when the 'nature or conduct of the defence is such as to involve imputations on the character of the prosecutor or the witnesses for the prosecution', the prosecution may cross-examine the accused on his bad character. An adequate interpretation of this provision can be found only if its rationale is first identified.

A Practice Lacking a Sound Principle

When an accused contends that a witness for the prosecution is mistaken in his account of events, he clearly does not cast imputations on the witness's character any more than he would by a simple denial of guilt or a suggestion that the witness was incapacitated by drink on a particular occasion. Such allegations do not seriously impair the witness's moral credibility. Difficulties arise in distinguishing between an attack on a witness which does justify cross-examination of the accused and an attack which does not, especially where the challenge to the witness's account implies that the latter has committed perjury in his testimony.

When an accused denies having made the confession attributed to him by the police, his denial inevitably implies that the policemen concocted the confession, conspired to pervert the course of justice (where more than one policeman was involved), and committed perjury at the trial. Under English law such denial exposes the accused to cross-examination on character and hence requires him to make an invidious choice.[45] The accused may deny the confession from the witness-box but be cross-examined on character and run the gauntlet of prejudice; he may testify but not contest the confession and accept that a verdict of guilty will most probably follow; or he may get his counsel to deny the confession, refrain from testifying and thus rob the denial of any force. An accused need only deny that he confessed or contend that his confession was obtained by improper means and everything that is inadmissible under the similar-fact rule becomes admissible.[46]

It was thought at one stage that as long as the accused or his counsel have not spelled out the implications of the denial, the defence need not be regarded as making imputations on the character of the witness for the prosecution.[47] The distinction between the implied and the explicit for the purpose of determining the occasion for cross-examination was soon rejected; referring to a denial of a confession Lawton LJ said:

---

[45] *Britzman* [1983] 1 All ER 369.

[46] This system facilitates unscrupulous behaviour by the police. A policeman intent on securing the conviction of an innocent suspect with a record has a relatively easy task; he can invent a confession, or distort one, with little fear because the accused will either not dare to contest the confession or, if he does, he will be discredited by his criminal record.

[47] *Nelson* (1978) 68 Cr App R 12. But it was added that if the accused elaborated his denial by suggesting, for example, that he was threatened in order to confess, cross-examination on the accused's character became permissible. This concession was made to accommodate *Clark* [1955] 3 All ER 29 and *Cook* [1959] 2 All ER 97. See M. Cohen, 'Challenging police evidence of interviews and the second limb of section 1(f)(ii)...' [1981] Crim L Rev 523.

The jury had to decide whether these officers had made up what they alleged had been said. If in any case that is the reality of the position and would be seen by the jury to be so, there is no room for drawing a distinction between a defence which is so conducted as to make specific allegations of fabrication and one in which the allegation arises by way of necessary and reasonable implication.[48]

The logic of this position is hard to flaw. If one takes 'imputations' to mean any allegation of fact which, if true, shows a prosecution witness in an unfavourable light, then there really is no difference between explicit attribution of perjury and a denial of the witness's testimony which implies perjury on the part of the latter. Behind this position lies the ubiquitous philosophy of literal construction whereby the words of the section 'must receive their ordinary and natural interpretation, and . . . it is not legitimate to qualify them by adding or inserting the words "unnecessarily" or "unjustifiably" or "for the purpose other than that of developing the defence", or other similar words . . .'.[49]

This philosophy is not only barren of principle, but there are numerous instances in which the courts have declined to follow it and adopt a literal reading. The subsection sanctions cross-examination if the conduct of the defence 'is such as to involve imputations'. Although this suggests that an unintended imputation would suffice,[50] this literal meaning was rejected.[51] The subsection refers to 'the nature or conduct of the defence'. On a literal interpretation 'nature' and 'conduct' should refer to different things, but no difference has been adopted.[52] Lastly, 'character' must mean something more than an isolated act, yet in *Britzman*[53] it was decided that the attribution of one act of concocting a confession was enough.[54]

The myth of a literal interpretation has forced the courts to

---

[48] *Britzman* [1983] 1 All ER 369, 372–3. See also *Tanner* (1977) 66 Cr App R 56 and *McGee and Cassidy* (1979) 70 Cr App R 247.

[49] *Hudson* [1912] 2 KB 464, 470.

[50] This suggestion is supported by the contrast with wording of the earlier part of the same subsection which uses the words 'with view to establish his own good character'.

[51] *Preston* [1909] 1 KB 568. See *Cross on Evidence*, 6th edn. (1985), 369–70.

[52] *Cross on Evidence*, 6th edn. (1985), 370.   [53] [1983] 1 All ER 369.

[54] It would appear that the literal philosophy is less persuasive when it is to the accused's advantage.

embrace discretion. It has been held that where the consequences of a literal interpretation are insupportable the trial
judge has a discretion to disallow otherwise permissible cross-
examination.[55] This proposition inevitably prompts the question: If the literal interpretation gives rise to insupportable
consequences, should this not cause us to reconsider the interpretation? Occasionally the courts have been prepared to face
this question[56] but on the whole they have preferred to avoid it
and let the excesses of their course be dealt with by discretion.
However, the practical need for a theory has not disappeared as
a result of the proclamation of discretion because a judge needs
a theory about the aim of the provision in order to know when
and how to exercise his discretion.

The poverty of the guidelines that have been evolved, in
the absence of a theory, for avoiding the worst excesses of this
rule may be observed in Lawton LJ's decision that discretion
should be exercised to disallow cross-examination on character
where the accused denies only 'one incident' or only 'a short
interview'.[57] It is difficult to see why the number of incidents, or
the length of the interview denied, should make a difference.
The claim that the police concocted a short confession is really
as serious an allegation as that they concocted a long one.[58]
And if it is unfair to expose the accused to character cross-
examination when he denies the occurrence of a short incident
it must also be unfair to do so when he denies the occurrence of
a long one.

The shortcomings of both the literal approach and the discretionary strategy were canvassed before the House of Lords in
the leading case of *Selvey* v. *DPP*.[59] One of the more interesting
aspects that surfaced in this debate was the existence of a
respectable line of cases favouring a construction reflecting the
legislative purpose. As Humphreys J put it:

[55] *Watson* (1913) 8 Cr App R 249; *Cook* [1959] 2 All ER 97.
[56] In one case it was held that 'some limitation must be placed on the words of
the section since to decide otherwise would be to do grave injustice never intended
by Parliament'; *Turner* [1944] 1 All ER 599.
[57] *Britzman* [1983] 1 All ER 369, 373. See also quotation in text corresponding to
n. 48 above.
[58] Assuming that there is no possibility of misunderstanding.
[59] [1968] 2 All ER 497.

For centuries the law has jealously guarded the right of an accused person to put forward at his trial any defence open to him on the indictment without running the risk of his character, if a bad one, being disclosed to the jury. It would be strange indeed if the Act of Parliament which allowed him, in most cases for the first time, to give evidence on oath had virtually deprived him of that right in the case of one serious felony by enacting that he could only do so at the risk of having his character exposed.[60]

In that case the accused was charged with rape and claimed that the victim had consented. At the time the imputation of consent reflected badly on the character of the complainant. A literal construction would have caused the defence of consent to a charge of rape to produce an automatic loss of the shield against cross-examination on character. This consequence of the literal approach did not escape the notice of the House of Lords in *Selvey* v. *DPP* but the only conclusion that it was prepared to draw was that a special exception had been recognized. Of the five Law Lords in the case only Viscount Dilhorne was aware of the inconsistency between holding that the words of the section must be given their literal meaning and, at the same time, deciding that meaning does not apply to the defence of consent.[61] If there is any merit in a literal approach, which is open to doubt, it must be that the natural meaning of the words governs all situations falling to be decided under the section. The moment one decides to make an exception to the natural meaning, one abandons this position and looks beyond the words to find a justification for the exception.

The House of Lords considered Channell J's dictum in *Preston* where he attempted to formulate a principled interpretation:

if the defence is so conducted . . . as to involve the proposition that the jury ought not to believe the prosecutor or one of the witnesses for the prosecution upon the ground that his conduct—not his evidence in the case, but his conduct outside the evidence given by him—makes him an unreliable witness, then the jury ought also to know the character of the prisoner who either gives that evidence or makes that charge, and it then becomes admissible to cross-examine the prisoner as to his

---

[60] *Turner* [1944] 1 All ER 599, 601.
[61] [1968] 2 All ER 508. He therefore left the correctness of decisions such as *Turner* [1944] 1 All ER 599 and *Sheean* (1908) 21 Cox CC 561 open to question.

antecedents and character with view to showing that he has such a bad character that the jury ought not to rely upon his evidence. That is the general nature of the enactment and the general principle underlying it.[62]

Two principal reasons were given by the House of Lords in *Selvey* v. *DPP* for rejecting this approach: first, that past attempts to give the words of the subsection a limited meaning have led to irreconcilable decisions,[63] and, second, that so 'liberal a shield for an accused is in many cases unfair to a prosecution'.[64] Neither of these reasons is convincing.

The fact that in different trials imputations of a similar content (e.g. 'He is a thief') are held to have different effects does not necessarily imply inconsistency. The test advocated by Channell J does not ask only whether the imputation made shows the witness in a bad light but also, and more significantly, whether the aim of the defence was to challenge the entire moral standing of the witness. This is a matter that very much depends on the way in which the defence has developed its case in the particular trial and cannot be governed solely by the phraseology of the remarks in question.

Furthermore, the argument from consistency in *Selvey* is at odds with the acknowledgment of discretion in the same case. If consistency were so important, we would have expected the House of Lords to commit itself to the literal interpretation. Instead, it declared that the trial judge has a discretion to forbid character cross-examination even where it is admissible under the subsection (in its literal interpretation). The House of Lords felt that by taking this course it could spare itself the effort of developing principles to discriminate between fair and unfair cross-examination on character. Lord Guest freely conceded that were it not for discretion he would have 'striven hard and long to give a benevolent construction to s.1, proviso (*f*)(ii)', which would exclude from its ambit cases in which the defence claimed that the witness for the prosecution was a liar

---

[62] [1909] 1 KB 568, 575; Prof. Cross considered this dictum to represent the law: *Cross on Evidence*, 5th edn. (1979), 433.

[63] [1968] 2 All ER 519 and 526. A similar view had been expressed by Devlin J in *Cook* [1959] 2 All ER 97, 101.

[64] [1968] 2 All ER 522, per Lord Pearce.

or that he had fabricated evidence. He went on to say that he did not believe 'that Parliament can have intended that in such cases an accused could only put forward such a defence at peril of having [h]is character put before the jury.'[65] One cannot help wondering: If it is possible to ascertain the legislative intention, why was no attempt made to fashion a construction of the subsection which reflects this intention and avoids the haphazard and uncertain exercise of discretion?

The second reason given for the rejection of the Channell J's approach was that the prevention of cross-examination of the accused in circumstances such as those of *Selvey* would be unfair to the prosecution. The accused, charged with buggery, testified that the complainant offered himself for money and said that he, the complainant, had done the same thing with another man earlier that day; the accused testified that he declined the offer. The trial judge allowed the prosecution to cross-examine the accused on previous offences of indecency. Lord Pearce felt that it would unfair to adopt an interpretation that did not allow such cross-examination.[66]

Wherein does the unfairness lie? Lord Pearce thought that the adoption of Channell J's interpretation would mean that provided the imputation 'was all linked up to the defence put forward by an accused there would be no limit to the amount of mud which could be thrown against an unshielded prosecutor while the accused could still crouch behind his own shield.'[67] This dictum discloses an odd notion of fairness. It suggests that a witness should be protected from harmful imputations of immorality by holding over the accused the threat of exposing before the jury his own moral blemishes. This is indeed a tit-for-tat principle, but it is hardly consonant with the ends of our system of criminal justice, which places in the forefront the need to protect the innocent from conviction.[68]

As a result of the *Selvey* decision an accused person cannot seriously contest a confession without exposing his criminal

---

[65] Ibid. 519.   [66] Ibid. 522.   [67] Ibid.

[68] If protecting of prosecution witnesses from derogatory suggestions is so important, it may be preserved by allowing the prosecution to adduce rehabilitating evidence.

record and the benefits of the discretionary jurisdiction have been paltry.[69]

Identifying the Principles Governing Imputations

To find a sensible construction for the second part of subsection (f)(ii) we must start by finding an explanation for why the accused's attack on the prosecution's witnesses should trigger off cross-examination on the accused's record. Separate consideration will be given to the two different situations comprised in the second limb of subsection (f)(ii). The first concerns imputations made by the accused in his own testimony (hereinafter 'testimonial imputations') and the second concerns imputations made by the defence without the accused adding his testimonial voice to them ('non-testimonial imputations').

Testimonial Imputations

This situation concerns an accused who, while not claiming to be of good character himself, has in his testimony cast 'imputations on the character of the prosecutor or the witnesses for the prosecution'. Since the attack on the prosecution's witness has been launched from the witness-box its success depends on the credibility of the accused. It could not have been the legislative intention to sanction cross-examination on character whenever there was a contest of credibility between the accused and a prosecution witness, for to do so would be to expose the accused almost every time he opened his mouth to defend himself.

Suppose, for instance, that a prosecution witness has testified that he saw the crime being committed and that he identified the accused from a distance of thirty yards. If the accused testifies that due to some defect the witness cannot see that far, the accused is not impugning the entire moral credibility of the witness and no question of cross-examination on character

---

[69] The soothing words with which Lord Pearce concluded his judgment in *Selvey* give one a sense of unreality: 'The courts have been right . . . in thinking that the question is whether *this* attack on the prosecution ought to let *these* convictions on the particular facts of the case, and on such a point rules are no substitute for a discretion in producing a fair trial.' [1968] 2 All ER 528.

arises. Suppose now that our accused goes on to say that the witness falsely claims to have identified the accused because the witness has a grudge against him. Although the acceptance of the accused's testimony has implications for the way in which we view the prosecution's witness, there does not seem to be any need for exposing the accused's entire moral antecedents to the jury's gaze. What is necessary is to investigate the credibility of the accused's specific claim against the witness. If such investigation discloses the accused's criminal record, the matter should be governed by subsection $(f)(i)$ because, according to the interpretation suggested earlier, this provision allows cross-examination on matters that tend to rebut the accused's defence and are of sufficient probative significance to outweigh the prejudicial effect.

So far we have considered attacks on the probative credibility of a prosecution witness. Suppose now that our accused takes his attack further and tries to undermine the witness's general moral standing, as well as his probative credibility, in order to persuade the jury that the latter's character is so flawed that no criminal verdict should be allowed to rest on his testimony. The question therefore arises whether this attack justifies the opening of a general contest between the accused's moral standing and that of the witness for the prosecution.

It is possible to argue that it is unjustified to allow a moral contest. It might be said that the criminal trial is not concerned with determining who is a nicer person as between the accused and the prosecution witness, but with whether the prosecution has proved its case beyond reasonable doubt. It might be added that to the extent that the moral credibility of the prosecution's witness comes into question it should be assessed on its own merits and not relative to the accused's moral standing.

This argument is not altogether realistic. When the moral credibility of a prosecution witness becomes a function of the credibility of the accused, it is difficult to expect a jury (or anybody else) to form a judgment about the former other than in terms that are relative to the latter. This is particularly the case where the prosecution's witness is the victim of the crime.[70]

---

[70] The legislature contemplated this when it referred to 'imputations on the character of the *prosecutor* or the witness for the prosecution'.

An attack on the victim could be calculated to deprive the victim of moral credibility not only as a witness deserving of credit but also as a victim deserving of the court's sympathy and protection.[71] When an accused chooses to appeal to the jury on a moral and extra-probative level it is right that the jury should be able to ascertain where the moral balance lies.

It is not suggested that trial by moral contest is desirable or that it should be encouraged. The argument put forward here is that as long as the accused is allowed to seek a favourable verdict by means of undermining the moral credibility (and not just the probative credibility) of the witnesses for the prosecution, the jury can reach a balanced verdict only if it is given information about the accused's own moral record. It has been pointed out by Seabrooke that if 'the accused attacks the character of a prosecution witness and there is no tit for tat response by the prosecution, the net effect will often be the creation of a false impression in the mind of a juror'.[72] What we must, of course, ensure is that a moral contest takes place only in those situations where it is abundantly clear that the accused has chosen to take his struggle for a favourable verdict beyond the realms of the strictly probative and failure to cross-examine him on his own record would be liable to distort the moral picture.[73]

Non-testimonial Imputations

Defence counsel may seek a moral contest even in the absence of any testimonial imputations from the accused, as the former practice in rape cases illustrates. Under this practice the defence would attempt to denigrate the complainant in order to induce the jury to transfer their sympathy from the complainant to the accused.[74] Whenever the defence seeks a verdict based on a moral contrast between the accused and the witnesses for the

---

[71] A tactic that used to be commonly deployed against rape victims; see text corresponding to n. 7 above.

[72] 'Closing the credibility gap: a new approach to s. 1(f)(ii) of the Criminal Evidence Act 1898', [1987] Crim L Rev 231, 232.

[73] The Court of Appeal has come close to adopting this principle in *St Louis and Fitzroy* (1984) 79 Cr App R 53.

[74] See text corresponding to n. 7 above.

prosecution, it is necessary to investigate the full moral record in order to enable the jury to reach a balanced conclusion.

Here too we have to distinguish between a defence that is designed to challenge the probative credibility of a witness and one designed to challenge his moral credibility. Suppose that the accused is charged with theft from his employer. Defence counsel cross-examines the employer suggesting that the latter has been systematically defrauding customers and that he has implicated the innocent accused in the missing property in order to divert attention from his own misdeeds. As the accused is attributing to the employer a specific motive for lying, cross-examination should be confined to this matter only, and disclosure of the accused's record should be sanctioned only if it has sufficient bearing on this particular issue.

The interpretation advocated is based on a notion of commensurate response: cross-examination must be in proportion to the breadth of the accused's defence. If the accused has attacked the probative credibility of a prosecution witness, the prosecution should be allowed to examine the accused about such discreditable deeds as are of sufficient probative significance to counter the defence claims. Only where the accused has taken matters further and has set out on a moral campaign designed to destroy the moral standing of the prosecution witnesses should he be exposed to a general onslaught on his record. As this last situation will be very rare the present interpretation will restrict greatly the scope for uninhibited attacks on the accused's character.

A possible argument against this interpretation has to be considered. Subsection (*f*) deals only with cross-examination of the accused. Where the accused stays away from the witness-box, the prosecution cannot reveal his record even if the defence has made the gravest allegations against prosecution witnesses.[75] If the moral balance were the central concern of the legislature, it might be argued, the legislature would have allowed disclosure of the accused's record even where he has not testified. In response it may be said that, first, in the 1898

---

[75] *Westfall* (1912) 7 Cr App R 176; *Biggin* [1920] 1 KB 213; *Butterwasser* [1947] 2 All ER 415.

Act the legislature was making provision for the accused who for the first time was allowed to testify in his own defence and that, consequently, the legislature addressed itself exclusively to arrangements for the accused as a witness. Secondly, when an accused has declined the witness-box a moral contest is unlikely to develop because a jury would be unlikely to attribute to the accused positive moral qualities. Hence there is unlikely to be any moral imbalance to redress.[76]

Some Practical Aspects of the Proposed Interpretation

As we have seen, the most pressing situation for redress is that of an accused who denies the confession attributed to him. It is clear that such an accused does not make any claim about the general moral record of the officers who took his confession; in the vast majority of cases the accused will be ignorant of the officers' personal history. Rather, the accused's contention is that they are lying on the issue of the confession. If the jury believe him they will inevitably conclude that the officers are of questionable morality. But, let it be noted, the officers' questionable morality is not the reason why the jury will believe the accused's account but the other way around: because they decide to believe the accused they will form a judgment about the officers' morality. Our accused does not seek a dispensation because the police is morally corrupt, he does not attempt to divert the adjudication from the factual issues, he merely contests the validity of an item of evidence adduced by the prosecution. Consequently, trial judges should forbid the exploitation of the accused's denial for the purpose of dragging into the trial his entire moral record.[77]

---

[76] See Lord Devlin's comment on Bodkin Adams's absence from the witness-box in Ch. 3, question corresponding to n. 36. A difficult problem arises where the accused calls evidence to show that as a result of their propensity third parties, who have not testified, were more likely to have committed the offence charged. Since these persons have not testified, the accused cannot be cross-examined on his record in order to show that his propensity was as strong as that of the third parties; *Lee* [1976] 1 All ER 570. It might perhaps be possible to adduce evidence in rebuttal for this purpose; *Anderson* [1988] Crim L Rev 297.

[77] It would be different if, in addition to denying the confession, our accused were to set out to show that the policemen involved in his case or the entire local police force were corrupt, that they had on many occasions obstructed the course of justice, that they are given to perjury, and susceptible to bribery.

At present decided cases pay no attention to the relationship between cross-examination on previous conviction and the nature of the accused's defence.[78] Guided by the need to maintain a commensurate response, a trial judge should allow cross-examination on the accused's previous convictions only if they have a strong probative bearing upon the accused's attack on the policemen giving evidence.[79] The fact that the accused has a previous conviction for a similar offence will not necessarily be sufficiently relevant to justify cross-examination on the grounds that it disproves his denial of a confession. If the conviction goes merely to show that the accused had a disposition for committing the offence in question, its admissibility should fall to be determined under subsection $(f)(i)$. A previous offence that is so similar to the offence charged as to render high probative support for the accused's commission of the latter would also tend to confirm the accused's disputed confession, but since it does so indirectly[80] it is better to deal with this situation under subsection $(f)(i)$.

It is possible that the judicial reluctance to abandon the literal interpretation of subsection $(f)(ii)$ emanates from an unfounded fear that by doing so the prosecution will lose the opportunity of cross-examination even when fairness demands it.[81] A realization that the principle of probative significance of subsection $(f)(i)$ provides a solution to the problem will allay such apprehension.

A further factor that has hampered recognition of the principle advocated here is the myth that cross-examination of the

---

[78] In *Britzman* [1983] 1 All ER 369, the accused denied having made the incriminating statements attributed to them by the police but went out of their way to establish that they were not attacking the general moral standing of the policemen involved. It was decided that the implicit suggestion that the policemen were committing perjury justified, of itself, the cross-examination of the accused on their criminal record.

[79] Admittedly, even conviction bearing a strong resemblance could have a prejudicial effect, but it is better to confine disclosure to convictions with a strong connection to the accused's defence than allow the indiscriminate introduction of every piece of discreditable information.

[80] That is, we say that he confessed because we believe that he committed the offence and not the other way around.

[81] *Selvey* v. *DPP* itself gave rise to such fear; see text corresponding to n. 66 below.

accused on his criminal record is strictly relevant to his credit and must not give rise to any inference of guilt.[82] By having to keep up the pretence that the sole purpose of character cross-examination is to test the accused's credibility the courts have created a self-imposed ban on stating the true reasons for their decisions.[83]

In *Watts*[84] the accused, a man of low intelligence, was charged with indecent assault on a woman. The victim did not identify him. The accused was arrested because he had a record for indecent assaults and lived near the scene of the crime. The prosecution's evidence consisted of a confession which the accused denied. His denial was held to have involved imputations and the prosecution was allowed to cross-examine him on his record for indecent assaults on very young girls. The trial judge instructed the jury as follows:

The fact that a person has committed an offence on a previous occasion does not make him any more or less likely to be guilty of committing an offence on a subsequent occasion. It is not evidence. It was only allowed to be brought to your knowledge because of the serious allegations of misconduct which are made by the defendant . . . against the police.

On this Lord Lane CJ commented:

The jury in the present case was charged with deciding the guilt or innocence of a man against whom an allegation of indecent assault on a woman has been made. They were told that he had previous convictions for indecent assaults of a more serious kind on young girls. They were warned that such evidence was not to be taken as making it more

---

[82] See, for example, *Inder* (1977) 67 Cr App R 143, 146; Pattenden, 'The purpose of cross-examination under section 1(f) of the Criminal Evidence Act 1898', [1982] Crim L Rev 714.

[83] It is implicit in the provision itself that cross-examination is not concerned with the accused's credibility. The accused becomes liable to character cross-examination even where he does not make imputations in his own testimony or where the imputations are in no way disputable, as where they concern the previous convictions of the witnesses for the prosecution. Where the allegations against the witnesses do not depend on the accused's veracity, it is clear that the cross-examination is not necessary to test the credibility of his allegations. Indeed, cross-examination is not even confined to those aspects of the accused's past which reflect on his record for truth-telling.

[84] [1983] 3 All ER 101.

likely that he was guilty of the offence charged, which it seems it plainly did, but only as affecting his credibility, which it almost certainly did not.[85]

The Lord Chief Justice went on to explain that while the trial judge's direction was 'sound in law', 'it would have been extremely difficult, if not practically impossible, for the jury to have done what the judge was suggesting'.[86] This is plain common sense, yet within three years the Lord Chief Justice no longer felt able to say that this was also the law. In *Powell*[87] his Lordship held that in *Watts* the court had 'overlooked the "tit for tat" principle' and that too much attention had been paid to 'the question whether the previous offences did or did not involve dishonesty in the ordinary sense of the word'.[88] He concluded in *Powell* that when the accused has been cross-examined on his previous convictions under section $1(f)$(ii) the judge must instruct the jury 'that the previous convictions should not be taken as indications that the accused has committed the offence'.

Had attention been paid to the differing justification for cross-examination in these two cases the explanations for the respective decisions of the Court of Appeal would have been more satisfactory. The accused in *Powell* was charged with living on the earnings of prostitution. Police witnesses testified that they observed prostitutes using the defendant's premises, paying him money, and being assisted by him. The accused admitted that his premises had been used by prostitutes but contended that it was done without permission. For the rest, his defence was that the police fabricated the entire story. The prosecution were allowed to cross-examine the accused about a number of previous convictions for similar offences. On the principles outlined above, the cross-examination was justified because the previous offences were highly disprobative, in view of the rest of the evidence, of the accused's denial of knowledge.[89] Furthermore, by claiming that he was a man of means

---

[85] Ibid. 105.   [86] [1983] 1 All ER 104.
[87] [1986] 1 All ER 193.   [88] Ibid. 198.
[89] See also *Burke* (1986) 82 Cr App R 156, where the accused contended that the police planted evidence in order to implicate him in a drug related offence; the prosecution was allowed to put to him previous involvement in drugs. Cf. *Owen* (1986) 83 Cr App R 100 where the accused also contended that the police fabricated the evidence against him, but his cross-examination stopped short of revealing that his previous offences were similar to the offence charged.

who did not need to seek money in prostitution, the accused in *Powell* relied on his non-criminal disposition and it was right that the prosecution should be allowed to put the record right in this respect.

The situation in *Watts* was altogether different. The evidence against the accused was weak. His low intelligence created considerable scope for misunderstanding about his statement in the police station. Furthermore, his previous offences were of little probative significance on the issue because they were of a different kind. Quashing the conviction the Court of Appeal in *Watts* stressed the point that the previous offences were not 'so similar to the offence which the jury were trying that they could have been admitted as evidence of similar facts on the issue of identity. In short, their prejudicial effect far outweighed their probative value.'[90] This suggests a balance of probative weight and prejudicial effect. Had the Lord Chief Justice approached *Powell* with this principle in mind he would not have had to withdraw his wise counsel.

Decisions in individual cases will turn on an assessment of the purpose of the accused's attack on prosecution witnesses. Trial judges will have to analyse, in the words of subsection (*f*)(ii), 'the nature and conduct of the defence' in order to determine if and how much of the accused's moral record should be divulged. A finding that the defence has engaged in a general moral contest will be very rare. In most cases the real question will be whether the disclosure of the accused's record is necessary to counter a specific allegation made by the accused in his evidence or a particular line of argument put forward by the defence. In these situations the trial judge's main concern will be to ensure that the cross-examination proposed by the prosecution is indeed necessary in order to meet the allegation or the arguments deployed by the defence. Naturally, having to justify a line of cross-examination by reference to its probative purpose will both reduce the scope for introducing evidence of bad character and make the trial judge's decision subject to appellate review.[91]

[90] [1983] 3 All ER 104.
[91] The implementation of these principles will rid the law of spurious distinctions, such as the distinctions between rule and discretion, between relevance to issue and relevance to credibility, and between a challenge to a short confession and a challenge to a long one.

CROSS-EXAMINATION OF ACCUSED BY A CO-ACCUSED:
PROBATIVE AND MORAL CONTESTS

Sub-section (f)(iii) of section 1 of the 1898 Act makes provision for the cross-examination of one accused by another accused who is jointly charged with the former. It provides that the restrictions on cross-examination of an accused are lifted when 'he has given evidence against any other person charged in the same proceedings.'[92]

Unlike the earlier parts of subsection (f) the present subsection has a clear rationale. It holds that it would be wrong to limit the co-accused's freedom to fight for an acquittal in order not to disadvantage the accused. Provided that the accused has given evidence which either supports the prosecution's case in a material respect or undermines the co-accused's defence, the latter has a right to cross-examine the accused as if he were a prosecution witness.[93]

Unfortunately the courts have refused to place any restriction on the co-accused's freedom to cross-examine the accused, once the latter has given evidence against the former, or to allow the trial judge any restraining discretion.[94] This puts an accused with a criminal record in a very difficult situation when he is jointly charged with a co-accused whom he wishes to blame for the offence attributed to him.[95] The justification given for condoning this result is that the law must not place any obstacle in the way of the co-accused's freedom to establish his innocence.

If the distinction between attacking probative credibility and moral credibility is a valid one, then there is room for a restriction on the freedom of cross-examination in these cases. When the accused has confined his testimony to a factual account of

---

[92] Originally this provision applied to giving evidence against a person 'charged with the same offence'. These words were considered too restrictive and have been replaced with the words 'the same proceedings' by the Criminal Evidence Act 1979. For background to the change see *Metropolitan Police Commissioner* v. *Hills* [1978] 2 All ER 1105 and Mirfield [1978] Crim L Rev 725.

[93] *Murdoch* v. *Taylor* [1965] 1 All ER 406, 416.

[94] Ibid. 406.

[95] Ibid. 408, Lord Reid commented that 'an accused person with previous convictions, whose story contradicts in any material respect the story of a co-accused ... will find it almost impossible to defend himself, and if he elects not to give evidence his plight will be just as bad ...'

the events, there is good reason why the co-accused should be allowed to cross-examine the accused in order to attack his probative credibility and thus undermine the probative force of the evidence that the accused has given.[96] But there is no reason in fairness why the co-accused should also be allowed in such a situation to launch a general attack on the accused's moral credibility where this has no significant probative bearing on the accused's testimony. Of course, it would be different where the accused has attacked the moral credibility of the co-accused and widened the dispute beyond the confines of the events with which the charges against the two accused are concerned. Where this has not happened, the trial judge should strive to contain the dispute within the bounds of fairness and propriety and not allow the trial to degenerate into a mud-slinging match which contributes nothing to the determination of the truth.

As it is, the operation of subsection (f)(iii) does not relieve the trial judge from exercising judgment. Far from it, on occasion his decision will require considerable intellectual effort. In *Murdoch* v. *Taylor* Lord Donovan explained that

what *is* 'evidence against' a co-accused is perhaps the most difficult part of the case. At one end of the scale is evidence which does no more than contradict something which a co-accused has said without further advancing the prosecution's case in any significant degree. . . . this is not the kind of evidence contemplated by proviso (f)(iii). At the other end of the scale is evidence which, if the jury believes it, would establish the co-accused's guilt . . .[97]

In between these two poles there may be many shades which could require considerable judicial energy in deciding on which side the case falls. The distinction between relevance to credit and relevance to the issue has lost its importance here.[98] But

---

[96] A co-accused may challenge the accused's version of the events by putting to him an incriminating statement made by the accused to the police, which would have been inadmissible as evidence for the prosecution: *Rowson* (1985) 80 Cr App R 218.

[97] [1965] 1 All ER 415.

[98] While orthodoxy continues to maintain the need for a distinction, appellate courts do not seem to be over-zealous to compel trial judges to mouth the worn-out incantation. See *Hoggins* [1967] 3 All ER 334, 336 and review in Pattenden, 'The purpose of cross-examination under section 1(f) of the Criminal Evidence Act 1898', [1982] Crim L Rev 707, 718.

Lord Donovan's dictum requires trial judges to examine the evidential purpose of the testimony given by the accused. The proposal advocated here builds upon this idea in that it requires the trial judge to confine the accused's cross-examination to what is necessary to counter the testimony he has given.

In one respect subsection (f)(iii) places too great a restraint on cross-examination. *A* and *B* are tried together; to defend himself *A* gives evidence against *B* and is cross-examined by *B*'s counsel on his criminal record. *B* then testifies but says nothing which amounts to evidence against *A*.[99] May *A* cross-examine *B* on his criminal record?[100]

Neither subsection (ii) nor subsection (iii) gives licence to *A* to cross-examine *B* in this situation. But if *A* may not cross-examine *B*, the outcome is very odd: when the conduct of *B*'s defence amounts to an imputation against a witnesses for the prosecution he may be examined under subsection (ii) but he is immune from such examination when the imputations are directed against *A* who is tried in the same trial. In fairness the trial judge should be able to grant permission to *A* to cross-examine *B* where, for example, the cross-examination of *A* by *B*'s counsel was calculated to depict a moral contrast between the two accused, notwithstanding that *B* has not given evidence against *A*.[101]

It is settled that when an accused has given evidence against a co-accused, the trial judge has discretion to allow the prosecution to cross-examine the accused on his record.[102] Such cross-examination may be required where letting the accused's allegations remain unchallenged may distort the factual picture of the events.[103]

The strategy proposed here will not completely eliminate the

---

[99] It is assumed that a bare denial by *B* of his own involvement would not count as evidence against *A*.

[100] These problems were drawn to my attention by Mr M. Gelowitz.

[101] A further variant to the problem is involved in the following situation: *A* testifies in his defence without involving *B*. *B* testifies and incriminates *A*. *A*'s counsel cross-examines *B* and attacks his moral credibility by depicting him as a ruthless criminal with many convictions. *B* has no way of redressing the balance because *A* has finished testifying.

[102] *Seigley* (1911) 6 Cr App R 106; *Murdoch* v. *Taylor* [1965] 1 All ER 406.

[103] See *Cross on Evidence*, 6th edn. (1985), 375.

conflict between the accused's interests and those of the co-accused and the danger of prejudice to one or both of them. Whenever the criminal record of an accused person emerges there is a risk of infringement of the two cardinal principles of criminal justice. This conflict can be more effectively obviated by splitting the indictment and conducting separate trials. The pressures against such a solution are, however, formidable. Where the prosecution's case is that several accused committed the offence together there is, as explained in the previous chapter, a social need to deal with all the accused in the same trial. Addressing an argument that severance should have been ordered because co-accused were liable to cross-examine each other on character, Lawton LJ explained:

The factor of the public [*sic*] and interest of the public in the proper administration of justice is a very powerful factor indeed, and in the majority of cases where men are charged jointly, it is clearly in the interests of justice and the ascertainment of truth that all the men so charged should be tried together.[104]

A similar sentiment has been recently expressed by Kilner Brown J who said:

The truth of the matter is that this was a case where two experienced criminals metaphorically cut each other's throats in the course of their respective defences. If separate trials had been ordered, one or the other or both might have succeeded in preventing a just result.[105]

It seems that, notwithstanding occasional protestations to the contrary, judges regard disclosure of criminal record as important to the ascertainment of truth. Furthermore, these dicta are indicative of a strong trend to give preference to the social desirability of trying several connected offenders together over the interests of the accused involved in the joint trial. However, it is very much to be doubted whether the interests of the public in seeing a criminal episode disposed of as a whole should be allowed to outweigh so easily the interest of accused persons in not being exposed to prejudice.[106]

---

[104] *Hoggins* [1967] 3 All ER 334, 336.
[105] *Varley* [1982] 2 All ER 519, 522.
[106] See Dawson, 'Joint trials of defendants in criminal cases: an analysis of efficiencies and prejudices', 77 Mich L Rev 1379 (1979).

14

Witnesses: Compellability and Privilege

THE DUTY TO DISCLOSE INFORMATION TO THE COURT

Witnesses are the principal source of evidence in the courts and it is therefore essential to the determination of truth that the law should impose a duty on every person within the jurisdiction to testify or to hand over evidence. Hence the law stipulates that, at the request of the parties before the court, the court will summon persons in possession of relevant information to come and give in evidence the information they possess.[1] The law gives priority to the need to secure information over other interests of the citizen. A person cannot excuse himself from giving evidence by saying that he is otherwise engaged, or that he has promised not to disclose the sought-after information, or that its disclosure would cause him embarrassment.[2]

Reflecting this principle, the Criminal Procedure (Attendance of Witnesses) Act 1965, lays down that a person served with a witness summons cannot exempt himself from his duty to attend the court unless he satisfies the court that 'he cannot give any material evidence or ... produce any document or thing

---

[1] The summoning of witnesses in criminal cases is governed by the Criminal Procedure (Attendance of Witnesses) Act 1965, which confers on the courts the power to order the attendance of witnesses by means of witness summons and, if necessary, to enforce its orders by means of arrest of recalcitrant witnesses; s. 4.

[2] *The Countess of Shrewsbury's Trial*, 2 How St Tr 769, 778. Bentham drew a vivid picture of the implications of this duty: 'Are men of first rank and consideration—are men high in office—men whose time is not less valuable to the public than to themselves—are such men to be forced to quit their business, their functions, and what is more than all, their pleasure, at the beck of every idle of malicious adversary, to dance attendance upon every petty cause? Yes, as far as it is necessary, they and everybody ... Were the Prince of Wales, the Archbishop of Canterbury, and the Lord High Chancellor, to be passing by in the same coach, while a chimney-sweeper and a barrow-woman were in dispute about a halfpennyworth of apples, and the chimney-sweeper or the barrow-woman were to think proper to call upon them for their evidence, could they refuse it? No, most certainly'; *Works of Jeremy Bentham*, Bowring edn. (1843), vol. 4, pp. 320–1.

likely to be material evidence'.[3] Once in the witness-box, a witness is duty-bound by his oath to tell 'the truth, the whole truth and nothing but the truth'.[4] The duty to disclose in the courts evidence of crime is still subject to a number of exceptions which can hinder the proof of crime. The main restriction consists of the privilege against self-incrimination which the law confers on persons suspected or accused of criminal offences. This privilege will be discussed in Chapter 15. This Chapter is concerned with the privileges of other groups. It will be argued that the privileges of certain groups constitute indefensible obstacles to the ascertainmet of truth.

UNIVERSAL COMPETENCE

The moral acceptability of the means of obtaining convictions plays an important role in the fashioning of the criminal process. It is therefore to be expected that the law should give expression to public precepts concerning the acceptability of certain groups of witnesses and to public opinion regarding the propriety of compelling certain witnesses to testify.

Until the nineteenth century English law was much occupied with the moral qualifications of witnesses. Certain classes of witnesses were thought to lack what Wigmore called the 'moral responsibility' to justify legal reliance on their testimony.[5] For instance, persons who had been convicted of infamous crime were altogether disqualified as witnesses.[6] The denial of competence was usually founded on considerations of unreliability, but it is fairly clear that the exclusion of entire classes of witnesses often had deeper roots. Non-Christians, for example, were excluded on account of their inability to take the oath on the Gospel. Although the oath was thought to provide a guaran-

---

[3] Section 2(2) of the 1965 Act. Under s. 3, '[a]ny person who without just excuse disobeys a witness order or summons requiring him to attend before any court shall be guilty of contempt of that court and may be punished summarily by that court . . .'

[4] *Archbold's Pleading, Evidence and Practice in Criminal Cases* 42nd edn. (1985), 372.

[5] *Wigmore on Evidence*, 3rd edn. (1940), vol. 2, s. 515.

[6] These disqualifications were abolished by the Civil Rights of Convicts Act 1828 and finally by the Evidence Act 1843.

tee of veracity, the hostility felt against other religions was probably the dominant reason.[7] The incompetence according to which those who had an interest in the outcome of the proceedings were excluded as witnesses lasted longer than the last two forms of incompetence. Most importantly, this exclusion disqualified the parties to the proceedings from testifying. By the late nineteenth century all traces of this incompetence were abolished.[8]

Few traces of class-incompetence remain in contemporary law. Children and persons of defective intellect are usually mentioned as providing instances of the remaining categories of incompetence. In fact neither children nor persons of defective intellect are invariably excluded as witnesses. Children may testify under oath, as long as they understand its significance.[9] In criminal proceedings children of tender years may testify without taking an oath, if they possess sufficient intelligence to make their testimony worthwhile.[10] The reception of the testimony of persons of defective intellect depends on their understanding of the significance of the oath and on their credibility as witnesses.[11]

One of the principal ramifications of the right against self-incrimination is, as we shall see, that the accused may not be called to testify by the prosecution. It is often said that the accused is incompetent to testify for the prosecution.[12] This usage is misleading because it is not the case that he cannot give evidence in support of the prosecution. The accused has a right to testify on his own behalf, if he so chooses.[13] An accused who has chosen to testify is duty-bound to answer truthfully all

---

[7] This hostility found expression in *Clavin's case* 7 Co 17, as cited in Best, *The Principles of the Law of Evidence*, 5th edn. (1870), 192: 'All infidels are in law perpetui inimici, perpetual enemies . . . for between them, as with the devils, whose subjects they are, and the Christians, there is perpetual hostility, and can be no peace.' This attitude was finally put to rest in *Omychund* v. *Barker* (1745) 1 Atk 21, discussed by Best, ibid. 196.

[8] The effective legislation consisted of the Evidence Act 1843, the Evidence Act 1851, the Evidence Further Amendment Act 1869, and the Criminal Evidence Act 1898, which made the accused a competent witness in criminal trials.

[9] *Brasier* (1779) 1 Leach 199; *Hays* [1977] 2 All ER 288.

[10] Children and Young Persons Act 1933. See *Campbell* [1956] 2 All ER 272.

[11] *Hill* (1851) 2 Den 254.

[12] See, for instance, *Phipson on Evidence*, 13th edn. (1982), 697; Cross on Evidence, 6th edn. (1985), 194.

[13] Criminal Evidence Act 1898, s. 1 (a).

relevant questions put to him by the prosecution, even if the answers will incriminate him[14] or incriminate a person jointly charged with him. The accused's testimony, if believed, may be used as evidence against him or his co-accused.[15] Thus, once the accused has waived his privilege not to testify[16] and has entered the witness box, he is no longer free to withhold information supporting the prosecution.[17]

Thus, in contemporary law, class-tests of competence have given way to personal rules of competence. The general principle is that all persons are competent to give evidence, may be lawfully summoned to testify, and must answer all relevant questions addressed to them while testifying. This is, in the words of Lord Wilberforce, a 'constitutional principle underlying our whole system of justice'.[18] Exemptions are afforded only in the form of freedom to refrain from giving evidence on certain matters.

INCOMPELLABILITY AND PRIVILEGE: LICENCE TO WITHHOLD INFORMATION FROM THE COURT

A conceptual distinction is often drawn between a witness who cannot be compelled to testify and a witness who possesses a

---

[14] Section 1(e) of the 1898 Act.

[15] *Rudd* (1948) 32 Cr App R 138; *Paul* [1920] 2 KB 183; and discussion in *Cross on Evidence*, 6th edn. (1985), 195–6.

[16] The accused has also a right to decline testifying when called to do so by a co-accused; Criminal Evidence Act 1898, s. 1; *Payne* (1872) LR 1 CCR 349. This position is preserved by the Police and Criminal Evidence Act 1984, s. 80(4).

[17] The accused is similarly said to be incompetent as prosecution witness against a co-accused. However, if a notice of *nolle prosequi* has been filed in respect of the accused or if he has already been convicted and sentenced he may be called on behalf of the prosecution. See *Payne* [1950] 1 All ER 102 and discussion by Gooderson, 'The Evidence of Co-prisoners', (1953) 11 CLJ 209. On the extent to which an accomplice against whom proceedings are pending may be called by the prosecution to testify against the accused see: *Pipe* (1966) 51 Cr App R 17; *Turner* (1975) 61 Cr App R 67; *R v. Governor of Pentonville Prison ex parte Schneider* (1981) 73 Cr App R 200.

[18] *Hoskyn* [1978] 2 All ER 136, 138. The Sixth Amendment of the American Constitution confers on every accused the right 'to have compulsory process for obtaining witnesses in his favor'. There are a few exceptions: the monarch may not be compelled to give evidence by process of law; *A-G v. Radloff* (1854) 10 Exch 84, 94; the Diplomatic Privileges Act 1964, relieves foreign ambassadors from compellable process; see *Phipson on Evidence*, 13th edn. (1982), 708.

privilege to refuse to answer questions on certain matters. However, this distinction lacks substance. The accused's wife cannot, generally speaking, be compelled to give evidence for the prosecution.[19] She is said to be incompellable. In contrast, a witness testifying in a civil or criminal trial is said to possess a privilege not to answer questions where the answers would tend to incriminate him of a crime. When we compare the position of the spouse with that of a witness, it is clear that they both enjoy a similar freedom to chose whether or not to testify on certain matters: a wife is free not to incriminate her husband and a witness is free to refrain from incriminating himself.[20] It makes little difference whether we describe these freedoms in terms of privilege or incompellability.[21]

The privilege against self-incrimination confers on the citizen the freedom to refuse to divulge information showing that he has committed a criminal offence. A person may assert his privilege on three different occasions. First, when a person is called as witness in a criminal or civil trial he may refuse 'to answer any question if the answer thereto would, in the opinion of the judge, have a tendency to expose the deponent to any criminal charge, penalty or forfeiture which the judge regards as reasonably likely to be preferred or sued for'.[22] Secondly, a suspect may refuse to answer questions put to him during police interrogation or other official investigation. Lastly, a person standing trial for a criminal offence has a choice whether or not to go into the witness-box and testify.

There is a procedural difference between the assertion of the privilege by a witness, by a suspect, and by an accused.[23] A witness has to assert his privilege in response to every question

---

[19] The position is, of course, identical for the husband of an accused wife.

[20] A witness testifying in civil proceedings is exempt from answering questions that might incriminate his or her spouse: Civil Evidence Act 1968. s. 14. This freedom is commonly categorized as a privilege although in essence it is no different from the freedom not to testify against a spouse in criminal proceedings.

[21] While in some contexts it will be convenient to speak of a privilege and in others of incompellability, these terms are used interchangeably.

[22] *Blunt* v. *Park Lane Hotel Ltd* [1942] 2 All ER 187, 189. The rules concerning penalties and forfeiture are relatively unimportant and will not be discussed; for their exposition see *Cross on Evidence*, 6th edn. (1985), 381.

[23] Cf. Glanville Williams *The Proof of Guilt* (1963). 37–8.

put to him[24] while an accused person may avoid being asked questions either by keeping silent when interrogated by the police or by staying out of the witness-box. This is a procedural difference necessitated by a difference of circumstance. When a witness testifies, neither the witness nor the court (and sometimes not even the party questioning him) can know in advance whether questions will tend to incriminate the witness. Consequently, before an issue of self-incrimination can arise, specific questions have to be put to the witness. The position of an accused is different: the entire trial is concerned with his alleged criminal conduct. If he is cross-examined, it is solely with a view to showing him to be guilty of the offence charged. In these circumstances it would be pointless (and quite possibly prejudicial) to seek his assertion of the privilege in relation to every single question. We may therefore say that a witness and an accused have a similar privilege but that different procedures for its invocation are provided.

THE PRIVILEGE OF THE ACCUSED'S SPOUSE: A HINDRANCE TO THE ASCERTAINMENT OF TRUTH

The exemption of the accused's spouse from the duty of testifying against the accused has a long history which is wrapped, as Wigmore put it, 'in tantalizing obscurity'.[25] The dispensation accorded to the accused's spouse is now governed by section 80 of the Police and Criminal Evidence Act 1984, and this discussion will be confined to the justification of the present arrangements.

Broadly speaking, the accused's spouse is always competent and may testify both for the accused and for the prosecution.[26] However, subject to a number of exceptions, the spouse is free to choose whether to testify for the prosecution or for a person

---

[24] *Allhusen* v. *Labouchere* (1878) 3 QBD 654, 660.

[25] *Wigmore on Evidence*, 3rd edn. (1940), vol. 8, 2227, p. 221. Wigmore speculated that the origin of the wife's incompetence to testify against her husband might have originated in her semi-servitudinal status: ibid. pp. 22–3.

[26] For simplicity of exposition I shall assume a male accused and a female spouse.

jointly charged with the accused. The justification for this exemption from the civil duty to testify is far from self-evident.[27]

Four principal reasons have been put forward at one time or another in support of the exemption. However, here we need only concern ourselves with the justification that is reflected in the present law.[28] The rationale underlying the spouse's privilege in section 80 of the Police and Criminal Evidence Act 1984 is that which also appealed to the Criminal Law Revision Committee and to the House of Lords, namely that compulsion to testify might lead to marital discord.[29] Section 80 confers on the spouse a choice of whether to testify for the prosecution or a co-accused.[30] The idea is that if relations between the spouses are poor, a spouse will not be deterred from testifying against the accused but, where harmony subsists, a spouse will decline to do so and thereby preserve the matrimonial accord. To emphasize this rationale section 80(5) of the 1984 Act provides that once the marriage is over, the ex-spouse 'shall be competent and compellable to give evidence as if that person and the accused had never been married'.

Marital harmony is doubtless very important but in view of contemporary public attitudes the force of this consideration is somewhat limited. When marriage was indissoluble, the souring of relations between the spouses would have condemned them

---

[27] The rationale of the exemption was considered by the Criminal Law Revision Committee, whose recommendations lead to the enactment of s. 80 of the Police and Criminal Evidence Act 1984; 11th Report, cmnd. 4991, paras. 143–57. The Committee's arguments for spouses' privilege were echoed in the House of Lords in the case of *Hoskyn* [1978] 2 All ER 136. The case dealt with the law as it stood before the Police and Criminal Evidence Act 1984, but its analysis of the rationale of the spouse exemption is still pertinent.

[28] For a survey see *Hoskyn* [1978] 2 All ER 136 and Criminal Law Revision Committee, 11th Report, cmnd. 4991, paras. 143 ff.

[29] Criminal Law Revision Committee, 11th Report, cmnd. 4991, para. 148; *Hoskyn* [1978] 2 All ER 139, 149. In *Hoskyn* the issue was whether a wife who, under the old law, was competent to testify against her husband, because he was charged with an offence of violence against her, was also compellable to do so. Since in such circumstances marital harmony will have already been disturbed, it seems incongruous to appeal to harmony as a justification for deciding that the spouse was not compellable.

[30] It should be noted that when husband and wife are jointly charged, they cannot be called to testify for the prosecution irrespective of their willingness to do so; s. 80(4) of the 1984 Act. They may, of course, testify on their own behalf.

to living together in enmity for the rest of their lives or, alternatively, to separation without the prospect of establishing another family. However, matrimonial morality and matrimonial policy have undergone radical transformation. If marital relations have deteriorated, the marriage can be brought to an end. Indeed, a very considerable proportion of marriages do in fact end in divorce. It is difficult to imagine that granting spouses immunity from having to testify against each other in criminal proceedings makes an appreciable contribution to the general stability of marriage in our community.

There are further considerations that weaken the justification based on matrimonial harmony. If the wife is accorded a freedom to choose whether or not to testify, her accused husband will in many cases bring pressure to bear on her to refuse to testify when invited to do so by the prosecution. Those who regard it as repugnant to call a wife to testify against her husband (or a husband against his wife) should reflect that the present law holds out a temptation to the accused to exercise unedifying pressure on his or her spouse to refrain from testifying.[31] If the wife succumbs to pressure from her accused husband and declines to impart incriminating information, she is in effect made an unwilling accomplice after the event in that she is helping her husband to escape punishment. A spouse who becomes an instrument in the accused's attempt to avoid conviction suffers moral degradation which is likely to undermine the couple's harmony.

Even where a spouse freely chooses to decline the prosecution's call to testify, the moral position of withholding information that may lead to the accused's conviction is highly ambivalent. One may perhaps be able to defend a failure to initiate a complaint but it could hardly be maintained that withholding incriminating evidence from the court, once the accused has

---

[31] Before the 1984 Act the general rule was one of not merely incompellability but also of incompetence; see *Cross on Evidence*, 5th edn. (1979), 173 ff. A spouse simply could not testify on behalf of the prosecution. Thus under the old system the spouse was at least spared the invidious moral position in which a spouse could easily be placed under the present law. The old law did, however, suffer from many other serious shortcomings; for criticism see Criminal Law Revision Committee, 11th Report, cmnd. 4991, para. 143 ff.

been charged, is morally acceptable, especially where the offence is a grave one.

Lastly, even if the privilege protects the marital harmony of
accused persons, it is doubtful whether this end provides sufficient justification for foregoing evidence of crime and, to that
extent, reducing the protection of the community from crime.[32]

It may, perhaps, be suggested that the privilege is intended to
relieve the spouse from facing an unpleasant choice when called
to testify for the prosecution of either testifying against the
accused, or committing perjury or committing contempt by
refusing to answer questions.[33] However, this justification fails
to provide a reason for exempting the spouse as distinguished
from other relations of the accused. It can hardly be supposed
that a similar repugnance is not experienced at the sight of a
mother forced, on pain of contempt, to provide incriminating
testimony against her son.[34] It might be said that when the
accused stands alone facing the machinery of the state which is
trying to obtain his conviction, it is unfair that the state should
involve the accused's spouse to advance its case. Like the previous argument, however, this does not explain why the privilege should be conferred only on the spouse and not on other
relatives, nor is it consistent with section 80 which confers the
choice on the spouse rather than on the accused.

There is little justification therefore for granting a person a
privilege to refuse to furnish evidence of crime by virtue of that
person's matrimonial status. Fortunately, the legislature seems
to have accepted that the need to determine the facts in a
criminal trial may override the argument from marital harmony
and has restricted the privilege in some important respects.

---

[32] See Bentham, *A Treatise on Judicial Evidence*, Dumont edn. (1825), 238.

[33] Viscount Dilhorne considered it objectionable to sanction universal compellability 'no matter how trivial [the charge] and no matter the consequences to her and
to her family'. *Hoskyn* [1978] 2 All ER 148. See also Lord Salmon, ibid.

[34] In some countries the compellability, to testify against each other, of parents
and children is restricted: the Israel Evidence Ordinance (New Version) 1971, cl. 4;
the Victoria Crimes Act 1958, s. 400. The Australian Law Reform Commission has
recommended extension of the privilege to informal spouses: Research Paper no. 5,
ch. 7.

LIMITATIONS OF THE SPOUSE'S PRIVILEGE

The accused's spouse is generally free to decline to testify for the prosecution or a person jointly charged with the accused, but the spouse must testify if summoned by the accused.[35] The prosecution and a co-defendant may also compel the spouse's testimony in certain circumstances. Section 80(3) makes the spouse a compellable witness for the prosecution if:

(*a*)   the offence charged involves an assault on, or injury to or a threat of injury to, the wife or husband of the accused or a person who was at the material time under the age of sixteen; or
(*b*)   the offence charged is a sexual offence alleged to have been committed in respect of a person who was at the material time under that age; or
(*c*)   the offence charged consists of attempting or conspiring to commit, or of aiding, abetting, counselling and procuring or inciting the commission of, an offence falling within paragraph (*a*) or (*b*) above.

The compellability of a spouse when the charge involves an offence of violence against him or her continues the common-law tradition in this respect. Given that offences between spouses are likely to be committed in private, a wife would be at the mercy of her husband if she were not compellable to testify against him.[36]

The compellability of the accused's spouse when the accused stands charged with an offence of violence or with a sexual offence against a person under sixteen breaks new ground. The legislature has signalled that the protection of children is more important than the promotion of marital harmony.[37] There is but a small step between this position and a wider provision of compellability encompassing all serious offences; for it can hardly be said that the protection of children from crime is

---

[35] See s. 80(1), (2).
[36] Until the House of Lords decision in *Hoskyn* [1978] 2 All ER 136, the spouse's competence was understood to imply compellability too. See *Cross on Evidence*, 5th edn. (1979), 176–7.
[37] Presumably, compelling the wife to testify in relation to such offences is not thought to create public repugnance or, if it does, the protection of children is more important than pandering to public feeling.

more pressing than the protection of other citizens.[38] Now that the legislature has conceded that the spouse's privilege is to be balanced against the need to protect other citizens from crime, it will be easier to remove the privilege in respect of further and more serious offences, such as murder and, indeed, to dismantle it altogether.

The importance attached to the need to secure convictions of the guilty may be observed in a further example. When a witness appears in a civil trial, section 14(1)(b) of the Civil Evidence Act 1968 confers on the witness a 'right to refuse to answer any question or produce any document or thing if to do so would tend to expose the husband or the wife of that person to proceedings for any . . . criminal offence or for the recovery of . . . a penalty'. When a witness testifies in a criminal trial, the witness has no right to refuse answering questions on the grounds that to answer would incriminate the witness's spouse who is not charged in those proceedings. It seems that the legislature is not prepared to allow proof of guilt in criminal trials to be impeded by the need to protect marital harmony of persons who are indirectly involved in the proceedings.[39]

In certain other respects, however, the legislature has been less sensitive to the need to determine the truth. A spouse is compellable to testify on behalf of a person jointly charged with the accused only in the same circumstances that would make spouse compellable for the prosecution. It is difficult to comprehend why a wife should be compellable for her husband's co-

---

[38] As far as offences of violence are concerned, old people are just as vulnerable as the young. The editor of *Cross on Evidence*, 6th edn. (1985), 200, has pointed out that 'the accused's wife will be compellable against him if he kisses a fifteen year old, . . . but not if he rapes and murders a sixteen year old'. The Criminal Law Revision Committee, proposed the limiting of the exception to young persons of the same house as the accused. The idea being that offences against family members would ordinarily not be witnessed by others and that the spouse's testimony should be compellable to protect young members of the family as well as the spouse. The Committee refused to extend compellability to offences against other children because 'the law has never, except perhaps in treason, made the seriousness of an offence by itself a ground for compellability': 11th Report, cmnd. 4991, para. 152. See also para. 151 and cl. 9(3) of the bill attached to the report.

[39] It is notable that when enacting s. 80 of the Police and Criminal Evidence Act 1984, the legislature declined to adopt the recommendation of the Criminal Law Revision Committee to implement the civil privilege in criminal proceedings too. See 11th Report, cmnd. 4991, para. 169.

accused when both men are jointly charged with an offence of violence against a person under sixteen but not in other cases. If the co-accused requires the wife's assistance in proving his innocence, the law should compel this assistance regardless of the consequences for the witness's marital harmony or, alternatively, should provide for separate trials.

The provision concerning comment on a spouse's failure to testify is also unsatisfactory. Subsection (8) of secton 80 provides: 'The failure of the wife or husband of the accused to give evidence shall not be made the subject of any comment by the prosecution.'

The prosecution is forbidden to comment not only on the fact that the spouse declined to testify for the prosecution, but also that the spouse declined to testify for a co-accused. Thus the prosecution may not comment on the accused's failure to call his wife to testify even where, in the circumstances, he might have been expected to do so, as when his alibi is that he was with his wife at the relevant time. It is possible that the provision in the 1984 Act was prompted by the fear that if the prosecution were able to comment, an accused wishing to avoid the adverse effect of such comment might be tempted to summon his wife to testify even when the latter was not in possession of evidence favourable to his case, and pressurize her to falsify her account.[40] Even if it were likely that the threat of comment would encourage accused persons to solicit perjury from their spouses, it is difficult to imagine that this would have added appreciably to the pressure that spouses are liable to face in any event.[41]

The prohibition on comment by the prosecution regarding the wife's failure to testify cannot be justified by appeal to marital harmony because a wife who has declined to testify will

[40] If that were the reasoning, we would have expected to find a similar restriction on the co-accused's right to comment adversely on the failure of the accused's wife to respond to the co-accused's invitation to testify or to comment on the accused's failure to call his own wife, when such comment can help the co-accused's defence. No such restriction exists. It is notable that the Criminal Law Revision Committee, upon whose recommendations the section is broadly fashioned, was against a prohibition upon comment by the prosecution; 11th Report, cmnd. 4991, para. 154.

[41] As the not-infrequent appeals to spouses for alibi support seem to suggest.

often have complied, presumably, with her husband's wishes.[42] It may perhaps be suggested that the refusal of a spouse to testify for the prosecution is probatively ambiguous; it may arise from the spouse's preference not to get involved in the proceedings rather than from the spouse's or the accused's desire to withhold incriminating information. If this is the case, the prohibition is too wide because it attempts to prevent legitimate inferences from the spouse's refusal as well as unfounded ones.

It has to be acknowledged, however, that in one respect a prohibition upon prosecution comment does contribute to marital harmony. The spouse in possession of relevant information is given an opportunity of maximizing the accused's prospects of acquittal and the couple's chances of continuing to enjoy each other's company. Whether this is what the legislature had in mind is, of course, another matter.

Given the flaw in the basic principle of spouse privilege, the definition of its scope is bound to be haphazard. Before long Parliament will have to consider the balance of policy again. In civil proceedings spouses are on the whole treated like any other witnesses and may be called to testify against each other without any limitation. The marital discord arising from such instances may be as great as it would be in criminal proceeding, and with far less justification from the point of view of the administration of justice. The 1984 Act already recognizes that the interests of marriage have to give way to the interest of securing convictions in some categories of cases. From now on there will be pressure to extend these categories whenever, in particular cases attracting public attention, the assertion of the privilege creates public outrage. These pressures will, in the long run, lead to a progressive narrowing of the privilege.[43]

---

[42] Section 80(8) is in line with s. 1(b) of the Criminal Evidence Act 1898: 'The failure of any person charged with an offence, or of the wife or husband, as the case may be, or the person so charged, to give evidence shall not be made the subject of any comment by the prosecution'. In the context of the 1898 Act, s. 1 makes sense because it was feared that if the prosecution's right of comment were not curbed, the accused's right not to testify would have been eroded.

[43] The law of Victoria has moved closer to this position by holding spouses generally compellable for the prosecution while laying down guidelines for discretionary exemption: Crimes Act 1958, s. 400 (Vic). A similar scheme was recommended by the Australian Law Reform Commission, Research Paper no. 5, p. 86.

THE PRIVILEGE OF A WITNESS TO WITHHOLD
SELF-INCRIMINATING INFORMATION

The principal manifestations of the privilege against self-incrimination take place during the questioning of suspects by the police and at the trial of accused persons, as we shall see in the next chapter. However, the privilege applies more widely and entitles a person to withhold self-incriminating information when he appears as a witness in civil or criminal proceedings.[44]

The privilege entitles a witness to withhold both answers that disclose the incriminating facts themselves, such as commission of a crime, and answers that disclose facts which may later be relied upon to establish his guilt.[45] Because the privilege belongs to the witness and in no way confers any rights on the parties, it is for the witness to claim it, though in practice he will often be advised by the judge of the potential self-incrimination which a line of questioning poses.[46] The witness is not, however, the sole arbiter of whether he has a right to refuse to answer a question. In the final resort, it is for the trial judge to determine whether a question creates a reasonable risk of self-incrimination.[47] Since a party has no business to object to a witness furnishing self-incriminating evidence, the fact that a witness was wrongly obliged to divulge such evidence is no ground for quashing a conviction.[48] However, wrongly compelled self-incriminating evidence may not be used against the witness in subsequent proceedings against him.[49]

In support of this privilege it is suggested that if witnesses were exposed to answering self-incriminating questions, they

---

[44] *Blunt* v. *Park Lane Hotel Ltd* [1942] 2 All ER 187. See also Evidence Act 1851, s. 3. The exemption also entitles a person to give answers that tend to expose him to penalty and criminal forfeiture. For the meaning of these terms see *Cross on Evidence*, 6th edn. (1985), 381–2.

[45] *Slany* (1832) 5 C & P 213.

[46] *Coote* (1873) LR 4 PC 599; *Thomas* v. *Newton* (1827) 2 C & P 606.

[47] *Boyes* (1861) 1 B & S 311; *Spokes* v. *Grosvenor Hotel Co* [1897] 2 QB 124; *Triplex Safety Glass Co* v. *Lancegay Safety Glass* [1939] 2 All ER 613; *Rio Tinto Zinc Corp* v. *Westinghouse Electric Corp* [1978] 1 All ER 434 See also *Archbold's Pleading, Evidence and Practice in Criminal Cases* 42nd edn. (1985), p. 974.

[48] *Kinglake* (1870) 11 Cox CC 499; but see n. 63 below.

[49] *Garbett* (1847) 1 Den 236.

might be reluctant to come forward and testify. Persons who have something to conceal will not voluntarily come forward, whether or not the privilege exists, because the assertion of the privilege is bound to draw attention to the matters which the witness wishes to conceal and put the investigative institutions (whether they be the police or the press) on the scent. We may assume with a fair degree of confidence that had the law not afforded a privilege to the suspect and the accused it would not have accorded one to a mere witness either.[50]

The witness privilege has often been overridden by legislation in order to secure necessary evidence. In some instances the witness's right is preserved in substance by a provision that his answers may not be used in evidence against him in later proceedings.[51] In other situations the legislature has been prepared to ride roughshod over the privilege by removing it altogether. Thus, for example, in matters concerning official secrets, taxation, and gambling a person may not only be required to provide self-incriminating information, but such information may also be deployed against him.[52]

The courts have also taken a hand in seeing that the privilege does not receive strong procedural backing. Although judges tend to warn witnesses of their right not to answer questions that might incriminate them, answers furnished in the absence of such warning and in ignorance of the right are admissible in subsequent proceedings against the witness as well as in the trial in which they are given.[53]

OTHER PRIVILEGES: AN OUTLINE

Two other major obstacles to the obtaining of evidence are recognized by the law: legal professional privilege and public

---

[50] The rationale of suspects and accused privilege is discussed in the next chapter.

[51] Theft Act 1968, s. 31; Supreme Court Act 1981, s. 72. See *Phipson on Evidence*, 13th edn. (1982), 319–20.

[52] Heydon, 'Statutory restrictions on the privilege against self-incrimination' (1971) 87 LQR 214; *Cross on Evidence*, 6th edn. (1985), 387–8.

[53] *Cross on Evidence*, 6th edn. (1985), 385. However, when the wife of an accused has testified against the accused in ignorance of her right to refuse doing so, the conviction of the accused may be quashed; *Pitt* [1982] 3 All ER 63, 66. See also *Acaster* (1912) 7 Cr App R 187.

interest immunity. Since the rules governing these matters give rise to little dispute in criminal trials, they will only be outlined.

Legal Professional Privilege

Professor Cross captured the position in the following statement:

In civil and criminal cases, confidential communications passing between a client and his legal adviser need not be given in evidence by the client, and, without the client's consent, may not be given in evidence by the legal adviser in a judicial proceeding if made either—(1) to enable the client to obtain, or the adviser to give, legal advice; or (2) with reference to litigation that is actually taking place or was in the contemplation of the client.[54]

Under the second head not only communications which passed between the lawyer and his client are privileged but also communications between the client's legal advisers and third parties, if made for the purpose of pending or contemplated litigation. Similarly, communications between the client himself and third parties are privileged if made for submission to the client's legal adviser in connection with litigation.[55] Material covered by legal professional privilege is, subject to certain exceptions, immune from search and seizure under the Police and Criminal Evidence Act 1984.[56]

The idea behind the rule is that the protection of confidentiality between the client and his legal adviser encourages candour on the part of the client and this, in turn, enables the lawyer to offer the client useful legal advice and effectively represent the client in litigation.[57] Much of the material covered by legal

---

[54] *Cross on Evidence*, 5th edn. (1979), 282.

[55] 16th Report of the Law Reform Committee, para. 17.

[56] See ss. 8–10. It is thought that for the purpose of search and seizure the scope of privileged material is somewhat extended by the Act; see *Cross on Evidence*, 6th edn. (1985), 395–6. See also Stone, 'PACE: Special procedures and legal privilege', [1988] Crim L Rev 498.

[57] Since the privilege is for the benefit of the client it is in the client's power to waive it. Once waived by the client, the lawyer has no right to refuse disclosure in a court of law; *Wilson* v. *Rastall* (1792) 4 TR 753. For the relationship between this exception and the special procedure set up by the Police and Criminal Evidence Act 1984, see *R.* v. *Central Criminal Court, ex parte Francis & Francis* [1988] 1 All ER 677. Nor can a lawyer withhold a document in circumstances in which his client would not have been entitled to do so; *R.* v. *Peterborough Justices, ex parte Hicks* [1978] 1 All ER 225.

professional privilege will also be beyond the reach of the state as a consequence of the privilege against self-incrimination.

There are two common-law exceptions of particular significance in criminal trials. The first is that communications between client and lawyer before a crime are not privileged if their purpose was to guide or help the commission of crime.[58] Secondly, the privilege is overridden where the information is required by an accused person to prove his innocence.[59]

Public Interest Immunity

In any legal proceedings a party may object to the disclosure of information on the grounds that disclosure would harm the public interest. In deciding whether to accede to a request for immunity (whether from an organ of the state or anyone else) the court has to balance, on the one hand, the public interest in the documents remaining immune from production against, on the other hand, the general interests of the administration of justice and the specific interests of the party seeking disclosure.[60] Only if the balance tilts in favour of non-disclosure will the court refrain from ordering disclosure.

In striking the balance in a criminal case the court will clearly have to give overriding force to the interest of the accused to establish his innocence. If a piece of evidence tends to prove the accused's innocence, we can expect the balance to tilt in favour of disclosure almost regardless of the disadvantage attendant on disclosure.[61] Indeed, the Crown tends not to claim public interest immunity in criminal cases.[62]

Although the doctrines of legal professional privilege and of public interest immunity obtain in criminal trials as well as in

---

[58] *Cox and Railton* (1884) 14 QBD 153. See discussion in *Phipson on Evidence*, 13th edn. (1982), 299. When a privileged document falls into the hands of a third party, a court will not prevent the prosecution from using such document where it tends to prove the accused's guilt; *Butler* v. *Board of Trade* [1970] 3 All ER 593.

[59] *Barton* [1972] 2 All ER 1192; *Ataou* (1988) 87 Cr App R 210.

[60] *Conway* v. *Rimmer* [1968] 1 All ER 874; and see my article 'Privilege and public interest', in C. F. H. Tapper (ed), *Crime Proof and Punishment*, Essays in Memory of Sir Rupert Cross, (1981), 248.

[61] *Richardson* (1863) 3 F & F 693; *Brown and Daley* (1988) 87 Cr App R 52; *Hardy* [1988] Crim L Rev 687; and discussion in my art.: 'Privilege and public interest', 293.

[62] 'Crime and crown privilege', [1959] Crim L Rev 10.

civil trials, they are liable to be overridden in the interest of protecting the innocent from conviction. This and the fact that the Crown is unlikely to seek evidence from the accused's legal advisers renders issues concerning these doctrines a rare occurrence in criminal litigation.[63]

[63] But see Andrews, 'Public interest and criminal proceedings', (1988) 104 LQR 410.

15

The Privilege against Self-Incrimination

The state is not only the prosecutor but also the investigator of crime. To facilitate such investigation the police-force is given considerable powers to search premises, arrest suspects, and interrogate them in custody. But in order to preserve our freedom from excessive state inferference these powers have to be strictly limited and assiduously supervised. Our constitutional law provides most of the instruments for that purpose, but the law of criminal evidence is also concerned with some aspects of this general constitutional problem. These include the protection of the suspect, which is the main subject of this chapter.

Custodial interrogation lays the suspect open to two particular risks of harm against which the law must protect him: the risk of abuse of his person or dignity and the risk of distortion or manipulation of his statements so as to implicate him in crime.

So far as the first of these risks is concerned, it is accepted in every enlightened society that no one may be subjected to physical violence upon his or her person, unless the exertion of physical restraint is necessary in order to prevent the commission of crime. The suspect and the convicted prisoner enjoy the same right not to be killed, injured, or physically abused as any other member of the community. Physical torture during interrogation is forbidden not by virtue of special provisions but by the general criminal law.

Infringement of this right in the course of the official investigation harms the system of justice as well as the individual; a conviction is stripped of its moral validity if it is arrived at by the kind of violation that the criminal process sets out to forbid and punish. Abuses falling short of criminal offences, such as insults and mental degradation of the suspect, can also undermine the moral legitimacy of the criminal process.[1] Accordingly, the Police and Criminal Evidence Act 1984, section 76 (2)(*a*), renders inadmissible a confession obtained as a consequence of oppression, irrespective of its reliability.[2] A similar philosophy lies behind Article 3 of the European Convention on Human Rights and section 8(2) of the Northern Ireland (Emergency Provisions) Act 1978.[3] To safeguard the suspect against abuse, section 78(1) of the 1984 Act establishes a safety-net against unacceptable investigation methods by conferring on the judge a discretion to exclude evidence that adversely affects the fairness of the proceedings.[4] Clearly, there is no conflict between the need to protect the citizen from crime and the policy of outlawing the fruits of torture and degradation because convictions based on these fruits would defeat the aims of the administration of justice.

The second of the principal risks to which suspects are subject, the risk that their statements would be distorted and manipulated so as to implicate them in a crime they did not commit, is more difficult to protect against. Questioning in the police station is often conducted under conditions of pressure and tension. Suspects under investigation are likely to experience considerable strain even when they are innocent, while those who have something to hide or fear may be doubly susceptible to confusion and manipulation. If one adds to this the not-unnatural tendency of the investigator to manipulate the suspect's responses and interpret them in a way that confirms his own suspicion, one realizes that the scope for unreliability of

---

[1] Verbal abuse of another does not generally constitute a criminal offence because the victim can usually spare himself indignity by walking away from the abuser. But a suspect under arrest is not free to do so; hence his abuse by insults and degradation is offensive to our sense of justice.

[2] There is a suggestion that the doctrine, which antedates the 1984 act, is designed to protect the privilege against self-incrimination; see Lord McDermott's definition cited with approval in *Prager* [1972] 1 All ER 1114. The doctrine has, however, independent moral force and should not be regarded as an incidental instrument for protecting the privilege.

[3] For a discussion of the Act see *McCormick* [1977] NI 105; *Milne* [1978] NI 110; *McGrath* [1980] NI 91, and Mirfield, 'The future of the law of confessions', [1984] Crim L Rev 63, 69.

[4] See Ch. 16 for a discussion of this aspect.

confessions is not insignificant.[5] However, the need to safeguard reliability does not necessarily create a conflict between the protection of the innocent from conviction and the need of the community to see offences punished because the latter only demands the conviction of the guilty, not of the innocent.[6]

From a practical point of view, however, confessions do present a serious problem. Under Anglo-American law the interrogation of suspects is carried out by policemen without outside supervision. The police have a motive for suppressing any transgression of propriety and the suspect has a motive for fabricating stories of malpractice if he regrets making a confession. Since the information about the circumstances of the interrogation comes exclusively from biased sources the courts are bound to have great difficulty in assessing the probative weight of confessions.

The Police and Criminal Evidence Act 1984 contains several important measures designed to reduce the pressures on suspects and improve the means for ascertaining what really took place during an interrogation.[7] Section 56 of the Act gives a suspect in police custody a statutory right to have someone informed of his arrest and of his place of detention. This is likely to lessen the pyschological pressures associated with isolation. More important is the right to legal advice conferred on persons in custody by section 58(1): 'A person arrested and held in custody in a police station . . . shall be entitled, if he so requests, to consult a solicitor privately at any time.'[8]

---

[5] See Skolnick, *Justice Without Trial*, 2nd edn. (1966), 182; Kassin and Wrightsman (eds.), *Psychology of Evidence and Trial Procedure* (1985), ch. 3, pp. 67; Gudjonsson and Lister, 'Interrogative suggestibility . . .', (1984) 24 Journal of Forensic Science Society 99; Gudjonsson and MacKeith, 'False confessions . . .', in Norsledt and Forlag (eds), *Reconstructing of the Past: The Role of Psychologists in Criminal Trials* (1982); Gudjonsson, 'Interrogative suggestibility . . .', (1984) 24 Medical Science Law 56; Gudjonsson and Clark, 'Suggestibility in police interrogation . . .', (1986) 1 Social Behaviour 83; R. Kee, *Trial and Error* (1986).

[6] To the extent that the insistence on a high standard of proof regarding the reliability of confessions makes it likely that guilty persons would escape conviction, the problem is a general one and not peculiar to the law of confessions; see discussion in Ch. 9.

[7] For a survey of these provisions see Gibbons, 'The conditions of detention and questioning by the police', [1985] Crim L Rev 558.

[8] It is important to note that both the right to have someone informed of one's arrest and the right to legal advice are subject to exceptions that allow the police, in certain circumstances, to deny both these rights; s. 56(5), 58(8) of the 1984 Act.

These rights are further buttressed by the Code of Practice which the Home Secretary issued in 1985 under section 66 of the Act. Paragraph 3 requires the custody officer to notify the detained person, as soon as he is brought to the police station, of his right to have someone informed, of his right to consult a solicitor, and of his right to consult the code of practice. Moreover, if the suspect does not know any solicitor he must be advised of the availability of duty solicitors.[9] Subject to certain exceptions, a suspect who asks for legal advice may not be interviewed until he has received the advice sought; and when interviewed he may have his solicitor present. To improve the means of reviewing the treatment of suspects in custody the Act makes detailed provisions for recording the history of the suspect's detention and the various decisions taken during its course, as well as provisions for the tape-recording of the interrogation itself.

In addition to the right of the suspect not to be physically or mentally abused and the right of the innocent not to be convicted the law recognizes a further right in the form of a privilege against self-incrimination. The privilege may be exercised in the face of police interrogation by a refusal to answer police questions or by a refusal to testify at one's own the trial.

It might be said that in the case of the suspect and the accused we cannot speak of self-incrimination because they must be presumed innocent. Their right, it might be said, is simply a right to silence. There is indeed a right of silence in that, broadly speaking, the citizen is free to withhold information from the police and anybody else. However, although the general right of silence is very important, it is, as a rule, overridden in the interests of the administration of justice. We hold, as we have seen, that a witness must disclose all information relevant to the case in which he is summoned to testify so that the court may ascertain the true facts. Consequently, the reason for treating the suspect and the accused differently cannot rely on the general right of silence. It is precisely because the right of the suspect is not a simple instance of the right of silence that

---

[9] Para. 6 and notes for guidance in paras. 6A, 6B.

special procedures are required to protect it; no similar procedures exist to protect the general right of silence.[10]

The privilege against self-incrimination confers on the guilty
a freedom to refrain from providing information that could
establish their guilt and thereby either to avoid conviction or
substantially to reduce its likelihood. Clearly, this right is at
odds with the aim of the criminal process of securing conviction
of the guilty. In practice, however, the conflict is reduced due to
two main factors that make it difficult for a suspect to insist on
his privilege and refuse to answer police questions: the mental
pressures generated by police interrogation and the fear that
silence would be construed as an admission of guilt.

When we have offended some moral or legal law and we are
taxed with it our natural moral reaction is to offer an explanation. There is, of course, nothing wrong in the requirement that
our moral sentiment makes on us; there are after all many
rights which we possess but which it would be morally wrong
for us to press, and which we are therefore morally required to
waive.[11] However, when the police interrogate a suspect they
have an opportunity to exploit this moral position and induce
the suspect to confess against his better judgment. Bentham
observed that the very fact that questions are put by a person in
authority exerts pressure on the suspect to comply: 'Silence
. . . on the part of the affrighted culprit, seems to his ear to call for
vengeance; confession holds out a chance for indulgence.'[12]

If the police were free to apply pressure to induce the suspect
to speak when he prefers to remain silent and if, in addition,
inferences could be freely drawn at the trial from the accused's
silence in the face of police questions and from his failure to

---

[10] It may be suggested that the right of suspects and accused arises from the
principle that the citizen should not be troubled to account for himself merely
because the state has decided that he might have committed an offence. However,
this principle only suggests that the state should prove a probable cause before the
suspect or accused is troubled to defend himself; it does not support the further
proposition that a suspect or an accused should be free to avoid self-incrimination
no matter how strong the case against him.

[11] See Donagan, 'The right not to incriminate oneself', in Paul, Miller, and Paul
(eds.), *Human Rights* (1984), 137.

[12] *Rationale of Judicial Evidence* (1827), vol. 5, bk. v, ch. 7, s. 1, p. 134; see also
Menlowe, 'Bentham, self-incrimination and the law of evidence', (1988) 104 LQR
286.

testify at the trial, then it could hardly be said that a suspect and an accused were free to maintain their privilege against self-incrimination. An effective legal support for the privilege would have to prevent such undermining of the privilege. However, if the suspect is given a free choice between confessing and not confessing he will often, if not always, choose the latter and thwart the police in their efforts to obtain evidence of crime. This consideration has led the courts, as we shall presently see, to give little practical backing to the privilege. In order to avoid too tight an enforcement of the privilege and the consequent loss in the fruits of interrogation the courts have had to weaken their supervision over custodial interrogation which, in turn, has reduced protection of the other rights of the suspect: the right not to have one's statement distorted so as to create an impression of guilt and the right not to be abused.

This chapter examines the process of attrition which the privilege against self-incrimination has undergone in Anglo-American law. It discusses the strength of the justification for the privilege and argues that, given that a good protection of the privilege is unattainable in practice, it is better to abandon it and concentrate on a protection of the suspect's other rights. Indeed, it will be shown that the English law is already taking large steps in this direction.

THE AMERICAN STRATEGY

The Fifth Amendment of the American constitution declares: 'No person . . . shall be compelled in any criminal case to be a witness against himself. . .'[13]

The protection of the suspect in the police station is crucial, as we have observed. It is there that the reluctant suspect faces the most acute pressures to confess and his privilege is most

---

[13] For reassessment see: Friendly, 'The Fifth Amendment tomorrow: a case for a constitutional change', 37 University of Cincinnati L Rev 671 (1968). See also Heidt, 'The conjurer's circle: the Fifth Amendment in civil cases', 91 Yale L J 1062 (1982); Note, 'The rights of criminal defendants and the subpoena duces tecum . . .', 95 Harv L Rev 683 (1982); Arenella, 'Schmerber and the privilege against self-incrimination: a reappraisal', (1982) Am Crim L Rev 31.

vulnerable. This factor has received its sharpest recognition in the famous American case of *Miranda* v. *Arizona*[14] where the Supreme Court set out to erect effective safeguards for the privilege. The court declared that 'the prosecution may not use statements, whether exculpatory or inculpatory, stemming from custodial interrogation of the defendant unless it demonstrates the use of procedural safeguards effective to secure the privilege against self-incrimination.'[15] The minimal requirements, the court held, were as follows:

Prior to any questioning the person must be warned that he has a right to remain silent, that any statement he does make may be used as evidence against him, and that he has a right to the presence of an attorney, either retained or appointed. The defendant may waive any of these rights, provided the waiver is made voluntarily, knowingly and intelligently. If, however, he indicates in any manner and at any stage of the process that he wishes to consult with an attorney before speaking there can be no questioning. Likewise, if the individual is alone and indicates in any manner that he does not wish to be interrogated, the police may not question him.[16]

It does not take much imagination to realize that a procedure that enables the suspect to make a voluntary, knowing, and intelligent choice whether or not to make an incriminating admission creates a conflict between the moral instinct to confess and the desire to escape punishment. A suspect who receives legal advice will be told that he is free to eschew any statement and will be given to understand that if he is guilty, his self-interest is often, if not always, best served by silence.[17] Consequently, the *Miranda* decision was greeted with a good deal of apprehension about its effect on the fight against crime.[18]

---

[14] 384 US 436 (1966).   [15] Ibid. 444.   [16] Ibid. 444–5.

[17] Justice Jackson once said: 'Any lawyer worth his salt will tell the suspect in no uncertain terms to make no statement to the police under any circumstances.' *Watts* v. *Indiana* 338 US 49, 59 (1949). See also Griffiths and Ayres, 'A postscript to the *Miranda* project: interrogation of draft protesters', 77 Yale L J 300 (1967). Situations of plea-bargaining and related practices present further complications which shall not be dealt with here.

[18] See the comments of the Senate Judiciary Committee in Senate Report (Judiciary Committee) No. 1097 (29 Apr. 1968), [1968] US Code and Adm. News, vol. ii, p. 2128.

This apprehension did not prove well founded because the police and the courts saw to it that *Miranda* had only limited success in generating a real sense of freedom of choice in the suspect.[19] The post-*Miranda* decisions stand in stark contrast to the high-minded spirit of that judgment and indicate that the Supreme Court is less than wholehearted in its commitment to curbing police pressures on suspects. A few instances will suffice to illustrate this point.

The court refused to apply the *Miranda* rule to a situation where, although the suspect was interrogated in the police station, he was not technically under arrest. In so deciding the court seemed unperturbed by the fact that the suspect's freedom of movement was merely theoretical and that he was otherwise subject to the pressures associated with custody. Nor was the decision affected by the fact that the suspect had been falsely told that his fingerprints had been found at the scene of the crime.[20]

In another case the suspect demanded to consult a lawyer as soon as he was arrested, but while he was being driven to the police station the officers said that they feared that the crime weapon might harm a child if not found promptly, whereupon the suspect disclosed the location of the weapon. The court held that this procedure did not amount to interrogation necessitating the *Miranda* safeguards.[21] Furthermore, the court has developed the 'inevitable discovery' exception whereby real evidence obtained in violation of the *Miranda* rule is admissible if

[19] For surveys about the effects of *Miranda* see: Wald *et al.*, 'Interrogation in New Haven: the impact of *Miranda*', 76 Yale L J 1519 (1967); Pepinsky, 'The theory of police reaction to *Miranda* v *Arizona*', 16 Crime and Delinquency 379 (1970); and Stone, 'The *Miranda* doctrine in the Burger court', [1977] Supreme Court Rev 99; Meese, 'Promoting truth in the courtroom', 40 Van L Rev 271 (1987).

[20] *Oregon* v. *Mathison* 429 US 492 (1977). More recently the Supreme Court decided that the roadside questioning of a motorist detained pursuant to a routine traffic check did not constitute 'custodial interrogation' for the purpose of the *Miranda* rule: *Sheriff of Franklin County, Ohio* v. *McCarty* 52 US LW 5023 (1984).

[21] *Rhode Island* v. *Innis* 446 US 291 (1980); see *McCormick on Evidence*, 3rd edn. (1984), 388. It has also been held that the police do not have to accede to a suspect's request to consult a probation officer before interrogation, even where the demand is prompted by mistrust of lawyers provided by the police, and that—having denied his request—the police were entitled to press the suspect with questions; *Fare* v. *Michael* 442 US 707 (1979).

the prosecution shows that the evidence would have been discovered in any event.[22]

Two lines of cases are of particular significance in cutting down the practical effects of the *Miranda* decision. First, it has been held that while a confession obtained in breach of the *Miranda* rule may not be given in evidence-in-chief it may nevertheless be used in cross-examination for the purpose of impeaching the accused.[23] Secondly, the courts seem willing to find a waiver of the privilege in dubious circumstances. In one case the interrogation ceased when the suspect refused to be questioned, only to be resumed a couple of hours later by another officer. It was held that the suspect's initial refusal to answer questions did not create an indefinite prohibition against further questioning, and that the second interrogation did not violate the rule because the suspect's responses amounted to a waiver of his privilege.[24] In another case the police, having obtained a clearly inadmissible confession without a warning, proceeded to administer a warning and, not surprisingly, obtained another confession. Despite the fact that the second confession was prompted by the knowledge that the cat was out of the bag, it has been held that the inadmissibility of the first confession did not render that subsequent confession inadmissible.[25] In *Moran* v. *Burbine*[26] the family of a suspect who was under arrest arranged for a lawyer to represent the suspect but the police refused to allow the lawyer access to the suspect and proceeded with the interrogation without informing the suspect of the availability of his lawyer. The Supreme Court held that no violation of the *Miranda* rule had taken place. Lastly, it has been held that waiver of *Miranda* rights in respect of a particular offence counts as a general waiver and the police

---

[22] *Crispus Nix, Warden* v. *Williams* 467 US 431 (1984).

[23] *Oregon* v. *Hass* 420 US 714 (1975). See also *Harris* v. *New York* 401 US 222 (1971).

[24] *Michigan* v. *Mosley* 423 US 96 (1975). To make the suspect more forthcoming the police started the second interrogation by questioning the accused on a graver offence and by falsely telling him that an accomplice had already implicated him. Cf. *Brewer* v. *Williams* 430 US 387 (1977) and *Edwards* v. *Arizona* 451 US 477 (1981).

[25] *Oregon* v. *Elstad* 470 US 298 (1985); see comment in 'The Supreme Court 1984 Term', 99 Harv L Rev 141 (1986).

[26] 106 S Ct 1135; 89 L Ed 2d 410 (1986).

may then proceed and interrogate the suspect of other and even graver offences.[27]

The post-*Miranda* history shows that the Supreme Court of the United States has found it unwise to pursue the philosophy behind that decision to its logical conclusion. Rather than seek to develop further measures for inspiring suspects with confidence in their possession of a genuine constitutional right against self-incrimination it has sought refuge in a technical interpretation of the *Miranda* rule, leaving the suspect with an opportunity to 'voluntarily, knowingly and intelligently' assert his privilege which is hardly greater than he had before.

THE ENGLISH STRATEGY PRIOR TO 1984

The same disparity between theory and practice was notable in English law before the coming into effect of the Police and Criminal Evidence Act 1984. The privilege against self-incrimination was acclaimed as an important right of the citizen. At the same time, however, English law gave as little practical support to the privilege as did its American counterpart. Interrogation procedures—as the Royal Commission on Criminal Procedure found—tend to exert, whether by design or otherwise, enormous pressure on suspects to speak.[28] The notification of the right to say nothing is no more than perfunctory and is unlikely to displace the indications to the contrary.[29]

Before the enactment of the Criminal Evidence Act 1984, English law had evolved a two-pronged approach for the pro-

---

[27] *Colorado* v. *Springs* 107 S Ct 851; 93 L Ed (2d) 954 (1987).

[28] Royal Commission on Criminal Procedure, Report, 1981, para. 4.73.

[29] The caution administered to suspects informs them that they need say nothing and not that they have a right to withhold incriminating information. As a result of this emphasis on the right to silence the untutored suspect is left in doubt as to whether his silence might not give the impression that he is guilty. However, emphasis on the right not to incriminate oneself would indicate to the suspect that his silence would necessarily imply guilt. In order to convey to the suspect the existence of a free choice he should be told that he may not be questioned without his consent and he should then be asked whether he agrees to questioning. This will certainly be more effective, but for exactly this reason it would in all probability be found unacceptable.

tection of a suspect against the exertion of police pressure. It established a rule of law for the admissibility of confessions and it pursued 'rules of practice'—the Judges' Rules—for the treatment of suspects in custody. The rule of law, the voluntariness rule, was formulated in *Ibrahim* v. *R.*[30] and later incorporated in the Judges' Rules as follows:

It is a fundamental condition of the admissibility in evidence against any person, equally of any answer given by that person to a question put by a police officer and of any statement made by that person, that it shall have been voluntary, in the sense that it has not been obtained from him by fear of prejudice or hope of advantage exercised or held out by a person in authority, or by oppression.[31]

Yet no more than four years after *Ibrahim*, Darling J felt no inhibition in saying that:

It would be a lamentable thing if the police were not allowed to make inquiries, and if statements made by prisoners were excluded because of a shadowy notion that if the prisoners were left to themselves they would not have made them.[32]

In applying the *Ibrahim* rule the courts sought refuge in the minutiae of technicalities rather than trying to develop a genuine jurisdiction for the protection of the privilege. This approach had been taken to such lengths that the House of Lords was driven to complain that '[a] whole body of case law seems to have been conjured out of what are essentially decisions on questions of fact' and that 'a somewhat pedantic approach seems to have been adopted'.[33] However, this complaint did not result in any improvement in the protection of the privilege. Rather than seek to analyse and clarify the purpose of the voluntariness rule and develop means of achieving it, the House of Lords contented itself—in the key decision of *DPP* v.

---

[30] [1914] AC 599. For a survey of the law preceding that decision see Mirfield, *Confessions* (1985), 42.
[31] Principle (e) of the Judges' Rules 1964.
[32] *Cook* (1918) 34 TLR 515, 516.
[33] *DPP* v. *Ping Lin* [1975] 3 All ER 175, 188 per Lord Salmon. See also Report on Northern Ireland, cmnd. 5185, paras. 59, 80 ff. There is in this respect an analogy with the treatment that the United States Supreme Court accorded to the *Miranda* decision.

Ping Lin[34]—with a desultory declaration that the rule provided a simple and straightforward factual test which did not necessitate an inquiry into its rationale. Simple or otherwise, the voluntariness test offered little succour to the suspect in the police station, as was discovered by the Royal Commission on Criminal Procedure:

The link between involuntariness on these criteria [the voluntariness rule] and unreliability is in legal terms exact; in psychological terms it is uncertain, to say the least. What our research suggests is that in psychological terms custody in itself and questioning in custody develop forces upon many suspects which . . . so affect their minds that their wills crumble and they speak when otherwise they would have stayed silent. Those forces do not fall within the legal definition of factors that would render a confession involuntary and therefore unreliable. In other words, legal and psychological 'voluntariness' do not match.[35]

Moreover, in the absence of independent evidence of what took place during interrogation judges could hardly gauge the true effects of police practices on voluntariness, with the result that even such limited value as the rule possessed could not be put to much practical use.

The second measure adopted by the English courts to protect the privilege—a set of rules for the conduct of interrogation—proved even less effective. The Judges' Rules required the police to caution the suspect at various stages of the interrogation. They provided for the taking down of statements, and for the right to consult a solicitor. However, the courts decided that breaches of these rules should not lead to automatic but only to discretionary exclusion of confessions obtained following a breach. Notwithstanding widespread breaches, discretion was rarely exercised in favour of exclusion.[36] The reason for the

[34] [1975] 3 All ER 175.
[35] Para. 4.73. There is a confusion in the passage between admissibility and reliability, but it does not affect the main point made. See also Report on Northern Ireland, cmnd. 5185, para. 84.
[36] Except in cases of failure to administer the warning, which were very rare indeed in view of the insignificant effect that the warning has on the incidence of confessions.

poor adherence to the Judges' Rules was explained by the Commission on Criminal Procedure in Northern Ireland:

> If applied strictly they would have the effect of rendering inadmissible any statement made by the accused after his arrest unless it was volunteered by him upon his own initiative without any pressure or encouragement by anyone in authority. Guilty men do not usually do this. If left to themselves they would prefer to remain silent.[37]

Despite the existence of the Judges' Rules the judiciary balked at backing its own rules with the sanctions at its disposal when dealing with proven and frequent infringements of the rules. Instead they took refuge in a jumble of technicalities which served only to maintain a semblance of protection. The result of this was that the courts forwent adequate supervision of the interrogation and, by and large, left suspects to the mercy of the police.

A wavering judicial commitment to a right as central as the privilege against self-incrimination is bound to have a degrading effect on the police. At the very start of an interview with a suspect, the aim of the police is to ensure that the suspect submits to interrogation. If this can be achieved by obtaining a free and well-informed waiver of the privilege so much the better. If not, means have to be found to ensure that the suspect does not exercise his privilege. Police practices that have recently come to light as a result of the safeguards of the Police and Criminal Evidence Act 1984 bear this out.

THE JUSTIFICATION OF THE PRIVILEGE

The weak support which has been given to the privilege reflects not only the exigencies of the criminal investigation but also the weakness of the justification for its existence. When discussing the origins of the privilege Bentham mentioned the unpopularity of the courts of the Star Chamber and High Commission which were empowered to put defendants to the oath and question them.[38] It was not unknown for these courts to subject

---

[37] Cmnd. 5185, paras. 81–2.

[38] *Rationale of Judicial Evidence*, vol. 5, bk. x, pt. 4, ch. 3, p. 241. For a discussion of Bentham's views see Menlowe, 'Bentham, self-incrimination and the law of evidence', (1988) 104 LQR 286.

reluctant defendants to torture in order to extract statements of faith which would then form the basis of their conviction; but, as Bentham observed, there are no laws or powers that cannot be abused. He believed that excesses should be tackled directly rather than by the adoption of a rule which was capable of thwarting good laws (i.e. the criminal laws that punish offenders) as well as bad ones (i.e. the laws that would otherwise allow suspects and accused persons to be abused). Notwithstanding Bentham's account, however, the origins of the privilege remain obscure.[39] For the present purposes it is unnecessary to conduct a historical survey.[40] We need only consider the reasons that could justify the continued retention of this particularly English institution.[41]

We have seen that the privilege may be asserted at two principal stages of the criminal process: at the police interrogation and at the trial. The arguments supporting the privilege are sometimes directed to the first aspect and sometimes to the second; the discussion below will deal with both.

The Accused's Dilemma

Bentham was the first to subject the privilege to critical examination. He identified a number of justifications for it, one of which is the 'old woman's reason'. 'The essence of this reason', he says, 'is contained in the word *hard*: 'tis hard upon a man to be obliged to criminate himself.'[42] Bentham argues that the hardness consists not so much in the making of an incriminating statement as in the likelihood of punishment created by the statement. He goes on to say that since we are prepared to inflict punishment it is pusillanimous to recoil from the lesser hardship of questioning the accused.

---

[39] Even the connection between the privilege and the accused's right not to testify is unclear; the privilege antedates the right of the accused not to testify because until 1898 the accused was altogether disqualified as a witness.

[40] For such surveys see: Wigmore, '*Nemo tenetur seipsum prodere*', 5 Harv L Rev 71 (1891); Morgan, 'The privilege against self-incrimination', 34 Minn L Rev 1 (1949); Kemp, 'The background of the Fifth Amendment in England law: a study of its historical implications', 1 William & Mary L Rev 247 (1958); Levy, *Origins of the Fifth Amendment* (1968); Bentham, *Rationale Of Judicial Evidence*, vol. 5, p. 250.

[41] For a survey of the reasons see: E. Ratushny, *Self-Incrimination in the Canadian Criminal Process* (1979).

[42] *Rationale of Judicial Evidence* (1827), vol. 5, p. 230.

Against Bentham's position it might be suggested that the core of the hardship consists not in bringing nearer the prospect of punishment but in the dilemma that the accused finds himself in: testifying truthfully and being convicted, or committing perjury in order to escape punishment. There are, however, several reasons why this suggestion does not dispose of Bentham's objection. The accused's dilemma is not that harsh if one remembers that prosecutions for perjury in the course of giving evidence in one's own defence are extremely rare.[43] Besides, the fear of conviction is likely to be the most dominant factor in the accused's mind when confronting the dilemma of truth or perjury. Lastly, a witness may face a similar dilemma when he is not an accused; e.g. a father may find it just as terrible a prospect to see his son convicted by his own testimony. But the law recognizes no general privilege not to be faced with such a dilemma because the duty to testify about crime serves to enforce the criminal law and to protect our well-being and therefore overrides the hardship.

Unlike the justification that we have been discussing, modern arguments in favour of the privilege are usually instrumental. They take the form that to the extent that the privilege against self-incrimination is an efficient means for countering some undesirable phenomena, it is sensible to uphold it even at the cost of some loss of useful evidence of crime.[44]

The Privilege Protects the Innocent

One of the principal instrumental arguments in favour of the privilege suggests that it is a useful instrument for protecting innocent persons from conviction. Addressing this kind of justification Bentham explained:

---

[43] Indeed, if the sanction for perjury were considered to present a serious problem, the liability of an accused to a charge of perjury could easily be abolished.

[44] The arguments advanced in this respect are many, varied, and not infrequently confused. Here we need only consider more prominent ones. For a survey see McNaughton, 'The privilege against self-incrimination: its constitutional affectation, raison d'être and miscellaneous implications', 51 Journal of Criminal Law Criminology and Police Science 138 (1960).

Can it be supposed that the rule in question has been established with the intention of protecting them [the innocent]? They are the only persons to whom it can never be useful. . . . What is his [the innocent's] highest interest, and his most ardent wish? To dissipate the cloud which surrounds his conduct, and give every explanation which may set it in its true light; to provoke questions, to answer them, and to defy his accusers.[45]

In reply to this point it is said that in practice there must be innocent accused who, through being inarticulate or having an unfortunate manner, are likely to make unconvincing witnesses and are therefore more likely to be convicted if they are exposed to cross-examination in the witness-box.[46] However, it is doubtful that there is a real risk of this kind or, if a risk does exist, that the option of not testifying provides much protection in view of the inevitably negative impression which failure to give evidence is likely to make on the jury.[47] As Professor Glanville Williams put it: 'The crux of the matter is that immunity from being questioned is a rule which by its nature can protect the guilty only. It is not a rule that may operate to acquit some guilty for fear of convicting some innocent.'[48]

The arguments that we need consider, therefore, are arguments that explain why it is in society's interest to afford this protection to the guilty.

Privilege Protects Suspects from Police Abuses

A civilized society should maintain standards of propriety in the interrogation of suspects. Since the police are under pressure to

[45] Dumont (ed.), *Judicial Evidence* (1825), 241.
[46] Clapp, 'Privilege against self-incrimination', 10 Rutgers L Rev 541, 548 (1956). Interestingly, the self-same argument was advanced against the 1898 reforms which rendered the accused a competent witness in his own trial; *Wigmore on Evidence* (1940), 3rd edn. vol. 2, para. 579.
[47] Trial judges would presumably restrain those prosecutors who set out to confuse and manipulate an uneducated or vulnerable accused. There is certainly a very difficult problem concerning the accused with a record. The present law is unjust in this respect and is capable of abuse, as we have seen in the previous chapter; this problem requires urgent solution quite apart from the privilege under consideration.
[48] *The Proof of Guilt*, 3rd edn. (1963), 53.

bring offenders to justice there is an ever-present temptation for them to deviate from the rules of propriety in order to obtain incriminating statements. Of course we could forbid such deviation on pain of criminal or disciplinary sanctions, but since in practice we ultimately depend on the police for the enforcement of such sanctions the prohibition is not likely to be effective.

A supporter of the privilege will argue that by providing the suspect with the right to remain silent the suspect is given an opportunity to resist abusive interrogation. However, it is difficult to see how the privilege affords the suspect protection against abuse. The suspect is still free to waive his privilege, submit to questioning, and make incriminating statements. Far from shielding the suspect from the more insistent investigator, the privilege against self-incrimination presents the investigator with the challenge of obtaining, in the first instance, a waiver of the privilege so as to clear the way to questioning.

This last point brings out a practical weakness in instrumental justifications of the privilege. A right that tends to be negated by the process of police investigation because the very nature of police interrogation creates almost irresistible pressures to answer police questions can hardly be regarded as an efficient instrument of policy.

Privilege Encourages Search for Independent Evidence

Supporters of the privilege have also turned in another direction. They argue that if the police can rely on the suspect as a source of evidence they would neglect the search for independent evidence. However, the privilege's existence does not seem in practice to spur the police to go to great lengths to obtain evidence independent of the accused.[49] The Royal Commission on Criminal Procedure found that the interviewing of suspects is at present a most important device for dealing with crime and concluded that 'there can be no adequate substitute for police

---

[49] This observation is based on general impression. We know that the police prefer to begin their investigation by questioning rather than by field investigation. What we do not know is to what extent the police resort to the other investigations when a confession is not forthcoming.

questioning in the investigation and, ultimately, in the prosecution of crime.'[50] The reason for this lies in the scarcity of police resources and in the fact that on many occasions there is little prospect of discovering further evidence by investigaton.

Efficiency and Fairness at the Trial

It is said that the privilege of the accused not to testify relieves the courts from false testimony because an accused who cannot bring himself to admit the crime has the option of refraining from testifying. However, experience shows that the accused's untruthful or evasive testimony will very often make a useful contribution to the ascertainment of truth, since proven lies and manifest evasion help to expose guilt as much as many other forms of incriminating evidence. At present most accused testify in their own defence. Since many are convicted, it seems that juries are not hindered in carrying out their duty by any confusion which the accused's testimony creates.

It is argued sometimes that the prosecution must prove the accused's guilt beyond reasonable doubt and that if the prosecution was allowed to call upon the accused to account for his actions, its probative burden would unjustifiably be lightened. It is difficult to see how the abolition of the privilege would lead to a reduction in the standard of proof. After all, it is already the case that in many trials the prosecution is able to rely on some statements made by the accused, but it is not suggested that in these trials guilt is proved by a lower standard than in cases where the accused has insisted on his privilege.

Another argument advanced is that, in an adversarial system such as ours, the parties should be left to their own devices and should not have the right to call on help from the opposite party. It is argued that the prosecution, commanding the resources of the law-enforcement agencies of the state, already has

---

[50] *The Royal Commission on Criminal Procedure, Report* (1981), para. 4.1. The Commission also observed that only a small proportion of offences was discovered as a consequence of police detection; para. 2.12. See also Zander, 'The investigation of crime: a study of cases tried at the Old Bailey', [1979] Crim L Rev 203.

considerable advantages over the defence in the preparation and presentation of its case.[51]

This argument seems to appeal to a purity in the adversarial system which does not exist. In civil proceedings the parties are under a comprehensive duty of mutual disclosure and it is not suggested that the civil trial has lost its adversarial nature. In criminal proceedings most suspects make statements to the police or at the trial, but this does not seem to be regarded as diminishing the adversarial nature of the criminal trial. Perhaps what lies behind the present appeal to the adversarial values is Bentham's 'fox hunter's' reason:

> This consists in introducing upon the carpet of legal procedure the idea of *fairness*, in the sense in which the word is used by sportsmen. The fox is to have a fair chance for his life: he must have (so close is the analogy) what is called *law*: leave to run a certain length of way, for the express purpose of giving him a chance for escape.[52]

A somewhat different line of argument finds justification for the privilege in the accused's right not to be troubled to defend himself unless the prosecution has made a *prima facie* case against him. The right to be acquitted when the prosecution has made an insufficient *prima facie* case against the accused is, indeed, an important right. By means of this right the law ensures that an accused is not troubled with criminal proceeding unless the prosecution has presented evidence capable of justifying a reasonable jury in returning a guilty verdict. However, the removal of the privilege against self-incrimination need not and should not affect this right. Even if the privilege is abolished the prosecution should continue to bear the burden of making a *prima facie* case before the accused is required to defend himself.

The Right of the Citizen Not to be Questioned by the Police Without Reasonable Cause

In support of the privilege it may be argued that the accused's right not to be asked to account for himself at his trial unless a

---

[51] This argument seems to amount to a claim that what is the case ought to be the case—what Bentham called *petitio principii*, 'which consists in the assumption of the propriety of the rule, as a proposition too plainly true to admit of dispute'. *Rationale of Judicial Evidence* (1827), vol. 5, p. 229.

[52] Ibid. 238–9.

prima facie case against him has been established would be greatly weakened if he had to account for himself during police interrogation. The prosecution would then be able to rely on his incriminating statements in order to establish a *prima facie* case at his trial or, in the absence of a statement, the prosecution would be able to rely on the suspect's failure to respond to police questions. This danger is all the more serious, it may be said, since the police need not give any information to the suspect before interrogating him, apart from telling him that he is suspected of having committed the offence in question.

It is true that to allow the police to interrogate the citizen without justifiable cause could well lead to random arrests of suspects on the off-chance that they may provide incriminating information. Such a practice would undoubtedly undermine one of the important features of a free society: the citizen's freedom from interference by the police in the absence of reasonable suspicion that he has committed a crime. The importance of this freedom and the curbs placed on police action in order to preserve it cannot be overstated, but the significance of the privilege against self-incrimination in this regard is questionable.

The police's powers of arrest and interrogation are defined independently of the privilege.[53] Moreover, a suspect who declares that he insists on his privilege may be arrested and detained for the purpose of seeking his waiver of the privilege and submitting him to interrogation.[54] It appears, therefore, that under existing law the privilege does little to protect the citizen from arrest and questioning. What protects the citizen from random arrest is our democratic political system, which curbs the power of the police and gives the citizen various remedies against abuse of this power.

The Privilege Helps the Rehabilitation of Offenders

It has been suggested that the existence of the privilege spares the self-respect of the suspect and the accused and thereby advances the prospect of their giving up a life of crime. To quote Gerstein:

[53] See Pt. III of the Police and Criminal Evidence Act 1984.
[54] As we shall see later.

Insofar as it [the absence of a privilege] means forcing the criminal to accept and publicly to affirm his own condemnation, it is a direct compulsion of the conscience which is at odds with the effort made through punishment to awaken the criminal's own capacity to understand the direction in which his past actions move him and to take responsibility for changing that direction.[55]

This argument would have been persuasive if the absence of a privilege inevitably resulted in the kind of compulsion for which the Inquisition was notorious. But this is hardly the likely result of abolition. A law that requires the suspect and the accused to account for themselves but which does not impose a criminal sanction on those who decline to do so merely requires the suspect and the accused to consider their best interest; whether to maintain silence or run the risk of such adverse inferences as the circumstances justify. After all, this is the kind of calculation which, as we shall see, the law already obliges the suspect to make.

THE ENGLISH STRATEGY SINCE 1984: REDUCING THE SCOPE FOR CONFLICT

The weakness of the arguments advanced in support of the privilege helps explain why the courts have been relatively uninhibited in undermining its effectiveness. Looked at from a historical perspective it is clear, as we have seen, that while offering little protection to the suspect in the police station the existence of the privilege has forced the courts to distance themselves from the process of custodial interrogation in order to leave the police reasonably free to question suspects. The absence of effective judicial control has weakened the tests of reliability of confessions and made the suspect easy prey to improper practices. To enable the courts to insist on better protection for suspects a choice has to be made between two alternatives.

The first is to embrace the privilege unreservedly. This will

---

[55] 'Punishment and self-incrimination', 16 American Journal of Jurisprudence 84, 88 (1971).

require devising a procedure that will effectively ensure that suspects are meaningfully informed of their rights and are freed from any police pressure in deciding whether or not to submit to interrogation. An effective procedure of this kind would be very simple. If the only ground for arresting a suspect is the desire to interrogate him, the suspect should be informed that he cannot be interrogated without his consent and asked whether he agrees to interrogation and, thereby, to arrest. If a suspect has been arrested for other reasons, the police should not be allowed to have any discussion with the suspect before he has been informed, in the presence of his solicitor or his family, that he may not be interrogated without his consent. The suspect should then be asked whether he agrees to interrogation. A procedure of this kind will undoubtedly guarantee suspects' freedom of choice; but it will also put an end to most police questioning.

This second alternative entails the removal of the privilege in its present form while, at the same time, securing the following objectives: the erection of safeguards against arrest and questioning by the police in the absence of adequate proof against the suspect; the protection of suspects from physical or mental abuse and from indignity; the prevention of interrogation designed to confuse the suspect and the promotion of accuracy in the reporting of the suspect's statements.

It is the second option that the courts have chosen to implement, ingeniously exploiting the provisions of the Police and Criminal Evidence Act 1984.

Police Powers to Question Suspects Who Prefer to Keep Silent

As the Police and Criminal Evidence Act 1984 was coming off the presses, the House of Lords considered the simple, yet oddly undecided, question of whether a constable who suspected a person of having committed an arrestable offence was empowered to arrest that person for the sole purpose of questioning him. In *Holgate-Mohammed* v. *Duke*[56] the House of Lords held

---

[56] [1984] 1 All ER 1054. The case was concerned with the power of arrest conferred by s. 2(4) of the Criminal Law Act 1967; this has now been superseded by the similarly worded provision in s. 24(5) of the 1984 Act.

that a police officer was authorized so to do. Legislative support for this conclusion was found in section 43(3) of the Magistrates' Courts Act 1980. The decision has now received further support from the Police and Criminal Evidence Act 1984, section 37(2), which authorizes detention if a 'custody officer has reasonable grounds for believing that his [the suspect's] detention without being charged is necessary . . . to obtain . . . evidence by questioning him.'[57]

This position gives rise to two questions. The first is a practical one. Suppose that on being arrested the suspect declares that he insists on his privilege against self-incrimination and that he will refuse to answer any questions. Suppose also that there is no danger that the suspect will abscond, interfere with the investigation, or do anything else to justify his arrest. Is a constable still entitled to proceed and arrest this suspect, and are detention and continued detention under the above provisions of the 1984 Act justified? If the answer is in the negative, then the decision in *Holgate-Mohammed* v. *Duke* is easy to sidestep; all that a suspect need do in order to avoid arrest, or further detention, is to declare that he does not wish to answer any questions.

If, however, the answer is in the affirmative—as is probable—then a difficult problem arises concerning the protection of the privilege against self-incrimination. The problem lies in the conflict between the public interest in bringing offenders to justice and the right not to provide self-incriminating information.[58] Lord Diplock referred to the recognition by the Royal Commission on Criminal Procedure of the necessity of detention for questioning,[59] but the Commission also pointed out, as we have seen, that 'in psychological terms custody in itself and questioning in custody develop forces upon many suspects

---

[57] The need for further questioning is now a ground for extending the period of detention: s. 42(1)(b) and s. 43(4)(a).

[58] Notwithstanding the fact that Lord Diplock saw the nub of the issue in a 'conflict between the public interest in preserving liberty of the individual and the public interest in the detection of crime and the bringing to justice of those who commit it'. [1984] 1 All ER 1059.

[59] Cmnd. 8092, 1981, para. 3.66.

which . . . so affect their minds that their wills crumble and they speak when they would have stayed silent.'[60]

If arrest is justified merely for the purpose of questioning, it follows that while the suspect has a right to refuse to answer questions put to him he has no right not to be questioned against his wish. The absence of the latter right undermines, in practice, the existence of the former.

Vigorous Implementation of the Suspect's Access to a Solicitor

We have seen that the new Act makes provisions for the monitoring of the events that occur during the suspect's detention and the steps taken to grant him his requests or withhold them. These provisions are worked out in the Code of Practice. Although breaches of the Code are specifically rendered immune from civil and criminal proceedings (section 67(10) of the 1984 Act), section 67(11) stipulates that the Code may be taken into account if the court thinks that it is 'relevant to any question arising in the proceedings'; but the Act is silent on what such relevance may be. The courts are given a discretion to exclude unfair evidence under section 78 and there are early indications that the courts are ready to exercise this discretion to give meaningful support to the suspect's right to have access to a solicitor.

In *Samuel*[61] the accused was arrested on suspicion of robbery and burglary. His request to see his solicitor was denied, *inter alia*, on the grounds that access to solicitor was likely to result in other suspects being inadvertently warned. According to section 58 of the Police and Criminal Evidence Act 1984, where a person is in detention for a serious arrestable offence[62] and a senior police officer believes, on reasonable grounds,

that the exercise of the right [to consult a solicitor] . . . will lead to interference with . . . evidence . . . or lead to interference with or physic-

---

[60] Para. 4.74. Indeed, the Commission concluded that the 'rarity of complete silence may not be altogether surprising in view of the psychological pressures that custody in the police station generates'. Para 4.46. A view identical to that expressed in the *Miranda* case; 384 US 457, 467.

[61] [1988] 2 All ER 135.

[62] As defined by s. 116 and ch. 5 of the Act.

al injury to other persons ... or will lead to the alerting of other persons suspected of having committed ... an offence ... or will hinder the recovery of any property obtained as a result of ... an offence,

then access to a solicitor may be prevented for a defined period. The Court of Appeal decided that in order to prevent access to a solicitor the officer must believe, and have reasonable grounds for doing so, that it is very probable that the solicitor will, if allowed to consult with a detained person, thereafter commit a criminal offence of interfering with the course of justice or inadvertently do something which will have such effect.[63] This is a stiff test and Hodgson J remarked that since solicitors are officers of the court it would be very rare for the police to be able to form such a belief. He concluded that:

Any officer attempting to justify his decision to delay the exercise of this fundamental right of the citizen will, in our judgment, be unable to do so save by reference to specific circumstances, including evidence as to the person detained or the actual solicitor sought to be consulted.[64]

The Court of Appeal appreciated that the real motive of the police for delaying access to a solicitor was that they feared that the solicitor would counsel silence. Indeed, the prosecution went so far as to suggest that 'delaying access to a solicitor could be justified on the ground that he might advise his client not to answer questions and thereby hinder the police in their efforts to recover firearms'.[65] Rejecting this argument the court drew attention to paragraph 2 of Annex B of the Code of Practice which provides: 'Access to a solicitor may not be delayed on the grounds that he might advise the person not to answer any question ... '

The Court of Appeal's attitude to the infringements of the suspect's right to consult a solicitor breaks new ground. We have seen that prior to the 1984 Act the Judges' Rules conferred

---

[63] [1988] 2 All ER 142.

[64] Ibid. There was also an infringement of the suspect's right to see a solicitor after he had been charged with burglary. It was held that the fact that the police wished to continue the suspect's interrogation on the robbery suspicion did not provide an excuse for refusal of access.

[65] [1988] 2 All ER 145.

on suspects the right to see a solicitor but that the courts declined to exclude confessions obtained in violation of this right notwithstanding that denial of the right was commonplace. Here the court had no doubt what its reaction should be. It exercised its discretion under section 78 of the Police and Criminal Evidence Act 1984 and excluded the confession because the accused 'was denied improperly one of the most important and fundamental rights of a citizen'.[66] It is of particular significance that the court thought that the fact that the accused would have maintained silence and would not have confessed, had his solicitor been allowed to see him, constituted a strong consideration for exclusion. Further, the Court of Appeal held that a discretion may be exercised in favour of exclusion even where no impropriety was involved in obtaining the evidence.[67]

This decision has already produced a crop of cases in which trial judges have excluded confessions in the exercise of their discretion for breaches of the suspect's right to consult his solicitor.[68] However, this newly found sympathy for the suspect's right to consult a solicitor is threatened by the privilege against self-incrimination. For if the courts become convinced that by their promoting the suspect's right to consult a solicitor the police are unduly hindered in the investigation of crime, a reaction is bound to take place.

The more recent case of *Alladice*[69] has already prepared the ground for a retreat, should it become necessary. The Court of Appeal has decided that exclusion on the grounds of denial of a

---

[66] Ibid. 147. For recent Canadian developments see McCrimmon, 'Developments in the law of evidence: the 1985–86 term', (1987) 10 Supreme Court L Rev 365.

[67] [1988] 2 All ER 146–7; see commentary by Birch in [1988] Crim L Rev 301.

[68] *Davidson* [1988] Crim L Rev 442; *Vernon* ibid. 445; *Barry Trussler* ibid. 446; *Parris*, official transcript, 1 Nov. 1988. See also the earlier case of *McIvor* [1987] Crim L Rev 409; the police prevented the accused, who was charged with conspiracy to steal dogs, from seeing a solicitor on the grounds that the offence was a serious arrestable offence and that access to a solicitor might 'prejudice enquires', in accordance with s. 58(8) of the Police and Criminal Evidence Act 1984. Sir Frederick Lawton, sitting in the Crown Court, decided that the theft of twenty-eight dogs worth £880, in relation to which the accused was charged, did not amount to a serious arrestable offence and that it was improper of the police to refuse access to a solicitor because the accused would be advised to remain silent.

[69] (1988) 87 Cr App R 380. Cf. *Delaney*, official transcript, 8 Aug. 1988.

right to consult a solicitor would by no means be automatic. Unless the police acted in bad faith, when the court would have little difficulty in ruling a confession inadmissible under section 78, exclusion will depend on the extent that the denial of the right is likely to undermine the fairness of the trial. Indeed, the Court of Appeal approved of the trial judge's decision to admit a confession, despite the fact that the police refused the suspect's request to consult his solicitor, on the grounds that:

Had the solicitor been present, his advice would have added nothing to the knowledge of his rights which the appellant already had. The police, as the judge found, had acted with propriety at the interviews and therefore the solicitor's presence would not have improved the appellant's case in that respect.[70]

The presence of a solicitor at the interrogation provides an unbiased source of information as to how effectively the suspect was informed of his rights and how well protected he was from the adverse manipulation of his statements. The above dictum seems to undercut this rationale and constitutes therefore a threat to the protection of the suspect's rights. However, the seriousness of this threat depends, as has been suggested, on the extent that the presence of a solicitor is thought to deprive the police of the suspect's co-operation in the interrogation. If the move that the Court of Appeal has made in *Alladice* in connection with the permissible comment on the suspect's silence is successful, the conflict between the interest of the police in obtaining the suspect's co-operation and his right to consult a solicitor will have been reduced and the threat to this right will have accordingly diminished.

Curtailment of the Suspect's Privilege by Means of Comment on Silence

The Court of Appeal in *Alladice*[71] was of the opinion

that the effect of section 58 [of the 1984 Act, conferring the right to consult a solicitor] is such that the balance of fairness between prosecution and defence can not be maintained unless proper comment is permitted on the defendant's silence in such circumstances. It is

---

[70] Ibid, 387.   [71] (1988) 87 Cr App R 380.

high time that such comment should be permitted together with the necessary alteration to the words of the caution.[72]

This is clearly calculated, in the words of D. J. Birch 'to secure a *quid pro quo* for the enforcement of section 58 rights, in terms of a new right to comment adversely on the suspect's failure to reveal a defence later sprung on the prosecution ... and the modification of the caution to enable inferences to be drawn'.[73] Even before the decision in this case, both the prosecution and the trial judge were free to comment about the suspect's silence in the police station provided they were careful not to imply that silence is tantamount to an admission.[74] But the *Alladice* decision will give fresh impetus to searching questions about a suspect's reason for failing to co-operate with his interrogators.[75] Juries will now be advised to question closely the reasons why an accused declined to inform the police of a defence which he subsequently presented at his trial.

The strategy produced by a combination of *Samuel* and *Alladice* is sensible. By strengthening the right to a solicitor before and during interrogation the courts will have reduced the scope for inappropriate pressures on suspects. A confession obtained from a suspect who has had the benefit of legal advice will be very unlikely to fall foul of the reliability test of section 76(2)(*b*). On the other hand a suspect who has decided to maintain silence will have to realize that this course is not free of disadvantage.

---

[72] Ibid, 385.   [73] [1988] Crim L Rev 452.

[74] It was possible, for example, to point out that failure to offer an exculpatory explanation before the trial deprived the police of the means of checking its veracity. See: *Raviraj and others* (1987) 85 Cr App R 93 and my note: 'Criminal Law Revision Committee 11th Report: right of silence', (1973) 36 MLR 509 and Cross, 'The evidence report: sense and nonsense ...', [1973] Crim L R 329, 333. Mr Colin Tapper has drawn my attention to *Mann* (1922) 56 Cr App R 750, where it was held that if in the course of a police interview the accused has answered some questions but refused to answer many others, the whole interview may be admitted in evidence; thus drawing the jury's attention to the questions that he declined to answer.

[75] The position regarding failure to testify remains unaffected by the above decision and is governed by s. 1(*b*) of the Criminal Evidence Act 1898 which forbids the prosecution from commenting on the accused's failure to testify in his own defence. However, the trial judge may comment, again, provided that he does not suggest that failure to testify amounts to an admission of guilt.

This boldly asserted authority to comment on silence needs to be exercised fairly. The possibility of comment should not be allowed to become an instrument in the hands of the police to force people to speak because a policeman has a hunch that a person might have done something. A suspect who is told nothing about the case against him, except that the police suspect him of having committed an offence, should be entitled, even encouraged, to refuse to account for himself. An inference from silence will be in order only if the police had a sufficiently strong case against the suspect to necessitate a response and had informed the suspect of the nature of this case.

Welcome as the present development is, it has to be recognized that the privilege against self-incrimination is liable to cause difficulty. Suppose that a suspect is confronted with a strong case by the police. The suspect consults his solicitor and then tells the police: 'I am innocent of the offence of which you suspect me. I have perfectly good explanations for the evidence that you have against me. But my solicitor tells me that I have a right to say nothing at this stage and I have decided to keep silent because I wish to exercise this right and not because I have anything to conceal.' At his trial the accused raises his defence for the first time. May the judge tell the jury that it is open to them to infer that the fact that the accused kept his defence to the last moment may have been designed to deprive the police of an opportunity to investigate its flaws? The point has been considered in the United States where the Supreme Court held that silence pursuant to a *Miranda* warning is 'insolubly ambiguous', because it could not be known whether the accused's silence was due to a sense of guilt or to a preference to exercise the constitutional privilege.[76]

This reasoning is not altogether convincing because it assumes that the exercise of the privilege because of consciousness of guilt and for its own sake are mutually exclusive or, at any rate, do not overlap significantly. There must, however, be a very substantial, if not overwhelming, overlap between the

---

[76] *Doyle* v. *Ohio* 426 US 610 (1976); see also *US* v. *Hale* 422 US 171 (1975). At the same time it seems that the prosecution may comment on the failure of the defence to produce any evidence, and it may indicate that particular evidence has not been contradicted by the accused. *McCormick on Evidence*, 3rd edn. (1984), 320–1.

two; the majority of persons who exercise the privilege do so because they wish to avoid being convicted for a crime they have committed. There is therefore no reason in logic why the trier of fact should not, in appropriate cases, infer that the suspect exercised his right in order to conceal his guilt.[77]

There is, however, a different reason against allowing comment and, indeed, inference from silence as things stand. The caution administered to the suspect before questioning is: 'You do not have to say anything unless you wish to do so, but what you say may be given in evidence.'[78] This informs suspects of their right not to speak and implies, as the Supreme Court of the United States recognized, an assurance that silence would carry no penalty.[79] After all, what other possible meaning can the caution have? It would be otiose for the purpose of suggesting that the police would not physically compel the suspect to speak, or as indicating that the suspect will not suffer some legal sanction, if he did not reply to police questions. The warning suggests one thing only: that the suspect is free to remain silent in the sense that the criminal process will not disadvantage him as a consequence of his silence.[80]

If the trier of fact is to give silence in the face of interrogation its appropriate probative weight, the caution must be altered so as not to give the suspect the impression that his silence will be overlooked at the trial.[81] The caution must explain that although no formal sanction is attendant on silence the court may take it into account in judging the strength of any defence that the suspect may later advance. A scheme along these lines is already being introduced into Northern Ireland and it is

[77] A person is free to decline to provide a hair sample for the purpose of analysis but his refusal may count as evidence against him and corroborate the testimony of an accomplice: *Smith* (1985) 81 Cr App R 286.

[78] Code of Practice for the Detention, Treatment and Questioning of Persons by Police Officers, para. 10.4.

[79] *Doyle* v. *Ohio* 426 US 610 (1976); hence comment may be made on pre-arrest silence by the accused and on his failure to answer questions when he has not been given the *Miranda* warning; *Jenkins* v. *Anderson* 447 US 231 (1980); *Fletcher* v. *Weir* 455 US 603 (1982).

[80] The phrase 'but what you say may be given in evidence' suggests that evidence will not be given of what you do not say.

[81] See *Alladice*, n. 72 above.

probable that before long it will also be embraced in England and Wales.

Tolerance of Police Tricks to Obtain Confessions

Judicial tolerance of police tactics designed to overcome the suspect's reluctance to answer police questions has continued after the 1984 Act.

In *Fulling*[82] the accused was suspected of fraud but when questioned by the police refused to co-operate with her interrogators despite persistent questioning. A day later she made a confession. At her trial, the accused contended that she confessed only because the police told her that her lover was having an affair with a woman whom they were holding in a cell next to that of the accused. This revelation, the accused said, was so upsetting that she found the proximity to her rival unbearable and she confessed in order to be allowed to get away from the police station. The confession was challenged on the basis of section 76(2)(*a*) of the 1984 Act which provides that the prosecution must prove beyond reasonable doubt that the confession was not obtained 'by oppression of the person who made it'. The trial judge found it unnecessary to investigate the truth of the accused's allegations since, in his view, even if they had been correct, the conduct of the police would not have amounted to oppression.

The Court of Appeal upheld the judge's decision. According to the Lord Chief Justice, 'oppression' in section 76(2)(*a*) should be given its ordinary dictionary meaning, which is, to quote the *Oxford English Dictionary*, 'Exercise of authority or power in a burdensome, harsh, or wrongful manner; unjust or cruel treatment of subjects, inferiors, etc.; the imposition of unreasonable or unjust burdens'. The Lord Chief Justice quoted the illustration in the dictionary: 'There is not a word in our language which expresses more detestable wickedness than *oppression*'—and went on to say that 'it is hard to envisage any circumstances in which such oppression would not entail some impropriety on the part of the interrogator'.[83]

---

[82] [1987] 2 All ER 65.   [83] Ibid. 69.

A perfunctory reference to a dictionary entry can hardly provide the police with guidelines for the conduct of interrogation. Nor is it self-evident that in our society the word 'oppression' represents the most 'detestable wickedness'. Indeed, the same dictionary mentions other definitions. One of these may easily be thought to capture what is meant by 'oppression' in the present context: 'The feeling of being oppressed or weighed down; bodily or mental uneasiness or distress'.[84] But even if the restrictive definition adopted by his Lordship is the correct one, we are still left to wonder why the alleged police conduct was not 'unjust or cruel treatment of subjects' and why, in the court's view, it did not involve impropriety?

One thing is, however, clear: the Court of Appeal does not regard the suspect's privilege against self-incrimination to be very important. It played no part in the Lord Chief Justice's reasoning.

The court's reaction to a police strategy of deceiving a solicitor in order to induce the silent suspect to speak has been very different. In *Mason*[85] the police suspected the accused of arson and arrested him although they had no evidence whatsoever. To obtain the suspect's reaction, the police falsely told his solicitor that the accused's fingerprints had been found at the scene of the crime; whereupon the accused was advised by his solicitor to make a statement. The Court of Appeal overturned the trial judge's decision to admit the confession and quashed the conviction.[86] Watkins LJ deprecated 'the deceit practised on the appellant's solicitor' and expressed the hope 'never again to hear of deceit such as this being practised on the accused person, and more particularly possibly on a solicitor whose duty it is to advise him, unfettered by false information from the police'.[87]

---

[84] No reason was given for the rejection of this sense of the word. We may speculate that this was due to its description as late Middle English, although the same definition is subject to no such qualification in more modern dictionaries; see *Chambers Twentieth Century Dictionary; Longman Pocket English Dictionary*.

[85] [1987] 3 All ER 481.

[86] It rejected the argument that s. 76 was exhaustive with regard to the admissibility of confessions and held that a judge always has a residual discretion under s. 78 to reject a confession.

[87] [1987] 3 All ER 484, 485.

On the face of it, it is difficult to see why the last two cases should have been decided differently seeing that in both deceit was employed in order to induce a confession. However, there are two important differences. First, in *Mason* the police deceived the suspect about the evidence they had against him and thereby represented that there was sufficient evidence to require his reaction. By doing this the police breached the important principle that a citizen must not be disturbed unless there is compelling reason for doing so. Secondly, the police manipulated the trust that a client has in his solicitor and caused the solicitor to influence his client to confess, thereby corrupting the principal source of support that a suspect can obtain in order to preserve his rights in the face of the police challenge.

New Confession Rule

The Police and Criminal Evidence Act 1984 has introduced an important change in the rule of admissibility which now emphasizes reliability. Section 76(2) provides:

If, in any proceedings where the prosecution proposes to give in evidence a confession made by an accused person, it is represented to the court that the confession was or may have been obtained—(a) by oppression of the person who made it; or (b) in consequence of anything said or done which was likely, in the circumstances existing at the time, to render unreliable any confession which might be made by him in consequence thereof, the court shall not allow the confession to be given in evidence against him except in so far as the prosecution proves to the court beyond reasonable doubt that the confession (notwithstanding that it may be true) was not obtained as aforesaid.

Oppression continues to be a cause for exclusion but beyond that the trial judge is no longer concerned with whether the suspect spoke as a consequence of something said or done by the police when he would have preferred to remain silent.[88] Instead, the trial judge is to consider whether the reliability of the confession has been undermined by the conditions of the accused's interrogation. As a result the confession rule ceases to be a guardian of the privilege against self-incrimination and

---

[88] Oppression will be discussed below.

becomes a bulwark for the protection of the innocent from conviction.

Unfortunately the new test contains a number of ambiguities.[89] According to section 76(2)(*b*) the judge must be satisfied that the circumstances of the interrogation were not 'likely . . . to render unreliable *any confession* which might be made by him [the accused] in consequence thereof'. It seems odd that the trial judge should be asked to consider a hypothetical question rather than a concrete one: the reliability of 'any' confession that the suspect may have made rather than the reliability of the one he did make. The judge's task is further complicated by the section's requirement that he should consider the likelihood of unreliability 'notwithstanding that it [the confession] may be true'.

Difficult questions of admissibility could arise in the *voir dire*. Before the Act, when the voluntariness of a confession was in issue, its truth or falsity was irrelevant and, consequently, the prosecution was not allowed to ask the accused whether his confession was true: *Wong Kam-Ming* v. *R*.[90] This made sense as long as the test for the admissibility of a confession was not its reliability but whether the accused spoke when he would have preferred to remain silent. Now the Act has reversed matters. In the parliamentary bill that preceded the 1984 Act there was a provision specifically allowing the court to admit, at the trial within a trial, evidence on the truth or falsity of the confession.[91] Does the absence of this provision from the Act leave the old rule intact? If it does, it would mean that the accused is not allowed to prove the falsity of his statements in order to establish that the pressures on him were such that he was prepared to say anything. Such a prohibition would be wholly unjust. But if, on the contrary, the accused is allowed to prove falsity, is the prosecution then allowed to show that the accused's statements to the police were in fact true? If the answer is yes, little will

---

[89] The admissibility procedure is activated when the defence represents 'that the confession was or may have been obtained' as a consequence of the factors set out in the section. Suppose that the defence altogether denies that the accused made the confession attributed to him. Is the judge still required to conduct a trial within a trial? Presumably he is.

[90] [1979] 1 All ER 939.   [91] Cl. 69(4).

remain of the rule that truth or falsity are inadmissible matters at this stage.

Falsity is clearly relevant and admissible evidence to the issue of whether the confession was obtained by oppression under subsection (2)(*a*). It might be said that, as a matter of construction, falsity must also be admissible when the issue is one of reliability under subsection (2)(*b*).

It is possible that the reason for choosing the hypothetical phraseology lay in the belief that questions as to the truth or falsity of the confession were in principle matters for the jury and not for the judge.[92] Thus if the court is confined to considering whether 'any' confession could have been rendered unreliable, it could be said that the judge does not impinge on the jury's function. But this is a poor reason because, even if the judge were to consider whether the circumstances were likely to render the actual confession unreliable, he would only be deciding whether the jury should hear of the confession, not what weight they should give to it.[93] In practice, however, the falsity of a confession will probably be taken to provide an important indication of the effect that the interrogation had on the suspect.[94]

It may be said that the legislature was using the hypothetical form in order to create a normative test rather than a factual one.[95] According to this view the aim of the hypothetical

---

[92] See Mirfield, 'The future of the law of confessions', [1984] Crim L R 63, 70.

[93] One suspects that a further reason for the Criminal Law Revision Committee's decision not to frame a straightforward reliability test was a reluctance to make a clean break with the voluntariness test which draws attention away from reliability and concentrates on whether any threat or promise made the suspect speak. Indeed, cl. 2(2)(*b*) of the Committee's draft Bill still refers to 'threat or inducement'.

[94] This was recognized by the Criminal Law Revision Committee when it remarked that 'although the fact that a particular confession seems clearly to be true will not make it admissible if the threat or inducement was of a sort likely to cause the accused to make an unreliable confession, yet evidence of the terms of the confession may throw light on the facts concerning interrogation.' Ibid. 44. It is difficult, however, to see how, if the confession is clearly true, the judge can still hold that it was rendered unreliable by the conditions of the interrogation. Once the judge asks himself whether any confession might have been unreliable, he is bound—as Mirfield observed—'to decide the issue of admissibility on the basis of his assessment of the reliability of the confession actually before him, even though s. 76(2) tells him that a confession inadmissible under either statutory head is to be excluded "notwithstanding that it may be true".' *Confessions* (1985), 114–15.

[95] Mr A. Stein drew my attention to this possibility.

phraseology is to encourage the court to concentrate its attention on the propriety of the standards of interrogation rather than on their effect on the particular accused. Thus the judge has to pass an evaluative judgment on whether the methods adopted by the police are likely, in the long run of cases, to have an adverse effect on the reliability of confessions. This interpretation receives some support from *Phillips*[96] where the Court of Appeal considered an inducement offered by the police to a suspect in order to obtain a confession to be by itself sufficient ground for exclusion under section 76(2)(*b*).

There is a further complication in the drafting of the section under consideration. It concerns the proper standard of proof in the admissibility of confessions; which has been the subject of controversy in the United States and the Commonwealth.[97] In passing the Police and Criminal Evidence Act 1984, Parliament might have been expected to clarify its position on this point. Instead it has provided that the prosecution must prove *beyond reasonable doubt* that nothing said or done was *likely* to render *any* confession unreliable. The expression 'beyond reasonable doubt' denotes a degree of probative strength: it is the highest measure required by the law. The word 'likely' also denotes a degree of probative strength; but one of lesser extent. This double reference to degrees of probative support is confusing. Does it mean that the prosecution has to prove to the highest degree of proof that there was no degree of the lesser kind (no degree of 'likely') that something said or done would render the confession unreliable? If Parliament wished to stipulate that the prosecution has merely to prove that the circumstances of the confession were highly unlikely (though not necessarily beyond reasonable doubt) to make the confession unreliable, we might have expected the draftsman to state this more simply.[98]

---

[96] (1988) 86 Cr App R 18.

[97] In *Lego* v. *Twomey* 404 US 477 (1972) the American Supreme Court decided that proof on the balance of probabilities was constitutionally sufficient. But in a number of states proof beyond reasonable doubt is required: *People* v. *Jimenez* 580 P 2d 672 (1978); *Magley* v. *State* 335 NE 2d 811 (1975). The Australian case of *Warren* [1982] 2 NSWLR 360, decides in favour of the balance of probabilities but the New Zealand case of *McCuin* [1982] 1 NZLR 13 requires proof beyond reasonable doubt.

[98] Except that the decision to ask the judge to consider whether '*any*' confession was likely to be rendered unreliable might have presented an obstacle.

However, if the test established by subsection 76(2)(*b*) is a normative one, what has to be proved beyond reasonable doubt is only that the confession was obtained in consequence of the act of which a complaint is made. The further factor, that the act in question 'was likely . . . to render unreliable any confession', is not an object of proof in the normal way but is something that the judge has to establish as a matter of evaluation.[99]

The range of application of section 76 has been thrown into doubt by the decision of the Court of Appeal in *Sat-Bhambra*.[100] The prosecution adduced a recording of the accused's interview by the police. The contents of the accused's statement was exculpatory but its effect was, as Lord Lane CJ described, 'to demonstrate that the appellant was evasive and prevaricating and that many statements which he made proved eventually to be false'. Clearly, the hearing of the recording by the jury did the accused's case no good at all. The Court of Appeal decided, *obiter*, that a purely exculpatory statement does not come within the definition of 'confession' in section 82(1) of the 1984 Act. Section 82(1) provides: '"confession" includes any statement wholly or partly adverse to the person who made it . . .'

As this definition is inexhaustive, the Court of Appeal had to provide an independent reason for not applying the requirements of section 76 to an exculpatory statement. The Lord Chief Justice provided the following explanation: 'The section is aimed at excluding confessions obtained by words or deeds likely to render them unreliable, i.e. admissions or partial admissions contrary to the interests of the defendant and welcome to the interrogator.'[101]

On this reasoning all exculpatory statements of the kind adduced in this case are henceforth to be considered as 'confessions' for the simple reason that all suspects are now put on notice that it is contrary to their interest to make an evasive and prevaricating statement which, on being adduced at the trial,

---

[99] This interpretation is not, however, free of doubt. If the reason for exclusion under s. 76(2)(*b*) is deviation from standards of propriety, then real evidence obtained by such deviation should also be excluded, but this is not the case. Subs. 76(4)(*a*) sanctions the admissibility of facts discovered as a result of an inadmissible confession.

[100] Official transcript of judgment delivered on 19 Feb. 1988.

[101] Ibid.; see discussion in Mirfield, *Confessions* (1985), 81.

may undermine their defence.[102] In the case under consideration the prosecution thought that the recording amounted to a
confession and adduced it as such; indeed, how else would it
have been admissible?

The Court of Appeal's decision has its roots in the old notion
that a confession is admissible as an exception to the rule
against hearsay. Best explained this exception as follows: 'the
universal experience of mankind testifies that, as men consult
their own interest, and seek their own advantage; whatever they
say or admit against their interest or advantage may, with
tolerable safety, be taken to be true as against them . . .'.[103]

But we have come a long way since. Today the law of
confessions is not a mere refinement of an exception to the
largely discredited hearsay rule. It is concerned with devising
safeguards for the protection of persons interrogated in police
custody. There is no reason why we should suspend enforcement of these standards just because the suspect thought, at the
time of the interrogation, that he was not incriminating himself.
This was accepted in the Canadian decision of *Piche* v. *R.*[104] and
in the famous American case of *Miranda* v. *Arizona*.[105] It is a pity
that the Court of Appeal saw fit to brush aside these well-
considered opinions.

The tendency to place technical limitations on section 76 may
be also gleaned form *Goldenberg*[106] where it was decided that the
words 'in *consequence of anything said or done* which was likely . . . to
render unreliable any confession . . .', in section 76(2)(*b*), 'do
not extend so as to include anything said or done by the person
making the confession'. It was therefore considered that there
was no need to apply the admissibility test where the suspect
claimed to have confessed because, being addicted to drugs, he
wanted to be released on bail in order to satisfy his need.
However, it is in these very circumstances that the suspect is
most vulnerable and that police practices require the most
careful supervision.

---

[102] Birch, 'The PACE hots up: confessions and confusion under the 1984 Act',
[1989] Crim L Rev 95.
[103] Best, *The Principles of the Law of Evidence*, 5th edn. (1870), 659–60.
[104] (1970) 1 DLR 700.   [105] 384 US 436 (1966).
[106] Official transcript of judgment delivered on 18 May 1988.

CONCLUSION

Recent Court of Appeal decisions provide early indication of the courts' solution to the conflict between the privilege against self-incrimination and the need to question suspects.

The courts are enforcing compliance with the rights of suspects as set out in the Police and Criminal Evidence Act 1984. The design of the Act is to protect suspects in custody from improper police behaviour and, above all, to erect procedural devices that will enable the courts to supervise police conduct towards suspects. Although the courts are still dependent on police sources for the facts regarding the treatment of prisoners, the records of such treatment are much improved.[107]

In marked contrast to the pre-1984 attitude, the courts are now insisting that the right of suspects to consult a solicitor is honoured. However, it would appear that the courts are not prepared to allow this right to be turned into an exemption from interrogation. The suspect may insist on his right to keep silent but this course of action is not going to be free from disadvantage in that the trier of fact will be encouraged to give such probative weight to the suspect's silence as the circumstances demand.

This approach will contribute towards achieving two aims: first, the suspect will be better protected from improper police pressure, but, at the same time, the obstructive effect of this protection on police investigations will be reduced. English law seems to have made admirable progress towards reducing the tension between the privilege against self-incrimination and the social need to interrogate persons against whom there is a well-grounded suspicion.

The new strategy leaves, however, a few questions unresolved, not least the connection between reliance on the privilege to refrain from providing information and the nature of the comment on the suspect's silence. Further, we have yet to see what steps are taken to safeguard against police questioning in the absence of a well-founded suspicion against the suspect.

---

[107] Indeed, the factual basis for most of the decisions reviewed here was derived from such records.

It may be necessary to legislate that the suspect's silence should be disclosable at the trial if, and only if, he has been adequately informed of the case and the evidence against him. If the accused is to be expected to put his cards on the table, it should be unlawful for the police to mislead a suspect or his solicitor about the nature of the evidence in its possession.[108]

Another aspect of the present law which requires reconsideration concerns the right of an accused not to testify. The Criminal Law Revision Committee recommended that, after the prosecution has made a *prima facie* case against him, the accused should be called upon to testify; and that the jury be informed that they may take into account a refusal to testify in determining the accused's guilt. This proposal seems excessive. There is no need to invest the accused's failure with dramatic effects. All that is necessary is to inform the jury at the end of the trial that, in law, the accused had the opportunity of rebutting the charges levelled against him under oath but that he declined to do so. It is unlikely that this piece of information will come as a surprise to the majority of jurors and it will not, therefore, constitute a sharp departure from the present position.[109] To avoid misunderstanding, the trial judge should make the jury understand that refusal to testify is not tantamount to an admission of guilt and that the accused's failure does not discharge them from weighing carefully the evidence presented by the prosecution and by the defence.

Addressing himself to this proposal Professor Cross wrote:

If for the loaded phrase 'self accusation' we were to substitute 'liability for cross-examination', the defendant at a criminal trial would be confronted with the choice between giving the court his version of the facts with the possibility of a cross-examination which might or might not be unpleasant, and running the risk of adverse inferences being drawn from his failure to testify, a risk the magnitude of which would

---

[108] On the need for disclosing incriminating evidence to accused persons see Whitebread, *Criminal Procedure* (1980), 396; Note, 'The prosecutor's duty to disclose to defendants pleading guilty', 99 Harv L Rev 1004 (1986).

[109] Nowadays defence counsel tend to fear that juries will draw adverse inferences from the accused's failure to testify and they therefore tend to ask trial judges to inform juries of the accused's right to stay out of the witness box; *Harris* (1987) 84 Cr App R 75.

vary considerably from case to case. If ... an accused with a criminal record is adequately protected from cross-examination on that subject, I fail to see how the choice can realistically be described as a cruel one.[110]

It may well be that Professor Cross's view is not far from being reflected in the reality of today's criminal trials.[111]

---

[110] 'An Attempt to Update the Law of Evidence', 19th Lionel Cohen Lectures (1973). This also disposes of the objection that it would be unseemly for the trial to deteriorate into a contest between the accused trying to avoid answering incriminating questions and the court trying to elicit his answers. No contest need take place, the accused's reticence would attract no active countermeasures.

[111] A limitation on the accused's freedom not to testify is already openly acknowledged where the accused is tried on several counts and he wishes to testify in relation to some but not others. It has been decided that the trial judge is not bound to accommodate the accused by ordering separate trials: *Phillips* (1988) 86 Cr App R 18.

16

Improperly Obtained Evidence

This chapter is concerned with a simple and age-old question: Should a court give judgment on the basis of evidence that has been procured by illegal or immoral means?[1] Although the question often comes up the courts find it difficult to confront it, except in relation to confessions. This is due to two principal factors: first, a failure to come to terms with the nature of the problem, and, secondly, a reluctance on the part of the courts to look beyond the immediate confines of the law of evidence.

The first factor is reflected in the disingenuous justification given for the traditional common-law principle that relevant and reliable evidence is admissible irrespective of its provenance:[2] the object of the trial is to ascertain the facts in issue, the proferred evidence helps ascertain these facts, *ergo* it is admissible. Since the appeal to relevance made in this justification is hardly sufficient when many a type of relevant evidence is excluded, supporters of this position, such as Wigmore, add that the trial is an unsuitable forum for trying violations of legality which are unconnected with the issue in the case and an investigation of the alleged illegality could confuse and delay adjudication on the main issue. Wigmore wrote:

a judge does not hold court in a street-car to do summary justice upon a fellow-passenger who fraudulently evades payment of his fare; and, upon the same principle, he does not attempt, in the course of a specific litigation, to investigate and punish all offences which incidentally cross the path of that litigation. Such a practice might be consis-

---

[1] This chapter is derived from my article: 'Illegally obtained evidence: discretion as a guardian of legitimacy', (1987) 40 Current Legal Problems 55.

[2] *Leatham* (1861) 8 Cox CC 498. *Wigmore on Evidence*, 3rd edn. (1940), vol. 8, s. 2183.

tent with the primitive system of justice under an Arabian sheik; but it
does not comport with our own system of law.[3]

This perception presupposes that the issue of illegality is
strictly one of evidence, straddling civil and criminal proceedings alike. In fact the problem assumes a wholly different nature
in criminal trials. The criminal trial has a special moral dimension. It is concerned with the determination of moral blame,
which may in turn justify the infliction of suffering and humiliation on an individual, as well as legal liability. The willingness of the public to accept the authority of the criminal court
as a dispenser of punishment depends on the extent to which
the public believes in the moral legitimacy of the system. The
morality or fairness of a system of adjudication hinges on many
factors, such as the impartiality and incorruptibility of the
judiciary. Amongst these must also be numbered a publicly
acceptable judicial attitude towards breaches of the law. A
judicial community that is seen to condone, or even encourage,
violations of the law can hardly demand compliance with its
own edicts.[4]

Where incidents of illegality are not recurrent or where they
emanate from individuals whose actions do not reflect on the
judicial institution as a whole, it may be feasible to dissociate
the admissibility of evidence from its legality.[5] Criminal judges
last century may have been right to divorce admissibility from
illegality, if they felt that the trial process was so detached from
the police investigation as to be insulated from any illegalities

---

[3] *Wigmore on Evidence*, 3rd edn. (1940), vol. 8, s. 2183, p. 5. See also *Fox* v. *Chief
Constable of Gwent* [1985] 3 All ER 392, 397, where the English version of the same
argument takes the simpler form: that it is not the courts' function to discipline the
police.

[4] Holmes and Brandeis stressed this in their dissenting judgment in *Olmstead* v.
US 277 US 438, 484–5 (1928): 'Our government is the potent, the omnipresent
teacher. For good or for ill, it teaches . . . by its example . . . If the government
becomes a law breaker, it breeds contempt for law; it invites every man to become a
law unto himself; it invites anarchy.' The need to keep a distance from illegitimate
activities has produced an entire body of law in relation to illegal contracts.

[5] It is thus possible to justify the admissibility of illegally obtained evidence in
civil litigation, where the transgressors are private citizens: see *Calcraft* v. *Guest*
[1898] 1 QB 759; *Ashburton* v. *Pape* [1913] 2 Ch 469. Even in civil proceedings the
illegality of the means is not always kept out of consideration, e.g. in relation to
illegal contracts.

that occurred in police stations.[6] However, today the investigative process is seen as part of the administration of justice, which explains why the debate regarding illegally obtained evidence has assumed such importance.[7]

The moral dimension is not the only distinguishing feature of the criminal trial. The public demands satisfaction of its sense of being protected from crime as well as of its moral sentiment. If, for instance, a court refuses to admit evidence conclusively implicating the accused in murder which has been obtained by illegal means, the public would feel that the court has betrayed its duty to protect the community from crime.[8]

There is an uncanny symmetry between the consequences of an admissibility and an inadmissibility rule. If applied consistently, each of these rules will undermine public confidence in the criminal process. If the court always admits illegally obtained evidence, it will be seen to condone the malpractice of the law-enforcement agencies. If it always excludes it, it will be seen to abandon its duty to protect us from crime. The first thing that we must therefore accept is that the criminal trial presents a dilemma which cannot be solved by an inflexible rule. An unwillingness to grasp the intractability of this dilem-

---

[6] *Warwickshall* (1783) 1 Leach 263; *Griffin* (1809) Russ & Ry 151; *Gould* (1840) 9 C & P 364; *Leatham* (1861) 8 Cox CC 498; *Berriman* (1854) 6 Cox CC 388. By 1955 even Lord Goddard CJ felt obliged to make some concession to this consideration when he declared the existence of a judicial discretion to exclude otherwise admissible evidence where it would 'operate unfairly against the accused'; *Kuruma* v. *R.* [1955] 1 All ER 236, 239. Justice Brennan has observed that the 'police and the courts cannot be regarded as constitutional strangers to each other; because the evidence-gathering role of the police is directly linked to the evidence-admitting function of the courts, and individuals' Fourth Amendment rights may be undermined as completely by the one as by the other' *US* v. *Leon* 468 US 897, 938 (1984); he described these functions as a 'single governmental action'.

[7] See s. 78 of the Police and Criminal Evidence Act 1984. The American Supreme Court held that the Fourteenth Amendment provides protection only against 'the activities of sovereign authority'; *Burdeau* v. *McDowell* 256 US 465 (1921); *Walter* v. *US* 447 US 649 (1980). Problems of illegality could of course arise in civil cases but there they are of a different dimension and I do not propose to deal with them here.

[8] As Mellor J observed: 'It would be a dangerous obstacle to the administration of justice if we were to hold, because evidence was obtained by illegal means, it could not be used against a party charged with an offence.' *Jones* v. *Owen* (1870) 34 JP 759. An illustration is provided by *Apicella* (1986) 82 Cr App R 295, where fluid obtained from a suspect for the purpose of diagnosis of disease was found to prove the suspect's vicious rape of three girls whom he infected with an unusual disease.

ma has contributed more than anything else to the backward-
ness of the law on illegally obtained evidence.[9]

THE SHORTCOMINGS OF THE EXCLUSIONARY PRINCIPLE

An exclusionary jurisdiction is clearly necessary and two theoretical bases for the jurisdiction are current.[10] The first is the
vindication or remedial theory, which holds that the object of
an exclusionary rule is to vindicate the accused for the infringement of his rights. The second is the deterrent theory, which
suggests that the object of exclusion is to deter the law-enforcement agencies from future abuses. I shall deal with each of
these in turn.

A person has a right not to have his person and premises
illegally searched, not to have his possessions illegally seized,
and not to be unlawfully arrested. It is suggested that by
imposing these restrictions the state has staked out the boundaries for lawful access to evidence and has indicated that
beyond these limits it is willing to forego evidence of crime in
deference to individual freedom.[11] Consequently, it is said, exclusion of evidence secured through illegal search, seizure, and
arrest puts the prosecution in the position where the constitution, or the legislature, meant to put it when it imposed those
restrictions: without the evidence.

This argument ignores a crucial factor in the situation that
we are considering: the evidence has been obtained, is now
available, and does tend to prove the accused's guilt. In devising the powers of search and seizure the lawmaker laid down
that an individual, who must be presumed innocent, should not
be disturbed without probable cause. Here, whether we like it
or not, we are no longer concerned with the question of whether

[9] See Zaltzman, 'The Israeli approach to evidence obtained in violation of the
right to privacy', (1983) 18 Israel L Rev 215.
[10] For an illuminating discussion see Ashworth, 'Excluding evidence as protecting rights', [1977] Crim L Rev 723.
[11] Loewy, 'The Warren court as defender of state and federal criminal law . . .',
37 Geo Washington L Rev 1218, 1236 (1969). See also dissent of Justice Brennan in
US v. *Leon* 468 US 897, 928 (1984).

we should disturb an individual against whom there is no probable cause but with the question of whether a person, in relation to whom evidence of guilt is now available, should be treated as if there were no increased probability of his guilt. The increased probability of guilt creates the need to protect the public from the crime, which makes a return to the *status quo ante* rather awkward.

The perception of the problem as purely one of admissibility of evidence at the trial has diverted attention from other areas in which a similar conflict of interests and rights takes place. If we look beyond the confines of the law of evidence we discover that the situation of *ex post facto* calculation is quite normal in relation to civil liberties. Section 24(5) of the Police and Criminal Evidence Act 1984 lays down: 'Where an arrestable offence has been committed, any person may arrest without warrant— (a) anyone who is guilty of the offence; (b) anyone whom he has reasonable grounds for suspecting to be guilty of it.'

This means that an otherwise groundless arrest is excused, if it turns out that the arrested person has in fact committed an arrestable offence.[12] This constitutes a choice of policy about the protection of civil liberties. A similar choice was made in relation to seizure when Horridge J held that 'the interests of the State must excuse the seizure of documents, which seizure would otherwise be unlawful, if it appears in fact that such documents were evidence of a crime committed by anyone . . .'[13]

Moreover, in the fight against crime our institutions are prepared at times to forgive a lesser crime in order to punish a more serious one, as the practice of immunity given to state witnesses shows.

Turning to the law of tort, we find that here too the tension between legality and just deserts has been resolved, to some

[12] Similarly, under s. 24(4), (7).
[13] *Elias* v. *Pasmore* [1934] 2 KB 164, 173. It was criticized by Lord Denning in *Ghani* v. *Jones* [1969] 3 All ER 1700, 1703, but the same sentiment was present in Lord Denning's own judgment. See also Lord MacDermott CJ's dictum in *Murphy* [1965] NI 138, 187–8: 'The appellant was . . . a serious security risk; this was revealed by the trick of misrepresentation practised by the police . . . and no other way of obtaining this revelation has been demonstrated or suggested.'

extent, in favour of the latter. Under the American Civil Rights Act a person may sue for damages for infringement of his constitutional rights.[14] However, if as a result of an infringement of rights, evidence is found that leads to the aggrieved person's conviction, that person loses his claim. The reason given is that immunity from action will encourage bolder and more efficient police action in combating crime.[15] While there is no direct English authority on the point, it is difficult to believe that, in practice, the guilty would secure any better remedies under English tort law.[16]

It would be odd if the consideration of the *ex post facto* realization that the infringement of the suspect's rights resulted in the discovery of his guilt were completely absent from the law of evidence, when it is so potent in the law of arrest, in the rules of search and seizure, and in the law of tort. It is, however, claimed that we need to remedy infringements of rights by the exclusion of evidence precisely because tort remedies are not taken seriously by the civil courts, where convicted plaintiffs find little sympathy.[17] This line of reasoning is unlikely to persuade the courts because the practical preferences that prevent an effective civil remedy cannot be neutralized simply by saying that we are dealing with a question of exclusion of evidence rather than with one of damages.

---

[14] 42 USCA s. 1983.

[15] *Pouncey* v. *Ryan* 396 F Supp 126 (1975); Harper and James, *The Law of Torts* (1956), s. 4.12, p. 347. Alternatively, a conviction could reduce the damages: *Long* v. *Mann* 65 So 2d 500 (1953); *Massantonio* v. *People* 236 P 1019 (1925).

[16] See L. Lustgarten, *The Governance of the Police* (1986), 133–4, 138.

[17] For American discussion see: *Bivens* v. *Six Unknown Named Agents of Federal Bureau of Narcotics* 403 US 388, 421–2 (1971); Comment, 'The tort alternative to the exclusionary rule', 63 Journal of Criminal Law Criminology and Police Science 256 (1972); Foote, 'Tort remedies for police violations of individual rights', 39 Minn L Rev 493 (1955); Plumb, 'Illegal enforcement of the law', 24 Cornell L Q 337, 385–91 (1939); Loewy, 'The Fourth Amendment as a device for protecting the innocent', 81 Mich L Rev 1229, 1265–6 (1983). Loewy also makes the point that if the civil remedy is taken seriously it might deter policemen from pursuing legal searches in cases where legality might be controversial or where the crime seems to them not serious enough to justify the risk of civil litigation. For the position in Australia see Australian Law Reform commission, Rep No 2 Criminal Investigation, 1975, paras. 287–302; and in Canada, Oakes, 'Studying the exclusionary rule in search and seizure', 37 University of Chi L Rev 665, 701–6 (1970). See also Lustgarten, *The Government of the Police* (1986), 135 n. 33.

Furthermore, the vindication theory runs up against the difficulty of maintaining a satisfactory balance between illegality and its remedy. In a criminal trial exclusion of evidence of guilt amounts to a contribution towards the acquittal of a person who may be guilty. It is by no means self-evident that acquittal of the guilty is an appropriate response to earlier police transgressions. Nor is a blanket exclusion capable of achieving a balance between the seriousness of the infringement and the benefit to the accused.[18]

Given these difficulties, the justification for the exclusion of illegally obtained evidence shifts to the second theory: the argument that exclusion is necessary not so much to vindicate the accused as to deter the police from unauthorized searches and thus protect the peace and privacy of individuals against whom there is no probable cause.[19] This theory flies in the face of the general willingness, just described, to detract from constitutional liberties in order to further crime control. In the absence of widespread resentment of the police, citizens are unlikely to feel that they require protection from the police by means which let guilty persons go free.[20]

From a practical point of view there are a number of reasons for doubting whether a general exclusionary rule would have significant deterrent effects.[21] First, police officers are subject to influences that may well outweigh the sanction of exclusion; for example, the expectations of peers and supervisors, and public pressure to apprehend offenders. Secondly, the violation of search rules would involve, at most, exclusion at some distant date and is therefore unlikely to constitute a serious brake on

---

[18] As Chief Justice Burger said: 'society has at least as much a right to expect rationally graded responses from judges in place of the universal "capital punishment" we inflict on all evidence when police error is shown in its acquisition'. *Bivens* v. *Six Unknown Named Agents* 403 US 388, 419 (1971).

[19] R. B. Dworkin, 'Fact style adjudication and the Fourth Amendment...', 48 Indiana L J 329 (1973).

[20] The situation is somewhat analogous to the enforcement of the privilege against self-incrimination; the innocent do not feel particularly disturbed by breaches because they are unlikely to wish to refuse to co-operate with interrogation.

[21] For a thorough examination of the deterrent argument in theory and in practice see Oakes, 'Studying the exclusionary rule in search and seizure', 37 University of Chi L Rev 665 (1970).

illegal searches.[22] Thirdly, even if officers were inclined to comply, it may be that the provisions of the search and seizure rules are not communicated to them effectively enough to secure compliance. Finally, if objections to unauthorized search turn out to be rare, or if police officers stand a good chance of concealing the breaches, the efficacy of an exclusion rule as a deterrent will be limited.

LEGITIMACY: A BALANCING EXERCISE

The manifest weaknesses of a pure vindication theory and of a pure deterrent one in justifying a rule of exclusion, and the shortcomings of an inclusionary rule, leave us with only one possible policy to pursue, that of avoiding the undesirable consequences of an absolute commitment to either exclusion or inclusion. We may refer to this as the principle of judicial integrity or the principle of legitimacy.[23] This principle has been criticized for lack of clarity.[24] It is, however, a mistake to assume that because individual decisions cannot be easily derived from a principle, the principle has no guiding force. The social need to balance two conflicting constitutional requirements is in itself a powerful consideration. Indeed, it is important that the courts should be seen to exercise a balancing jurisdiction, for this will inform the public of the difficulty of choosing between admissibility and inadmissibility and will secure support even from those who might have preferred a different result in an individual case.

That this is the direction in which a solution should be sought is demonstrated by the recent fluctuation of the American law and the clamour for discretion in the Common-

---

[22] Besides, the gathering of admissible evidence may not be a paramount objective in violating the search rules.

[23] It should be noted that the appeal to judicial integrity has been used in the United States as a justification for a strict exclusionary rule. The argument advanced here takes a different form and the use of the term 'legitimacy' will perhaps cause less confusion.

[24] *McCormick on Evidence*, 3rd edn. (1984), 462. See also *Stone* v. *Powell* 428 US 465, 485 (1976). Judicial integrity has even been equated with deterrence: *Janis* v. *US* 428 US 433, 458 n. (1976).

wealth.[25] By 1961 the old rule of universal admissibility had been completely replaced in the United States by a new rule of universal exclusion.[26] Within a decade, the United States Supreme Court began to appreciate that total exclusion was socially unacceptable. Just as the American court could not abide the strictures of the *Miranda* principle, it could not maintain unwavering faith to the exclusionary rule of the Fourth Amendment. Ways have had to be contrived in order to limit the scope of exclusion.[27] Instead of a consistent policy of exclusion American decisions indicate that both the remedial and deterrent policies have a part to play in the judicial strategy.

The remedial policy may be seen at work in decisions holding that the exclusionary rule does not apply in situations where search and seizure violations were directed against a third party and not the accused.[28] At the same time, the American courts

---

[25] In fact the problem of illegally obtained evidence is not confined to common-law systems. For a survey of the position in the major European systems see W. Pakter, 'Exclusionary rules in France, Germany and Italy', (1985) Hastings International and Comparative Law Rev 1.

[26] In the landmark decision of *Mapp* v. *Ohio* 367 US 643 (1961) the Supreme Court ruled that all evidence obtained by illegal searches and seizures was inadmissible in a criminal trial. The origins of the rule are in *Weeks* v. *US* 232 US 383 (1914). The rule applies to illegalities involving violation of the Federal Constitution, mainly violation of the Fourth Amendment which provides: 'The right of people to be secure in their persons, houses, papers, and effects, against unreasonable searches and seizures, shall not be violated, and no warrants shall issue, but upon probable cause, supported by oath or affirmation, and particularly describing the place to be searched, and the persons or things to be seized.'

[27] Justice Cardozo foresaw this development back in 1926 in *People* v. *Defore* 242 NY 13, 150 NE 585 (1926). The exclusionary rule has been cut down by decisions to sanction exclusion only where the benefit, in greater future observance of legality by the police, outweighs the disadvantage of loss of relevant evidence; *McCormick on Evidence*, 3rd edn. (1984), 465. It has been held, for example, that the exclusion of illegally obtained evidence would not provide sufficient incremental benefit where the evidence is merely used for impeaching an accused who is giving evidence; *Harris* v. *New York* 401 US 222 (1971). For similar reasons it has been decided that the exclusionary rule does not apply to grand jury proceedings; *US* v. *Calandra* 414 US 338 (1973); or in situations where the police made an excusable mistake about the legality of search or seizure; *US* v. *Leon* 468 US 897 (1984), where the Supreme Court has categorically stated that 'an assessment of the flagrancy of the police misconduct constitutes an important step in the calculus' and that 'suppression of evidence obtained pursuant to a warrant should be ordered only on a case-by-case basis and only in those unusual cases in which exclusion will further the purposes of the exclusionary rule'. See also Stuntz, 'The American exclusionary rule...' [1989] Crim L Rev 117.

[28] *McCormick on Evidence*, 3rd edn. (1984), 514.

have distanced themselves from any commitment to the idea that exclusion is a remedy to which the accused is entitled as a matter of right.[29] Simultaneously, considerations of deterrence are to be found behind the principle that exclusion is appropriate only where it is likely to lead, in the long run, to some incremental deterrence.[30]

The legitimacy principle has found its clearest statement in the new Canadian Constitution which provides:

Where . . . a court concludes that evidence was obtained in a manner that infringed or denied any rights or freedoms guaranteed by this Charter, the evidence shall be excluded if it is established that, having regard to all the circumstances, the admission of it in the proceedings would bring the administration of justice into disrepute.[31]

THE ENGLISH APPROACH

Section 78 of the Police and Criminal Evidence Act 1984 empowers the court to exclude prosecution evidence if its admission 'would have such an adverse effect on the fairness of the proceedings that the court ought not to admit it'.[32] However, so far there has been little inclination to elucidate the principles which should govern the exercise of this discretion.

This state of affairs is the result of a legal methodology, fast becoming the exclusive preserve of the English profession,

---

[29] *Elkins* v. *US* 364 US 206 (1960); Note, 'The Fourth Amendment exclusionary rule: past, present, no future', 12 Am Crim L Rev 507, 508–10 (1975).

[30] For instance, it has been held that little will be gained from excluding illegally obtained evidence used by the prosecution solely for the purpose of impeachment and such evidence is therefore admissible: *Harris* v. *New York* 401 US 222 (1971). See also n. 27 above.

[31] Constitution Act 1982, s. 24(2). Armed with this jurisdiction the Supreme Court lost no time in discarding the old common-law doctrine that was embodied in *Wray* [1971] SCR 272, 11 DLR (3d) 673, and began to evolve principles for the exercise of discretion: *Rothman* v. *R.* (1981) 59 CCC (2d) 30; *Therens* [1985] 4 WWR 286. See review by McCrimmon, 'Developments in the law of evidence: the 1984–85 Term', (1985) 8 Supreme Court L Rev 249.

[32] The exercise of discretion is not confined to instances of illegality or impropriety; *O'Leary* (1988) 87 Cr App R 387. In the latter case it was used to exclude unsatisfactory evidence of identification; see also *Delaney*, official transcript, 8 Aug. 1988, such a wide notion of 'fairness' is unhelpful since it can refer to a multitude of aspects and merely furnishes an excuse for achieving whatever result is wanted without rigorous justification.

according to which major problems of principle receive the kind of treatment that is more appropriate to the interpretation of technical tax provisions. *Sang*[33] is a case in point. On the issue of exclusionary discretion five Law Lords devoted their energies to reconciling dicta in previous cases, while leaving untouched the questions of principle: Should there be discretion and, if so, what role might it fulfil? In the event the decision only succeeded in throwing doubt on the very existence of discretion.[34]

A recent House of Lords pronouncement on exclusionary discretion is to be found in *Fox* v. *Chief Constable of Gwent*.[35] On finding a car at the scene of an accident, the police unlawfully entered the driver's house and asked him to provide a specimen of breath. When the accused refused, he was arrested and taken to a police station where he was made to provide a breath specimen which showed that the amount of alcohol in his breath exceeded the prescribed limit. The accused was convicted, first, of failing to provide a breath specimen contrary to section 7(4) of the Road Traffic Act 1972, and, secondly, of driving with excess alcohol contrary to section 6(1) of the same Act.

The first conviction was quashed because, according to *Morris* v. *Beardmore*,[36] as trespassers, the policemen could not make a legally valid request for a breath specimen. Against the second conviction the accused argued that, since the specimen had been obtained as a result of a wrongful arrest, it should have been excluded as a matter of discretion. Rejecting this argument Lord Fraser said:

the Divisional Court was ... right in treating the fact that the appellant was in the police station because he had been unlawfully arrested merely as a historical fact, with which the court was not concerned. The duty of the court is to decide whether the appellant has committed the offence with which he is charged, and not to discipline the police for exceeding their powers. I note in passing that there were several reasons any one of which might have accounted for the appellant's being in the police station perfectly lawfully. He might have been there

---

[33] [1979] 2 All ER 1222.
[34] See Polyviou, 'Illegally-obtained evidence and *R* v *Sang*', in Tapper (ed.), *Crime Proof and Punishment*, 175.
[35] [1985] 3 All ER 392, originally tried before s. 78 came into force.
[36] [1980] 2 All ER 753.

because he had been lawfully arrested. Or he might have gone there voluntarily etc.[37]

This extraordinary reasoning bodes ill for the section 78 jurisdiction; if followed, hardly any evidence would be excludable because it would almost always be possible to postulate hypothetical circumstances in which the evidence could have been obtained otherwise than by the impropriety in question.[38] Turning a blind eye to proven acts of illegality and pretending that the evidence might have been obtained with propriety is unlikely to enhance respect for the administration of justice.

There was some appreciation of the problem in Lord Fraser's remark that: 'Of course, if the appellant had been lured to the police station by some trick or deception, or if the police officers had behaved oppressively towards the appellant, the justices' jurisdiction to exclude otherwise admissible evidence ... might have come into play.'[39]

Yet the terms used here are not self-explanatory and one might wish to know why, if the accused was made to go to the police station by being falsely told that he was under lawful arrest, this did not amount to a trick or a deception? Similarly, why does not false imprisonment amount to oppression? These were the real issues in the case, but they went unanswered.

A POLICY OF ACCOUNTABILITY

Courts in the USA, Australia, Canada, and other common-law jurisdictions are addressing themselves to the very issues that

---

[37] [1985] 3 All ER 397. To this inexhaustive list one may add, for instance, the possibility that it was not the police that obtained the accused's breath specimen.

[38] Why not, after all, also draw a 'historical' divide between the police entry and their subsequent request and thus uphold their initial request as valid? Indeed, that was the very point that the House of Lords in *Morris* v. *Beardmore* refused to accept. There the prosecution tried to draw a veil between the constables' entry as trespassers and their request for the specimen, claiming that the former was a fact of the past leaving the subsequent request unaffected. Rejecting this approach Lord Diplock said: 'I find it quite impossible to suppose that Parliament intended that a person whose common law right to keep his home free from unauthorised intruders had been violated in this way should be bound under penal sanctions to comply with a demand which only the violation of that common law right had enabled the constable to make to him.' [1980] 2 All ER 753, 757.

[39] [1985] 3 All ER 397.

our courts decline to take seriously. Much can be learnt from their decisions.[40] The High Court of Australia, for instance, has been developing an exclusionary theory by setting out the type of considerations that have to be taken into account.[41] They include the following: whether the transgression was mistaken or intentional, whether the illegality affected the probative value of the evidence, the ease with which the law might have been complied with in order to obtain the evidence, and the nature of the offence charged.[42]

It would be wrong to claim that these considerations present simple choices. Indeed, some of them point in different directions at once. On the one hand, it could be said that if an officer acted under a mistaken belief in the lawfulness of his action, the reception of the evidence would not undermine legitimacy since the court would not be perceived as condoning intentional violations of legality. Nor, it could be argued, is exclusion necessary for deterrence, since an innocent officer would not be deterred by the knowledge that illegality may result in exclusion. But the opposite case could also be made, for if ignorance were to excuse infringement of individual rights, the police would have no incentive to inform officers of the limits of their powers.[43]

A similar ambiguity is involved in the consideration that the evidence could have been lawfully secured. It might be said that, since the evidence could have been obtained in any event, the accused has not lost much by the illegality; but if this is accepted, the police would have no incentive to conform with the legal requirements.

---

[40] *Welsh* v. *Wisconsin* 466 US 740 (1984), which deals with a situation identical to that of *Fox* v. *Chief Constable of Gwent*, stands in stark contrast to the English decision. The American Supreme Court showed no reluctance to face the real point of difficulty: the conflict between the right to privacy in one's own home and the public interest in being protected from drunken drivers.

[41] *Bunning* v. *Cross* (1977) 141 CLR 54, 78–80.

[42] In Canada too the courts have been refining the balancing strategy; *Therens* [1985] 4 WWR 286; *Collins* (1987) 56 CR (3d) 193; *Hamill* ibid. 220; *Sieben* ibid. 225.

[43] A premium will thereby be placed on the ignorance of the police officer, as the McDonald Report in Canada pointed out; Commission of Inquiry Concerning Certain Activities of the Royal Canadian Mounted Police, Second Report: Freedom and Security Under the Law (1981), 1046. See also Kaplan, 'The limits of the exclusionary rule', 26 Stan L Rev 1027, 1044 (1974).

The consideration relating to the seriousness of the offence might also be a source of conflicting conclusions. On the one hand, the more serious the offence, the more difficult it is to justify exclusion and thereby risk acquittal of a guilty and possibly dangerous person. On the other hand, the more serious the consequences of conviction the higher should be the moral rectitude of the means by which it is achieved.

This takes us back to Wigmore's objection, mentioned at the outset. How, it may be asked, can the trial judge be expected to address difficult questions of policy while having to conduct criminal proceedings efficiently and expeditiously? It must be realized from the outset that an exclusionary jurisdiction cannot have satisfactory results without a willingness on the part of the superior courts to develop suitable principles. Once policies and priorities have been clarified by these courts, the jurisdiction would be exercisable along well-charted paths. Yet we must not delude ourselves into believing that policy in this area can be satisfactorily shaped once and for all. A defensible attitude towards illegality requires the continuing development of the legal and moral limits of police investigation.

Even if the trial judge has to grapple with difficult problems in this regard, the exercise of a discretionary jurisdiction is of sufficient value to justify the judicial effort. The most salutary aspect of the exclusionary jurisdiction is the subjection of police practices to judicial scrutiny. A judicial discretion to exclude illegally obtained evidence renders the investigative process liable to judicial scrutiny in much the same way as other executive activities. The very exercise of judicial review gives public notice that the police are not above the law, brings out the constitutional dimension involved, and advances its development.[44] The concept of reasonableness, for instance, is fundamental in defining the constitutional powers of search, seizure, and arrest. The same parameters have important implications for the admissibility of evidence. The admissibility stage seems

---

[44] By its very nature, scrutiny has to be continually asserted and its principles periodically reviewed in response to institutional and social changes. As Justice Blackmun observed in *US* v. *Leon* 104 S Ct 3405, 3425, 'the scope of the exclusionary rule is subject to change in the light of changing judicial understanding about the effects of the rule outside the confines of the courtroom'.

particularly suitable for dealing with the constitutional issues involved here because it makes scrutiny much more likely than it would be if the matter were left to the sidelines of civil litigation.[45]

The exclusionary policy will doubtless give rise to some tricky problems. It will have to concern itself with violations of moral standards, as well as with those of express legal prohibitions, and the superior courts will have to develop criteria to identify those police measures that are considered morally unacceptable. English courts have decided, for instance, that evidence obtained by an *agent provocateur* is not excludable.[46] In America the Supreme Court devoted much thought to evidence obtained by means of surreptitious listening devices and other infringements of privacy.[47] But the theory of immorality is still very rudimentary and much more has to be done.

It sometimes happens that an impossible burden is imposed on a party in order to resolve the issue against that party without seeming so to do.[48] This might happen here if it were held, for instance, that an accused objecting to illegally obtained evidence must prove that the police make a practice of conducting unlawful searches.[49] Since the object of the jurisdiction is to seek justification from the law enforcement agencies for their practices it should be for them to satisfy the courts that they have acted lawfully.[50]

This leads on to the distinction between what is and what is not provable. In formulating guiding principles the courts have

---

[45] Lustgarten, *The Governance of the Police* (1986), 145–6.

[46] *Sang* [1979] 2 All ER 1222. Though one suspects that it would be as difficult to maintain unconditional admissibility here as it is in relation to other kinds of questionable methods.

[47] See *Katz* v. *US* 389 US 347 (1967); *US* v. *Karo* 104 S Ct 3296 (1984) and discussion in *McCormick on Evidence*, 3rd edn. (1984), 466–72.

[48] For example, according to *Air Canada* v. *Secretary of State for Trade* [1983] 1 All ER 910, where the government claims public interest immunity in respect of relevant documents in its possession, the courts will not inspect them unless the litigant seeking disclosure proves that they can materially help his case. Since the documents are in the government's hands the litigant is not in a position to prove their content and this rule effectively denies discovery. See [1983] All ER Rev 205.

[49] Cf *US* v. *Leon* 104 S Ct 3430, 3437–8.

[50] The original proposal for s. 78 of the Police and Criminal Evidence Act 1984, imposed an onus on the prosecution to justify admissibility of illegally obtained evidence. Lustgarten, *The Governance of the Police* (1986), 145.

to have regard to the consequences of their decisions. Sometimes these consequences will be empirically discoverable, but not always. If the courts adopt a vigorous policy of exclusion because of widespread transgressions by the police, prosecuting authorities should be free to show that the bad practices have ceased. But considerations such as the likely effect of admissibility or inadmissibility on public sentiment are not capable of proof in the ordinary sense.[51] In relation to such issues the courts will have to make a judgment that combines social and moral considerations. They will have to consider what, in a society with high moral standards, should be the public reaction to institutional violations. In other words, decisions will be taken by reference to a normative model as well as a factual one.

It may be argued against the discretionary policy advocated here that this is too tortuous and indirect a method for securing our social and constitutional goals. These are, as will have become clear, to deter the police from infringing our constitutional rights, to compensate adequately individuals whose rights have been infringed (especially when they are innocent), and, lastly, to convict the guilty. It has been suggested that it would be more effective to attempt to achieve each of these goals by independent steps.[52] First, it might be said, we could set up an effective disciplinary court, under judicial supervision, to try and punish infringements of individual rights by the police. Secondly, the law could explicitly provide for compensation in respect of such infringements and establish a cheap and easy procedure that would encourage aggrieved persons to sue. These two measures, it might be suggested, would make any further action during the criminal trial redundant; evidence will be admissible and the guilty punished.

It is, however, doubtful whether independent procedural devices of this kind could avoid the need for constitutional mechanisms for dealing with the ubiquitous conflict between individual rights and the community's interest in the protection

---

[51] Cf. McCrimmon, 'Developments in the law of evidence: the 1984–85 term', (1985) 8 Supreme Court L Rev 249; *US* v. *Leon* 104 S Ct 3430, 3437.

[52] See contrib. by R. Schlesinger, *Exclusionary Injustice* (1977).

from crime. A disciplinary court would still have to devise an adequate compromise to this conflict and to draw an imperfect line between failure to comply strictly with the rules and unacceptable conduct.[53] Furthermore, since we want to prevent not only violations of explicit rules but also immoral methods of investigation, a disciplinary court would still have to evolve a normative theory of police behaviour. Similarly, compensatory civil procedures would have to have regard to the normative problems that now beset admissibility. It is unlikely that a substantive law of damages could solve these problems at a stroke, as the American case law on civil-rights violations shows.[54]

It is not suggested that present disciplinary procedures could not be improved. Nor is it argued that civil remedies are satisfactory at the moment. Much can be improved, quite apart from the question of illegal police action. For instance, if the police detain the goods of an innocent person on reasonable suspicion that they were stolen, the lawfulness of the detention prevents the owner from obtaining compensation.[55] While police action in such circumstances may be supported, it does not follow that the loss should fall on the individual rather than be borne by the public.[56] However, improvements in these respects will not obviate the need for developing criteria of legitimacy.

The tension between strict observance of constitutional rights and the protection from crime is ever present but it is possible to sweep manifestations of police transgression under the carpet.

---

[53] Justice Renquist observed in *Michigan* v. *Tucker* 417 US 433, 446 (1974): 'Just as the law does not require that a defendant receive a perfect trial, only a fair one, it cannot realistically require that a policeman investigating serious crimes make no errors whatsoever. The pressure of law enforcement and the vagaries of human nature would make such an expectation unrealistic. Before we penalize police errors, therefore, we must consider whether the sanction serves a valid and useful purpose.' See also *Scheuer* v. *Rhodes* 416 US 232, 241–2 (1974) per Chief Justice Burger.

[54] See n. 57 below. It is to be noted that a compensatory jurisdiction already exists in English law. An aggrieved person can sue for trespass to person or property and may even be able to obtain exemplary damages. See also *George* v. *Metropolitan Police Commissioner*, *The Times*, (31 Mar. 1984); *Connor* v. *Chief Constable of Cambridgshire*, ibid. (11 Apr. 1984).

[55] *Chic Fashions* v. *Jones* [1968] 1 All ER 229.

[56] See Weir, 'Police power to seize suspected goods', [1968] CLJ 193, 195.

In a moment of candour Lord Denning hinted at this strategy when, commenting on the law as it then stood, he said:

No magistrate...has the power to issue a search warrant for murder....The police have to get the consent of the householder to enter if they can; or, if not, to do it by stealth or by force. Somehow they seem to manage. No decent person refuses them permission. If he does, he is probably implicated in some way or other. So the police risk an action for trespass. It is not much risk.[57]

The trouble with this method is that in the long run it is likely to cast doubt on the impartiality of the judiciary. If a compromise has to be found it is better to do so in a publicly accountable fashion rather than by a wink and a nod. The conflict should be brought into the open so that we can develop a suitable theory for underpinning the legitimacy of the administration of justice.

---

[57] In *Ghani* v. *Jones* [1969] 3 All ER 1700, 1702. Today a magistrate may issue a search warrant in the circumstances described: Police and Criminal Evidence Act 1984, s. 8.

Bibliography

ADAMS, *Criminal Onus and Exculpations* (1968)

ALLAN, 'Similar fact evidence of disposition: law, discretion and admissibility', [1985] MLR 253

ALLEN R. J., 'Structuring jury decision making in criminal case...', 94 Harv L Rev 321, (1980)

——'Structuring jury decision-making in criminal cases...', 94 Harv L Rev 321, 1798 (1980)

——'Rationality, mythology, and the "acceptability of verdicts" thesis', 66 Boston University L Rev 541 (1986)

ANDENAES, 'General prevention: illusion and reality, 43 Crim L

——'The general preventive effects of punishment', 114 University of Pennsylvania L Rev 949 (1966)

ANDREWS, 'Public interest and criminal proceedings', (1988) 104 LQR 410

ANSCOMBE E., 'On brute facts', (1958) 18/3 Analysis

Archbold's Pleading, Evdience and Practice in Criminal Cases, 42nd edn. (1985)

ARENELLA P., 'Rethinking the functions of criminal procedure: the Warren and Burger courts' competing ideologies', 72 Georgetown L J 185 (1983)

——'Rethinking the functions of criminal procedure: the Warren and Burger courts' competing ideologies', 72 Georgetown L J 185 (1983)

——'Schmerber and the privilege against self-incrimination: a reappraisal', (1982) Am Crim L Rev 31

ASHFORD and RISINGER, 'Presumptions, asumptions and due process in criminal cases...', 79 Yale L J 165 (1969)

ASHWORTH and PATTENDEN, 'Reliability, hearsay evidence and the English criminal trial', (1986) 102 LQR 292

——'Reliability, hearsay evidence and the English criminal trial', (1986) 102 LQR 292

ASHWORTH, 'Excluding evidence as protecting rights', [1977] Crim L Rev 723

Australian Law Reform Commission has recommended extension of the privilege to informal spouses: Research Paper No. 5

Australian Law Reform commission, Rep No 2 Criminal Investigation, 1975

362 *Bibliography*

BABCOCK, 'Fair play: evidence favourable to an accused . . .', 34 Stan L Rev 1133, 1135 (1982)

BAKER, *The Hearsay Rule* (1950)

BALDWIN and MCCONVILLE, *Jury Trials* (1979), 135

BALL, 'The moment of truth: probability theory and standards of proof', 14 V and L Rev 807, 813–4 (1961)

BARTON and COWART, 'The enigma of hearsay', 49 Mississippi L J 31, 33 (1978)

BASTEN, 'The court expert in civil trials', (1977) 40 MLR 174

BAYLES, 'Principles for legal procedure', 5 Law and Philosophy 33 (1986)

BENNION, 'Statutory exceptions: a third knot in the golden thread?' [1988] Crim L Rev 31

BENTHAM, *A Treatise on Judicial Evidence*, Dumont ed. (1825)
———*Rationale of Judicial Evidence*, 1827
———*Works of Jeremy Bentham*, Bowring ed. (1843)

BEST, *The Principles of the Law of Evidence*, 5th edn. (1870)
———*The Principles of the Law of Evidence*, 12th edn. (1922)

BIRCH D. J., 'Hearsay logic and hearsay fiddles: Blastland revisited, in P Smith (ed.), Criminal Law: Essays in Honour of J. C. Smith (1987) 24
———'Hunting the snark: the elusive statutory exception', [1988] Crim L Rev 221
———'The evidence provisions in the Criminal Justice Act 1988', [1989] Crim L Rev 15
———'The PACE hots up: confessions and confusion under the 1984 Act', [1989] Crim L Rev 95

BLACK E., 'Why Judge Samuels sent Gary Dotson back to prison', 71 ABAJ 56 (1985)

BLACKSTONE, *Commentaries*

BRIDGE, 'Presumptions and burdens', (1949) 12 MLR 273

BUXTON, 'Some simple thoughts on intention', [1988] Crim. L. Rev. 485

CARTER, 'Forbidden reasoning permissible: similar fact evidence a decade after *Boardman*', (1985) 48 MLR 29
———'Hearsay relevance and amissibility: declarations as to state of mind . . .', (1987) 103 LQR 106
———*Cases and Statutes on Evidence* (1981)

CLAPP, 'Privilege against self-incrimination', 10 Rutgers L Rev 541, 548 (1956)

CLARKE, 'Corroboration in sexual cases', [1980] Crim L Rev 362

COBB S., 'Gary Dotson as a victim: the legal response to recanting testimony', 35 Emory L J 969 (1986)

COHEN L. Jonathan, *The Probable and the Provable* (1977)

COHEN, M., 'Challenging police evidence of interviews and second limb of s. 1(f)(ii)—another view', [1981] Crim L Rev 523

Comment: 'The presently expanding concept of judicial notice', 13 Vill L Rev 528 (1968)

Comment: 'The Supreme Court 1984 Term', 99 Harv L Rev 141 (1986)

Comment: 'The tort alternative to the exclusionary rule', 63 Journal Criminal Law Criminology and Police Science 256 (1972)

Commission of Inquiry Concerning Certain Activities of the Royal Canadian Mounted Police, Second Report: Freedom and Security Under the Law, 1981

CORNISH and SEALY, LSE Jury Project, Juries and the rules of evidence, [1973] Crim L Rev 208

COWEN and CARTER, *Essays on the Law of Evidence* (1956)

'Crime and crown privilege', [1959] Crim L Rev 10

Criminal Law Revision Committee, 11th Report, para 257

Cross on Evidence, 5th edn. (1979)

Cross on Evidence, 6th edn. C. Tapper ed. (1985)

CROSS, Rupert, 'An Attempt to Update the Law of Evidence', 19th Lionel Cohen Lectures (1973)

——'The evidence report: sense and nonsense etc', [1973] Crim L R 329

——'The golden thread of the English criminal law', Rede Lecture (1976)

——'The periphery of hearsay', (1969) 7 Melbourne Univ L Rev 1

DAMASKA, 'Evidentiary barriers to conviction and two models of criminal procedure...', 121 University of Pennsylvania L Rev 506 (1973)

——*The Faces of Justice and State Authority* (1986)

DARLING, *Scintillae Juris* (1914)

DAVIS K. C., 'A system of judicial notice based on fairness and convenience', in Perspectives of Law (1964), 69

——'An approach to problems of evidence in the administrative process', 55 Harv L R 364 (1942); 'Judicial notice', 55 Colum L R 945 (1955)

——'Facts in lawmaking', 80 Col L Rev 931 (1980)

————*Administrative Law Text*, 3rd edn. (1972)

DAWSON, 'Joint trials of defendants in criminal cases: an analysis of efficiencies and prejudices', 77 Mich L Rev 1379 (1979)

DENNING, 'Presumptions and burdens', (1945) 61 LQR 379

DENNIS, 'Corroboration requirements reconsidered', [1984] Crim L Rev 316

Devlin Committee Report on Evidence of Identification in Criminal Cases, 1976

DEVLIN, Easing The Passing (1985)

————*The Judge*, (1981)

————Trial by Jury, (1956)

DONAGAN, The Right Not to Incriminate Oneself, in Paul, Miller, Paul (eds.), *Human Rights* (1984), 137

DUFF, 'The obscure intentions of the House of Lords', [1986] Crim. L. Rev. 771

DWORKIN, *A Matter of Principle* (1985)

————'Fact style adjudication and the Fourth Amendment...' 48 Indiana L J 329 (1973)

EGGLESTON, *Evidence, Proof and Probability*, 2nd edn (1983)

EISENBERG, 'Participation, responsiveness and the consultative process, etc.', 92 Harv L Rev 410 (1978)

EKELOF, 'Free evaluation of evidence', 8 Scandinavian Studies in Law, 47 (1964)

ELLIOT, 'Rape complainants' sexual experience with third parties', [1984] Crim L Rev 4

ELLIOTT and WAKEFIELD, 'Exculpatory statements by accused persons', [1979] Crim L Rev 428

ESTRICH, 'Rape', 95 Yale L J 1087 (1986)

Federal Rules of Evidence, The Advisory Committee's Note on Rule 201, 56 FRD 183, 201

FINKELSTEIN, *Quantitative Methods in the Law* (1978)

FINNIS, *Natural Law and Natural Rights* (1980)

FLETCHER G., 'Two kinds of legal rules: a comparative legal study of burden of persuasion practices in criminal cases', 77 Yale L J 880 (1968)

————*Rethinking Criminal Law* (1978)

FLOUD, 'Dangerousness and criminal justice', (1982) 22 British Journal of Criminology 213

FOOTE, 'Tort remedies for police violations of individual rights', 39 Minn L Rev 493 (1955)

FORTESCUE, *De Laudibus Legum Angliae*

FRANK, Jerome, *Courts on Trial* (1949)

———*Law and the Modern Mind*, Anchor books edn. (1963), 195 Criminal Law Revision Committee, 11th Report, cmnd. 4991

FRIENDLY, 'The Fifth Amendment tomorrow: a case for a constitutional change', 37 University of Cincinnati L Rev 671 (1968)

FULLER L., 'The forms and limits of adjudication', 92 Harv L Rev 353 (1978)

GALLIGAN, 'More scepticism about scepticism', (1988) 8 Oxford Journal of Legal Studies 249

———*Discretionary Powers: A Legal Study of Official Discretion*, (1986)

GARDINER, 'The purposes of the criminal punishment', (1958) 21 MLR 117

GERSTEIN, 'Punishment and self-incrimination', 16 American Journal of Jurisprudence 84 (1971)

GIBBONS, T.' 'The conditions of detention and questioning by the police', [1985] Crim L Rev 558

GODJONSSON and MACKEITH, 'False confessions...', in Norsledt and Forlag (eds.), *Reconstructing of the Past: The Role of Psychologists in Criminal Trials* (1982)

GOFF, 'The mental element in the crime of murder', (1988) 104 LQR 30

GOODERSON, 'Previous consistent statements', [1968] CLJ 64

———'The Evidence of Co-prisoners', (1953) 11 CLJ 64

GRAHAM, 'Stickperson hearsay: a simplified approach to understanding the rule against hearsay', (1982) University of Ill L Rev 887

GREEN, Verdicts According to Conscience', (1985)

GRIEW, 'Directions to convict', [1972] Crim L Rev 204

GRIFFITH, 'Ideology in criminal procedure of a "Third Model" of the criminal process', 79 Yale L J 359 (1970)

GRIFFITHS and AYRES, 'A postscript to the *Miranda* project: interrogation of draft protesters', 77 Yale L J 300 (1967)

GROSS, 'Loss of innocence: eyewitness identification and proof of guilt', 16 Journal of Legal Studies 395 (1987)

GUDJONSSON and CLARK, 'Suggestibility in police interrogation...', (1986) 1 Social Behaviour 83

GUDJONSSON and LISTER, 'Interrogative suggestibility...', (1984) 24 Journal of Forensic Science Society 99

GUDJONSSON, 'Interrogative suggestibility...', (1984) 24 Medical Science Law 56

GUEST S., 'The scope of the hearsay rule', (1985) 101 LQR 385

HAMMELMANN, 'Expert evidence', (1947) 10 MLR 32

HARNON, 'Examination of children in sexual offences: the Israeli law and practice', [1988] Crim L Rev 263

———'The need for corroboration of accomplice testimony and the need for "something additional" to the testimony of someone involved', 6 Israel L Rev 81 (1976)

HARPER and JAMES, *The Law of Torts* (1956)

HART and McNAUGHTON, 'Evidence and inference in the law', in D. Lerner (ed.), Evidence and Inference (1958)

HART H. L. A., *The Concept of Law* (1961)

HEALY, 'Proof and policy, no golden threads', [1987] Crim L Rev 355

HEIDT, 'The conjurer's circle—the Fifth Amendment in civil case', 91 Yale L J 1062 (1982)

HEYDON, 'Statutory restrictions on the privilege against self-incrimination' (1971) 87 LQR 214

———'The Corroboration of accomplices' [1973] Crim L Rev 264

———*Evidence, Cases and Materials*, 2nd edn. (1984)

HOFFMANN, 'Similar facts after *Boardman*', (1975) 91 LQR 193

HOFFMANN, Book Review, (1978) 94 LQR 457

HOHFELD, *Fundamental Legal Conceptions* (1923)

HOLDSWORTH, *A History of English Law*

HUTCHESON, 'The judgment intuitive: the function of the "hunch" in judicial decisions', 14 Cornell L Q 274 (1929)

ISAACS N., 'The law and the facts', 22 Col L Rev 1, 6 (1922)

JACKSON, 'Expertise or evidence?' (1982) 98 LQR 192

———'Questions of fact and questions of law', in Twining (ed.), Facts in the Law (1983)

JACOB J., *The Fabric of English Civil Justice* (1987)

JAMES, 'Relevance, probability and the Law', 29 Calif L Rev 689 (1941)

JEFFRIES and STEPHAN, 'Defences, presumptions and the burden of proof in criminal cases', 88 Yale L J 1325 (1979)

JENKS, 'According to the evidence', in *Cambridge Legal Essays* (1926)

JOY, *Evidence of Accomplices* (1844)

KADISH and KADISH, *Discretion to Disobey* (1973)

KALVEN and ZEISEL, *The American Jury* (1971)

KAPLAN, 'Decision theory and fact finding process', 20 Stan L Rev 1065, 1074 (1968)

———'The limits of the exclusionary rule', 26 Stan L Rev 1027 (1974)

KASSIN and WRIGHTSMAN (eds.), *Psychology of Evidence and Trial Procedure* (1985)

KAYE, 'The paradox of the gate-crasher and other stories', [1979] Ariz St U L J 101

KEANE, *The Modern Law of Evidence* (1985)

KEE, R., *Trial and Error* (1986)

KEETON and MARSHALL, 'Bentham's influence on the law of evidence', in *J. Bentham and the law*, (1948), 79

KEMP, 'The background of the Fifth Amendment in English law: a study of its historical implications', 1 William

KUHNS, R. B., 'The propensity to misunderstand the character of specific acts evidence', 66 Iowa L Rev 777 (1981)

LACEY, N., *State Punishment* (1988)

Law Reform Committee, 16th Report

Law Reform Committee, 17th Report, Evidence of Opinion and Expert Evidence (1970), cmnd. 4489

Learned Hand, 'Historical and practical considerations regarding expert testimony', 15 Harv L Rev 40 (1901)

LEMPERT and SALTZBURG, *A Modern Approach to Evidence*, 2nd edn (1982)

LEMPERT, 'Uncovering "non-discernible" differences: empirical research and the jury-size cases', 73 Mich L Rev 643 (1975)

———'Modeling relevance', 75 Mich L Rev 1021, 1035 (1975)

LEVIN and LEVY, 'Persuading the jury with facts not evidence: the fiction-science spectrum', 105 University of Pennsylvaniaa L Rev 139 (1956)

LEVY, *Origins of the Fifth Amendment* (1968)

LLEWELLYN, *Jurisprudence* (1962)

LOEWY, 'The Fourth Amendment as device for protecting the innocent', 81 Mich L Rev 1229 (1983)

———'The Warren court as defender of state and federal criminal law . . .', 37 Geo Washington L Rev 1218 (1969)

LUSTGARTEN, L., *The Governance of the Police* (1986)

MacCORMICK D. N., 'Coherence in legal justification', in Krawietz *et al.*, *Theorie der Normen*, (Berlin 1984), 37

MACKIE J. L., *The Cement of the Universe* (1974)

MANCHASTER, 'Judicial notice and personal knowledge', (1979) 42 MLR 22

MAY, R., 'Fair play at trial: an interim assessment of section 78 of the Police and Criminal Evidence Act 1984', [1988] Crim L Rev 722

McBAINE, 'Burden of proof: degrees of belief', 32 Calif L Rev 242 (1944)

McBARNET D. J., *Conviction* (1981)

———'Pre-trial procedures and the construction of convictions', P. Carlen (ed.), *The Sociology of Law* (1976), 172

McCONVILLE, 'Directions to convict: a reply', [1973] Crim L Rev 164

McCormick on Evidence, 3rd edn. (1984)

McCRIMMON, 'Developments in the law of evidence: the 1984–85 Term', (1985) 8 Supreme Court L Rev 249

———'Developments in the law of evidence: the 1985–86 term', (1987) 10 Supreme Court L Rev, 365

McEWAN J., 'Child evidence: more proposals for reform', [1988] Crim L Rev 813

McNAMARA, 'Cross-examination of the complainant in a trial for rape', (1981) 5 Crim L J 25

———'The canons of evidence: rules of exclusion or rules of use?', (1985–6) 10 Adelaide L Rev 341

McNAUGTON, 'The privilege against self-incrimination—its constitutional affectation, raison d'etre and miscellaneous implications', 51 Journal of Criminal Law Criminology and Police Science 138 (1960)

MEESE, 'Promoting truth in the courtroom', 40 Van L Rev 271 (1987)

MENLOWE, 'Bentham, self-incrimination and the law of evidence', (1988) 104 LQR 286

MICHAEL and ADLER, 'The trial of an issue of fact', 34 Col L Rev 1224 (1934)

MILSOM, 'Law and fact in legal development', (1967) University of Toronto L J 1

MIRFIELD, 'Meaning of the "same offence" under section $1(f)(iii)$', [1978] Crim L Rev 725

———'Similar facts: *Makin* out?', [1987] CLJ 83, 94

———'The future of the law of confessions', [1984] Crim L R 63

———'The legacy of Hunt', [1988] Crim L Rev 19

———*Confessions* (1985)

Model Code of Evidence in 1942

MONTROSE, 'Basic concepts of the law of evidence', (1954) 70 LQR 527

MORGAN, 'Presumptions', 12 Washington L Rev 255 (1937)

———'Judicial notice', 57 Harv L Rev 269 (1944)

———'The privilege against self-incrimination', 34 Minn L Rev 1 (1949)

MUNDAY, 'Stepping beyond the bounds of credibility: the application of section 1(*f*)(ii) of the Criminal Evidence Act 1898', [1986] Crim L Rev 511

MUREINIK, 'The application of rules: law or act?' (1982) 98 LQR 587

NESSON, 'The evidence or the event? On judicial proof and the acceptability of verdicts', 98 Harv L Rev 1357, 1370 (1985)

NEWARK and SAMUELS, 'Refreshing memory', [1978] Crim L Rev 408

NICOL, 'Official secrets and jury vetting', [1979] Crim L Rev 284

NOAKES, 'Real evidence', (1949) 65 LQR 57

NORTH P. M., '*Rondel* v. *Worsley* and criminal proceedings', [1968] Crim L Rev 183

Note: 'Inadmissible evidence as a basis for expert opinion', 40 Van L Rev 583 (1987)

————'Preserving the right to confrontation: a new approach to hearsay evidence in criminal trials', 113 University of Pennsylvania L Rev 741 (1965)

————'The Fourth Amendment exclusionary rule: past, present, no future', 12 Am Crim L Rev 507 (1975)

————'The prosecution's duty to disclose to defendants pleading guilty', 99 Harv L Rev 1004 (1986)

————'The prosecutor's duty to disclose to defendants pleading guilty', 99 Harv L Rev 1004 (1986)

————'The rights of criminal defendants and the subpoena duces tecum . . .', 95 Harv L Rev 683 (1982)

OAKES, 'Studying the exclusionary rule in search and seizure', 37 University of Chi L Rev 665 (1970)

————'Studying the exclusionary rule in search and seizure', 37 University of Chi L Rev 665 (1970)

PACKER, 'Two models of the criminal process', 113 University of Pennsylvania L Rev 1 (1964)

————*The Limits of the Criminal Sanction* (1968)

PAKTER, W., 'Exclusionary rules in France, Germany and Italy', (1985) Hastings International and Comparative Law Rev 1

PALEY, *Principles of Moral and Political Philosophy* (1817)

PARK, 'A subject matter approach to hearsay reform', 86 Mich L Rev 51, 55 (1987)

————'McCormick on Evidence and the concept of hearsay', 65 Minn L Rev 423 (1980)

PATTENDEN, 'Expert opinion evidence based on hearsay', [1982] Crim L Rev 85
———'The character of victims and third parties in criminal proceedings other than rape trials', [1986] Crim L Rev 367
———'The purpose of cross-examination under section 1(*f*) of the Criminal Evidence Act 1898', [1982] Crim L Rev 707
———'The purpose of cross-examination under section 1(*f*) of the Criminal Evidence Act 1898', [1982] Crim L Rev 707, 713
———'The submission of no case to answer . . .', [1982] Crim L Rev 558
———*The Judge, Discretion, and the Criminal Trial*, (1982)
PEPINSKY, 'The theory of police reaction to *Miranda* v. *Arizona*', 16 Crime and Delinquency 379 (1970)
Phipson on Evidence, 13th edn (1982)
PIRAGOFF, *Similar Fact Evidence, Probative Value and Prejudice* (1987)
PLUMB, 'Illegal enforcement of the law', 24 Cornell L Q 337, 385–91 (1939)
POLYVIOU, 'Illegally-obtained evidence and *R* v. *Sang*' in Tapper (ed.), *Crime Proof and Punishment* (1981), 175
POSNER, 'An economic approach to legal procedure and judicial administration', 2 Journal of Legal Studies 399, 410 (1973)
POSTEMA, *Bentham and the Common Law Tradition*, (1986)

RATUSHNY, E., *Self-Incrimination in the Canadian Criminal Process'* (1979)
Report on Evidence of Identification in Criminal Cases, 1976
Report on Northern Ireland, cmnd. 5185
ROMILLY, *Observations on the Criminal Law of England*, 1810, Note D, quoted in Howell, 7 State Trials (32 Charles II, 1680), 1529, n.
Royal Commission on Criminal Procedure, Report, 1981

SAMUELS A., 'Judicial misconduct in the criminal trial', [1982] Crim L Rev 221
SANDERS, A., 'Rights, remedies, and the Police and Criminal Evidence Act', [1988] Crim L Rev 802
SCHEFLIN and VAN DYKE, 'Jury nullification: the contours of a controversy', 43 Law and Contemp Prob 51 (1980)
SCHLESINGER, R., *Exclusionary Injustice* (1977)
SCOTT K. E., 'Two models of the civil process', 27 Stan L Rev 937 (1974–5)
SEABROOK, 'Closing the credibility gap: a new approach to section 1(*f*)(ii) of the Criminal Evidence Act 1898', [1987] Crim L Rev 231
Senate Judiciary Committee in Senate Report (Judiciary Committee)

No. 1097 (29 Apr. 1968), [1968] US Code and Adm. News, vol. II, p. 2128

SHAPIRO B., 'To a moral certainty': theories of knowledge and Anglo-American juries 1600–1850', 38 Hastings L J 153 (1986)

SIMON W. H., 'The ideology of advocacy', [1978] Wis L Rev 29

SKOLNICK, *Justice Without Trial*, 2nd edn. (1966)

SMITH J. C., 'The admissibility of statements by computer', [1981] Crim L Rev 387

———'The presumption of innocence', (1987) 38 NILQ 223

SPENCER, 'Child witnesses, corroboration and expert evidence', [1987] Crim L Rev 239

———'Child witnesses, video-technology and the law of evidence', [1987] Crim L Rev 76

STEIN, A., 'Bentham, Wigmore and freedom of proof', 22 Israel L Rev 243, 269 (1987)

STEIN, P., *Legal Institutions, The Development of Dispute Settlement* (1984)

STEPHEN, *A Digest of the Law of Evidence*, 12th edn. (1946)

———*History of the Criminal Law of England* (1883)

STONE, J., 'A comment on Joseph Constantine Steamship line Ltd v. Imperial Corporation Ltd', (1944) 60 LQR 262

———'Res gestae reagitata', (1939) 55 LQR 66

———The *Miranda* doctrine in the Burger court, [1977] Supreme Court Rev 99

STONE, R. T. H., 'PACE: Special procedures and legal privilege', [1988] Crim L Rev 498

STREET, *The Law of Torts*, 7th edn. (1983)

STUNTZ, J. S., 'The American exclusionary rule and the defendants' changing rights', [1989] Crim L Rev 117

SUMMERS, 'Evaluating and improving legal process—a plea for "process values"', 60 Cornell L Rev 1 (1974)

SWIFT, 'Abolishing the hearsay rule', 75 Calif L Rev 495, 504 (1987)

TAPPER, 'Proof and prejudice', in Campbell and Waller (eds.), *Well and Truly Tried* (1982), 185

———'Similar facts: peculiarity and credibility', (1975) 38 MLR 206

———*Computer Law*, 3rd edn. (1983)

———'Corroboration from an independent source', (1973) 36 MLR 541

TEMKIN, 'Regulating sexual evidence history: the limits of discretionary legislation', (1984) ICLQ 942

———*Rape and the Legal Process* (1987)

TEN, *Crime, Guilt, and Punishment*, (1987)

TENNYSON Jesse, 'The Ratenbury trial', in J. Mortimer (ed.), *Famous Trials* (1984), 15

THAYER, 'Bedingfield's Case: Declarations as part of the Res Gestae', 15 American Law Rev 1 (1881)

———'Law and fact', 4 Harv L Rev 147 (1890)

———*A Preliminary Treatise on Evidence At Common Law* (1898)

———Ezra R., 'Observations on the law of evidence', 13 Michigan L Rev 355, 360 (1915)

THOMPSON E. P., 'Subduing the jury', *The London Review of Books* (4 and 18 Dec. 1986)

TILLERS, P., 'The value of evidence in the law', (1988) 39 NILQ 167

TRIBE, *American Constitutional Law* (1978)

———'Trial by mathematics: precision and ritual in the legal process.' 84 Harv L Rev 1329 (1971)

———'Triangulating hearsay', 87 Harv L Rev 957 (1974)

TWINING, 'Debating probabilities', [1950] 2 Liverpool L Rev 51

———Identification and misidentification in legal processes: redefining the problem, in Lloyd-Bostock and Clifford (eds.), *Evaluating Witness Evidence*, (1983)

———*Theories of Evidence: Bentham and Wigmore* (1985)

ULMAN-MARGALIT, 'On presumptions', (1983) 80 Journal of Philosophy 143

UNDERWOOD, 'The thumb on the scales of justice . . .', 86 Yale L J 1299 (1977)

Uniform Rules of Evidence in 1953

VENNARD and RILEY, 'The use of peremptory challenge and stand by of jurors and their relationship to trial outcome', [1988] Crim L Rev 731

WALD *et al.*, 'Interrogation in New Haven: the impact of *Miranda*', 76 Yale L J 1519 (1967)

WALDMAN T., 'Origins of the legal doctrine of reasonable doubt', 20 Journal of the History of Ideas 299 (1959)

WASIK, 'Shifting the burden of strict liability', [1982] Crim L Rev 567

WEINBERG, 'Multiple counts and similar fact evidence', in Campbell and Waller (eds.), *Well and Truly Tried* (1982), 250

WEINSTEIN, 'Some difficulties in devising rules for determining truth in judicial proceedings', 66 Col L Rev 223 (1966)

———'The probative force of hearsay', 46 Iowa L Rev 331 (1961)

————Mansfield, Abrams and Berger, *Evidence, Rules and Statutes* (1984)

WEIR, 'Police power to seize suspected goods', [1968] CLJ 193, 195

WESTEN, 'Confrontation and compulsory process: a unified theory of evidence for criminal cases', 91 Harv L Rev 267 (1978)

————'The future of confrontation', 77 Michigan L Rev 1185 (1979)

WHITE A., 'Fact in the law', in Twining (ed.), Facts in the Law (1983)

WHITEBREAD, *Criminal Procedure* (1980), 396

Wigmore on Evidence, 3rd edn. (1940)

Wigmore on Evidence, Chad Rev.

Wigmore on Evidence, McNaughton Rev.

Wigmore on Evidence, Tillers Rev.

WIGMORE, '*Nemo tenetur seipsum prodere*', 5 Harv L Rev 71 (1891)

————*Rationale of Judicial Evidence* (1827)

WILLIAMS C. R., 'The problem of similar fact evidence', (1979) 5 Dalhousie L J 281

WILLIAMS, GLANVILLE, 'Child witnesses', in P. Smith (ed.), *Criminal Law, Essays in Honour of J C Smith* (1987)

————'Corroboration: accomplices', [1962] Crim L Rev 588

————'Corroboration: sexual cases', [1962] Crim L Rev 662

————'Law and fact', [1976] Crim L Rev 472

————'Letting off the guilty and prosecuting the innocent', [1985] Crim L Rev 115, 116

————'Offences and defences', (1982) 2 Legal Studies 233

————'The application for a directed verdict', [1965] Crim L Rev 343

————'The evidential burden: some common misapprehensions', 127 NLJ 156

————'The logic of exceptions', (1988) 47 Cambridge L J 261

————'The new proposals in relation to double hearsay and records'. [1973] Crim L Rev 139

————'The proposals for hearsay evidence', [1973] Crim L Rev 76

————*Criminal Law, the General Part*, 2nd edn. (1961)

————, *The Proof of Guilt*, 3rd edn. (1963)

WILLS, *Theory and Practice of the Law of Evidence* (1894)

WILSON W. A., 'Questions of degree', (1969) 32 MLR 361

WINTER, 'The jury and the risk of nonpersuasion', 5 Law and Society 335, 340 (1971)

WOLCHOVER D., 'The right to jury trial', 136 NLJ 530 (1986)

WOOD J. C., 'The submission of no case to answer in criminal trials—the quantum of proof', (1961) 77 LQR 491

WYDICK, 'Character evidence: a guided tour to the grotesque structure', 21 U C Davis L R 123 (1987)

ZALTZMAN, 'The Israeli approach to evidence obtained in violation of the right to privacy', (1983) 18 Israel L Rev 215

ZANDER, 'The investigation of crime: a study of cases tried at the Old Bailey', [1979] Crim L Rev 203

ZUCKERMAN, 'Similar fact evidence: the unobservable rule', (1987) 104 LQR 187

———'Criminal Law Revision Committee 11th Report—right of silence, (1973) 36 MLR 509

———'Illegally obtained evidence: discretion as a guardian of legitimacy', (1987) 40 Current Legal Problems 55

———'Law, act or justice', 66 Boston University L Rev 487 (1986)

———'Privilege and public interest', in C. F. H. Tapper (ed.), *Crime Proof and Punishment, Essays in Memory of Sir Rupert Cross* (1981), 248

———'Relevance in legal proceedings', in Twining (ed.), *Facts in Law* (1983)

———'The third exception to the Woolmington rule', (1976) 92 LQR 402

Index